MIND OVER MEDIA

NORTON BOOKS IN EDUCATION

MIND OVER MEDIA

PROPAGANDA EDUCATION FOR A DIGITAL AGE

RENEE HOBBS

W. W. NORTON & COMPANY
Independent Publishers Since 1923

Note to Readers: Models and techniques described in this volume are illustrative; neither the author nor the publisher can guarantee the efficacy or appropriateness of any particular suggestion in every circumstance. Nothing contained in this book should be construed as legal advice, and neither the author nor the publisher should be deemed to endorse any website, web page, blog, or other online content source that is not operated or provided directly by the author or the publisher, respectively.

Printed in the United States of America
First Edition

For information about special discounts for bulk purchases, please contact W. W. Norton Special Sales at specialsales@wwnorton.com or 800-233-4830

Manufacturing by Sheridan Books
Production manager: Katelyn MacKenzie

Library of Congress Cataloging-in-Publication Data

Names: Hobbs, Renee, author.
Title: Mind over media : propaganda education for a digital age / Renee Hobbs.
Description: First edition. | New York : W. W. Norton & Company, 2020. | Includes bibliographical references and index.
Identifiers: LCCN 2019057929 | ISBN 9780393713503 (paperback) | ISBN 9780393713510 (epub)
Subjects: LCSH: Mass media and propaganda. | Disinformation. | Fake news.
Classification: LCC P96.P72 H63 2020 | DDC 303.3/75--dc23
LC record available at https://lccn.loc.gov/2019057929

W. W. Norton & Company, Inc., 500 Fifth Avenue, New York, N.Y. 10110
www.wwnorton.com

W. W. Norton & Company Ltd., 15 Carlisle Street, London W1D 3BS

1 2 3 4 5 6 7 8 9 0

Access the special online features of this book at www.mindovermedia.us

for my ghostman

Contents

Foreword

I suppose it's fitting that our era's most important book on propaganda should come disguised as a teacher's guide to the subject. After all, this is the era of insiders. We all see behind the curtain, all the time. We are no longer mere consumers or voters; we are amateur product spokespeople and political commentators. We don't simply read the headlines or watch television; we tweet captions and make YouTube videos.

You may think that in this context, to read a book about propaganda would be almost pointless. A purely academic exercise. It may have sufficed in era when propaganda was a form of media content—something we could deconstruct in order to neutralize. But what about when propaganda is no longer relegated to the content of media, but becomes the context itself? Books, radio, and television offered us mostly self-contained universes we entered voluntarily. A TV show or news report could influence us, but it did so largely through storytelling. The sentencing of a criminal at the end of *Dragnet* or *Law & Order* taught us that crime doesn't pay. The editing of war footage into narratives let broadcasters choose which side we should root for.

We ended up living in a world of stories, each of which is fed back into reality. Everything we saw on TV influenced our behavior, which in turn influenced what happened in the real world. If local news stories convinced us that the streets were dangerous, we stayed inside at night, making the streets more empty and dangerous. If a public relations professional could convince us that holding a cigarette was a symbol of female power, more women would actually choose to smoke in public, abolishing a former stigma.

But this sort of public relations always depended on elite media professionals capable of crafting a story and then delivering it to us through newspapers, movies, or TV. This was the province of Woodrow Wilson and FDR, William

Randolph Hearst and Rupert Murdoch, or Ed Bernays and Howard Rubinstein. And all we really had to do in order to defuse the power of stories, from *Triumph of Will* to *Top Gun*, was to analyze the content and maybe look at the companies behind the scenes.

Today, the story behind the scenes is the story. In reality TV, the story is inconsequential—it's the setup that matters. The context. *Cops* isn't about any particular arrest, but the nature of law enforcement in working-class America. (What you gonna do when they come for you?) *American Idol* doesn't highlight its individual performers so much as the primacy of corporate pop and the willingness of artists to surrender to the judges and remake themselves in more commercial packages. *Survivor* epitomizes the cutthroat ethos of the competitive marketplace. And reality television, as a genre, promotes the notion that getting on TV—by any means necessary—is worth the humiliation and self-degradation. The footage may be real, but the producers get to assemble whatever reality they choose from it. It's like the news, except with no obligation to the truth.

Our collective ignorance of how this new propaganda landscape functions matters. It's why we elected a reality television star as president: we mistook *Cops* for America, *American Idol*'s popularity contest for democracy, and the star of *The Apprentice* for a successful businessman.

Media literacy used to mean being able to read the media, deconstruct the story, and decode what "they" mean for us to believe or do. But in a digital environment, media literacy means being able to engage with the environment, tools, and platforms of media itself.

When you watch a YouTube video, the content of that clip is only one small part of its influence over you. Less recognized but equally influential are its number of views, search ranking, description, and comments. YouTube exercises its propagandistic pull less through individual videos than through the sequence of videos recommended by its algorithms. Those algorithms are watching us much more intently than we're watching the videos. And their sole objective is to get us to click on more.

Likewise, where we may have once valued our ability to look at a Facebook post and understand its rhetorical power, that is no longer sufficient. Facebook is not like a TV channel or newspaper; it is an entire environment, designed to change the way we think and act. Only an analysis of the platform as propaganda will reveal to us the way Facebook really works. The network uses data we leave behind in order to put us into statistical buckets of people who are likely to behave in a certain way. Then, they use everything at their disposal to make sure we behave true to our algorithmically derived statistical profiles.

So, say Facebook determines that you are in a group of people who have an 80% likelihood of going on a diet in the next three weeks. The next thing you know, you'll begin seeing particular kinds of posts fill your newsfeed—articles about people who have died from obesity or clogged arteries, posts from friends of friends who went on a successful diet, and so on. The objective is not simply to advertise a particular marketer's diet products, but to increase the accuracy of their predictions—by whittling down the 20% of people who may have done something other than going on a diet. The platform means to increase our predictability. Or compare your Google search results to those of your best friend or your parents. Search for the same words and see how differently Google responds. Better yet, log in through an IP address in a different neighborhood or country. Take a look at the difference between the Google search results for the word "Jew" in America, Europe, and Jordan. Those are the sorts of experiences that change your understanding of the media architecture we are inhabiting. And they're the sorts of experiences Renee Hobbs offers us, our students, and our children in this book. Media is no longer something we watch; it is something we do. The only way for us to have a fighting chance at autonomy in such a constructed reality is to gain our bearings through experiential learning. There is no map; there is only territory. You have to walk it to know it.

And when you do, you'll be rather surprised to find out that there may not really be anyone in charge. There's no Big Brother at the top of the media hierarchy, crafting messages to trickle down through the mass media we consume. No, there's no one at the wheel. The companies responsible for mediating and representing our reality are run largely by people who have no aim other than to collect our data and get us to click on more stuff. And they've relinquished authority over their networks and content to the algorithms, which are just doing whatever they can to trigger our brain stems and get us to click. Whether that means showing us a shark attack, a racist diatribe, or fake news from Russia, it doesn't matter. We're no longer living in a world where propaganda is being used against us, so much as one made of propaganda itself.

That's why this book is so important. This is the first step toward regaining human comprehension and control over the tools and platforms that comprise our shared communication space. It is at once an engaging chronicle of how we got here, a handbook for understanding propaganda, a course in experiential learning, and a collection of ways to discuss and confront the greatest challenges to human flourishing in the coming century. Reading *Mind Over Media* should convince you that it's not too late to take back control—not just of the media but also of our own thought processes. The power to change everything is in your hands right now.

Douglas Rushkoff
New York, 2019

Preface

Let's admit it. Propaganda is a word with a bad reputation. Perhaps you think that the word has been thrown around indiscriminately in the past few years. You may be inclined to think that propaganda is something associated with totalitarian regimes from the past. Or perhaps you think of propaganda as government-sponsored spreading of lies and misinformation. Perhaps you think of propaganda as unethical effort to distort people's sense of social reality through the endless display of ever-changing tweets and memes in a world where Instagram, Facebook, Twitter, and Google seem to rule. You have certainly encountered many purposefully manufactured stories from politicians, governments, businesses, activists, and special interest groups who aim to sway public opinion, quash critics, or sow discord. For many people, propaganda is a term of abuse to hurl at rivals and opponents. If you really dislike a particular news story, social media post, or YouTube video, if it outrages or offends you, or if you think it's harmful, dangerous, irresponsible, or just flat-out wrong, just call it propaganda.

But propaganda is so much more interesting and complicated than all that. Propaganda contributes its share to the infodemic, a term the World Health Organization has used during the coronavirus pandemic to describe the avalanche of information that people must sift through to make decisions about their health and safety. Propaganda can be found in entertainment, education, and the management of public opinion, where ideas about moral character and ethical values become embedded into the fabric of culture. Propaganda has helped to shape your sense of personal identity through religious, commercial, or entertainment narratives that depict what it means to lead a good life. Depending on your point of view, the good life may include caring for your family, travelling the world, honoring people with disabilities, or even appreciating the timeless beauty of expensive watches.

In schools, many educators keep discussions of propaganda comfortably in the past, exploring it only when studying World War II Germany. As one critic put it, "Propaganda is something most of us read about in history class and wondered how people were so easily duped" (Ali, 2018, p. 1). And although teaching and learning about historic propaganda is important, this book primarily addresses the propaganda that is a part of everyday life.

There's never been a more important time to learn about contemporary propaganda. New digital forms of propaganda are influencing both the public and policy makers, as bots amplify certain ideas to create an illusion of popularity and trolls attack people with the goal of silencing or marginalizing ideas they hate. Propaganda is big business, disseminated through personalization algorithms and machine learning. Digital platforms make it easier than ever to use techniques like sentiment analysis, where natural language processing, text analysis, and computational linguistics help propagandists identify, evaluate, and respond to people's expression of emotion in ordinary online interactions (Hobbs, 2020).

Today, many people are engaged in the production of compelling propaganda. Political leaders around the world make use of it to influence public opinion. Conspiracy theories and lies have been used to demean leaders of foreign countries, government agencies, and political foes alike. Sometimes, propagandists use anger or outrage to grab attention. Other times, they repeat simple slogans over and over until they become mindless but memorable clichés. Others use more sophisticated techniques. Disinformation specialists are adept at online manipulation campaigns that trick journalists into reporting false information. Some propagandists even create think tanks and build up their authority by producing research that supports their preferred position. This kind of propaganda may influence policy makers, who end up with a distorted perception of issues that are important to the public.

Propaganda thrives on conflict. Mass media and social media can cultivate us-versus-them narratives that dehumanize the other and increase people's willingness to participate in conflict. Sadly, many people have embraced hate speech as part of political discourse. We have become desensitized to it and even experience outrage as a form of entertainment. You may barely recall the shock of reading about Donald Trump's insistence that President Barack Obama was not a U.S. citizen. Today, you may shrug when he labels immigrants as criminals and tells Americans that their elected political leaders and military generals are "morons" and "babies." Propaganda has contributed high-octane gas to accelerate the growing political polarization we are seeing all around the world. Some days, it can be exhilarating; other days, it can feel tragic. As *Los Angeles Times* TV critic Lorraine Ali pointed out, "It's the mark of a country we never wanted to be: a nation that divides its own people and pits them against one another" (2018, p. 1).

Throughout history, propagandists have chosen whether to unify or divide people, depending on their strategic goals. Demagogues simplify complex realities by making wild promises, using the power of emotion to activate people's feelings of trust and loyalty. Anyone who opposes the demagogue is labeled an enemy, which then incites a spirited us-versus-them energy that can be difficult to unravel. This kind of leadership can be appealing to many, but it is anathema to democracy. Scapegoating is used to focus blame. By insulting and trying to damage the reputation of anyone who dares to challenge them, demagogues aim to silence or marginalize opponents. The ancient Greeks warned us that demagogues intentionally widen social cleavages, "playing one group of citizens against another" (Raymond, 2019, p. 1). The result can become a tyrannical abuse of power.

On key public issues like poverty, health care, education, immigration, the federal debt, foreign policy, and more, propaganda plus demagoguery spells trouble. As Raymond (2019, p. 1) explains, "Political divisions become almost impossible to bridge, which dissuades elected officials with differing viewpoints from deliberating together." Without consensus, the democratic process does not work. Sadly, as we are seeing now in the public sphere, it's far easier to divide than to unite.

Given the complex political context of today, how can propaganda be productively studied in the elementary school, the high school or the college classroom? Ironically, the first step involves appreciating propaganda instead of demonizing it. Propaganda, as a powerful form of expression and communication, must not be positioned as the fall guy for all the world's woes. Propaganda is a vital part of the democratic process, providing opportunities for exposure to diverse ideas and inducing people to act together. Activists create propaganda when they stage a protest march, a rally, or any other public event filled with songs, chants, and inspiring speeches. Public health officials create propaganda when they develop targeted ad campaigns to help people make informed decisions about their health. Documentary filmmakers create propaganda when they explain why urgent attention is needed to address the climate emergency resulting from the 40 billion tons of carbon dioxide humans pump into the atmosphere each year. You may contribute to propaganda's viral nature when you like or share a social media post about police brutality and racism or even when you share a compelling political campaign ad.

When propaganda appeals to genuinely democratic values, it can increase people's awareness of the dangers of authoritarian and fascist ideologies. In fact, there is a long history of public conversation regarding "how a society aspiring to democracy may balance the right to persuade with the right of the public to free choice" (Sproule, 1997, p. 271). Because it simplifies information and ideas, propagandists can help people experience moral clarity about issues and events that most concern them. Propaganda that speaks to people's deepest values bypasses the head and goes straight for the heart. It breaks through the clutter of everyday life.

As we will see in the pages that follow, teaching and learning about propaganda can be a transformative experience for both students and teachers alike. When done well, the study of propaganda can embody fundamental practices of literacy and civic education in the context of inquiry learning. Propaganda education can activate intellectual curiosity. It can promote multiperspectival thinking and help people more accurately read the digital environments we inhabit, helping us make better decisions. It can be a means to resist demagoguery and even help to cure the disease of political polarization.

But there's no magic wand, no defensive armor, vaccine, or potion that can inoculate people against the pernicious influence of propaganda. Education alone cannot solve the epistemological crisis of the present time, when social media amplifies false, dangerous, and repugnant ideas, and political leaders lie with impunity. Education alone cannot erase the fear that leads people to become vulnerable to false but emotionally resonant messages. Education alone cannot eliminate the damage caused by inequality, racism, greed, and the long-standing abuse of power by institutions and individuals with authority and expertise. But education about contemporary propaganda is essential for people of all ages who want to hold on to their democracy in the face of threats.

Propaganda predates the Internet by millennia, and this book acknowledges that people have been recognizing, resisting, and falling for the allure of propaganda since well before the time of the Sophists in ancient Greece. Responsible leaders themselves have navigated the dilemma of trying to be an ethical communicator when, as one scholar put it, the business of manipulating public opinion "inevitably pushes towards the use of whatever techniques 'work'" (Merton, 1946, p. 270).

The study of propaganda provides plentiful opportunities to address values, ethics, and morality. In this book, I argue that as people activate critical thinking skills in recognizing and responding to propaganda, they increase autonomy and personal freedom. As the emotional jolts and the promise of simple solutions and easy answers become easier to spot, people can use the power of inquiry, dialogue, and reflection to evaluate propaganda's explicit and implicit claims. They can appreciate how propaganda can be interpreted in different ways.

As people understand how propaganda works, they are empowered to become propagandists themselves by creating and sharing media. In using the power of communication and information to make a difference in the world, they have an opportunity to deepen awareness of the moral and ethical tensions that are built into the practice of persuasion. People can learn to discern between propaganda that is designed for personal benefit and propaganda that is trying to benefit society.

But because no one is immune from the power of propaganda, the pedagogy of propaganda education can be controversial and it must be designed and implemented with care, so that it does not turn into indoctrination. When done well, propaganda education does not increase cynicism, suspicion, distrust, and alienation. In the pages that follow, you'll discover that an optimistic and empowering approach to teaching and learning about propaganda is relevant for every learner, in every discipline or field of study, from kindergarten to graduate school, and across the life span, in and out of school.

MIND OVER MEDIA

1
Mind Over Media

Propaganda is responsive to changes in culture, technology, and society

When the staff of the National Archives Museum in Washington, D.C. were developing an exhibit entitled, "Rightfully Hers: American Women and the Vote," they wanted to examine the history of the struggle of women to gain the right to vote. In developing a way to connect the present to the past, they created a unique and attention-getting display for the elevator lobby. They combined a large historic image of a 1913 photo of a women's demonstration on Pennsylvania Avenue with an image from the 2017 Women's March in Washington, D.C. using a lenticular printing technique, which enables viewers to see the 1913 photo from one vantage point and also see the contemporary photo by looking at the image from a slightly different point of view.

Since the election of President Donald Trump in 2016, thousands of demonstrators have gathered annually in Washington, DC and 250 other cities for a protest. These boisterous annual gatherings feature people of all ages carrying provocative signs, chanting slogans, and wearing those now famous "pussy hats." But when the *Washington Post* reported in early 2020 that the image of the Women's March at the National Archives exhibit on women's protests had been edited to remove certain words on the signs held by the protest marchers, it reminded some of *Nineteen Eighty Four*, the dystopian novel by George Orwell. There, the protagonist Winston Smith's job is to revise history on behalf of Big Brother. As a non-political federal agency, the National Archives staff decided to obscure the protest signs that commented on Trump's misogyny and they removed words relating to female genitalia. They blurred a sign that stated, "God Hates Trump" and one that read "Trump & GOP — Hands Off Women." In their careful design of the exhibit's promotional materials, the staff at the National Archives simply wanted to avoid political controversy (Heim, 2020).

The government employees at the National Archives were not intending to create propaganda, but their editorial decision was perceived by some as an intentional distortion of history for propaganda purposes. Their action seemed to neutralize the highly partisan nature of political expression at the Women's March. When the news about the altered photo was released, a firestorm of criticism erupted on social media as a wide variety of people were infuriated that the federal agency responsible for preserving our nation's history would distort photographic evidence. Soon after, the National Archives issued a formal apology letter and removed the display, noting that the photo they used was not an archival record, but one they had merely licensed to use as a promotional graphic. But one critic explained, "The photographs of the Women's March are not only photographs of events in our history. They are the artifactual records we have of our freedom of speech and assembly—the documents showing hundreds of thousands went into the streets that day to raise their voices about their worries and their dreams" (Clancy, 2020).

Such a simple form of image manipulation may seem pale in comparison to the more sophisticated and radical forms of image manipulation that now circulate online. Deepfake videos take advantage of machine learning to create highly convincing unreal realities, making someone appear to say or do something he or she did not say or do. For example, in Europe, many Dutch-speaking viewers saw a short Facebook video of Donald Trump making a speech that asked Belgium to withdraw from the Paris climate agreement. In the video, which is in English but has Dutch subtitles, a very realistic-looking fake Trump says, "As you know, I had the balls to withdraw from the Paris climate agreement, and so should you." At the very end of the video, the fake Trump says, "We all know climate change is fake, just like this video." But this last line is not translated into Dutch in the subtitles. For the many Facebook viewers who watched the video without volume, reading only the subtitles, it looked very real indeed (Von de Burchard, 2018).

Since then, hundreds of news stories have claimed that deepfake technology is a new kind of propaganda that will soon be sweeping the Internet. Naturally people fear that the software could be used to cause political damage. One expert explained, "If deepfakes make people believe they can't trust video, the problems of misinformation and conspiracy theories could get worse" (O'Sullivan, 2019). A convincing deepfake could further diminish our trust in audio and video as reliable sources of information. Fortunately, computer scientists are finding ways for machine learning to detect deepfakes, and Facebook is already using a system to filter for doctored video at the point of upload (Brandom, 2019).

Some critics point out deepfakes haven't taken off as propaganda because the public can be manipulated much more easily without all those technological bells and whistles. When a video of U.S. House Speaker Nancy Pelosi circulated online, showing her with artificially slowed speech, reporters pointed out that the Pelosi video did not use deepfake technology, but much simpler audio editing tools.

Propaganda videos have created havoc round the world. One video depicted a person being burned alive. The video was relabeled multiple times to make it look like it came from Ivory Coast, South Sudan, Kenya, and Burma. In each case, the mislabeled video led to violent actions in each country and caused harm to innocent people (B. Johnson, 2019).

Although videos using these simple techniques have been called cheapfakes, they are not new. You may remember that in 2010, Fox News aired a highly edited video created by Andrew Breitbart of a speech by Shirley Sherrod, an official in the Obama administration, that made it appear as if she was a racist. The resulting brouhaha led to Sherrod getting fired from her position at the U.S. Department of Agriculture in 2010. Only after the damage was done was it discovered that the video was intentionally designed to harm Sherrod's reputation and manipulate public opinion. Since then, this form of propaganda has become commonplace.

And doctored photos, deepfakes, and cheapfakes are just the tip of the iceberg. Propaganda comes in wide variety of forms and genres because it is an inescapable feature of everyday life. As we will learn in the pages that follow, it may be created intentionally or unintentionally. It may occur when people try to influence attitudes and behaviors by evoking strong emotions, attacking opponents, simplifying information, and appealing to the deepest hopes, fears, and dreams of a target audience. But first, we must consider how definitions of propaganda reflect changes in culture, technology, and media, and see how contemporary propaganda takes many forms, including some that can be challenging to spot.

The Propaganda Formula

There's a timeless pattern to many forms of propaganda, one that's rooted in both problems and solutions. As a propagandist, when you are promoting a solution, you intensify it using repetition, positive feelings, and careful design and composition. You make that solution seem like the best thing in the world. When you have a problem on your hands, you downplay it through omission, diversion, and creating confusion. Downplaying and intensifying are neither good nor evil: they are rhetorical practices that aim to influence people to accept a version of reality that meets the needs of the person doing the persuading (Rank, 1991).

You might be inclined to blame social media and the Internet as the cause of propaganda's cultural dominance today. From an economic point of view, propaganda is rising in visibility and influence due to the attention economy, where an explosive array of choices are now available to us as both consumers and creators of media. In this global information network, anyone can produce digital content. People can easily use the classic formula of sensationalism (with its focus on sex, violence, children, animals, and the mysterious unknown) to profit from viral sharing, where more clicks equal more revenue.

When people use emotionally intense words or images, their messages spread to reach a larger audience. Delight, surprise, anger, and outrage are not merely emotions: they are attention-getting tools. The impact of these strategies is evident in the home, the workplace, and in public life.

Not only does digital propaganda evoke strong feelings, but today, we're often not sure what kinds of content we can trust. When we hear the same ideas and phrases over and over, they begin to seem true. Finding and evaluating the source of information can be challenging. Often the real funder of propaganda is disguised or hidden, as when organizations that deliver messages choose not to reveal the funding sources that support them. Because most Americans get their news from social media, we often experience content as headlines and snippets, without source information or context clues to assist in interpretation. Today, propaganda takes new digital forms that blur the lines between entertainment, information, and persuasion.

If you look around, you'll see that people who use the propaganda techniques of intensifying and downplaying are often the most respected people in a community simply because they are compelling, effective communicators. Ministers, community leaders, elected public officials, educators, media professionals, and even celebrities are aware that, as professional communicators who aim to coalesce public opinion, they face important ethical questions in their relationship with audiences. They make their case using the power of language to engage audiences emotionally and intellectually. They also choose whether to tell the truth, to stretch the truth, to lie by omission, or to make stuff up. Everyone knows that an educator can inspire with positive words and expressions of emotion or use threats or negative evaluation to gain compliance. A politician makes a choice to inspire and unify people or divide by lying, bullying, and name calling. An activist who speaks at a public event can use inspire people by painting a mental picture of the changed world they seek, or attack opponents with a withering critique.

Intensifying and downplaying can occur through visual symbols as well as words. Consider the graphic designer who creates an infographic on global energy. She may rely on factual information to depict the differing levels of consumption of coal, gas, hydroelectric, wind, and other forms of energy. She will inevitably use subtle visual messages to signify the value of coal (or solar) in the design, color, and layout of the images and charts. Readers generally cannot directly interrogate the author to determine authorial intent. But clues in the language, imagery, color, design, and choice of informational content all provide tacit evidence of the author's point of view and strategic goals.

While it's critically important to analyze propaganda, it's also important to learn how to create it. When you create propaganda, you discover that it's a challenging task that requires discipline, imagination, and tenacity. You also learn that propaganda is not always effective. Learning to create propaganda prepares students for life in a democratic society because propaganda is a major way that people try to influence public opinion and make social change.

Although many people think propaganda is purely negative, the term also applies to messages that are intended to be used for beneficial and socially desirable purposes. Perhaps you have seen the inspiring YouTube video that features Asian American singer-songwriter Clara Chung, who describes her favorite middle school music teacher, a woman who helped her realize that she could make choices to achieve her dreams (Jubilee, 2010). This video on the power of teaching was funded by the White House Department of Education's Initiative on Asian Americans and Pacific Islanders. Produced by Jubilee, a media company "by changemakers, for changemakers," the music and the story combine to evoke feelings about the importance of teachers in the lives of young people. Videos like this may provide viewers with positive feelings about the role of educators in American society. By touching the heartstrings and reminding us of the importance of good teachers, you may be more likely to share a link to the video with your circle of friends and family. You may not think of videos like this as a form of propaganda, but they are.

The study of propaganda is profoundly linked to the mission of education and civic learning in American schools. If schools are to fulfill their social purpose of preparing people for life in a democratic society, there's a need to help learners make sense of contemporary propaganda and use the power of inquiry to explore it. I'm deeply committed to this goal. That's why you'll find a wide variety of learning activities, like the one below, that offer examples of how to integrate propaganda education into any curriculum. At the companion website (www.mindovermedia.us), you'll find additional online learning resources. In an appendix, you'll find a complete list of Learning Activities presented throughout the book. These Learning Activities have two purposes: they are designed to help general readers visualize the instructional practices of media literacy education and they may also jump-start the creativity and imagination of educators who are looking for creative strategies for exploring the topic of propaganda with their students.

LEARNING ACTIVITY

The Formula for Propaganda

Explore the power of language to make something seem terrific or awful by using Hugh Rank's intensify/downplay scheme. Many forms of propaganda and persuasion use this formula.

Activity: Can you make someone love a topic or hate it through the use of the techniques? Pick a topic of interest to you and compose a message that uses the intensify and downplay formula. Share examples on a digital bulletin board and notice the patterns that reoccur.

Intensify: Make something look good. The significance of an idea, product, or person can be increased through repetition, association, and composition.

- ***Repetition.*** Repetition of words or images makes messages more memorable, and it also leads people to accept what is being repeated as being true.

- ***Association.*** Persuaders link an idea, product, or person with something people naturally desire or fear.
- ***Composition.*** Creative use of design, variations in sequence, and patterns to help attract and hold the audience's attention.

Downplay: Make something look small, bad, or unimportant. Something can be made to seem insignificant by diverting attention from it, or reducing people's attention to it by distracting them with something more interesting.

- ***Diversion.*** Provide something more entertaining, interesting or important for people to focus on.
- ***Omission.*** Do not call attention to a message you dislike; instead, simply ignore it.
- ***Confusion.*** Shower people with too much information on a topic you want to downplay, so that they feel overwhelmed and their attention is diminished.

The Takeaway: The creative use of language can shape people's perceptions and interpretations of reality.

–Adapted from H. Rank (1991), The Pitch

Persuasion, Information, Entertainment, and Power

The relationship between propaganda and persuasion is complicated. These two terms are very closely related and have been debated and discussed for thousands of years. Both refer to efforts that use communication and symbolic expression to influence people's beliefs, attitudes, and behaviors. Scholars have defined persuasion in relation to a communicator's intention to change or reinforce the beliefs, attitudes, or behaviors of another (Jowett & O'Donnell, 2012). To identify elements of persuasion, terms from classical Greek rhetoric are often used to acknowledge how persuasion occurs through these modes: the credibility and character of the speaker (*ethos*), the quality of ideas presented (*logos*), and the emotions activated in the listener (*pathos*). Persuasion also occurs in a particular context, at the right moment in time (*kairos*).

The term propaganda refers to a form of persuasion that aims to influence the beliefs, attitudes, and behaviors of a large audience, not just a single individual or small group. Before the rise of social media, some scholars used to generally think of persuasion as part of interpersonal communication, while the term propaganda referred to mass communication (Ross, 2002). You would typically use the term persuasion to describe how you convinced your friends to try that new restaurant, while you could use the term propaganda when referring to a television public service announcement on the importance of preventing forest fires.

But today, you probably see the blurriness between the two terms. With the rise of the Internet and social media, the distinction between mass communication and interpersonal communication is eroding because so many of our important social relationships are now mediatized. We now interact daily with friends and family through social media, sharing images, textual language, and recorded music and sound. Your text messages may reach a few people or many; a photo that you share on your Facebook may reach a large audience under some conditions. Misunderstanding and confusion can result when content intended for a single individual is read or seen by a mass audience. In some cases, it can even create dangerous risks and potential harm. When interpersonal and mass communication collide, the meaning of a message in one context can be transformed by its shift into another context, a concept that has become known as context collapse (Marwick & Boyd, 2011). When people share content online, nearly any message has the capacity and potential to go viral and reach a wide, diverse audience.

Propaganda is not merely a type of persuasion: it also stands at the intersection of information and entertainment. The versatility of propaganda to inform, entertain and persuade is why it is used by those in power or those who seek power. Throughout history, military, religious, and political leaders have all used informational propaganda to accomplish their goals. For example, the Athenian naval commander Themistocles tricked his opponent with false information about the location and movement of his troops. Julius Caesar created his own fantastic and entertaining legends about himself to make him appear to be supernatural, inspiring the awe of the public. The Catholic popes told atrocity stories about Muslims to inspire the Crusades while Protestant reformer Martin Luther used entertaining dialogues in his printed sermons to expose the corruption of the pope, activating people's emotions (Auerbach & Castronovo, 2013b).

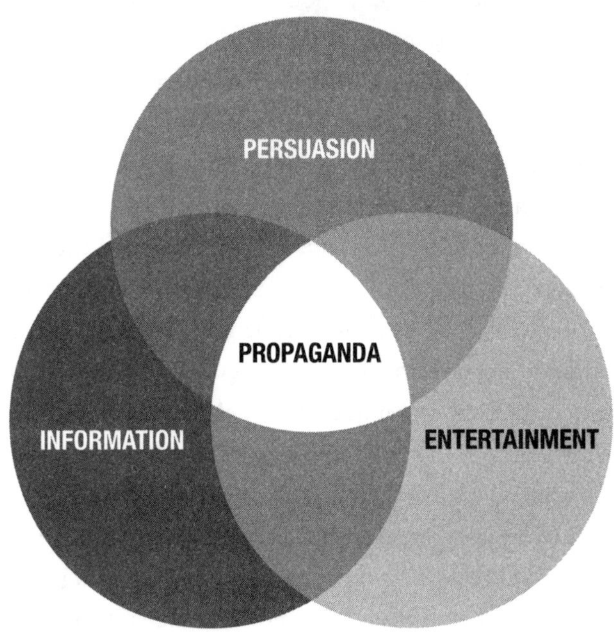

Propaganda at the Intersection of Persuasion, Information, and Entertainment

Information, art, culture, and entertainment can all function as propaganda. Writers, artists, and activists use stories, music, paintings, photography, or film to express ideas about possible worlds in the hope that they will shape and influence public opinion. Through propaganda, people can connect new information to people's existing beliefs, strategically using information to create unreal realities. The information provided by a propagandist may be true, partly true, false, or even pants-on-fire false. During the Enlightenment, propagandists used satire and political cartoons to express their ideas. American colonists portrayed minor skirmishes (at Lexington and Concord) as major victories and even the Declaration of Independence was designed as a form of propaganda to influence public opinion and justify the need for political independence (Jowett & O'Donnell, 2012).

A variety of 19th-century popular American authors (like Harriet Beecher Stowe and Mark Twain) used the power of fictional stories to imaginatively blend realistic events into fictional narratives in ways that addressed larger emotional truths about racism and inequality. During the Civil War, photography was a new technology that enabled people to see the horrors of the battlefield. Some photographers expressed their sentiments about the tragic loss of life by moving the dead bodies into dramatic positions and occasionally adding props to intensify the drama of the visual image. By the 19th century, propaganda was fully institutionalized as part of the democratic political process and it was fueled by the rise of newspapers and magazines, which enabled politicians to more easily reach vast audiences. Political philosophers began to comment on the ways in which the increasingly sophisticated activation of both emotion and reason was influencing the practice of civic decision making.

Entertaining fictions can sometimes function more effectively as propaganda than information. While the greater availability of political information enables people to learn more about politics and the political process, many people take advantage of greater choice of content to tune out of politics completely (Prior, 2005). The blurring of entertainment and propaganda can be observed by simply noticing how entertainment techniques have become commonplace in political discourse and how political and social topics are embedded in music, movies, TV shows and video games. Creative producers, musicians, athletes, and celebrities often embed political messages into movies, television, music, sports, and art. Because people let down their critical guard when they are being entertained, they may fail to notice how deeply propaganda messages are embedded in spectacle or amusement.

Entertainment storytelling has long helped to shape social norms. At the turn of the 20th century, audiences thrilled to D. W. Griffith's *Birth of a Nation* (1915) because of its epic and visually compelling storytelling. But the film also depicted post–Civil War Reconstruction in ways that presented Black leaders as dangerous and evil. The racist political ideology expressed in the film outraged many African American leaders and white liberals. But the film's emotional power emboldened white politicians and inspired efforts to quash the political and social rights of African Americans through overtly discriminatory practices in law, real estate, education, business, transportation, and public life (Lehr, 2014).

Storytelling can be used to sell lifestyles. In the 1930s, Hollywood studios released sponsored films that were disguised advertising for cars, clothes, and new houses. By the middle of the century, critics observed that entertainment film could convey powerful ideological messages about society and politics (Sproule, 1994). Today, first-person military shooter games prepare children and young people for combat training. Video games also connect the military with potential recruits; journalists have documented the relationship between U.S. military recruiting and the video game industry. Even professional soldiers easily recognize how first-person shooter games function as propaganda for war (Romaniuk & Burgers, 2017).

The Internet and meme culture bring even more entertaining propaganda to our doorstep. According to artist and activist An Xiao Mina, it's the silly stuff of the Internet that opens the door to social activism. Selfies, YouTube parodies, and cat videos are intertwined with human rights and social justice issues, storytelling, and culture. For example, in the spring of 2016, during the debate about whether the United Kingdom should leave the European Union, the hashtag #CatsAgainstBrexit was popular for a time. It started with a post that featured a sad-looking cat, with the phrase, "My cat is sad because #Brexit. If you agree RT w/ your cat." Through creating, sharing, and liking emotionally evocative and playful online content, we let others know who we are and what we value. These messages may have special persuasive power when they are shared by family members, friends, and co-workers via social media. The repetition and affirmation of playful messages can also lead to the synchronization of opinion, which is a function of propaganda (Mina, 2019). Yet, people may not be fully aware of how they acquire shared attitudes and beliefs through propaganda that blurs the boundaries between persuasion, entertainment, and information.

Definitions of Propaganda

Definitions of propaganda are situational and contextual, rooted in time and space. In Germany and around the world, the term is closely linked to the Third Reich. For those in eastern Europe, the word is deeply nuanced with cultural memories of life under communism. In the United States, public relations professionals have worked hard to distance themselves from the word, even though it was the original term used for the profession (Bernays, 1928/2005). People of different cultural and political backgrounds may differ in their use of the term, and those of different generations may also have nuanced and sometimes divergent interpretations. That's why Neil Postman (1979) once wrote that of all the words we use to talk about talk, the word "propaganda" is the most mischievous.

Propaganda originally had a meaning that was rooted in Truth with a capital T. As used by the Catholic Church in the 17th century, propaganda referred to the propagation of the faith, spreading the good news of the gospel of Jesus Christ. Religious scholars have pointed out that the missionary spirit of spreading the good news is a form of beneficial propaganda, and it is baked into the very foundations of early Christianity through the Apostle Paul's systematic efforts to deliberately to extend the gospel across all parts of the known world through land and sea

(Bowers, 1980). In his many travels to reach early Christian audiences, Saint Paul was a pioneering propagandist. Even today, Christian propaganda can be understood as bringing the world a gift of spiritual redemption through advancing an ideology of love and forgiveness.

During and immediately after World War II, communication scholars reflected on how the power of propaganda helped to strengthen democracy and fight fascism. In the U.S., Hollywood played an active role in supporting the war effort, working in close coordination with the government. After the war, the process of de-Nazification in Germany involved actively promoting democratic values by repealing Nazi laws, obliterating swastikas, and changing street names. The U.S. government also created libraries in many German cities to help with the re-education process. As a result, some scholars described propaganda in quite positive terms, as "one means by which large numbers of people are induced to act together" (Lasswell, 1948).

But later in the 20th century, definitions of propaganda began to take a narrower focus, emphasizing intentional political manipulation through untruths and lies. One English philosopher described propaganda as the "cold-blooded manipulation of popular impulse and thought by professional politicians" (Qualter, 1962). In the 1960s, when television's cultural and economic power was rising and advertisers were tapping into psychoanalytic thought to persuade, propaganda was defined in relation to human psychology, as "a form of information that panders to our insecurities and anxieties" (Ellul, 1973). As concerns about commercial culture flooded into every sector of cultural life, propaganda was defined as "intentionally-designed communication that invites us to respond emotionally, immediately, and in an either-or manner" (Postman, 1982).

When new approaches to public relations were being pioneered in the 1980s, propaganda was defined in relation to it as "the deliberate, systematic attempt to shape perceptions, manipulate cognitions, and direct behavior to achieve a response that furthers the desired intent of the propagandist" (Jowett & O'Donnell, 1986). In the 21st century, as corporate and special interest lobbyists were accelerating the scope of their incursion into Washington, DC politics, definitions of propaganda acknowledged its indifference to ethics, truth, and morality, as "strategic communication that uses any means to accomplish its ends" (Cunningham, 2002).

Today, some people think that propaganda and public lying are synonymous while others blame digital technologies for the rising influence of propaganda. Propaganda has been defined in relation to the abuse of power, as "shaping perceptions and actions through the manipulation of information, often involving some form of deception, lying, omission, distortion or misdirection" (Robinson, 2015). The term computational propaganda has been used to refer to "the manipulation of public opinion through platforms and digital devices" (Wooley & Howard, 2019). Algorithmic personalization enables propaganda to spread through personalized advertising and entertainment as well as the differential display of filtered search results on search engines.

But one person's propaganda can be another person's art, education, or news. Perhaps you have encountered a person who believes that your most reliable news source is a form of propaganda. Many forms of propaganda are designed for beneficial public purposes and rely on the delivery of truthful information and the transparent display of persuasive purpose. But philosophers like to point out that some forms of propaganda are rooted in flawed ideologies or false beliefs (Stanley, 2015). Some forms of propaganda present structural inequalities, cultural hierarchies, and other social power dynamics as "natural." Since we are inevitably positioned within these systems, we may accept attitudes and beliefs that prevent us from seeing these hierarchies and inequalities in all their complexity. For this reason, it takes considerable self-awareness and humility to engage in the examination of contemporary propaganda.

Some forms of propaganda are straightforward, while other forms can be deviously sophisticated and tricky. Propaganda may appear to appeal to public values while actually seeking to undermine those values. For example, when Republican politicians claimed that America had a significant voter fraud problem, they proposed the use of tactics designed to suppress the vote. In this case, they used a particular social value (the integrity of elections) to actually undermine the integrity of elections (Stanley, 2015).

The study of persuasion and propaganda can help us better understand the myriad ways that humans seek to influence each other using the power of communication and expression. The expression of a world view (about democracy, feminism, capitalism, automation, racism, globalization, or a million other topics) functions as a form of social power. Becoming aware of how power relations are baked into the meaning-making process is an important dimension of lifelong learning. But inherent subjectivity is also involved in the study of persuasion and propaganda because we are situated within it, as both audiences and authors.

Think of it this way: Propaganda is in the eye of the beholder. You may have interpreted that doctored National Archives image of the Women's March as a form of political propaganda, while I may see it merely as an innocent marketing display. You may see that video game as an entertaining thrill ride, while I may see its gratuitous display of violence as a dehumanizing spectacle that encourages people to love war. Although scholars and experts may quibble about the precise scope of their definitions, most agree that:

1. Propaganda appears in a variety of forms.
2. It is strategic and intentional.
3. Propaganda aims to influence public opinions, attitudes, and behaviors.
4. It can be beneficial or harmful.
5. It may use truth, half-truths, or lies.
6. To be successful, propaganda taps into our deepest values, fears, hopes, and dreams.
7. Propagandists may use any means to accomplish their goals (Luckert & Bachrach, 2009).

Definitions of propaganda like this have their merits, but they have their disadvantages, too. Through trial and error in the classroom, I have discovered that it shortchanges the learning experience to merely offer students a definition of propaganda on a PowerPoint slide or in a handout. Learners benefit from opportunities to wrestle with the various definitions that have developed over time and identify the features or elements that make sense to them. This helps them own their understanding of the term. When they appreciate that definitions of propaganda are constructed by people situated in a particular moment in time and space, they are more willing to construct definitions that relate to their lived experience. As they learn more about the topic, they are able to revise their personal definitions. This is why I like to engage learners in constructing their own definition of propaganda at the beginning and at the end of the semester. I like to ask learners to review a variety of definitions and underline or highlight ideas that resonate with them. They then remix phrases and ideas from the work of previous scholars and thinkers, selecting those that make sense to them. I then ask learners to discuss their choices with a partner to explain which elements of the definitions are most important to them.

One student may call attention to the idea that propaganda taps into people's existing values, which also helps explain why propaganda is not always effective. Propaganda is not a magic bullet that affects all people in the same way. Another learner may point out that propaganda may use factual information, carefully selected and arranged. When a student points out that propaganda may use any means to accomplish its goal, there's an opportunity to introduce the importance of framing the study of propaganda through an ethical lens. The study of propaganda enables us to consider the moral and social responsibilities of communication by demonstrating respect for the whole human person. The study of contemporary propaganda is a near-perfect entrée to explore ethics and moral philosophy because it helps learners reflect on the social responsibilities of both the people who create messages and those who consume them.

But in order for genuine learning to occur, we must shed some of the negative connotations of the term itself. One thing is certain: debating whether a particular message is or is not propaganda is educationally unproductive. People can't really wrestle with issues concerning the ethics of communication if they simplistically believe that propaganda is by definition bad or that the use of propaganda is inherently immoral or unethical. The topic must be approached with intellectual curiosity and an open mind.

LEARNING ACTIVITY

Remix a Definition of Propaganda

Because propaganda changes in response to media, technology, and culture, definitions of propaganda are situated in time and space.

Activity: After reviewing these definitions of propaganda, identify the most meaningful phrases and ideas. Then craft your personal definition by using the most relevant elements from older definitions along with ideas that reflect your own experiences with propaganda as part of everyday life.

Propaganda is . . .

1. . . . a form of communication aimed toward influencing the attitude of a population toward some cause or position (Wikipedia, entry on propaganda, 2009)
2. . . . a form of information that panders to our insecurities and anxieties (Jacques Ellul, author of *Propaganda: The Formation of Men's Attitudes*, 1962)

3. . . . indifferent to truth and truthfulness, knowledge and understanding; it is a form of strategic communication that uses any means to accomplish its ends (Walter Cunningham, author of *The Idea of Propaganda*, 2002)
4. . . . the deliberate, systematic attempt to shape perceptions, manipulate cognitions, and direct behavior to achieve a response that furthers the desired intent of the propagandist (Garth Jowett and Victoria O'Donnell, authors of *Propaganda and Persuasion*, 1986).
5. . . . a form of purposeful persuasion that attempts to influence the emotions, attitudes, opinions, and actions of specified target audiences for ideological, political or commercial purposes through the controlled transmission of one-sided messages (which may or may not be factual) via mass and direct media channels (Richard Alan Nelson, author of *A Chronology and Glossary of Propaganda in the United States*, 1995).
6. . . . intentionally designed communication that invites us to respond emotionally, immediately, and in an either-or manner (Neil Postman, author of "Propaganda," 1979).

The Takeaway: Definitions of propaganda shift in response to changes in society, technology, and culture. People's definitions of propaganda will vary depending on their media use experiences, cultural background, values, and other factors.

–Adapted from Mind Over Media: Analyzing Contemporary Propaganda (Media Education Lab, 2018)

Where Propaganda Can Be Found

Propaganda appears in a variety of forms: it can be found in news and journalism, advertising and public relations, and education—and in all aspects of daily life. It is present in information from government, business, religious and nonprofit organizations, and in many forms of entertainment including music, TV shows, movies, video games, and social media like YouTube, Facebook, and Twitter. Let's look at propaganda in six different places: advertising, journalism and public relations, activism, education, government, and entertainment.

Journalism and Public Relations

Journalists have long recognized how to exploit the formula, "If it bleeds, it leads." Conflict, crime, and controversy are key factors that define what journalists consider to be newsworthy. But the rise of the Internet has hobbled the business model for journalism, as the economic base of an independent press—advertising—has shifted toward online media. All daily newspapers have experienced declining revenues for more than a decade, and some broadcast news media outlets have survived by becoming more partisan in an effort to attract and hold key target audiences. Beginning in 1996, some television news stations shifted away from a focus on local crime news towards conservative topics, which had long been a successful formula in AM talk radio. Fox News appealed to viewers who were neglected by other journalistic enterprises, and their strategy of presenting partisan news helped an industry struggling with profitability to gain market share and persuade its viewers that they were "fair and balanced." Other cable television news stations followed in their lead.

Around the same time, philanthropists discovered they could influence the news agenda of public broadcasting. Joan Kroc, the wife of the fast food founder of McDonald's, bequeathed more than $200 million to National Public Radio (NPR) to ensure that Americans have access to quality news and journalism. There was never any suggestion that her gift came with strings attached. But after a philanthropy that strongly supported the Iran nuclear deal gave NPR a $100,000 grant, it seemed to many observers that NPR's coverage was noticeably skewed in favor of the deal. In fact, a large number of analysts and experts who were directly funded by that same philanthropy made it on the air to discuss the Iran nuclear deal, without NPR's disclosing that connection. Leaders of the network admit that they have not always been transparent about who funds its journalism and how much the public is told about it (Jensen, 2016).

Few Americans understand how news and journalism benefit from the practice of public relations (PR), whose practitioners use many strategies to shape perceptions and influence public opinion on behalf of a business client. In the U.S., there are four PR professionals for every working journalist. Many people are surprised by that fact. Public relations people feed journalists information based on their client's agenda. For example, many local newspapers and TV news organizations reported on JetBlue's stunt for Mother's Day when they decided to reward passengers on a particular flight from JFK in New York to Long Beach, California, based on the number of times a baby cried. If four babies cried, all passengers on the flight got a free return ticket for their next JetBlue flight (Griner, 2016). By using events, stunts, contests, video news releases, blogging, newsletters, policy documents, and more, businesses send messages that carefully represent their interests, often by linking their products or services to particular emotions, values or feelings.

Advertising and Marketing

You may wonder about the similarities and differences between advertising and propaganda. Advertising is a type of propaganda that supports sales and marketing goals. Commercial products play a meaningful role in people's lives, and we derive emotional satisfaction from certain products and promotional messages. Advertising relies on building inferential bonds between products and human values. It links feelings and images with companies and products to create brands. Some people think of a brand as a logo, but it's more precisely defined as a person's perception of a product, service, person, or organization. In 2016, the Target store chain spent $1.4 billion to buy advertising placements on television, billboards, radio, and magazines. For many customers, the big red bull's eye means getting the stuff that you need for daily life at a cheap price. Your favorite brand addresses your identity in relation to the aspirational lifestyle you seek. One marketer explained that brands help "you become more you" (Serazio, 2013, p. 166).

Today, advertisers track your clicks and likes when you are online to deliver highly customized messages that are designed to appeal to your desires. In doing so, they place you in a category based on who they think you are. For some people, this may satisfy the need for a common culture by connecting people together through products. Young mothers may be proud and happy to receive online ads for diapers and baby products, feeling like they are part of a small but important tribe. After all, advertising offers a sense of identity and community in an increasingly isolating and unstable world. In his book *The Attention Merchants*, Tim Wu (2016) points out that while advertising can increase people's personal freedom by helping them become more aware of the choices available to them, it simultaneously serves up propaganda that perpetuates the centrality of consumer culture as a key facet of personal identity. In an important way, advertising is a form of propaganda for capitalism itself.

Government and Politics

Governments use propaganda in both very large, noticeable ways and in very small and often unnoticeable ways. At various times in American history, the United States has generated war propaganda by defining battles as epic conflicts between good and evil, leading the public to accept its decision to use armed conflict as rational and justified. But local and national government also use nudges, which are small ways of structuring choice so that people make socially desirable decisions. For example, your water bill might include a chart showing how much water is used by an average family of various sizes so that you can compare your costs to others. You are being presented with information that offers a set of social norms. You're responding to influence if you actually change your behavior by taking shorter showers or watering the grass less frequently after seeing the chart. In many countries, nudges are used to implement public policies. In his book *The Ethics of Influence*, Cass Sunstein (2016) points out that nutrition labels, fuel economy labels, and disclosures about the real cost of taking out a loan are tools that encourage a certain sort of good behavior. Such nudges are forms of propaganda that aim to shape someone else's beliefs and actions. Because we may not recognize their purpose, nudges can violate personal autonomy (Wilkinson, 2013).

The government also uses propaganda in more overt and recognizable ways. You may be familiar with public service announcements (PSAs) that aim to alter your behavior. In 2016, the Los Angeles Police Department launched a major campaign to increase public awareness of domestic violence. These billboards were eye-popping. One billboard was covered in bridal lace with the phrase, "You may now hit the bride," written to look like a wedding invitation. Another showed a stream of smartphone text messages that went from heart emojis to the controlling demand, "Where are you?" (Prince Street, 2016). The campaign was designed to increase public awareness of the many forms of controlling behavior that characterize domestic violence.

PSAs are no silver bullet for social problems, of course. Research has shown that some public service campaigns are highly effective, some are simply unmemorable, and others can have negative effects. Martin Fishbein conducted research on many of those antidrug ads that you may remember, including the one that features a frying egg: "This is your brain on drugs." He found a wide variation in the effectiveness of the antidrug PSAs produced by the the U.S. government. Most of the PSAs did, in fact, make adolescents think that they and their friends would be less likely to use drugs or that they would be more confident about how to handle situations in which drugs were offered or available. But there were several PSAs that had little or no effect. Some even had negative effects, causing adolescents to feel that they and their friends would be more likely to try drugs (Fishbein et al., 2002). Propaganda does not influence everyone the same way because people interpret media messages differently, based on their life experience and world view. Propaganda is not so powerful as to transform thinking human beings into mindless automatons (USHMM, 2007).

Entertainment

Another place where propaganda can be found is in performance and entertainment. In colonial times, songs and poems were used to interpret and offer meaning on the political issues of the day. Often, music can have a unifying effect on large groups of people. Samuel Adams, in particular, used protest songs in public demonstrations to rile up the public against the British. Music can inspire many people to feel patriotic or rebellious, or it can encourage people to reject war. The 17th century Scottish political activist Andrew Fletcher once said: "Let me make the songs of a nation, and I care not who makes its laws" (Alford & Rozbicka, 2018). When Childish Gambino released "This is America," it was an African American protest song that struck a deep chord among many people. The music video featured lyrics and choreography that critically examined police brutality, machismo, systems of racial oppression, and the entertaining distractions that keep Americans "from noticing how the world around them is falling apart" (Amoako, 2018).

Songs, books, and movies can show us how to feel. Stories offer characters, ideas and information about good and evil, right and wrong. Through such moral framing, values and ideology are expressed. Throughout the history of American film, a lot of movies have justified violence. In the war film, *Fury,* an American tank crew battles Germans toward the end of World War II. When one soldier hesitates to shoot a German boy, the tank commander, played by Brad Pitt, tells the young soldier that he must without hesitation kill anyone—even "a baby with a butter knife" (Ayer, 2014). Many American movies deliver a propaganda message that in war, soldiers must do terrible things like killing children.

Comedy news programs from celebrities like Trevor Noah, Jimmy Kimmel, Stephen Colbert, and Seth Meyers can also be seen as entertainment propaganda. These shows use ridicule to inform, persuade, and entertain. Whether or not these shows are beneficial or harmful propaganda is a matter of debate. Since the election of President Trump, some comedians have targeted not just the Republican politicians who support him, but the people who voted for him, leading some people to interpret the harsh jokes as evidence that "the entire media landscape loathes them, their values, their family, and their religion" (Flanagan, 2017).

Other companies outside of Hollywood are also creating propaganda by intentionally blurring the boundaries between entertainment, information, and persuasion. For example, in 2014, the restaurant chain Chipotle launched an online comedy series about the agriculture industry. That show aired on Hulu, an online streaming video service. Using comedy, the show reflected certain values about sustainable agriculture and the humane treatment of animals used for meat (Young, 2014).

Education

From kindergarten to college, some forms of education are explicitly designed to lead people to accept a particular worldview. Religious education helps people embrace the values of a faith community. But propaganda enters the public schools, too. Reciting the Pledge of Allegiance is an educational practice designed to instill feelings of patriotism. When librarians and educators carefully select appropriate books and media for children, they make choices that may function as propaganda. For example, they may use children's picture books that depict a typical family as consisting of a man, a woman, a boy, and a girl, or they may select works that represent more diverse family types. Students may read about how immigrants worked hard to build American communities, embracing democratic practices and contributing to society. They may learn about the profound injustices of slavery and the legacy of inequalities that resulted from it. Lessons about climate change may offer the point of view of coal companies or emphasize the value of alternative energy sources like wind and solar power. Biotechnology firms provide videos, lesson plans, and other materials for science teachers to explain about genetically modified vegetables.

Most teachers recognize how education can become a form of indoctrination when certain ideas, information, values, and beliefs are not permitted to be questioned. In higher education, indoctrination can occur when people do not get to access a wide range of ideas about social values or when one particular ideology or worldview dominates over others. Jacques Ellul (1973) pointed out that educators and intellectuals are actually more susceptible to propaganda because of their inflated sense of confidence that they are immune to its influence.

Activism and Advocacy

Civic action cannot occur without propaganda. Of course, you're familiar with how political communication is used to influence you to vote for (or against) a candidate. But activists can address broader social goals, too. People who are trying to improve society use a variety of persuasive genres to influence public opinion. Activists try to promote social, political, economic, or environmental causes through using communication activities and public events that attract attention, evoke emotion, and influence people's knowledge, attitudes, and opinions.

On social media, activists rework the trends and currents of popular culture for purposes of social change, connecting their goals to what people are paying attention to. Creative media activism helped create powerful visual symbols including the rainbow flag, the raised fist, the yellow ribbon, and Pepe the Frog, all familiar markers of different social causes. People can indicate their affiliation with a social cause very simply through using such symbols. Because of their emotional resonance, the use of such propaganda may strengthen feelings of connection to the cause.

Controversial actions of all kinds can function as propaganda. The videotaped murder of George Floyd by Minneapolis police activated widespread public outrage in 2020. When violent protests erupted in some cities, coverage of fires and looting might have led white people to reject the aims of the Black Lives Matter movement. But the excessive police response to peaceful protesters stimulated even more crowds as people all over the world came together to show their support for dismantling systemic racism in law enforcement. Media coverage depicted protesters who suffered brutality at the hands of police officers, intensifying sympathy for protesters. When political leaders dispersed Washington, D.C. crowds with tear gas and created photo opportunities featuring U.S. political and military leaders, this action helped activists build a highly effective narrative about the dangerous abuse of power by a corrupt government.

Activists use public protests to express their ideas about a better world, and this can inspire and motivate civic engagement and civic action. Perhaps you have even been a propagandist yourself when promoting a cause, a group, or an event that is meaningful or important to you. Perhaps you even designed a poster or a large sign with a clever phrase designed to attract attention and express your point of view. Being a propagandist is part of the job of being an active and engaged citizen in a democracy.

LEARNING ACTIVITY

Beneficial or Harmful Propaganda

Explore examples of propaganda and evaluate them, considering the potential benefits or harms of media messages.

Activity: Visit the Mind Over Media website, where users are invited to view, rate, upload, and comment on propaganda. This crowdsourced website contains thousands of examples of propaganda found in advertising, journalism and public relations, activism, education, government, entertainment. Visit www.mindovermedia.gallery and find an example of propaganda that interests you. After you rate it, you will see how others have rated it. After reading the comments of others, share your own interpretation of the example by adding a written comment on the website. Consider these questions:

- ***Who*** might see this propaganda as beneficial? ***Why*** might they value it?
- ***Who*** might see this propaganda as harmful? ***Why*** might they see it as potentially dangerous?

For Discussion: Assessing the potential benefits or harms of propaganda is complicated. When people interpret propaganda, they may choose to consider its potential impact on themselves alone. But they can also imagine its potential impact on members of their family, neighbors, and people in their community. They can even imagine influences on a larger scale as propaganda shapes public opinion in a country and even around the world.

The Takeaway: Talking about how values are embedded in propaganda helps people think more deeply about how social benefit and social harm are conceptualized in relation to both individuals and society.

–Adapted from Mind Over Media: Analyzing Contemporary Propaganda (Media Education Lab, 2018)

Mind Over Media: What to Expect

Many adults from all walks of life are fascinated with propaganda because of the intriguing ways it reflects and shapes the public mind. There has never been a more urgent time to learn about propaganda, as digital platforms are weaponized by a variety of agents. Readers with an interest in the topic of propaganda may be fascinated with its rhetorical, legal, political, literary, philosophical, sociological, or business dimensions. In this book, you will get a chance to see how critics, scholars, and researchers from many disciplines have interrogated the many ways that humans are now influencing each other in a digital age through the use of symbols, including language, image, sound, music, interactivity, algorithms, and more.

This book offers many examples of how elementary and secondary educators, school leaders, and college faculty are using the study of contemporary propaganda to build critical thinking and communication skills while advancing people's sense of social responsibility and community connectedness. Because propaganda enters into all disciplines and discourses, every educator needs to be knowledgeable about propaganda.

In order to help readers visualize the pedagogy of media literacy education when applied to the study of contemporary propaganda, this book describes a variety of strategies used by teachers from around the world who are strengthening the cognitive, social, and emotional competencies of students who are increasingly expected to be both savvy consumers and creative producers of media messages. As you read on, you'll see how the critical analysis of propaganda can apply to all subject areas from grade school to graduate school.

In Chapter 2, I examine the past, present, and future of propaganda education in the United States in relation to the theory and practice of media literacy education. The history of media literacy education in the United States reveals how, through trial and error, educators have developed and implemented instructional practices that build people's resilience to propaganda. You'll get a look at the many different ways that propaganda education enters the curriculum across the college and K–12 education system, in subjects including history, civics, English language and literature, the arts and sciences, and communication and media. We'll then unpack some myths of propaganda to better understand why some educators have fears and concerns about teaching students about it.

In Chapter 3, the focus is on understanding the economics of propaganda. Attracting and holding people's attention is at the heart of propaganda's power. Because advertising is the engine of media industries, it is critical for learners to understand the business model that makes propaganda so important in society. In elementary school, students can learn about the various forms of advertising that are part of their everyday life. They can appreciate how likes and shares are a form of data currency that have economic value in the media marketplace. Propaganda that gets digitally amplified via disinformation spread by fake accounts can create an illusion of popularity. This distortion can be exploited for political and economic gain. Learning activities can help students understand how attention is hijacked through attention-getting headlines that are specially designed to appeal to people's fundamental interests, values and needs.

In Chapter 4, we consider the practice of teaching news and current events in the increasingly polarized political climate of today. Students and teachers can use strategies that depolarize the classroom through establishing ground rules for responsible communication, reflecting on the web of belief, developing empathy, and recognizing the impact of partisanship on civil discourse and democracy. We also explore the six paradigms now being used by educators, journalists, and librarians to help students navigate the increasing variety of so-called fake news they encounter online. I show how teaching about propaganda involves a deep understanding of one's own ideological commitments in relation to many different forms of institutional power.

In Chapter 5, we'll learn more about propaganda's dark side, including a focus on intolerance, hate speech, disinformation, election interference, conspiracy theories, and, finally, terrorism. You'll get a chance to learn why people are so fascinated with potentially harmful propaganda and how it may activate certain feelings of pleasurable transgression. Teaching about harmful propaganda can be tricky in the classroom, but it offers great opportunities to address timely debates about the regulation of the Internet. Learners can evaluate the forms of regulation that are under discussion in the public sphere to explore how content moderation and government regulation may (or may not) help alleviate the problems caused by the most dangerous forms of digital propaganda.

In Chapter 6, the focus is on beneficial propaganda, including art, activism, and elections. Propaganda helps consensus to emerge. In a democratic society, the use of emotionally compelling propaganda can build support for new policies or help someone to get elected. Even as propaganda's power to shape and influence public opinion is undeniable, it must be understood as a form of artistic and creative expression that is protected under the First Amendment. Propaganda is legally protected speech because the democratic process of self-governance relies on the robust interchange of ideas. Artists and activists engage people's feelings about social issues that matter to them. Intense competition in the political arena has led to the development of political spin. Election propaganda is used by politicians to target potential voters using strategies that make people feel a sense of belonging. Learning activities can help to build students' understanding of the interplay between election propaganda, campaign funding, and public mistrust of government.

In Chapter 7, we consider the idea that propaganda is in the eye of the beholder, looking closely at how entertainment and education creates a shared sense of community and articulates social values. In the arena of popular culture, movies, TV shows, and video games may also function as sociological propaganda. Fictional stories activate strong emotions to convey particular values and ideologies that are generally not interrogated or questioned. In schools, propaganda can be found in climate science education, history textbooks, and even the literary canon. And by presenting particular depictions of history, public architecture, monuments and memorials express persuasive messages that resonate across generations, shaping how we think about and remember the past. In important ways, the study of entertainment and education propaganda offers opportunities for dialogue and inquiry on ethical values that may sustain and advance the strength of communities. In the epilogue, I reflect on how teaching and learning about propaganda cultivates self-awareness, curiosity and humility in ways that promote lifelong learning.

For thousands of years, people all over the world have understood that control over symbolic expression—storytelling, art, music, news, and information—can change the world, for better or for worse. Symbols and emotions are powerful. They shape our perception of ourselves, our communities, and possibilities for the future. People who are media literate recognize that propaganda is not all powerful and that we don't need to be afraid of it. By creating propaganda, people discover how creativity and strategy combine to influence public opinion. In the next chapter, I introduce you to the generations of educators who appreciated the value of studying propaganda and persuasive genres in school. Their stories enable us to reflect on the role that teachers play in helping learners understand both the power and responsibility of public communication.

2

Propaganda Education

Educators have long understood the importance of helping people critically analyze propaganda

Perhaps you remember the startling announcement on Facebook, just before the 2016 presidential election, from WTOE 5 News: "Pope Francis Shocks World, Endorses Donald Trump for President, Issues Statement." I will never forget the day I saw that message on my Facebook feed. I really was shocked. It looked so real that I was tempted to share it with my friends, but I thought better of it. I immediately gathered additional information to try to confirm the statement, learning that WTOE 5 was not a real news outlet and Pope Francis did not endorse either American presidential candidate. But in those heated days before the 2016 election, nearly 1 million people shared that particular story, making it one of the top so-called fake news stories of 2016. And of course, there were hundreds of other examples of false and misleading information circulating online as the fake news phenomenon spread like wildfire, not just here in the United States but in Germany, Italy, and around the world.

Since the concept of fake news erupted on the scene, there's been a lot of talk about the importance of teaching students to critically analyze news and information. Researchers have found that most adults can't accurately judge the truth or falsity of an online news story. They can't identify sponsored content on a website. Most people assume that content that aligns with their existing beliefs is automatically accurate. However, research evidence reported in the *American Educa-*

tional Research Journal from Joseph Kahne and his colleagues shows that teens and young adults who have had some exposure to media literacy and civic education in school are better able to judge misleading content as false, even if it is aligned with their existing political beliefs (Kahne & Bowyer, 2017). They have also found that students who get digital civic engagement opportunities while in school are later more likely to engage in online practices that foster democratic participation. For example, youth who had more than three class periods to create and share media in school were more likely to support an online petition or contact a government office, company, or organization. Those students were more likely to send an email or post a comment on a website or Facebook page (Kahne & Bowyer, 2019).

There are many good reasons to implement digital and media literacy education in schools and universities, where students are learning to be citizens in a democracy. It takes practice to sort out how to analyze and evaluate all the media messages that are part of everyday life. By creating media to share with audiences, young people gain confidence that their opinions and ideas have real value and worth to others. They take up the practice of self-governance. As both creators and consumers of media content, students develop the social and civic responsibilities to thrive in a digital age.

Many media literacy educators struggle with the term "fake news," which is a phrase that conceals more than it reveals. In the 1980s, the term was originally used to describe entertainment-oriented television news magazine shows and, later, comedy journalism like *The Daily Show with Jon Stewart.* At the time, some people worried that comedy journalism would degrade people's trust in TV news. But perhaps the rise of comedy journalism was simply a reaction to the loss of trust that resulted from the decades-long infusion of entertainment values into journalism (Postman, 1986). The term fake news shifted its meaning rather quickly when President Donald Trump began repeatedly using the term in rallies and tweets to disparage the press. Whenever journalists reported on his behaviors and policies in ways he did not find flattering enough, he labeled them with the phase, saying "You're fake news." Others began using the term even more broadly to refer to partisan journalism and political spin.

Media literacy educators and school, public and academic librarians have certainly benefitted from the visibility that the term has provided. It has given us the opportunity to highlight the urgent need to help all Americans critically analyze information, news and media. But I sometimes resist using the term "fake news" precisely because it has been used to focus attention solely on news and journalism. Learners should acquire strategies that help them understand and evaluate the many different types of messages that are part of daily life, including entertainment, advertising, social media posts, satire and parody, conspiracy theories, pseudoscience, and more. In this chapter, I take a close look at the past, present, and future of propaganda education in the context of media literacy, English language arts, and civic education. Teaching and learning *about* propaganda can support the development of a set of habits of mind that support literacy and lifelong learning.

Propaganda Education as Media Literacy

Scholars emphasize that literacy is a historically, socially, and culturally situated practice, part of people's everyday lives and central to the process of teaching and learning (Jewitt, 2008). While print texts are at the center of the institutional construction of literacy in schools and universities, people's experience at home and at work involves a much wider array of forms and genres, including plenty of popular culture, digital, and multimedia content. Reading for work and school, reading for pleasure, viewing movies and TV shows, watching videos on YouTube, looking at photos on Instagram, reading, creating, and commenting on social media posts on Facebook, reading and composing text messages, listening to music in the car or in the subway, playing video games with family and friends, reading or viewing the news, researching potential purchases online—these are the literacy practices of daily life. In all of these contexts, people are likely to experience propaganda.

For literacy to be culturally responsive to people's lived experience, educators cannot neglect the inherently political dimensions of literacy, including Paulo Freire and Donaldo Macedo's (2005) construction of literacy as "reading the word and reading the world." This is why educators who embrace media literacy education value the process of helping students see themselves as active participants in society and agents of social change (Mihailidis, 2019). This theme is particularly important for exploring the topic of propaganda, which is itself designed to influence public opinion.

Media literacy education advanced significantly in the 1980s as scholars and practitioners integrated key ideas from a variety of academic disciplines and fields, including media studies and communication, literary theory, psychology, and cultural studies (Hobbs & Mihailidis, 2019). Media representations are understood as socially situated practices that are invariably intertwined with issues of both aesthetics and social, political and economic power (Luke & Freebody, 1997). In one way or the other, power enters in to all elements of the spiral of cognitive and social competencies that are activated when we engage in practices of reading and writing with messages and media in a wide variety of forms. The following media literacy competencies help learners move through a cycle of inquiry learning:

- ***Access:*** Using media and technology tools skillfully and finding and sharing appropriate and relevant content with others;
- ***Analyze and evaluate:*** Comprehending messages and using critical thinking to analyze message quality, veracity, credibility, and point of view, while considering potential effects or consequences of messages;
- ***Create:*** Composing or generating content using creativity and confidence in self-expression, with awareness of purpose, audience, and composition techniques;
- ***Reflect:*** Applying caring, social responsibility, and ethical principles to one's own social identity and lived experience, communication behavior, and conduct;
- ***Take Action:*** Working individually and collaboratively to share knowledge and solve problems in the family, the workplace and the community, and participating as a member of a community at local, regional, national, and international levels (Hobbs, 2010).

On a practical level, there are numerous instructional practices that facilitate the development of media literacy competencies. Some classic strategies for teaching and learning media literacy have become time-honored techniques for educators at all levels. For example:

- ***Media diary*** activities involve careful documentation and record-keeping activities that help people reflect on their choices and decisions in how they use media and technology.
- ***Inquiry, search, and research*** activities that involve asking questions and finding, evaluating, and sharing content from a variety of sources helps people explore diverse sources of information. Using inquiry strategies appropriate to one's needs helps people make discriminating choices about content, quality, and relevance.

- ***Reading, viewing, listening, and discussing*** involve the active interpretation of texts, which helps people acquire new ideas, perspectives, and knowledge and make sense of it in relation to lived experience. Dialogue and sharing help deepen understanding and appreciation.
- ***Close analysis*** activities that involve careful examination of the constructed nature of particular texts encourage people to use critical questioning to examine the author's intent and issues of representation.
- ***Cross-media comparison*** activities involve comparing and contrasting two (or more) texts to develop critical thinking skills. By examining genre, purpose, form and content, and point of view, people recognize how media shape message content.
- ***Gaming, simulation, and role-playing*** are playful activities that promote multiperspectival thinking and cultivate imagination, creativity, and decision-making skills, advancing reflective thinking about choices and consequences.
- ***Media composition*** activities that involve learners in collaborating and creating media to address a particular audience in a specific context for a particular purpose or to accomplish a stated goal.
- ***Civic action*** is the practice of using communicative power to make a difference locally, regionally, nationally or globally. By creating media that expresses values and goals, students gain respect for the democratic process.

Learning about propaganda inevitably involves thinking about oneself in relationship to a larger community or communities where mutual influence occurs. We are all part of a variety of different publics and propaganda has helped to forge our identities and allegiances. Through discussing our interpretations of propaganda, learners share ideas and listen to the ideas of others. Through this process, reciprocal influence occurs. This give-and-take dynamic helps cultivate civic culture. It helps create consensus. Guided by a teacher, learners can engage in activities and interventions that articulate their values and achieve real and meaningful goals for themselves and their communities. When done well, the process can be truly magical and it's why I believe that media literacy education can advance the kind of critical consciousness and embodied learning that can have far-reaching implications for society.

LEARNING ACTIVITY

Memes as Propaganda Posters

It has been said that memes are modern-day propaganda.

Activity: Consider the memes shown below. Working individually or with a partner, choose one or more to discuss.

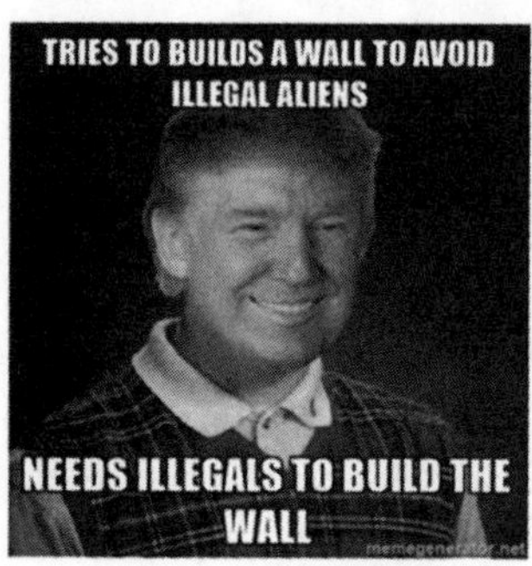

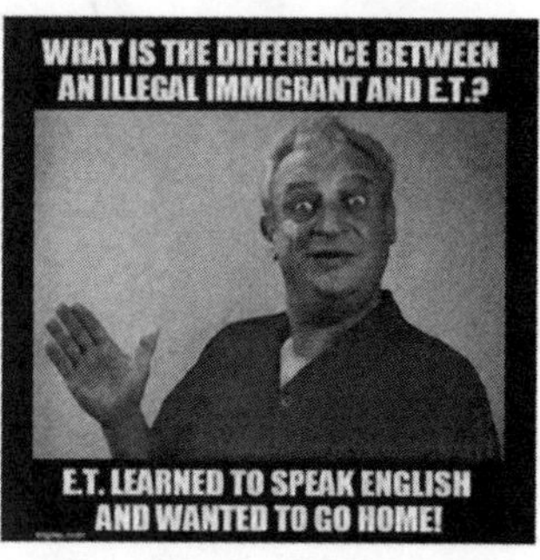

1. ***Message:*** What ideas are being expressed? What visual elements are used?

2. ***Context:*** What hopes, fears, or grievances are present in society at this point in time? Consider the economic, political, and social climate.
3. ***Point of View:*** What visual and verbal evidence in the text offers ideas concerning the author's point of view?
4. ***Audience:*** Who is the target audience? What is it about this message that would be appealing to this group? What reactions might different audiences have?
5. ***Creator:*** Who is the propagandist? Why was this message created? What do they hope that the audience will think, feel, and do?
6. ***Consequences:*** What potential beneficial or harmful effects could this message have on individuals and society?

For Discussion: Are memes like propaganda posters? Why or why not? Explain some of the many similarities and differences and reflect on the potential implications for audiences and authors.

The Takeaway: When pictures and words are combined in creative ways that respond to the ongoing issues in the contemporary social and political climate, they may express complex ideas and influence target audiences in ways that may be beneficial or harmful.

A Short History of Propaganda Education

As media have changed over time, educators have found creative ways to help students to recognize propaganda in print, audio, visual, and digital forms by exploring news, advertising, literature, and political communication. Most people think they know about how propaganda was used in Nazi Germany. When pressed, many people seem familiar with Nazi patriotic propaganda films like Leni Riefenstahl's epic *Triumph of the Will*. They may recall having studied Nazi propaganda posters in school or hearing about *The Eternal Jew*, a fake documentary film created by the Nazis. Hitler first used propaganda to gain political power, and then used it to justify war, mass murder, and genocide. Some know that, as Führer, Hitler took over all aspects of culture, education, and the arts with a centralized propaganda ministry, led by Joseph Goebbels.

But too many students today think propaganda only happened in the past and it only happened in the German Third Reich. They don't realize that Hitler was inspired by British and American approaches to propaganda used in World War I. Many Americans are unfamiliar with how emotional imagery was first used by the U.S. government to depict Germans as threatening, menacing animals. But the American approach to propaganda during World War I also included more subtle forms that relied on the power of thought leaders, those influential community members known for their leadership qualities. These individuals, known as the Four-Minute Men, were a carefully selected group of 75,000 white men who delivered war updates at theaters and other public gatherings throughout the country (Jowett & O'Donnell, 2012). Of course, American schools were also used to promote the Great War, with 75 million pieces of literature provided to public schools across the United States in a two-year span, enrolling teachers as propagandists to explain why Americans needed to fight (Axelrod, 2009). These messages activated feelings of patriotic duty that inspired people to support the war effort.

After World War I, people discovered how to use propaganda for commercial purposes. When Edward Bernays got upper-middle-class women to walk around New York City carrying and smoking their "torches of freedom" during the 1929 Easter Sunday Parade, it was a sensation. Working on behalf of his tobacco industry client, pictures of the event were sent to newspapers all around the world (Bernays, 1928/2005). These images linked cigarettes to women's growing aspirations for a better life. Women themselves were attracted to the idea that they could display their feminist impulses for emancipation and equality through smoking. This form of propaganda was highly effective. In 1923 women only purchased 5% of cigarettes sold but in 1929 that percentage jumped to 12%, more than doubling the number of women smokers (Welch, 2013). The success of Bernays's staged public event inspired cigarette manufacturers to explicitly target women with messages about the desirability of smoking, and the field of public relations was born.

I must disclose a small bit of personal connection to this slice of propaganda history. My interest in propaganda started when I was a young scholar, when I had a once-in-a-lifetime opportunity to meet the legendary Edward Bernays, who called himself the father of public relations. I got to have dinner with him at a Boston-area dinner party hosted by a colleague. By that time, he was in his 80s, a little hard of hearing but still sharp as a tack. When I asked him about the torches of freedom campaign, he acknowledged that it was a significant accomplishment; he pointed out that at that time, people did not understand the health risks of smoking. When he later became aware of the dangers in the 1940s, he refused to work for tobacco companies. At the dinner, he said to me, "To be a good propagandist, you have to truly believe that your product or idea has real value for people."

When Bernays said he was a "good" propagandist, I recognized the ambiguity inherent in the statement. He was an advocate for the ethical practice of propaganda, which he called public relations. When a critic accused him of manipulating the public like a puppet master, Bernays countered that propaganda was truly democratic because anyone could use it, not just those with wealth and power. As he saw it, propaganda could be used by educators, labor unions, and reformers, to fight for good causes and to fight against intolerance and tyranny. He knew that propaganda was not a magic bullet that affected everyone the same way. He believed that truth seeking and propaganda were not incompatible, and that propaganda, or the mass promotion of ideas, is necessary to change society in beneficial ways (Bernays, 1929).

By midcentury, movies were also becoming more widely used for propaganda purposes. Audiences were captivated by film, and their widespread public dissemination became an increasingly important way to influence the public. Hollywood glamour, depicted in movies of the 1920s and '30s, was cultivating an entire generation's interest in fashion, music, and dance. But innovation in film was also occurring outside the orbit of Hollywood. Under the New Deal, thousands of unemployed people were put to work through federal programs that affected nearly every city and town in the United States. Some of these people were filmmakers, writers, and artists. They made films about erosion control and land improvements, educational and social programs, and issues of poverty and inequality. For example, one 9-minute documentary film produced by the National Youth Administration depicted a program for teen boys at Camp DeSoto in Tampa, Florida, where they worked on motors and in wood shops, metal shops, and classrooms. Hundreds of these inspiring short films helped to document how American ingenuity was helping people recover from the Great Depression (Orgeron, Orgeron & Streible, 2011).

When filmmakers tried to persuade, they could be very effective indeed. In 1940, famed documentary director Pare Lorentz made *The Fight for Life* about an urban maternity clinic. The director was aware that the people living in the slums of Pittsburgh could be depicted in ways that could lead viewers to either hate them or love them (Lorentz, 1992). Filmmakers of the era began to develop an ethic of social justice and accountability for the social impact of their work. Both Hollywood entertainment and documentary film could help to shape Americans' sense of public identity and renew their commitment to shared values. Films produced with support from the federal government played a key role in helping to unify national public opinion (Uricchio & Roholl, 2005).

LEARNING ACTIVITY

Advocacy Documentary Past and Present

Compare and contrast the work of two documentary filmmakers who used film to inspire public awareness and shape public policy.

Activity: View "Pare Lorentz: FDR's Filmmaker," a short video that describes the work of Pare Lorentz, a West Virginia filmmaker who created important documentary films in the 1930s about the Dust Bowl, environmental degradation, and urban maternal health. Sponsored by the U.S. government under the administration of Franklin Delano Roosevelt, Lorentz used film to inspire public awareness through skillful use of imagery, storytelling, music, and narration.

Then listen to "Michael Moore on Documentaries and Propaganda," a short segment from NPR's *Talk of the Nation* radio program, in which the filmmaker Michael Moore explains how his social issue documentaries on health care and other topics offer balance to the dominant opinions and perspectives offered by government and corporate media.

For Discussion: How are the films of Pare Lorentz and Michael Moore similar? How are they different? Neither Pare Lorentz nor Michael Moore thought of themselves as propagandists. Discuss the reasons why they rejected the term. Then offer your interpretation on whether or not you see their work as a form of propaganda.

The Takeaway: Documentary filmmakers offer a distinct point of view on social and cultural issues. When their interpretation of public events is effective, it can have a substantial effect on public opinion and public policy.

Philanthropies Recognize the Power of Propaganda

Research on propaganda in news, radio, and film gradually became an important field of study during the 1930s and '40s, as scholars with interests in the intersections of political science, psychology, and sociology began to study the new communications technologies of the era. Their work attracted the interest of leaders of major foundations, who believed that studies of radio listeners could build a foundation of social science research by documenting audience behavior. Using new methods for examining the content and impact of media messages, it might be possible to increase the value of public communication for public good. In helping to develop propaganda research by providing both coordination and financial support, a Rockefeller Foundation executive explained in 1936, "Both radio and motion pictures are recognized as instrumentalities potentially of great importance alike for formal education and for the general diffusion of culture. But they have so far been exploited for the most part for purposes of entertainment" (Rockefeller Foundation, 2016, p. 1).

The Rockefeller Foundation's support for research on propaganda certainly jump-started the emerging field of communication and media. Lasswell's landmark content analysis of wartime propaganda techniques, published in 1938, revealed the power of appealing to diverse target audiences by connecting to audience needs and values. Propagandists also learned to create a variety of messages from multiple sources, which helped to create an illusion of diverse perspectives all converging upon a shared consensus.

Propaganda education has its origins in a by-product of this important work, when a group of academics, educators, and professional communicators came together to pull back the curtain on the structure and function of wartime propaganda, political communication, and commercial advertising. A group of scholars gathered under the aegis of the Rockefeller Foundation Group on Mass Communication Research, including Columbia University sociologist Robert S. Lynd; George Gallup, a leader of public opinion polling; Frank Stanton, future president of CBS; and Paul Lazarsfeld, a social scientist who became a leader in communication research. They all recognized the value of research in communication to address the nature of mass communication, the rise of advertising and public relations, and its impact on the political process (Glander, 2000).

At the same time, the growing cultural influence of Hollywood caught the attention of well-placed individuals in Washington and New York. In an article published in 1940, Donald Slesinger, director of the American Film Center (which was funded by the Rockefeller Foundation), observed that the leaders of the American movie industry had three interrelated goals: art, commerce, and politics. For this reason, he said, it was important for people to be alert to how their objectives and motives might influence public opinion.

Perhaps the growing concern about moving image propaganda could be addressed through education. Although films were actively used for propaganda purposes during the 1930s, Slesinger believed that intentionally "persuasive films fall far short of an educational objective" because an "audience that is swept off its feet by one film has its critical faculties so dulled that another film can sweep it right back on." He wrote, "Any successful propaganda makes an audience receptive to all propaganda." Thus, educators should focus on the development of students' attitudes and abilities that base social action on critical analysis rather than on emotion, building up people's "propaganda resistance" (Slesinger, 1940, p. 265).

Another group with interests in propaganda resistance emerged during this time, but these individuals were not university researchers. Instead, they were a group of journalists and high school teachers working with business and civic leaders who were concerned about the rise of propaganda and demagoguery in the United States. They founded the Institute for Propaganda Analysis (IPA) in 1937 in New York City. The IPA created resource materials for educators and librarians to help the public detect, recognize, and analyze propaganda. This work, housed at Columbia University, was the first large-scale media literacy education initiative in the United States. For six years, this group was involved in designing and delivering resources to help educators introduce propaganda analysis into the classroom. They developed lesson plans, worksheets, and readings for high school students and their teachers, to help young people develop critical thinking skills in responding to contemporary propaganda (Hobbs & McGee, 2014).

This group decided to focus their outreach on high school teachers, their students, and the patrons of public libraries. But selecting educators and students as a target audience was unusual in many ways. During this time period, American public education was in a state of crisis. Declining school budgets were part of the legacy of the Great Depression. Although there were plenty of ambitious experiments to modernize the curriculum to address the needs of the increasingly diverse population, school budgets had been slashed. Educators were concerned about the loss of health education, music, art, home economics, and school libraries. They worried that the back-to-basics movement was negatively impacting the quality of learning for children and young people.

Some educators realized that they and their traditional approaches were becoming irrelevant to the fast-paced contemporary world, where film and radio were reshaping the cultural values of a new generation. A growing number of educators wanted teaching and learning to be more directly relevant to the real-world experience of growing up in "new times."

The activities of the Institute for Propaganda Analysis were made possible by funding from Edward Filene, the business leader and philanthropist who owned Filene's department store in Boston. Filene spent more than $1 million to support the IPA between 1937 and 1941 in creating and distributing educational materials helping teachers engage students in critically analyzing propaganda. As the son of a Jewish immigrant, he was deeply aware of anti-Semitism and the growing persecution of Jews in Europe and around the world (Hobbs & McGee, 2014).

Heading the IPA was Clyde Miller, a journalist who oversaw the IPA's editorial operations and helped published the first five issues of the magazine *Propaganda Analysis*. Miller believed that education was "the American way of dealing with disinformation," noting that propaganda cannot be censored by government due to the First Amendment. In a 1939 speech, he also pointed out that learning to critically analyze propaganda does not diminish the effectiveness of potentially beneficial propaganda messages. Instead, it simply allows learners to consider the many ways that propaganda aims to influence people without their conscious awareness (Schiffrin, 2018).

In his new magazine, Miller and his team developed short informational articles with titles including "How to Detect Propaganda" and "How to Analyze Newspapers." This publication attracted 10,000 subscribers and was mailed to thousands of high schools, colleges, and public libraries throughout the United States. By the late 1930s, 1 million students were using IPA's instructional materials and methods to analyze propaganda, and 2,500 teachers had corresponded with Miller and his team.

But propaganda education turned out to be controversial once the U.S. entered World War II and accelerated its own wartime propaganda initiative. In 1941, many of the IPA's board and supporters joined the war effort. The IPA decided to disband, fearing its work could be misunderstood as critical of the war. After the war, the United States government included programs in propaganda education as part of military training. Army trainers emphasized that knowledge of propaganda's varying mechanisms and the ability to critically analyze it would be the best defense to help protect people's rights to freedom of expression (U.S. Department of the Army, 1954)

Sadly, as anticommunist hysteria started to rise in America in 1947, the IPA was wrongly listed by the House Un-American Activities Committee as a communist front organization (Schiffrin, 2018). Still, the organization made important inroads into American public education: it helped the American public to recognize the importance of teaching about propaganda as a part of the process of learning to be an informed and skeptical consumer.

Certainly, the most important legacy of the IPA is its list of seven devices or techniques used to identify propaganda (Lee & Lee, 1939). You may even have learned about these techniques when you were in school. These seven techniques are rooted in classical theories of rhetoric and they were attuned to the rise of radio as a dominant medium of social influence. They offer catchy labels like "glittering generalities" and "card stacking" that let learners in on some of the tricks used by those who try to manipulate them.

The list of seven rhetorical devices is explicitly presented as the knowledge needed to avoid being victimized by a presumably powerful and manipulative persuader. According to the IPA, awareness of these devices "keeps us from having our thought processes blocked by a trick" (Miller & Edwards, 1936, p. 24). Today, teachers continue to be concerned about young people's vulnerability to media influence, aware that those who create propaganda target anyone perceived to be susceptible to messages that evoke strong emotions, attack opponents, simplify information, and appeal to people's deepest hopes, fears, and dreams.

LEARNING ACTIVITY

Update the Seven Propaganda Devices

Multiple generations of Americans learned to spot propaganda by using this list of persuasive techniques.

Activity: Review the seven propaganda devices and find updated examples from the present day. Advanced learners might be invited to reframe and redefine each technique from the point of view of the public relations professional, the political campaign consultant, the philanthropist, the activist, or even a foreign enemy.

Seven Propaganda Devices

- ***Name calling:*** Using labels with a negative connotation to simplify information and evoke strong emotion in ways that favor a specific agenda.
- ***Bandwagon:*** Emphasizing the popularity of a person, idea, or practice in ways that tap into people's need for belonging.
- ***Glittering generalities:*** An attempt to sway emotions through the use of ideals or virtues (such as freedom, justice, truth, education, democracy) in a large, general way.
- ***Card stacking:*** Using omission, distortion, lies, or false testimony to create an unreal reality that deceives people through the presentation of information.
- ***Plain folks:*** Presenting an image of personal identity that emphasizes the similarities between oneself and the group being targeted.
- ***Flag waving:*** Building a symbolic connection between the authority, respect, and prestige of a particular symbol, individual, or institution to promote another person, idea, or practice. This propaganda technique is also sometimes called transfer.
- ***Testimonial:*** Using the voices of established celebrities, authorities, community leaders, and well-respected individuals to offer their support.

For Discussion: Some of these rhetorical techniques of propaganda are more ethically defensible than others. Some may be used in unfair, manipulative and even dangerous ways. Which ones do you think are most problematic? Which are least likely to cause harm?

The Takeaway: Recognizing propaganda techniques helps us be alert to the many strategies people use to influence each other through symbolic expression.

–Adapted from A. Lee & E. Lee (1939), "The Fine Art of Propaganda"

History Educators Offer Propaganda Education

As the American government ramped up propaganda targeting American citizens in order to produce widespread support for World War II, they were responding to the work of survey researchers of the time, who had found that many Americans were ambivalent about the war and did not understand the rationale for fighting it. As the war drew to a close, both soldiers and the American public had concerns about what would be different when the war ended. The U.S. military asked American history professors for assistance in influencing soldiers and the general public to be more optimistic about the postwar future.

Historians and history educators were happy to comply. Under the direction of the Army's Division of Information and Education, the American Historical Association produced a series of pamphlets in a series called G.I. Roundtable "to increase the effectiveness of the soldiers and officers as fighters during the war and as citizens after the war." In order to improve morale, they emphasized the value of military service as key to building the future of the nation. In 2002, in one of the first digital history projects, Robert Townsend of the American Historical Association digitized the collection of pamphlets and made them available online. One of the goals of this pamphlet series was to communicate to soldiers about what a postwar world would look like. The government wanted to reassure soldiers that they would be able to establish careers and families when they returned from military service. These pamphlets were widely distributed to service men and women and offer a glimpse of the social issues people were discussing and debating at the time, including crime, jobs, foreign policy, and the role of women in society.

Today, it's easy to see the racial, gender, and social class bias of these documents. Produced between 1944 and 1946, the pamphlets seem to depict a future without working women or racial minorities. Topics included exploration of family decisions like "Shall I Build a House After the War?" and "Do You Want Your Wife to Work After the War?"

Historians knew that the subject matter of propaganda itself needed to be explained in ways that helped the public understand why it was justified as part of the war effort. That's why the very first pamphlet in the series was titled, "What Is Propaganda?" Created in 1944 by Ralph Casey, a professor of journalism at the University of Minnesota, the pamphlet series also provided specific and detailed information and advice for discussion leaders. After making the pamphlet available for group members, discussion leaders were invited to give a 10-minute introductory talk about propaganda, defining the term and suggesting the question of whether a propagandist needed a conscious purpose. Might someone be a propagandist without being aware of it? Another suggested opening question was the issue of whether there is such a thing as "good propaganda" or how propagandists could make unethical use of rhetorical devices to befog rather than clarify issues (Casey, 1944).

Four pieces of practical advice were offered to discussion leaders. Because for many persons propaganda was "a smear word," discussion leaders were urged to challenge this belief. In defining propaganda, an important distinction was made between forms of propaganda whose authorship is concealed and those that are open and avowed. When propagandists are transparent about their goals, their work contributes to democratic deliberation and may help advance the public interest.

Distinguishing between propaganda and education was the second piece of advice offered for teaching about propaganda. Teachers, parents, scientists, and government officials are all agents of socialization who also aim to influence people's knowledge, opinions, and beliefs. An important function of education is to "train individuals to be immune to the distortions, the biases, the omissions, and the prejudices found in the various types of propaganda material" (1944, p. 1). Education could liberate people from the risks of propaganda by advancing critical thinking skills.

Another important distinction concerned the differences between the use of propaganda in a democracy and in an authoritarian nation. In educating adults about propaganda, it is important to consider the system of governance in place in a particular society. In a capitalistic democracy, advertising is an important form of propaganda, but consumers are free to accept or reject the messages they encounter. In an authoritarian dictatorship, the immediate threat of peer pressure, intimidation, and even violence creates an intense pressure toward conformity. In Germany, at the time, political loyalty was narrowly reframed in relationship to a focus on upholding the leader at all costs. The propaganda apparatus that was available to Hitler, including the press, film, radio, magazines, the education system, museums, and cultural institutions, was buttressed by a massive military force with a predilection for brutal violence. This made it very difficult for German citizens to reject or critique the ideological messages of the Third Reich.

Finally, the importance of provoking discussion was emphasized. Participants learned that genuine dialogue and deliberation can be a safeguard against propaganda because it activates multiple points of view that demand both reflective and critical thinking. In activating people's capacity for deliberative dialogue, the following questions were suggested:

- How does differential access to specific information and facts influence public opinion?
- How does the element of prestige work in fixing or altering attitudes and opinions?
- If people get fed up with propaganda, will that reduce its influence on them?
- Do many individuals support propaganda that is in the public interest and not solely in line with their own selfish interests?
- True or false: "Although propaganda is pervasive and will be persistent, it need not be fatal to intelligent popular decisions." (Casey, 1944, p. 1)

Both educators and government officials clearly hoped that public discussion of the question "What is propaganda?" would inoculate citizens against it while enabling them to deepen their respect for freedom of expression in a diverse society.

Critical Viewing and Critical Literacy

Less than ten years after the end of World War II, a new medium emerged that inspired educators to want to teach about the commercial propaganda that was reaching into living rooms to reach the youngest Americans. Early on, educators recognized that television's potent mix of entertainment, information, and persuasion could be used for propaganda purposes. In the 1960s and early '70s, a sharp rise in commercial culture was erupting as watching television became a dominant part of childhood. At this time, children were watching more than 20 hours of television per week, and adults watched even more. The barrage of ads and promotion, the violent actions of characters, the presentation of superficial stereotypes, and the overstimulating fast pace of the programming was a concern to parents across the nation.

Inspired by the zeitgeist of the times, some parents became activists to pressure government and the media industry for regulation. Others took up the challenge of educating teachers and parents. In 1977, Elizabeth Thoman created *Media&Values*, a magazine that targeted general interest readers, helping them understand the discussions, debates, and controversies associated with television, culture and society. For parents who were troubled by the high volume of noisy commercials that activated children's pester power, the magazine was a godsend. Articles examined the power of racial and gender stereotypes in the media to reinforce or challenge discrimination. Readers could learn how radio and television were regulated; they were encouraged to participate in "talking back" to regulators and businesses about the quality of TV content. It explained scholarly work in media and communication in accessible short articles that helped people gain knowledge about media's cultural power. *Media&Values* magazine reached thousands of readers across the United States and helped build a national community of media literacy activists and educators (RobbGrieco, 2018).

As interest in the topic grew, educators and developmental psychologists also began to explore the idea of teaching students about television. James Anderson and his colleagues were exploring something they called receivership skills in the mid-1970s (Anderson & Ploghoft, 1980). By 1978, Dorothy and Jerome Singer of Yale University developed a curriculum for children called Creating Critical Viewers. With funding from the ABC television network, they developed, implemented, and assessed a curriculum for children ages 8 to 10. They wanted to help children understand these ideas:

1. There are many different types of TV programs.
2. They are created by writers, producers, directors, and other personnel.
3. TV content uses a variety of techniques including fantasy, pretend, and special effects.
4. Advertising is a form of expression that is designed to sell products.
5. It influences people's emotions and provides ideas in ways that affect self-concept and identity.
6. Television can be a source of information about people, countries, and occupations.
7. Stereotypes are representations that oversimplify.
8. In TV shows, characters' violent behavior rarely depicts the aftermath and consequences that would occur in real life.
9. People make choices about what and how often to view television.
10. People can express their opinions to aim to influence networks, producers, and TV stations (Rapaczynski, Singer & Singer, 1982).

Critical viewing lessons were effective with young children. Experimental results showed that even four months after the lessons, children remembered the knowledge they had gained from the critical viewing skills curriculum and were able to define words like fiction, animation, sponsor, and prejudice. The instructors noted that children were highly aware of the differences between the way a toy is depicted on TV commercials and what it's like to actually play with it. But researchers also noted that most of the children's parents were not very interested in participating in TV critical viewing workshops, believing that "television was a problem for other children, especially children less privileged than their own" (Singer & Singer, 1980, p. 92).

Over time, however, parents and teachers became more deeply engaged in this work, and with support from the National Parent Teacher Association and the National Academy of Television Arts and Sciences, trainings were offered to thousands of parents and adults across the country (Cherow-O'Leary, 2014). The cable television industry also supported similar initiatives including Know TV and Assignment Media Literacy, which I created (Hobbs, 1994; 1999). The media literacy movement coalesced during the 1990s as educators, scholars, and policy makers came together to form a national organization for the growing community, originally called the Partnership for Media Education and later renamed the National Association for Media Literacy Education. I consider myself very fortunate to have been a team member in advancing this movement as the community grew larger and more diverse.

At the same time, a controversy erupted over the issue of audiovisual propaganda in American public education that implicated the entire media literacy community and all those interested in using the power of visual media as tool for teaching and learning about news and current events. Beginning in 1989, Channel One offered schools access to a daily current events news program targeted to teens ages 12 to 17. The program was available to schools for free and was subsidized by 2 minutes of advertising. The U.S. government was the single largest advertiser, reaching young audiences with military recruiting ads and public health messages. School districts who agreed to the free service received television monitors in every high school and middle school classroom. Many schools leaped on the opportunity to bring Channel One into the classroom because, at the time, access to television technology in school was expensive and the use of video for learning was considered desirable. Also, certain beliefs had saturated public consciousness about the value of both advertising and news. Among them was the idea that exposure to current events is important for the development of young people's citizenship skills and that advertising is not significantly harmful to adolescents.

Some educators, including myself, believed that the media industry had a social responsibility to bring media literacy lessons into the curriculum, and that Channel One could be a vital resource to help students analyze news, advertising and propaganda. But other educators believed that exposure to advertising was harmful and that seeing ads in school could not be countered by critical analysis activities. They believed that advertising in public schools represented a form of coercion, because students were required to watch both the 10-minute news program and its 2 minutes of advertising (Heins & Cho, 2003).

Because advertising is a form of propaganda that uses nonrational techniques to build image-driven associations between products and feelings, its harms may not be obvious at first glance (Rozendaal, Lapierre, van Reijmersdal, & Buijzen, 2011). Advertising is such a ubiquitous propaganda for capitalism that learners might not recognize that the display of materialistic values may cause "economic harms (debt cycle, stress) and psychological harms (anxieties, frustrations) to individuals and families" and encourage consumption and waste, contributing greatly "to the global problems of pollution, environmental destruction, and social justice" (Rank, 1992, p. 32). Controversy about the role of the media industry in media literacy education caused great debate in the American media literacy community that continues to this very day.

Another set of controversies emerged over the development of critical literacy, a term that explicitly addresses cultural and social issues related to social justice and power inequalities. Some educators want to raise students' awareness about political and social issues they experience in everyday life. Through close analysis of popular culture, students learn how ideologies of power are depicted in familiar movies and TV shows, including Disney animation. They begin to notice voices and points of view that are not well represented in the media. They learn to recognize and resist the status quo norms that reproduce social injustices related to race, class, and gender. Finally, they engage in actions that help them develop powerful voices that could transform the world into a more socially just one (Odrowaz-Coates, 2016). For example, in one classroom, students decided to take action through "designing slogans and using them to protest against violence in the village streets, or writing letters-of-critique to politicians or authors of sexist stories" (Hayik, 2011, p. 98). The practice of critical literacy engages students in learning to be activists who use the power of communication and information to transform society.

But the question of whether critical literacy is liberating or a form of indoctrination may depend upon your point of view. When teachers try to interrogate cultural norms and values in relation to contemporary political issues, it can seem like values education to some students, and indoctrination to others. Because the pedagogy puts the instructor in a key intervening role, lessons often reproduce the instructor's existing beliefs and world view (Wooldridge, 2001). Students may choose to simply agree with the teacher in order to get a good grade. Others may evade or resist participation. But when done well, critical literacy enables students "to authentically express the ideologies they hold and respectfully disagree with each other and the teacher" (Brayton & Casey, 2019, p 182).

This short historical tour has revealed how educators understand the value of examining propaganda as a means of developing critical thinking and communication skills. People of all ages benefit from experiences that deepen their understanding of how their attention is monetized through advertising and how agendas are shaped through news and public relations. It's important to be able to "discriminate between legitimate talk about controversial issues and the type of propaganda that conceals fact and reason in a cloud of prejudice and fear" (Casey, 1944, p. 1). A series of scaffolded learning experiences about advertising, persuasion, and propaganda can help aid the development of critical autonomy, which is defined as the desire and capacity for independent thinking and the set of skills to rationally assess the significance, truthfulness, and value of media messages in a wide variety of forms.

Propaganda Education in Schools and Colleges Today

We don't know much about whether the topic of propaganda gets the attention it deserves in American secondary schools, colleges, and universities. Given that there are 5,300 colleges and universities in the United States and 3 million teachers now working in 15,000 school districts in elementary and secondary education, it is difficult to arrive at an estimate across such a diverse landscape.

You may be able to recall how you first learned about propaganda in the context of formal education. At the university level, a review of college course titles shows that propaganda is generally taught by historians or scholars of political science, rhetoric, or mass communication. In high school, the study of propaganda may be led by the social studies or English language arts faculty. The study of propaganda can be infrequently found in courses in public health or medicine, science, technology, information science, or business.

Many people never get the chance to encounter the topic in any part of their formal education, and if this represents your experience, you may be reading this book to satisfy your curiosity on the topic. Others may have been introduced to propaganda education if they take specialist courses in writing and rhetoric, political science, public relations, or communications. A few college students may even encounter the study of propaganda in science classes. For example, at the University of Queensland in Australia, students can take a free online course titled Making Sense of Climate Science Denial, which introduces them to pseudoscience, propaganda, and climate change denial rhetoric.

Disciplinary frames shape the study of propaganda in higher education. A college course may target general education students with a course description that focuses on literacy like this one from the City College of New York:

> *This course introduces students to methods of understanding a highly developed and pervasive discourse: propaganda. Emphasis is placed on reading materials that use the persuasive and argumentative language of politics, advertising, cultural discussions and the media. Political speeches, essays, editorials, and articles are used to enlarge the student's experience with the materials and tools of propaganda. The student will acquire the intellectual framework and sophisticated level of literacy needed to recognize and respond to the aims of propaganda.*

In political science, a course on media and politics may focus on propaganda as part of the political process, as in this course description from Rutgers University–Camden College of Arts and Sciences:

> *How the media covers American politics, and how different forms of media (newspapers, blogs, TV news) cover politics differently. How politicians, parties, and interests use the media, especially through advertising (both positive and attack ads).*

At the University of Massachusetts, Amherst, a course titled Media, Public Relations and Propaganda uses critical cultural studies to frame the inquiry:

> *This course looks at how the industries of media and public relations have been used as instruments of social control and propaganda by economic and political elites. Examined will be the following: the historical roots of the public relations industry in government propaganda efforts; the contemporary influence of the public relations industry on public debate of social issues; the role of public relations in distorting discussion of the military/industrial complex; the effects of structuring media systems around the needs of advertisers; the role of media and public relations in how the public understands both domestic and international issues (such as war).*

High school students may get opportunities to discuss propaganda in English, social studies, science, or health class. For example, high school students in Indiana might gain exposure to propaganda by taking an elective social studies course titled Current Problems, Issues and Events, a course that gives students the opportunity to apply inquiry techniques to the study of significant problems or issues. Students develop competence in (1) recognizing cause-and-effect relationships, (2) recognizing fallacies in reasoning and propaganda devices, (3) synthesizing knowledge into useful patterns, (4) stating and testing hypotheses, and (5) generalizing based on evidence. Students examine issues of contemporary significance from the viewpoint of the social sciences. Or they might enroll in a course titled Mass Media, which may include a focus on analyzing news, entertainment, and persuasive messages in everyday life. But the subject of propaganda is not formally included in required English courses for high school students in Indiana (Indiana Department of Education, 2017).

When college students are asked to recall their precollege exposure to propaganda education, most only ever remember learning something about Nazi propaganda in high school. In the next few pages, I share what I've learned about how propaganda education may enter into American schools and colleges today.

Elementary School

Learning to recognize persuasion is a developmental process. In the primary grades, young children may first learn about the purpose of media messages with PIE, an acronym for learning to identify texts that persuade, inform, and entertain. Some children learn to recognize advertising techniques as part of a media literacy lesson on visual symbols, since children don't reliably recognize television advertising as persuasive until the middle of childhood (Zarouali, Walrave, Poels & Ponnet, 2019). Such lessons may help children learn to recognize different forms of advertising and marketing messages. Because children's exposure to advertising is extensive and ever increasing, some educators have explored the topic as part of library and technology instruction.

Rachel Kidder, a library media specialist at the Sunderland Elementary School in Deerfield, Massachusetts, helps children recognize ads on children's game websites. She has taught students about product placement by looking at examples from television and film and asking children to create a drawing with an example of product placement in it.

Teachers and librarians may also teach about persuasion to the youngest readers through the use of children's picture books. To introduce persuasive techniques, Kidder reads *The Pigeon Wants a Puppy* by Mo Willems. As she reads, she invites children to consider two different ways that Pigeon tries to persuade: with feelings and with facts. As they read and listen to the story, children are able to distinguish between the two persuasive strategies. As Kidder explained to me, one child even noticed how, in his zeal to persuade, Pigeon used "facts" that were not correct (Kidder, personal communication, March 1, 2019).

A variety of children's books and films include themes directly related to propaganda. For example, In *Harry Potter and the Order of the Phoenix*, propaganda techniques are used by the Ministry and the wizarding world's newspaper, the *Daily Prophet*, to position Sirius Black as a central villain in the wizarding world. Readers see how character assassination is used by newspapers to question Black's motivations and behavior through exaggeration, innuendo, and lies. Harry Potter, once "the boy who lived," is referred to in the *Daily Prophet* headlines as "The Boy Who Lies." A headline about headmaster Albus Dumbledore, Harry's chief advocate, reads: "Daft or Dangerous?" (Elder, 2018, p. 918). Readers are thus introduced to the idea that, through the skillful use of language, people can symbolically attack their opponents.

Outside of school, children's media is sometimes perceived to be a form of propaganda when it aims to represent the full diversity of family relationships. Alabama Public Television censored *Arthur,* a popular, long-running animated children's program broadcast nationally on PBS, when an episode included a plot about Arthur's teacher, who has a same-sex wedding.* Conservative voices protested the program, and an intern at the conservative *National Review* wrote that the question of whether the two types of marriage are identical "is far from settled in the minds of many Americans," especially in Alabama, the only state where a majority of citizens remain opposed to same-sex marriage (Leary, 2019). Angered by the show, Christian evangelist minister Franklin Graham publicly asked his nearly 2 million Twitter followers to challenge federal funding for PBS. Both conservatives and liberals who perceive children's media to be a form of propaganda

* Censorship by local public television stations happens occasionally when program content is perceived as controversial. Five years after *Obergefell v. Hodges*, the 2014 Supreme Court case that required all states to recognize same-sex marriage, Alabama public TV station executives stated that they wanted to avoid complaints from viewers who would be likely to interpret the episode as a form of pro-gay propaganda targeting young children.

also may engage in community campaigns to remove books from school and public libraries (Doyle, 2016).

History and Social Studies

It is simply impossible to teach about the 20th century without exploring the topic of propaganda. History faculty generally include material about propaganda in Nazi Germany as part of the study of the Holocaust. Students learn that Nazi Germany invested significant resources in the indoctrination of youth. Germans even tailored toys, games, and books toward the desired ends of the Third Reich, ensuring that children would believe in the goals and values of the Führer.*

Many history scholars with interests in the pedagogy of teaching history may use digital texts and media literacy concepts in their work (Kelly, 2013). Some take an explicitly hands-on and digital approach to teaching and learning about propaganda. For example, professor Glenn Kranking has created a website called We Want You! to feature the work of his students who critically analyze historical and contemporary propaganda in an upper-level history course at a small liberal arts college in Minnesota. Each week during the semester, his students contribute an example of propaganda to a curated digital collection, using tags to help organize artifacts by theme, region, and medium. They write short essays that demonstrate their ability to interpret and analyze propaganda in relation to the themes being discussed in the course. At the end of the semester, students work in creative teams to create propaganda as a way to demonstrate their developing knowledge and skills.

University-school partnerships can also be effective in helping students to develop visual literacy and communication skills. In Vilonia, Arizona, ninth grade civics students visited the local Museum of Veterans and Military History with their teacher, Michael Slicer. Working with them for the session was a group of college students from the University of Central Arkansas and their professor, John H. Saunders. Using posters from the World War II era, the college students helped the high school students to understand that propaganda is a

* At the website of the United States Holocaust Memorial Museum, there are lesson plans, videos, and educational materials available to help students to learn about the history of Nazi propaganda. These resources examine how propaganda was used in the democratic process of German elections, how it was used in a dictatorship, and how it was used to promote war and mass murder.

form of communication that uses media to persuade a mass audience to believe or behave in a specific way that is desired by the author of the message. In this session, college students offered their interpretation of various Nazi posters from all across Europe. One student showed an Italian propaganda poster depicting Hitler standing tall and prideful, clutching the Nazi flag. The student called attention to the halo effect around Hitler's head. That plus the use of gold leaves, oak trees, and soldiers standing behind Hitler offering the Nazi salute led the student to see the message of Hitler as a divine leader, mirroring Christ in a biblical reference. Students also demonstrated the analysis of a British poster with the words "Keep Mum, She's Not So Dumb," reminding men to be mindful of talking freely about the war effort around women who might be spies.

Many history faculty adopt the stance of warning students not to be influenced by propaganda. Said Saunders to the high school students, "You are exposed to more propaganda now than ever. I would encourage you to learn and use your skills to understand the world you live in today and to protect yourself. You shouldn't let propaganda determine your mindset or what is in your heart" (Vilonia Schools, 2017, p. 1). However, this position inadvertantly reinforces the perception that propaganda is solely negative and denies the ways in which propaganda enables democratic process of coalition building and the formation of public consensus.

Science, Health, Math, and Business

In these disciplines, it is common for students to encounter corporate-sponsored curriculum. Sponsored curriculum has been part of the U.S. education system for well over 100 years. These educational materials are developed by a private company or an industry trade organization and given to a teacher or school for free or at a minimal cost. Depending on your point of view, you may see this as beneficial or harmful propaganda. Education has long relied on business and industries for curriculum resources. For most of the 20th century, local businesses have supported schools with contributions in cash, time, expertise, or even equipment. In Montana, the Cisco Networking Academy program is offered in more than one in four public high schools across the state, providing a corporate-sponsored ICT curriculum for students interested in technology careers (Gottwig, 2013). In Canada, a pharmaceutical company sponsors curriculum resources that teach children about physical fitness, health, and wellness (Robinson, Gleddie, & Shaefer, 2016).

Pro-business propaganda learned in childhood may influence knowledge, attitudes, and beliefs across a lifetime.* In Oklahoma, a state agency funded by oil and gas producers has spent $40 million over 20 years on K–12 education with a pro-industry bent, including hundreds of pages of curricula, a speaker series, and an afterschool program—all provided free to educators. In Ohio, students even learn how to "frack" Twinkies using straws to drill for the cream filling (Werz, 2017). To encourage public allegiance to the coal industry, the Illinois Department of Commerce and Economic Opportunity distributed a curriculum including "From the Coalfields to the Power Lines," hosted a yearly art and essay contest for students, and offered an all-expenses paid educational seminar for teachers at a lakeside resort (Richart, 2014). Only after substantial pressure from environmental activists did the state of Illinois suspend this taxpayer-funded program that promoted the coal industry in public schools.

The scale of corporate involvement in education has increased dramatically with the Googlefication of the classroom. Today, Google's G Suite for Education software dominates K–12 education. More than half the students in American public schools now use Google education apps. Students are getting acclimated to sharing their data in the Google environment, using Google search, YouTube, Maps, and other Google products. This does not just build consumer loyalty, but it also advances their company profitability. Google's success in the education marketplace came from providing easy-to-use, low-cost services directly to educators. They encouraged educators to beta-test Google products without approval from their school district leaders and showcased these individuals as forward thinkers, enrolling teachers in marketing their products. Eventually, large school districts like Chicago formally adopted Google products, becoming a test lab for the company (Singer, 2017).

Today, Google is deeply committed to shaping school district and state level policies, with the welcome support from leaders in the educational technology community. New York City students in 99 schools were involved in a pilot-test of Google's virtual reality curriculum with Google in charge of training educators and school leaders (NYC Mayor's Office of Media and Entertainment, 2018). Google also offers lesson plans on digital citizenship for young learners that emphasize

* I've been influenced by pro-business propaganda, as have many Americans. As a teen, I participated in Junior Achievement, an afterschool program that teaches work readiness, entrepreneurship, and financial literacy to young people all over the world. For me, at the impressionable age of 13, I saw it as just a way to meet boys. But I was influenced by the spirit of entrepreneurship and creativity embodied in the learning experience.

the harms of bullies and malware and the need for individuals to take personal responsibility when using digital platforms. In the curriculum, which is entitled Be Internet Awesome, students do not learn about the company's data-handling practices or consider the pros and cons of the tracking of user actions online. There's no focus on understanding the role of algorithmic personalization in filtering search results, customizing advertising displays, or influencing public opinion (Stanley, Ciccone, & Hobbs, 2020).

Like propaganda, the harms and benefits of corporate involvement in education and sponsored curricula are in the eye of the beholder. American public schools face wide variations in resources due to near-complete reliance on local funding. When digital resources are offered to a community for free, it may be hard to refuse them. Perhaps that is why research on public attitudes toward the use of free technology platforms or sponsored curriculum in schools reveals no consensus about its appropriateness: in one survey, teachers were almost evenly split on whether or not using materials provided by a company is ethical or not. Most teachers did not think that parents should be informed if commercially sponsored material was used in their classroom, and most felt that they could use corporate materials within the classroom without influencing students' views on the brand (Lightfoot, 2015).

Communication, Media, Technology, and Library

For students majoring in public relations or communications and for students with interests in digital and media production, propaganda may be studied in relation to advertising and the political economy of media systems in society. Propaganda is sometimes taught as a content course, where students gain knowledge about various theories and scholars. Sometimes the study of propaganda is embedded in courses in media studies and media literacy. The Media Education Foundation has produced dozens of advocacy documentaries on social issues, offering films that promote progressive ideologies and inspire critical thinking about the social, political, and cultural impact of American mass media.

In a few college courses, students get opportunities to create propaganda as a way to develop digital and media literacy competencies, or as professional preparation for careers in public relations or advertising. At the high school level, school librarians are moving away from a "read-only" model and toward supporting various forms of media production, using create-to-learn principles. For example, at Monticello High School in Charlottesville, Virginia, the school library has a music studio, a genius bar, and a hacker room for students, in which students can produce music, learn computer programming, and help repair technology in the school. When school libraries offer audio and video production facilities for learners, students may participate in lessons like the production of "Thirty-Second Propaganda" videos, where as part of Digital Learning Day, students demonstrate their critical understanding of complex concepts by using media production tools to create propaganda (Wolf, Jones, & Gilbert, 2014).

The Arts

Music and art are key vehicles of propaganda, and they always have been. Some music educators explore forms of patriotic music to help their students recognize the power of music to arouse emotions and create a shared sense of community (Phillpott & Spruce, 2012). Visual arts educators may explicitly tune in to the emotional and persuasive power of art. This approach may challenge other forms of art education that are rooted in the fine arts tradition. Some art educators believe it is important to situate the arts in relation to social and cultural issues in ways that help students "to recognize and understand the ambiguities, conflicts, nuances, and ephemeral qualities of social experience, much of which is now configured through imagery and designed objects" (Freedman & Stuhr, 2004, p. 821).

Nora Bates Zale developed a propaganda project in her high school art class at a private school in Massachusetts, asking students to examine historical propaganda in relation to the work of Barbara Kruger, whose work combines powerful text with strong graphic design sensibilities. Right away, her students noticed the similarity between the work of the fine artist and the skateboard brand Supreme. Students appreciated the chance to reflect on the connections between the fine arts and popular culture.

Zale then asked students to create a propaganda poster on an issue of their choice using lithography, an artistic medium they had not been exposed to before. In explaining this choice, Zale said, "I do feel that it is well-suited for this project because the ability to reproduce the same image endlessly speaks to the potential for a widespread impact." The combination of handmade lino block printing combined with Sharpie-drawn elements gave each piece its own human-touched individuality, something that a digitally printed poster would not possess. As they brainstormed current events or topics for their projects, students were clearly pushing back against boundaries they felt imposed upon them, according to Zale. She said, "One student who has had repeated run-ins with authority figures made one that had a recycling symbol and the words 'Respect Goes Both Ways.' Another student who made a poster with the message to 'Unplug' had an extreme dependency on his phone, and this student acknowledged that his work was just as much a message to himself as it was to others."

But when students create propaganda as part of a class assignment, teachers can have concerns about the content of the messages they choose to share. While Zale felt comfortable permitting a conservative student to create an anti-NAFTA poster (with the slogan "NAFTA is Nast-a!"), she did not feel comfortable with another student's plan to make a poster about how people shouldn't be offended by the Confederate flag, and so she encouraged him to select another topic (Zale, personal communication, June 14, 2019). Educators must make decisions about the "appropriateness" of student creative work with sensitivity to school and community culture.

Language and Literature

Educators who are teaching foreign languages or English to nonnative speakers have long made active use of popular culture materials, including print and moving-image media, to support language learning skills while also improving critical thinking (He, 2019). Some foreign language teachers also explicitly embed media literacy pedagogies into their classes, critically analyzing advertising, news, and issues of representation. In one case, new immigrant students learned to critically analyze advertising as they learned to speak English. When Michael Robb-Grieco was teaching new immigrants in a Philadelphia high school, he developed a unit of instruction designed to build their language skills through the critical analysis of advertising. To meet the needs of his newcomer learners just getting familiar with English, he selected ads that communicate clear visual messages in a powerful way. He used ads for familiar products because these ads gave students an opportunity to apply prior knowledge in analyzing the message. Exploring advertising with explicit and implicit messages, students were able to practice speaking and listening using the texts of their everyday experiences. High school students were able to spontaneously apply critical questions to visual texts. These activities aimed to strike a balance between learning a new language and connecting with students' life experiences (Hobbs, He, & RobbGrieco, 2015).

English educators are generally familiar with the topic of propaganda, as it is a theme of much of the literature that is emphasized in courses for high school and college students. For many teachers, it may seem as if dystopian young adult novels have become the default genre of a generation. Huxley's *Brave New World* and other works critique mindless consumption, instant gratification, reliance on technology, and the resulting atrophy of language and critical thinking. When reading this novel, one teacher asks her students to reflect on these questions: "Is life easy for us today? Is it too easy? How do people escape from everyday life? Is it necessary to do so? Why or why not?" (Wilkinson, 2010, p. 24).

M. T. Anderson's young adult novel *Feed* is a popular work that considers the ubiquitous nature of advertising as propaganda. The novel uses satire, humor, and exaggeration to depict the world of the future, where the Internet is implanted into your brain as the Feed. As people grow up, their brains cannot function without the Feed. They attend a classroom run by corporations where students learn how to use technology, find bargains, and decorate a bedroom. Through education, in this dystopic world, students are trained to be consumers.

Today's learners are growing up in a time period marked by political polarization, a global health and economic crisis, environmental degradation, and the dehumanization and oppression of minorities and immigrants. Books and movies like *The Hunger Games* series explicitly address the power of propaganda in relation to the anxieties of the current age. The setting for the series is an oppressive society in which teenagers are selected to participate in annual televised survivalist competitions to the death. These brutal spectacles are required viewing. The protagonist, Katniss Everdeen, has been immersed in propaganda her whole life. But as she struggles and survives in the games, she also begins to understand and appreciate the usefulness of the media as a tool for revolution. In discovering the value of propaganda to shape public opinion as part of the revolution, the book demonstrates how information and media literacy competencies are "powerful tools of resistance for people oppressed by totalitarian governments" (Latham & Hollister, 2014, p. 34).

While teachers of literature may teach novels that include themes related to propaganda, they may also struggle with the challenges of teaching about propaganda at a time when it is rampant. After all, students are swimming in a sea of advertising and promotion. As a high school English teacher in Maryland puts it, "Young people love advertising, consuming, entertainment, and technology. If we attack these trappings of modern life, we risk nurturing defensiveness" (Wilkinson, 2010, p. 24).

Here is a startling fact: despite the relevance of the subject and a wealth of literary resources on the topic the study of propaganda in English Language Arts Education is not as common in 2020 as it was in 1940. In fact, since the rise of the

Common Core State Standards in English language arts, the study of persuasive genres has virtually disappeared. Those standards call for students to be able to:

- Determine the central ideas or themes of a text and analyze their development; summarize the key supporting details and ideas.
- Interpret words and phrases as they are used in a text, including determining technical, connotative, and figurative meanings, and analyze how specific word choices shape meaning or tone.
- Analyze the structure of texts, including how specific sentences, paragraphs, and larger portions of the text (e.g., a section, chapter, scene, or stanza) relate to each other and the whole.
- Integrate and evaluate content presented in diverse media and formats, including visually and quantitatively, as well as in words.
- Delineate and evaluate the argument and specific claims in a text, including the validity of the reasoning as well as the relevance and sufficiency of the evidence.
- Read and comprehend complex literary and informational texts independently and proficiently.

The framing offered by the Common Core standards may explain why many English teachers focus exclusively on argumentation and do not pay much attention to persuasion, advertising or propaganda. Notice that none of these bullet points includes any attention to examining how language activates emotions or shapes perceptions of social reality.

In his compelling historical and critical analysis which traces the "fear of persuasion" over the course of academic scholarship in English language arts education, David Fleming (2019) shows how, by the middle of the 20th century, persuasive genres were gradually included in the curricula of college writing programs as faculty embraced the revival of classical rhetoric. After 1990, however, a focus on argumentation led writing and composition scholars to ignore persuasive genres.

How did the study of argumentation push out the study of persuasion? The Common Core State Standards denigrates the art of persuasion while lionizing argumentation. Indeed, an "explicit bias" against persuasive genres is evident in the CCSS reading and writing standards (Fleming, 2019, p. 522). The document sets forward a binary opposition between persuasion and argumentation, stating that persuasive writing may appeal to the credibility, character, or authority of the writer as well as appeal to the audience's self-interest, sense of identity, or emotions, while argument convinces the audience because of the perceived merit and reasonableness of the claims, evidence and proofs.

According to Fleming, this kind of framing substantially misrepresents the 2,000-year-old history of rhetorical scholarship on persuasion. In analyzing examples of lesson plans and typical K–12 classroom practices, Fleming offers evidence to show the many substantial ways in which English language arts educators have privileged *logos* over *pathos* and *ethos*. Indeed, a generation of educators has been taught to position argumentation as uniquely "truth seeking" and thus superior to persuasion, which uses mere emotion and appeals to character as a (presumably unethical) form of influence. As a result, "In one stroke, the key insight of Aristotelian rhetorical theory, that persuasive argument is a matter of ethos, pathos, and logos, is overturned, making argument in schools an exclusively "logical" affair and practically banishing writing that appeals to 'emotions' or 'character' " (Fleming, 2019, p. 522).

An English teacher may go to great lengths to point out that argumentative writing activates logic and reasoning to prove a point; from this perspective, persuasion merely appeals to the reader's emotions, and propaganda is seen as downright evil (Taithe & Thornton, 1999). This is a truly distressing situation. In one lesson plan for high school students, bright crisp lines are drawn to help learners distinguish between the concepts. In a handout for students, argument's purpose is described as the search for "truth," while persuasion is defined as "the promotion of an opinion." Propaganda is defined as "political advertising that may distort the truth or include false information" (Henning, n.d.). This lesson vastly oversimplifies the nature of persuasive influence by establishing a strict hierarchy of rhetorical forms. Such efforts are an exercise in labeling that do little to promote critical thinking.

Some critics may argue that the study of propaganda has disappeared from English education because the skills involved in analyzing it are not part of the SAT test. While analyzing propaganda may be highly valuable for daily life, it is not yet considered a central component of college readiness. But when informational texts were given special status by the Common Core State Standards and the testing companies, many media literacy educators cheered. Finally, students could read and analyze a news story in *The New York Times* and apply media literacy concepts as part of the reading comprehension process. Optimists hoped that this would increase the likelihood that students would be exposed to media literacy instructional practices.

But when concerns about students' ability to express ideas in academic language are narrowly positioned in the context of college readiness, reading and writing for the real world often gets short shrift. To do well in college, competence in reading and writing academic texts is considered a requirement for success. Students must learn to write academic essays because academic prose is authoritative, detached, and dense with formal language (Snow & Uccelli, 2008). Argumentation relies on the construction of authority through the presentation of a neutral, dispassionate stance, using reasoning and evidence to make knowledge claims.

Against this background, it's no surprise that propaganda analysis has disappeared from contemporary English education in the secondary grades. If argument is seen as high culture, then propaganda is seen as low culture. If argumentation is seen as academic and sophisticated, propaganda can be seen as popular, simple and inferior.

Propaganda may well be the absolute opposite of academic prose. Propaganda is subjective and emotional: It responds to the needs of readers and viewers, and it relies on familiar symbols accessible to all. The analysis of propaganda is unlikely to meet rigid Common Core guidelines about the required complexity of texts now that text complexity has become a mantra in English education. Propaganda that targets teens is unlikely to have a Lexile level of 1200, with advanced vocabulary and complex sentence structure. As a result, many students get little opportunity in a school context to analyze the most powerful and emotionally resonant messages that circulate in contemporary culture.

The consequences of ignoring the study of propaganda for more than 20 years are beginning to be felt in society as a whole, and educators are beginning to feel a little guilty that they have not paid more attention to it. Fortunately, new momentum on the need to incorporate the study of propaganda and persuasion is beginning to develop. After the U.S. presidential election in 2016, a number of professional organizations responsible for teaching writing, composition, and speech reaffirmed their commitment to teaching the responsible use of language as a form of social power.

In 2019, the National Council of Teachers of English issued a resolution on critical literacy in English education, calling for educators to promote pedagogy and scholarly curricula in English and related subjects that instruct students in analyzing and evaluating "sophisticated persuasive techniques in all texts, genres, and types of media, current and yet to be imagined." They also urge members to

- ***Support classroom practices*** that examine and question uses of language in order to discern inhumane, misinformative, or dishonest discourse and arguments;
- ***Prioritize research and pedagogies*** that encourage students to become critical thinkers, consumers, and creators who advocate for and actively contribute to a better world;
- ***Provide resources*** to mitigate the effect of new technologies and platforms that accelerate and destabilize our information environment;
- ***Support*** the integration of reliable, balanced, and credible news sources within classroom practices at all levels of education;
- ***Resist attempts*** to influence civic discussion through falsehoods, unwarranted doubts, prejudicial or stereotypical ideas, attempts to shame or silence, or other techniques that deteriorate the quality of public deliberation; and
- ***Model civic literacy and conversation*** by creating a supportive environment where students can have an informed discussion and engage with current events and civic issues while staying mindful and critical of the difference between the intent and impact of their language (NCTE, 2019).

These practices are not yet normative among English language arts educators in American public schools, but with leadership from educators in the field, they could be. Teachers all over the world are feeling a need to demonstrate how attention, emotions, and evidence are all fundamentally responsive to the search for truth. One scholar explained, "Rhetors must know the facts in order to mislead through lies; they must recognize the truth in order to deceive through fallacies, and they must understand reality in order to manipulate through doublespeak" (McComiskey, 2017, p. 8). The careful and systematic study of propaganda and persuasion must no longer be neglected in American public schools.

True or False? Considering Some Ideas About Propaganda

By now, some of your previously held opinions and beliefs about propaganda may have been disrupted. While some people hold beliefs about propaganda that are outdated, inaccurate, or false, most people simply have a partial view of propaganda that is just not the whole story. You can use Table 2.1 to check your comprehension of some key ideas presented so far.

TABLE 2.1

STATEMENT	TRUE OR FALSE?
Propaganda is harmful.	**False.** Propaganda may be beneficial or harmful.
Propaganda is used only during political campaigns and elections.	**False.** Propaganda is used to influence public opinion and to advance social power, which happens on an ongoing basis in all sectors of society, not just in the political realm.
Propaganda is unethical.	**It depends.** Propaganda can be ethical when the creators of the message are transparent about their goals. It can be unethical when intentional deception, half-truths, or false information are involved.
Advertising is a form of propaganda.	**True.** Advertising may be designed to sell goods and services, but it also validates consumption and commodity capitalism. Some (but not all) ads can be propaganda when they advance specific ideological positions that aim to influence public opinion beyond a specific sales goal.
Propaganda and persuasion are synonyms.	**False.** Propaganda is a subset of all three modes of expression: persuasion, information, a nd entertainment. It is a mode of communication designed to influence public opinion and gain social power. Persuasion is a more general process of communication designed to influence attitudes and behavior.

(TABLE 2.1 continued)

STATEMENT	TRUE OR FALSE?
Any media message that activates your emotions is a form of propaganda.	**False.** Expressions of emotion in art and culture function as propaganda when they influence public opinion on issues of public importance. Some propaganda uses facts and information, not emotion, to influence people.
Propaganda is in the eye of the beholder.	**True.** It's easier for people to recognize propaganda when it does not align with existing beliefs. When it does align with existing beliefs, we may see it as information or entertainment.

LEARNING ACTIVITY

Create a Propaganda Poster

When students create propaganda, they consider their own social responsibilities to be change agents in society.

Activity: First, students examine a variety of propaganda posters from throughout history and then look at the contemporary artwork of Barbara Kruger, an artist who is best known for her aggressively directive slogans presented over black-and-white photographs from magazines. Her famous pieces include *I Shop, Therefore I Am* (1987) and *Your Body Is a Battleground* (1985), works that critique consumerism and desire.

Create to Learn: After analyzing the design features of propaganda art, students choose a current or ongoing topic of interest to them, research the topic, and then design a propaganda poster. As part of their project, they must create a linoleum block for use in their poster. Posters are assembled and displayed for the whole school, as shown below.

The Takeaway: Creating propaganda using strong and simple language and distinctive visual imagery can be an emotionally powerful learning experience.

–Developed by Nora Bates Zale, Academy at Charlemont

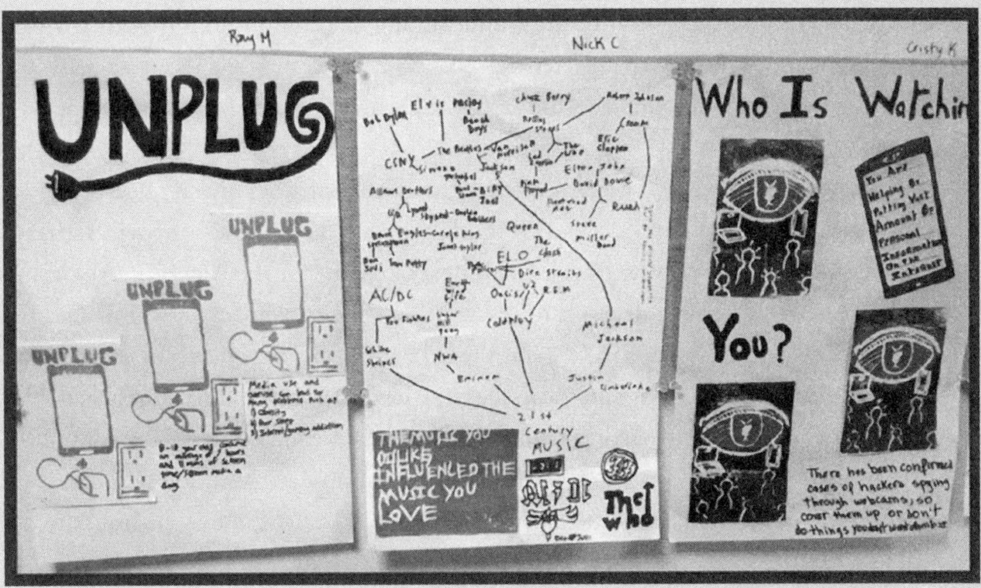

Fears About Teaching Propaganda

Since you are reading this book, you obviously understand the value of learning about propaganda, but if you are an educator or parent, you may also be wondering about the challenges of teaching it. You may already be wondering what can go wrong. It may be risky to bring emotionally compelling, controversial, and contemporary texts and topics into the classroom. What if students want to create propaganda that comments and reflects on the enduring emotional power of symbols like the Confederate flag, white nationalism, or other controversial subjects? Educators don't want to inadvertently increase the problem of political polarization. They don't want students to create potentially harmful propaganda. They don't want to get fired. So what can go wrong? Here's a short list of potential challenges.

The emotional intensity of propaganda may inspire both educators and students to behave badly on social media in ways that may cause harm. In one case, an adjunct professor posted a critical comment on her Facebook page about Otto Warmbier, the Ohio college student who, after traveling to North Korea with a tour group and stealing a propaganda poster from a restricted area in his hotel, was sentenced to 15 years in prison. Warmbier was returned to the United States suffering from botulism and in a coma; he died six days after his release. On Facebook, the instructor wrote that Otto Warmbier was "a clueless white male" who "got what he deserved," noting that he grew up thinking "he could get away with anything he wanted." Though she deleted the post soon afterward, she received death threats for her comments, and the University of Delaware decided not to rehire her (Alkousaa, 2017, p. 1).

Professors and teachers who examine controversial topics have been targeted by activist groups for what they say and do inside the classroom. Professor Brian Katz was put on a conservative watchlist for writing a blog post for the American Mathematical Society about his decision to discuss the white supremacy terrorism that occurred in Charlottesville, Virginia, on the first day of his math class in order to demonstrate that math is not apolitical. He explained that many of his students do not see how math is connected to issues of identity and equity. He describes how even something as simple as 1 + 1 = 2 is an artifact of human invention and intercultural communication, as mathematical notation was brought to Europe from the Arabic-speaking world.

Supervisors or members of the local community may challenge particular examples of propaganda used in the classroom. If an educator's own political ideologies are out of step with community views, the results can even make headlines. In Janesville, Wisconsin, a high school teacher in a marketing and business class showed her class an episode of a comedy news show called *Newsbroke*, hosted by comedian Francesca Fiorentini from AJ+, the Al Jazeera Media Network. The episode was called "Why the Rich Love Destroying Unions." In an examination of the history of unions in the United States, the video explains why children don't work in coal mines anymore and how the 40-hour work week was established.*

* In this video, there is a crisp historical timeline of the rise and fall of unions in the United States, interspersed with funny, sharp, and mean-spirited criticism of some politicians (including Mitch McConnell and Donald Trump). The video explains how so-called right-to-work laws have weakened both workers and unions while strengthening business competitiveness. The topic of right-to-work laws was especially controversial in Wisconsin, because Act 10, enacted in 2011, took away some legal rights of teachers and other public employees (Shultz, 2018).

A parent who complained to the principal about the screening of the video perceived it to have a demeaning and bullying manner, as if other viewpoints on the topic were not legitimate. The parent called the video "outrageous" and "propaganda," explaining that politicians should not be smeared in a high school classroom. But the school principal defended the teacher's choice, noting that since economics is taught in marketing, the teacher used this video to introduce a discussion about the cost of labor, in which unions play a role. The parent then called the newspaper, which reported on the issue and also wrote an editorial that supported the parent, noting the district's policy on teaching controversial issues. This policy requires teachers to notify administrators of their plans to introduce a controversial topic. Because of the content of the video, the newspaper wrote that the high school teacher "was out to indoctrinate students rather than help them consider all sides of an issue." The newspaper editorial then offered a glowing review of the state's right-to-work law, which they claim "was instrumental in getting the state's fiscal house in order," noting that "taxpayers aren't vessels to be drained for union purposes" (*Gazette Extra*, 2018, p. 1).

The ironies shouldn't be missed here: the newspaper offered its own propaganda about a controversial community issue by writing an editorial warning about the dangers of propaganda. Clearly, discussing controversial issues in schools can challenge the status quo. What's clear from this example is that a considerable amount of knowledge, courage, confidence, and humility are needed when using instructional practices that connect the classroom to contemporary culture.

In the next chapter, we'll consider the political economy of propaganda to understand why it's become so very profitable to be a propagandist in a digital age. Media literacy educators have long aimed to pull back the curtain to show learners how human attention is exploited to achieve economic goals. Every citizen should be more aware of how the economic structures of media enterprises ensure that everyone, all around the world, receives a steady stream of exposure to propaganda.

3

Propaganda and the Attention Economy

Propaganda can be profitable when it taps into people's deepest hopes, fears, and dreams

When I saw the meme in my Facebook feed, it stopped me dead in my tracks. Titled "American Terrorists," it shows images of six men's faces. It reads, "We have a problem in this country, and they didn't cross the border." The intended meaning of the meme is contingent upon the audience's awareness that the six white males depicted are American terrorists who have committed mass murder. One of these images depicts the 20-year-old man who murdered 26 children at Sandy Hook Elementary School. The meme, shown on the next page, brings together two different topics (gun violence and immigration) in a way I had not considered so directly before. The emotional jolt I got from this surprising meme aroused my itchy fingers: I had a strong urge to share it with my friends and colleagues in my social network. Many of my friends agree with me that gun violence is a far bigger problem in our country than immigration across the Mexican border.

But something stopped me from sharing it. I reflected on the way that the meme uses the images of the killers as a symbol. I realized that I simply didn't feel comfortable giving those murderers any more attention or notoriety by sharing their photos. But since I want to help my readers truly understand the power of propaganda in an attention economy, I feel the need reproduce it here.

The small decisions we make about liking and sharing digital content may seem trivial, but they exert a powerful force in shaping how propaganda spreads. Many times a day, I scan the virtual environment, look for novel items, and decide whether or not to like or share them with my online tribe. This is an activity that I find pleasurable. Plus, I benefit from the amazing resources that others share with me.

Many people like or share a message after only a quick scan of the headline and image, without making reflective decisions about what to share or not share. Some people might share online content more or less automatically. They might share content when it activates strong feelings or when aligns with their values. Novel, surprising or unconventional content inspires some people to share. People may choose to share content that offers the promise of increased status among their peers.

Peer-to-peer sharing drives the viral spread of propaganda. The solution is simple: think before you share. When people share content without first reading or viewing it, they may inadvertently contribute to the spread of propaganda. Unfortunately, my students often see their online liking and sharing behavior as unproblematic. They often say that when they see something newsworthy or shocking, of course they simply must share it with their network because they want others to know what they have just learned. When it comes to sharing novel or surprising digital content, they see themselves as merely links in a chain. They do not see themselves as responsible for spreading propaganda.

To be honest, some content does seem to compel people to like or share it. Perhaps it is the feeling of authenticity that is associated with the message (Matsushima, 2016). When online propaganda gets you to share it, it's like a clever card trick has been performed. One writer explained, "Good propaganda campaigns are like a Vegas act, replete with sexy assistants, ordinary misdirection, and lots of good old-fashioned bait and switch. Great campaigns play all sides to the user's advantage." For example, when a social media post seems scary, perverse, disgusting, or frightening, it's likely to have been intentionally designed to activate those emotions (Davis, 2018, p. 1).

In this chapter, we learn how attracting and holding people's attention is at the heart of propaganda's economic power. There are four key features of propaganda that represent the heart of its attention-getting power. To understand the profitability of propaganda, a good understanding of the digital economy of information and entertainment is needed. As we will see, American consumer culture weaves its transactional values into the relationships, dreams, and ideas we hold most dear.

The Four Keys of Propaganda

What's the best way to change hearts and minds? Propagandists have discovered four primary keys that unlock people's attention, emotions, and values, often in ways that bypass critical thinking. Not all propaganda uses all of these keys, of course. But in general, much propaganda can be identified by the presence of one or more of the following keys.

1. Activate Strong Emotions

Propaganda plays on any and all human emotions—love, the need to belong, hope, fear, anger, frustration, sympathy—to direct audiences toward a desired goal. In the deepest sense, propaganda is a hearts-and-minds game. The skillful propagandist activates strong emotions to break through the clutter of everyday life and connect to what matters most to you. Successful propagandists understand how to psychologically tailor messages to create an emotional response. When people are feeling excitement and arousal, they are unlikely to engage in critical thinking.

2. Simplify Information and Ideas

Many forms of communication simplify information and ideas—it's part of the art and craft of creative expression. When information is not simplified, users themselves often must take extra steps to sort, organize and synthesize. When information is simplified, it can be packaged for maximum appeal. As every teacher knows, simplifying information can contribute to advancing knowledge or understanding. Because people naturally seek to reduce complexity, propaganda taps into our human bias toward fast information processing (Kahneman, 2011).

Through simplifying, accurate information can be framed to help tell a story that fits the predetermined narrative of the propagandist. This can make a message more attractive to key stakeholders, including business and political leaders. Lies and falsehoods can also be used to simplify the state of the world in ways that align information with the worldview of the propagandist. Simplification can be dangerous when compelling images and catchy and memorable short phrases substitute for knowledge and real learning.

3. Respond to Audience Needs and Values

Effective propaganda conveys messages, themes, and language that appeal directly, and many times exclusively, to specific and distinct groups within a population. Propagandists may appeal to your sense of humor, for example. Propaganda can easily be inserted in entertainment messages of all kinds, including jokes, stand-up comedy, pop songs, music videos, movies, TV shows, and memes. Propaganda can activate your feelings of pride about your racial or ethnic identity, your hobbies, your pets, your favorite celebrities, your beliefs, and values, or even your personal or collective aspirations for the future. By creating messages that appeal directly to the needs, hopes, and fears of specific groups, propaganda becomes personal. When messages are perceived as relevant and meaningful to your personal identity, you pay much more attention to them.

4. Attack Opponents

Propaganda can serve as a form of political and social warfare to identify, vilify, and trivialize opponents. It can call into question the legitimacy, credibility, accuracy, and even the character of one's opponents and their ideas. Because people are naturally attracted to conflict, a propagandist can make strategic use of controversy to get attention. Attacking opponents also encourages either-or and us-versus-them thinking, which suppresses the consideration of more complex information and ideas. Propaganda can also be used to discredit individuals, destroy their reputation, exclude specific groups of people, incite hatred, or cultivate indifference. Such attacks can have disastrous consequences for both individuals and society.

Noticing how the four keys of propaganda are used to attract attention helps people recognize how their emotions, values, and sense of personal identity can be engaged or exploited. As learners come to recognize and use these keys for themselves, it's important to address the special social responsibility that they entail.

LEARNING ACTIVITY

To Share or Not to Share

People make propaganda spread through their use of social media.

Activity: Review examples of contemporary propaganda and make strategic decisions about which examples you might like to share (or not share) with your social network. Visit the Mind Over Media website to access examples of propaganda (www.mindovermedia.gallery) and complete these tasks:

1. ***Share.*** Find an example of content that you would be willing to share with your social network. Explain which of the four keys of propaganda are operating in the content you selected. Compose a comment on the example you selected.
2. ***Or Not to Share.*** Find an example of content that you would not be willing to share with your social network. Compose a comment on the example you selected.

For Reflection: Consider how your decisions about sharing may reflect your perceptions of the message in relation to your own values as well as the interests and priorities of your peers. How might your online sharing affect how others perceive you?

The Takeaway: Because people trust their friends more than they trust people they do not know, sharing and discussing propaganda is an important way to engage in dialogue about social issues.

–Adapted from Mind Over Media: Analyzing Contemporary Propaganda (Media Education Lab, 2018)

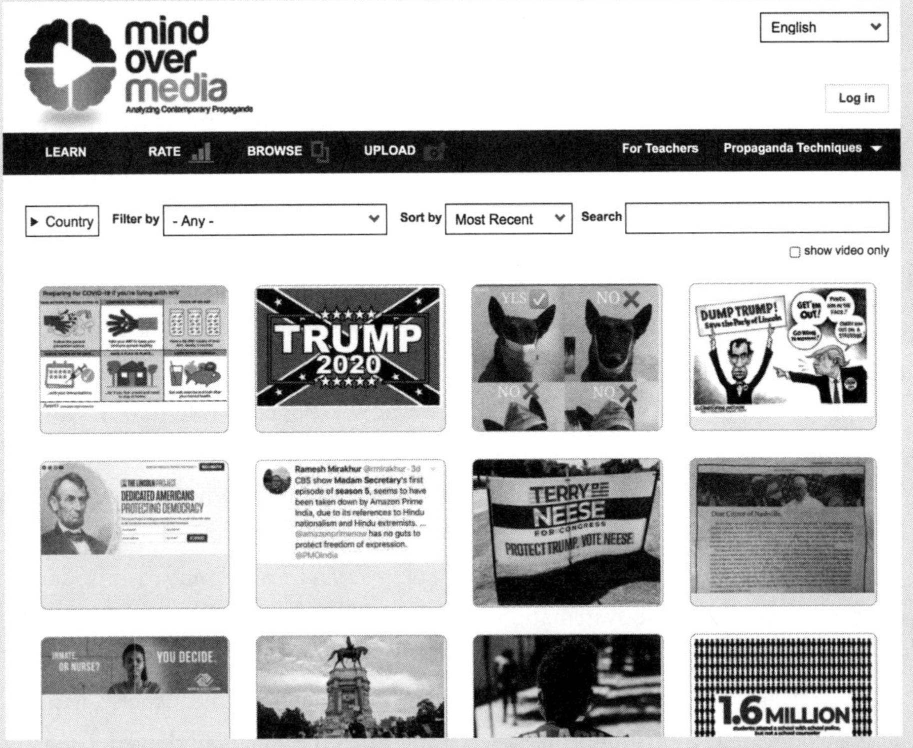

Mind Over Media: The Gallery

Learning to Analyze Advertising

Many advertising formats playfully and intentionally blur the lines between commercial message and entertainment content, which can make it difficult to recognize persuasive intent. Marketers spent $4.2 billion on advertising to children and teens in 2018, an all-time high. Nearly one-third was spent on digital advertising, raising concerns about privacy issues, parental mediation, and regulation required to address the new ways that advertisers target children and youth (Nelson, 2018).

If you watch YouTube, you may have seen a 90-second movie trailer for *Web of Fries*. It was a mystery thriller that included both government cover-ups and scary clowns. This fake movie trailer was actually an ad to promote the launch of Taco Bell's nacho fries with cheese. By blending entertainment and persuasion through branded trailers, advertisers try to override people's skepticism about advertising.

Exposure to advertising begins at home, where the youngest children encounter advertising as a part of everyday family life. But today's parents do not have the same kinds of co-viewing opportunities with their children as those in earlier generations, because of the widespread use of cell phones and tablets. Many parents are becoming cord-cutters, relying less and less on broadcast and cable television and using more individualized video streaming services including Netflix, Amazon Prime, and YouTube. Children may watch PBS, YouTube, or Cartoon Network on small screens while parents multitask daily chores, check social media, or use other forms of media that interest them. Without as many co-viewing opportunities for parents and children to talk about advertising at home, researchers have found that there is less informal learning about advertising. In one study, although parents of young children talked about TV advertising, they rarely mentioned the many types of digital marketing children now experience (Nelson, Atkinson, Rademacher, & Ahn, 2017).

Advertising has been studied as a genre since the 1960s, when educators first began exploring media literacy. Back then, many were influenced by the work of Vance Packard, whose 1957 best-selling book *The Hidden Persuaders* introduced the general public to the systematic manipulation of emotion by advertisers. The book offered a powerful report on how manufacturers and politicians were using psychological techniques to influence readers and viewers. The American public gained awareness of subliminal advertising after the FCC conducted a test in Washington in January 1958 that demonstrated it was not effective. Still, despite the evidence, many members of the public believed that subliminal advertising was being used to persuade, as popular culture and news reports described other experiments where very brief exposures of images of popcorn, soda and sexually arousing images were edited into film or airbrushed into print advertising (Zanot, Pincus, & Lamp, 1983). *The Hidden Persuaders* may have activated a conspiracy consciousness among some members of the public because, before reading the book, "viewers of television had conditioned themselves to believe that their choices were still their own, whatever commercials might be telling them to do" (Wu, 2016, p. 148).

Although Packard recommended that people avoid all advertising, most educators didn't think that was a particularly realistic solution. Instead, they began to explore how to teach about advertising as a way to reduce its power over individuals and society. Fifty years later, a rich body of scholarly and practical work in media literacy, with insights from the fields of education, media psychology, and communication, now demonstrates the value of teaching even very young children how to read, critically analyze, and create their own advertising messages (Hobbs & Mihailidis, 2019).

Today, teaching and learning about the genre of advertising may occur in elementary, middle, or high school, and in the context of a variety of subject areas. In general, advertising analysis activities for children may focus on examining (1) the content of ads, (2) the visual language, rhetorical strategies, and production techniques used to promote ideas and values, or (3) the economic structure of the media industry (Hwang, Yum, & Jeong, 2019). Some educators believe that advertising literacy helps children protect themselves from the undue influence of advertising. When children understand the purpose of advertising, they may be more able to activate cognitive defenses. Such approaches emphasize how advertising may trick or mislead people, examining how ads distort information or use images, sound, and language to link branded products to deep-seated human values.

In the absence of large-scale survey research, we don't know much about how likely it is that elementary school students will get an introduction to these topics before middle school. We do know how a teacher's own attitudes and beliefs about advertising will shape whether or not they feel it is important for learners in the elementary grades (Hobbs & Moore, 2013).

Around the age of eight, the majority of children are able to recognize the difference between television advertising and programs, and they demonstrate an increasing understanding of the intent of advertising (Young, 1990). Researchers who have developed and assessed media literacy programs for elementary school students have found that young learners can experience dramatic gains in knowledge that helps them better understanding advertising (Nelson, 2016). Media literacy expert Frank Baker has noted that because many middle school teachers recognize how ads are shaping students' values, they feel more compelled to help students engage in critical thinking about advertising. Such efforts can be easily aligned with state and national standards in English language arts, civics, and health and wellness (Baker, 2017).

Some researchers have designed educational programs that intentionally cultivate the dislike of advertising, explicitly trying to persuade children to view ads as harmful (Rozendaal, Opree, & Buijzen, 2016). They have designed interventions that are designed to stimulate psychological reactance, the feeling of loss of freedom that comes from the awareness of being persuaded. As researchers explained, they aim to arouse "an unpleasant feeling within the viewer that they are being unfairly manipulated" (Rozendaal, Buijs, & van Reijmersdal, 2016, p. 1187). This practice may result in less favorable thoughts and attitudes about a brand. But in my mind, this is suspiciously like a disguised form of propaganda itself. Such an approach to media literacy is unlikely to build the habits of mind that lead to critical autonomy, or the ability to think for oneself.

Some educators make an effort to ensure that the study of advertising does not simply demonize advertising. Instead of using words like "tricks" and "manipulation," these lesson plans and activities help students to identify the target audience and the implicit message suggested by the imagery, language and narrative of ads. In emphasizing the value of reading nutrition labels and making rational choices, this approach to media literacy education is oriented toward consumer rights and responsibilities. Ten years ago, the Federal Trade Commission created Admongo, an online game to help children recognize the persuasive techniques used in advertising. Through an online game and a set of lesson plans for classroom use, students discovered how advertisers use humor or fear to appeal to target audiences. They learned how advertisers try to transfer people's feelings about attractive images or ideas to a product, and how a sense of urgency is constructed to get people to take action. Today, the website is obsolete and outdated. But it demonstrated the point that, in teaching kids how to swim in the ocean of advertising, it's not necessary to make advertising the enemy (Elliott, 2010).

LEARNING ACTIVITY

Create Advertisements for Different Target Audiences

For young learners, the study of advertising is a foundational skill needed to understand how persuasive genres influence people.

Activity: Let's pretend we have been asked to create a cereal ad–for space aliens! If you want the ad to appeal to space aliens, but you don't know anything about them, what can you do? Advertisers often use research to learn about their target audience. Imagine that aliens were interviewed and surveyed to find out what they like. How would the audience research data below affect the design of an ad campaign?

TABLE 3.1: Space Aliens Audience Research

LIKES	DISLIKES
Flying in space	Swimming
Slimy food	Crunchy food
The color green	The color red
Magazines about rocket ships	Computers

Read the Chart: To understand how decisions about advertising are influenced by research on consumer preferences, practice reading the chart, using reasoning to explain your interpretation:

1. What's the better choice–a magazine ad or an Internet ad?
2. What's a better image–an alien flying in space or an alien swimming?
3. Which would be the best color for the ad?

Create to Learn: After analyzing the market research on space aliens, create a cereal box or cereal ad for space aliens, using what they learned from the research along with some persuasive techniques, including repetition, humor, fear, testimonials, and call to action.

The Takeaway: Careful research and creative expression are both used to ensure that advertising messages address people's perceived needs.

–Adapted from Federal Trade Commission, Admongo (2010)

Popular Culture in the Classroom

American teachers who are knowledgeable about advertising are more likely to be comfortable teaching about it. But research evidence offers additional reasons why teachers may perceive this work as challenging. When classroom talk turns to advertising, children generally have specific knowledge about current advertising campaigns that are often unfamiliar to their teachers. In the classroom, teachers themselves may use examples of advertising from past decades that their students have not encountered (Hobbs & Moore, 2013). When elementary students start explaining what they learned about digital advertising on *Game Shakers*, a Nickelodeon TV series about a group of seventh grade kids who start a video game app company, teachers who are unfamiliar with the show may not know how to respond. Some teachers make a substantial effort to be up to date on an ever-changing popular culture, but for many, this practice is simply too time-consuming. And even for teachers who highly value the practice of keeping up with popular culture trends, events and controversies may not be able to understand how their students use media in the context of their everyday lives (Moore, 2011). Of course, teachers do not need to be popular culture experts. Instead, educators can adopt the stance of a social anthropologist, asking students themselves to explain and share their experiences with digital advertising and other forms of media.

Educators may believe that the values of popular culture and the values of the school are in direct competition. At school, teachers emphasize the value of respect, while at home, children watch ads, TV shows, and movies that advance the themes of competition, one-upsmanship, pride, greed, and humiliation. In some communities, talking about popular culture is simply not "appropriate" for school. Some students have already learned from previous teachers about topics they cannot talk about, leading them to be quite cautious in describing their encounters with movies, TV shows, video games, and the online media they experience at home.

Nearly every elementary teacher I have ever talked to has experienced situations where a child has been exposed to entertainment or advertising messages that a teacher believed was not age appropriate. For example, first grade teachers worked with young girls whose watching of YouTube beauty tutorials created an intense interest in makeup and beauty products. Because of the unpredictability of these conversations, some teachers expressed fears about not wanting to "get in trouble" for including aspects of media and popular culture in the curriculum (Deal, Flores-Koulish, & Sears, 2010).

That's ironic, because at the heart of it, advertising analysis activities activate reading, writing, speaking, listening, and critical thinking by connecting the classroom to contemporary culture. While some educators want to protect young children from advertising's compelling persuasion, others emphasize the wonder and delight at how ads respond to the ever-changing cultural environment (Hobbs & Tuzel, 2017). When I observed educators in an urban elementary school, I saw a classroom practice designed to activate the skill of asking questions in response to advertising, using the Question Game. Because it showcases the practice of wondering, this flexible activity can be effective with learners of all ages, from kindergarten to graduate school. During the game, one student wondered about Coca-Cola. She and her partner engaged in a battle of questions, and as the game went on, more and more questions were generated. Did people's feelings about the product relate to the shape of the bottle or the can? When was the Coke bottle invented? This led to an Internet search activity, where the student generated keywords and sifted through several websites, reading for comprehension to discover the answer, and proudly reporting what she learned. Because the student controlled the learning experience in generating both the questions and the answers, her confidence and intellectual curiosity increased (Hobbs & Moore, 2013). Such inquiry activities prepare students for a lifetime of learning.

LEARNING ACTIVITY

The Question Game

Discover the power of generating questions and promote reflection on the inquiry process in a playful one-on-one dialogue that goes back and forth in a type of questioning battle.

Activity: Choose any popular culture topic or artifact as a stimulus. Two participants sit in a fishbowl-style seating arrangement, with other class members in a circle around them. In this activity, one person starts with a question and the other person responds with another question, allowing no more than 30 seconds between questions. The two participants generate as many questions as possible about the artifact under examination. Observers take notes to identify the most interesting questions generated by the questioning process.

Observers stop the game when someone makes a statement or repeats a question that has already been asked.

Reflection and Search: What were the most interesting questions generated by the activity? Students may be asked to distinguish between closed-ended questions (which have a right or wrong answer) and open questions, which require discussion. The teacher may model the search process to demonstrate one or two key information literacy practices. Then learners get a short period of time to independently search for answers to a question that most interested them, as the teacher observes and supports this work. After the search time has concluded, results are briefly shared and discussed.

The Takeaway: Asking questions about popular culture activates intellectual curiosity. When students get plenty of guided practice in generating questions and searching for information, they become more confident learners.

How Attention and Relationships Are Monetized

Attention matters significantly in the nature of human relationships. When Dale Carnegie codified his sales techniques in the 1912 book, *How to Win Friends and Influence People*, he offered an alternative to the hard-sell of face-to-face persuasion that dominated the business community at the time. He showed how being generous with your attention was a key factor in business success. Be positive, don't criticize. Ask questions. Show your concern for others. Admit when you're wrong. Be kind. Cultivate relationships, because people matter more than things. At the time he wrote the book, these were radical ideas for people in business and sales, where the high-pressure sales pitch was predominant. Carnegie demonstrated to his readers that the soft sell was a far better and more effective way to reach hearts and minds.

In his seminal book on propaganda, the French theologian Jacques Ellul recognized the power dynamics inherent in social relationships that are aligned with propaganda. He called it horizontal propaganda, noting that it can emanate from "inside the group (and not from the top), where, in principle, all individuals are equal and there is no leader" (Ellul, 1973, p. 82). Relationship driven persuasion can even be coercive when people are required to pay attention to certain topics and issues as a result of social pressure from peers. In Russia and China, study groups socialize people from all strata of society to accept the fundamental principles of communism. But this type of propaganda does not only occur in communist societies. It is an ordinary part of workplace culture everywhere. As one writer succinctly put it, "Groups are pressure cookers of conformity" (Patrick, 2012, p. 83). Such coercion limits human freedom in the service of social cohesion. Propaganda is one of the many communication strategies that help people unify their thoughts and actions in order to work together.

When Google and Facebook decided to adopt advertising as the heart of their business models, they understood the importance of relationships. They use tracking and measurement to understand how people behave in social networks. To profile users, small text files (called cookies) are placed in the user's computer to create an identification code that documents the clicks made by that user (Turow, 2017). User profiles are then created and digital ads are shown to people based on that data. Today, Google, Facebook, *The New York Times* and many other companies gather and use information about people's online behavior. From their point of view, these companies pay attention to what you and your friends pay attention to in order to give you more of what you like, thus leading you to spend more time on their platforms.

To monetize human attention, data scientists use the term engagement as a means to measure the value of online content. Online content that attracts more attention has more economic value. To be sure, they don't examine the quality of the content itself, or its usefulness to users. They simply measure the amount of attention it attracts. Any website owner or platform user can measure website traffic by counting likes and clicks. Advertisers value precise measures of engagement because it makes their job easier and more effective (Wu, 2016).

Measures of online engagement inevitably conflate popularity with quality: if something is popular, it must be good. The rise of user-generated content has led to a conceptualization of the audience as "a collective of active agents whose labor may generate alternative forms of market value" (Jenkins, Ford, & Green, 2013, p. 116). Thus, participatory culture, which is generally understood as the social practice of engaging in online communication and creative expression, is also a vital part of the information economy. Since online participation is the engine of the digital economy, platform companies will naturally cultivate and support any and all activities that lead people to spend more time with technology and media. They'll avoid ever suggesting that people disconnect from digital devices or spend less time online.

The personalization of entertainment, information, and persuasion forces us to think about propaganda in new ways. In previous eras, shared exposure to media and communication messages helped to forge common cultural bonds between members of a diverse population. Today, each individual sees a never-ending stream of digital content that is uniquely personalized. Online experiences rely on algorithmic curation to supply people with content that meets their particular needs and interests. Because the Instagram photos that I see have been algorithmically selected based on my previous behavior on the platform, the content I encounter is unlikely to be similar to what you may experience.

This poses real challenges for media literacy educators by making it difficult for one user to compare his or her media experience with that of another user. Each user gets a "private, personalized pipeline of media" based on the media content and the creators that they tend to pay attention to (Rose-Stockwell, 2017, p. 1). Because we encounter information and entertainment on personalized handheld devices, media consumption feels more relevant and personal than ever before. When you use TikTok, the content presented will be different from what your students are likely to see. Today, an educator's front page of the Internet is different from that of his or her students. With rising levels of political polarization, we are seeing the cultural consequences of this kind of fragmentation. For educators, the implications of this phenomenon may affect how we create and sustain learning communities. Consider the implications of this reality:

- Your Google search results are different from my Google search results.
- Your Netflix does not display the same movies as my Netflix.
- Your Amazon does not present the same types of merchandise as my Amazon.

How might online personalization enable new forms of propaganda to flourish? My German colleague Christian Seyferth-Zapf and I wanted our students to understand how Google searches are structured and personalized in ways that might enable so-called "filter bubbles" to form. This term originated ten years ago when Eli Pariser introduced readers to the algorithms used to shape search engines. Algorithms use signals provided indirectly by users to select and display content that people are predisposed to agree with. As a homework activity, we asked students to use Google to search on a keyword and then make a screenshot of the search engine results page. We used keywords like Germany, United States of America, and Finland. Students posted their images on a digital bulletin board.

What did we discover? A number of German students were disproportionately exposed to news from Russian news agencies like RT and Sputnik when they searched for news about the United States. Many American students also got news from foreign sources including Al Jazeera and the *Jerusalem Post.* Perhaps because many American news media sources like *The New York Times* and the *Washington Post* are behind a paywall, they were much less frequently shown to them (Hobbs, Seyferth-Zapf & Grafe, 2018). Through this activity, students learned that algorithms serve as a nonhuman editor in selecting news stories for users, differentially shaping their understanding of the world around them.

You might want to blame platforms for the rise of digital propaganda, but the platforms alone are not the source of the problem. Despite the power of Google to shape the information and advertising you receive, the quality and diversity of political propaganda in the United States is not merely an algorithm problem. Researchers who study political partisanship analyzed the market reward systems in place for partisan-confirming news over truth. They explain, "Technology interacts with institutions and ideology to shape how we make meaning, how we organize our affairs across economic, political and personal domains, and how we make our culture and identity" (Benkler, Faris, & Roberts, 2018, p. 381). Digital platforms do not have just one effect on democracy, news media, or on people's ability to tell truth from fiction.

LEARNING ACTIVITY

Reading Charts: Social Media Economics

To understand the digital economy, it's important to "follow the money." Charts and graphs about financial trends help business leaders make important decisions.

Activity: The chart on the next page displays data collected by App Annie, a data analytics platform, about Snapchat, a social media platform. After reading and interpreting the chart, write a short paragraph that expresses your understanding of the main ideas presented.

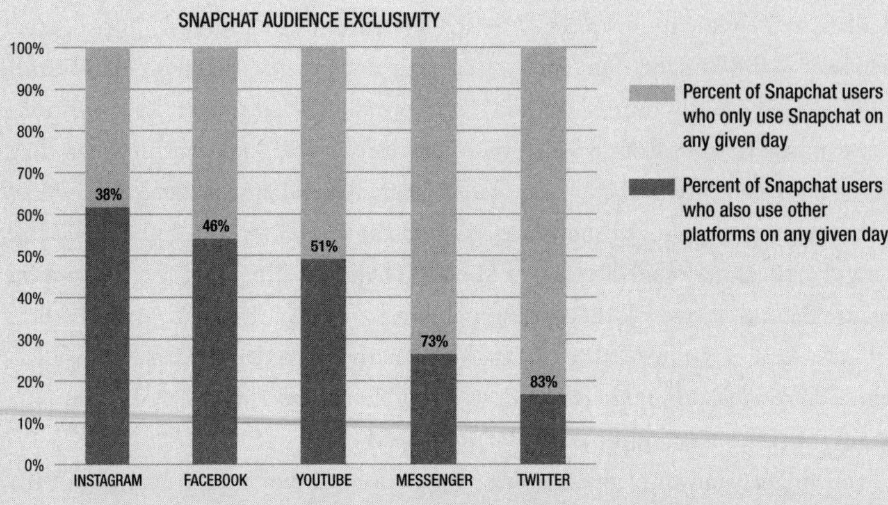

REVENUES IN MILLIONS	Winter 2017	Spring 2018	Summer 2018
NORTH AMERICA	219	170	177
EUROPE	40	33	40
REST OF WORLD	26	27	45
TOTAL	286	231	262

Snapchat Economics

Questions for Analysis:

- What is the main message of the chart?
- Why was this chart probably created? What is the purpose?
- Who would be most interested in this information? How might this information be useful?
- What was surprising to you about this chart?
- What other questions does this chart raise for you?

The Takeaway: Snapchat makes millions of dollars from digital advertising on the platform. Many young people use Snapchat as their only form of social media, which means that advertisers interested in reaching teens may be highly motivated to buy advertising on this platform.

–Adapted from App Annie (2019)

Understanding and Creating Clickbait

Clickbait is a relatively new form of advertising propaganda. It's usually recognizable by its eye-catching headlines that are designed to make money for their producers by exploiting the curiosity gap between what the headline promises and what the article delivers. One familiar clickbait formula is the question, where a combination of headline and image is supposed to attract audience attention. For some users, clickbait can lead to disappointment when the link yields content unrelated to the intriguing headline.

The art of creating clickbait comes from strategic omission. Ironically, the withholding of information can inspire curiosity through the activation of suspense. All great storytellers know this. As one reporter points out, "Great journalism at every point on the information-entertainment spectrum has long relied on curiosity to draw people into a story that they otherwise wouldn't care about" (Hamblin, 2014, p. 1).

Because people naturally strive to make sense of their world, clickbait content can be compelling to readers. But clickbait may also encourage impulsive online scrolling. Clickbait relies on the appeal of emotional subjects or controversial political and social issues. People may experience pleasure in aligning themselves with certain ideas that reflect their existing beliefs and attitudes, especially if these ideas are presented in a novel or surprising way.

While surprising and sometimes deceptive headlines are used to create clickbait, the content may also feature disinformation that is intentionally false and designed to mislead. Clickbait's influence is intensified as people increasingly encounter news via headlines on social media streams. As one researcher explained, "On social media sites like Facebook, an article from *The New York Times* looks just like an article from *The Onion* and either may come with the endorsement of the friend who shared it" (Chen, Conroy, & Rubin, 2015, p. 2). Political ads can look like information shared by your neighbors and friends. Lack of contextual clues impairs people's ability to evaluate the source and quality of information. The sheer volume of all this misleading information creates a new form of manipulation that has been called "censorship through noise" (Coppins, 2020).

Educators are exploring instructional strategies to advance students' understanding of clickbait as a form of propaganda. One history teacher at the International School of Toulouse was inspired by a clever list of clickbait headlines written about historical events, so he created a learning activity that involves students summarizing an aspect of their most recent study topic as a clickbait headline for a trashy website blog post (Tarr, 2016). Studying and creating clickbait may help learners develop metacognition by reflecting on what activates their curiosity (Bruce, 2019).

To collect examples of clickbait, I asked my students to make screenshots of some typical, outrageous or even bizarre examples of clickbait, sharing these images on a digital bulletin board. From this collection of artifacts, it was easy for them to see how gender, age, and interests shape the types of advertising and sponsored content that are presented via people's social networks. But it takes practice to learn to deconstruct, decipher, and resist clickbait headlines that are designed to hijack attention. Web marketing expert Jaelithe Guillette designed Portent's Content Idea Generator, a simple digital tool for generating clickbait headlines. The tool offers a way to explore the power of language to attract and hold attention. You simply type in a topic of interest, and you are shown many ways that the topic could be turned into a clickbait headline. One of my students, a fan of the video game Fortnite, typed in the name of the video game and got this list of suggested clickbait titles:

- Why You'll Never Succeed at Fortnite
- How Low Can Fortnite Go?
- How Fortnite Can Keep You From Fortnite
- How Fortnite Changes How We Think About Death
- 6 Ways That Fortnite Can Make You Rich

In the Title Generator, each of these examples also includes a brief bit of deconstruction. For example, consider the clickbait headline, "15 Facts About Fortnite That Will Keep You Up at Night." The platform points out that the phrase "15 Facts" unconsciously activates feelings of trust. People automatically think facts are objective and neutral. In considering the phrase "will keep you up at night," we're reminded of the power of fear as a means to drive attention. Portent's Title Generator explains, "Anxiety-inducing headlines are like horror movies. They are effective but easy to overdo."

Creating clickbait headlines is fun—and the pleasure it offers can be an excellent way to inspire deeper curiosity about how clickbait works. Creating clickbait may also offer a creativity jolt for some learners. For example, one of my students found that the experience of playing with the Title Generator tool unleashed creativity. It wasn't long before my Fortnite fan found an angle for his writing and composed a detailed article on professional gamer Tyler Blevins and his tremendous financial success with Fortnite. In writing it, he was careful not to create fake news about getting rich playing Fortnite. All the information in his blog post was accurate. But it was just packed with emotional wallop because of the way he activated curiosity about the complex process of becoming a professional player while simultaneously appealing to an adolescent boy's competitive ego. For some learners, creative writing experiences may help to demystify the ubiquitous clickbait headlines we encounter online.

LEARNING ACTIVITY

Creating and Analyzing Clickbait Titles

Creating clickbait helps learners better recognize and understand the "hooks" that grab attention.

Activity: Search online for Portent's Content Idea Generator and use it generate a sample of at least 15 titles on a topic of interest to you. Read the explanation of each title that is provided on the website.

Create to Learn: Select one of the clickbait titles you like best and write a short blog post, using one or more propaganda strategies to create clickbait content of your own that compels reader attention.

The Takeaway: Although clickbait may be designed to discourage critical thinking, people can be attentive to how it exploits curiosity to attract and hold attention.

Influence Marketing and Authenticity

Marketers have found many different ways to monetize human relationships. Today, the term of art for this form of propaganda is influence marketing. Companies pay people to promote their products online. Influence marketers are the beauty bloggers, BookTubers, and micro-celebrities who receive products or compensation for promoting a product or service on videos, podcasts, or blogs. Influence marketers are highly visible on YouTube and many other digital platforms today.

Influence marketing is popular because companies value the authenticity of connecting their brand with a celebrity, of course, even a minor one. The increased use of ad-blocking tools has fueled the rise of influence marketing because 40% of consumers find ads to be annoying (Conick, 2018). Influence marketing is considered valuable to advertisers because unlike other forms of advertising, the post or video cannot be skipped over, ignored, or bypassed. As people do more shopping online, they like to get information and have conversations about products and services. When specific products and services are mentioned by Internet personalities, it doesn't seem like a hard sell. Although celebrities like Kim Kardashian promote products by reaching millions, marketers are reaching out to people with a smaller following on social media, those between 10,000 and 100,000 followers (Maheshwari, 2018).

Many elementary and secondary students are quite familiar with influencers, and some have strong positive opinions about them. In Finland, a number of young YouTubers have created personal brands, and media literacy educators there have introduced the subject of influence marketing on YouTube to their students. Sonja Hernesniemi of the Finnish Society on Media Education developed a workshop for teens, where students explore the commercial side of YouTube content production and influence marketing.* In her workshop with teens, Sonja started with a Walk the Line warm-up activity where students indicate their opinions on several statements about influence marketers. Students who agree with the statement stand on an imaginary line in the classroom, with "strongly agree" at one end of the line and "strongly disagree" at the other end. They volunteer to share their reasons for agreeing or disagreeing with statements like, "Influencers on YouTube are more trustworthy than people who don't promote products on their channel." The activity gives students a playful way to share their ideas about a topic while helping the teacher increase knowledge of students' existing attitudes and beliefs.

* The Finnish Society on Media Education promotes and develops media literacy education in Finland by raising awareness and spreading information and best practices of media literacy to teachers, child and youth workers, librarians, early childhood educators, representatives of media and culture, researchers, and students of the field.

Another activity involves learning key marketing and advertising terminology and discussing the ethical and legal boundaries of advertising. Working in small groups, students analyze a marketing case in which the Council of Ethics in Advertising in Finland received a complaint about the lack of fiscal transparency of an online content provider. In a simulation activity, small groups learn more about influence marketing by playing one of three roles: a business or company that wants to promote products using influence marketing, a YouTube content provider, or a multichannel network organization of YouTube content providers. During this activity, the groups research and evaluate the marketing process from the perspective of their assigned role. After gathering information online, they share their insights with the whole group.

The study of influence marketing inevitably leads to deeper ethical questions about the practice of monetizing relationships and selling authenticity. My students enjoyed reading and discussing an article in *The New York Times* that explained how some Instagrammers create "fake" sponsored content in hopes they might be perceived by their peers as an influencer. For example, one Instagrammer pretended to be on a sponsored trip to Miami, promoting brands and providing a stream of content (Lorenz, 2018). This practice embodies the cultural belief that you should "fake it until you make it."

In a rich discussion, my students had quite diverse perspectives on this topic. I even learned that one of my students aspired to be an influencer. She explained, "My dog has a growing following and although he creates a lot of traffic, that traffic hasn't yet led to much business for the companies we collaborate with." But another student was troubled by "fake" influencers, explaining, "The strategy really upsets me. It proves to me that people really do not care about being themselves anymore as long as there is money involved." Another student acknowledged that although faking it seems like a creative idea to get to the top, if brands become more aware of this, "they will start to do more research before giving someone a sponsorship. As the trend becomes more exposed, the value of influencers may start to decrease." Educators know that discussions like this help to create a classroom climate of trust and respect when diverse perspectives are truly welcomed.

Fake Friends

Manipulating people's need for belonging and social connection can be a form of propaganda. Many social media users receive requests from unknown individuals who seek to friend them on Facebook, which can be hard to resist. You see a name and a face, and you are presented with the option of confirming or deleting. You may feel a bit of curiosity or even a sense of delight when other people seek your friendship. I know I do. Who doesn't want more friends? For many people, it feels easy and natural to confirm these new friends, to welcome them into our lives. But fake friends can also be destabilizing and can even lead people to experience paranoia and existential distrust.

People send fake friend requests for a variety of reasons. Some are harmless, while others are malicious. Scammers may send a friend request in order to access the personal information you share with friends only. These people may post content with malicious links to malware or phishing sites. Catfishers may be looking for love (or money) by creating elaborate online profiles featuring beautiful men or women and sending out random friend requests to huge numbers of people before finding a willing victim. Even a current or ex-boyfriend or girlfriend may create a fake account in order to unobtrusively monitor your Facebook page.

Many fake accounts are created for political purposes. A large proportion of the followers of politicians come from fake accounts. For example, when one company analyzed the 54 million Twitter followers of @realdonaldtrump, they found that more than 50% of Trump's followers had seven or more red flags that suggest a fake account (Fishkin, 2018). During the congressional hearings on Facebook in 2017, Facebook business leaders estimated that at least 60 million of their accounts were fakes. According to one expert, "Spammers and bad actors are getting better at making themselves look more real" (Shane & Isaac, 2017, p. 1).

Some fake accounts are created for scams and frauds. In analyzing the authenticity of one particular Facebook account, Greg Johnson looked for clues to determine who was posting. He observed that every other post was a promotion of a book called *The Gold Road to Plenty*. Within one click, you can discover that the author of the book, Maksim Zaslavskiy, presents himself as "one of the world's leading currency decentralization proponents." A Bitcoin entrepreneur, he was cultivating Facebook friends to build an audience for his ideas (Johnson, 2017). By first taking the extra step of typing a particular name into a search engine, you can often learn a lot. In this case, Johnson discovered that this particular individual had been convicted of securities fraud for the misuse of Bitcoin marketing.

Still, fake accounts are big business. An investigation in *The New York Times* reported on a company that has collected millions of dollars by selling Twitter followers and retweets to celebrities and businesses. The company controls more than 3.5 million automated bot accounts, some of which closely resemble real people, using the names, profile pictures, hometowns, and other personal details of real Twitter users (Confessore, Dance, Harris, & Hansen, 2018). These Twitter bots can be programmed to automatically amplify a client's tweet, so that whenever a particular B-list celebrity tweets, her bot followers immediately retweet. Each bot may retweet content on a wide assortment of topics and in several languages.

Fake accounts spread potentially harmful propaganda. One of the first reported cases of this occurred in 2009, when more than a hundred stem cell research scientists were victims of Facebook imposter accounts. Attackers stole their identities to create a convincing fake network, which is used to create an impression that "a certain set of ideas is more accepted (or under more fire) than it really is" (Laursen, 2009, p. 1089).

Computer scientists are developing algorithms to automatically detect fake accounts. Although they have devoted a lot of effort to designing programs that can identify and stop the rise of fake accounts, they cannot yet reliably design software tools to detect fake social media accounts (Koll et al., 2017). That's because humans sometimes behave in ways that bots do. For example, many people sign up for a new social media account, fill out no information, post very few or no messages, follow some accounts, and then abandon the platform.

Students may experience a sense of empowerment through being able to recognize and spot fake Twitter bots or identify fake friends on Facebook. There are a variety of strategies for identifying fake social media accounts, but one easy way is to simply review an individual's public content for the type of content, pictures, and interactions that occur there.

Students can learn how to determine the authenticity of online accounts. In one compelling video, Johnson (2017) shows how to use reverse image search to identify a fake account. We see an account depicting a K-9 police officer and his police dog, but with a little bit of searching, we learn that it was one of several created by a man in Albania who maintained a network of many fake police officer Facebook accounts. Learning to detect fake Facebook accounts can provide people of all ages with a powerful opportunity to understand the problems with authenticity embedded in our current information ecosystem. For learners, such hands-on, minds-on explorations can intensify their perceptions of the need to be vigilant when using the Internet.

LEARNING ACTIVITY

Find Fake Facebook or Instagram Accounts

When used as an intergenerational media literacy learning experience with family members, this activity helps everyone to develop media literacy competencies.

Activity: Working together with a family member, teacher, or peer, review a list of friends on Facebook or followers on Instagram until you find a name you do not recognize. Then use one or more online digital tools that help you identify fake followers.

1. ***Review posts.*** What kind of content does this individual post? Is a lot of the same content posted from one particular website to different groups or hashtags? If so, this user might be getting paid to spread content.
2. ***Review pictures.*** Do the pictures include a lot of stereotypical or generic images? If so, this user might be constructing a fake identity using easily available online images or images of real people. Use a reverse image search to reveal the origins of pictures.
3. ***Review friends.*** Fake Instagram and Facebook accounts may be part of a network of fake accounts. Review the accounts of the user's friends to see how many of them are real people or constructed fake accounts.

For Discussion: Reflect upon the emotional insights of exploring fake Instagram and Facebook accounts. What different thoughts and feelings did you experience while examining the authenticity of people's Instagram and Facebook accounts?

The Takeaway: Being an online detective can sometimes be exhilarating, or it might make you feel creepy. When encountering fake accounts, people may experience a mix of different emotions including surprise, sadness, disgust, delight, and other feelings.

Microtargeting through Algorithmic Personalization

Advertising subsidizes many forms of media by making it free to consumers in a system called the indirect revenue stream. Terrestrial radio and television are free to listeners and viewers. Instagram, Facebook, and Google don't charge fees either. When you listen to a podcast, it may be free, but you will hear ads that urge you to visit a website to get a special discount for making a purchase there. In this business model, the advertiser pays to gain access to the consumer's attention. In effect, for these media companies, you (as the viewer, reader, or listener) are the product that is sold to advertisers.

Social media platforms rely on digital advertising as their primary revenue stream. These companies design their products and services to encourage people to spend the most time possible using the platform. Data collected on user behavior enables personalized search results, advertising displays, and price discrimination (Turow, 2017). Recommendation engines offer content that people are likely to find relevant and interesting, which leads to more media use. On social media platforms, ads are sold via an auction system that matches advertisers to their desired target audiences. Digital advertising is generally appreciated by consumers who find it to be more relevant than advertising on TV, radio, or print media. Plus, online ad buying is democratic: it's something that anyone with a social media account can do. Individuals and small businesses can target audiences with advertising for a wide range of commercial and educational purposes.

Digital advertising can be used for very precise targeting and this has been shamefully exploited by some. In 2016, politicians could target Facebook audiences with terms like "Jew haters" (Coppins, 2020). Microtargeting is defined as the use of user profiling based on psychological or other characteristics of consumers. To place an ad on Instagram, you can target exactly the type of people you want to reach. Do you want to reach people who have purchased a car in the past year? Or people who watch *American Idol*? Or perhaps just people who are interested in pets like hamsters and other small rodents?

Another form of microtargeting enables advertisers to customize advertising based on GPS data, reaching individual users in specific physical locations on their mobile phones, computers, and TVs. Ads can be delivered to individuals in specific locations through social media (Nix, 2017). Ads can appear when you're at an airport or walking in the vicinity of a new restaurant. But ads for a political candidate can even appear on people's mobile phones as they walk out of a local church and head to the parking lot.

The American public first learned about microtargeting when it affected the 2016 election, after Cambridge Analytica championed strategies for targeting potential voters based on identifying personality characteristics that might influence voting behavior. They aimed to customize political advertising based on attitudes like openness, conscientiousness, extroversion, agreeableness, and neuroticism (Nix, 2017). An ad sponsored by the National Rifle Association and designed for people with high levels of neuroticism might depict owning a gun as a type of insurance policy in case of a burglary. For conscientious types, an ad could talk about values associated with tradition, family, and cultural heritage.

President Donald Trump has mastered the art of political ad spending on Facebook, using highly customized ads to appeal to constituents. In the last days before the 2016 Presidential election, Trump's campaign team tried to suppress turnout among Black voters in Florida by slipping provocative ads into their News Feeds that read, "Hillary Thinks African-Americans Are Super Predators" (Coppins, 2020). And well in advance of the 2020 election, between January and May of 2019, Trump spent nearly $4.5 million on Facebook ads, far outspending other political candidates (Kaplan & Almukhtar, 2019).

Platform companies are now engaged in heated discussion about whether and how to regulate online political advertising. Other than certain federal campaign finance regulations, there are no federal laws that directly regulate online political advertising. But in response to congressional pressure, Facebook created the Ad Library in 2018. This online library offers increased transparency about targeted political advertising through a searchable collection of all political ads running on Facebook or Instagram. This important resource is a useful resource for educators and students exploring the role of advertising in political campaigns. People can access all ads, even ones that may not have been shown to you because you weren't part of the intended target audience.

Social media platforms have responded in different ways to the misuses of microtargeting in political advertising. Political advertising is an important source of revenue for social media platforms. But in response to concerns about the risks of microtargeting, Google decided to outlaw political ads directed at specific audiences based on public voter records or political affiliations. Twitter has refused to allow political ads at all. Only Facebook has not changed their policies on political advertising. Mark Zuckerberg believes that social media gives people "the power to express themselves at scale" (Isaac & Kang, 2020). Facebook has declared that they will allow political microtargeting because they do not want to police the accuracy of political ads. It was feared that if Facebook changed its policies on microtargeting, it could differentially influence political groups and potentially hurt smaller grassroots organizations. For example, if Facebook had raised the minimum number of people who could be targeted to 1,000 from 100, smaller organizations might be at a disadvantage (Isaac, 2019).

As we have seen in this chapter, the idea of buying and selling people's attention and capitalizing on people's relationships has become normalized, first by the rise of advertising and now through social media. Educators who aim to pull back the curtain on how human attention is exploited for political and economic goals need to be sensitive to the complex range of feelings that such work can create for learners. Learning about advertising propaganda, fake followers, and political microtargeting can raise complicated feelings. We may experience delight, appreciation, cynicism, anger, denial, paranoia, or even disgust. Being transparent about your own mix of feelings in exploring the emotional power of propaganda and its function in the context of our social relationships can help to deepen your appreciation of the complexity and nuance of these issues. Armed with a good understanding attention economics, we are in a better position to examine propaganda in the context of news and information.

4

Teaching the News

Propaganda in news and information shapes perceptions of reality

Entrepreneurship is alive and well in the field of journalism. Take a look at Ken LaCorte's small website company. He and his small team put out only 15 stories per day, but they reach 30 million readers. His websites include Conservative Edition News and Liberal Edition News, which both offer highly differentiated partisan content for a politically divided country. Ken LaCorte's unique approach to journalism is merely taking advantage of the growing popularity of politically divisive partisan news content. Developing his business model from the one used by young Macedonians in 2016, LaCorte has profited from the use of Google AdSense, which enables him to place pay-per-click ads next to stories with eye-popping headlines like "Austin Sex-Ed Curriculum Teaches Kids How to Obtain an Abortion" (Perlroth, 2019).

Or consider the plight of radio listeners in Kansas City, Missouri, where the owner of three local stations decided to put Russian government news and talk shows on the airwaves, subjecting listeners to messages designed to deepen resentment, confusion, and doubt about the American political system. For 42 hours a week over the next three years, the nearly half a million residents of Kansas City can hear Radio Sputnik's point of view on the news, thanks to the Russian government paying $324,000 to the owner of the local station (MacFarquhar, 2020).

Such examples of propaganda disguised as news and information may be profitable, but you may be surprised to learn that a another type of "fake news" has also been intentionally used by teachers and librarians in public school classrooms as far back as the 1990s, when the Internet was new. Perhaps you have heard about microwave ovens as a form of mind control, the new toy for activist girls called Hacker Barbie, the dangerous chemical called dihydrogen monoxide, or even the elusive Pacific tree octopus? Such fake websites have long been used to teach media and information literacy. Consider the Male Pregnancy website, which first appeared online in 1999. On the website, a video documents the case of Mr. Lee Mingwei, who had a series of operations to enable his pregnancy. Visitors to the website could inspect a variety of documentary evidence about the pregnancy, including news reports, pictures, video clips, an EKG, ultrasound images, and even blood pressure measurements. The site was a compelling hoax created by artist and filmmaker Virgil Wong, whose art projects examine themes from contemporary medicine. Librarians and educators found sites like this to be valuable to teach students how to evaluate credibility, accuracy, reasonableness, and factual support.

Many different types of hoax websites have become useful as teaching tools. But hoaxes are generally most effective when they are plausible, and not easy to spot. One such website is Lip Balm Anonymous, a website that offers online support for those who find themselves addicted to Chapstick. This website is packed with advice about treating dry lips and overcoming the use of lip balm as a compulsive behavior. Is it a real website or a hoax? It's hard to tell for sure.

You may think of children and teenagers as the victims of fake news. But they can also be the perpetrators. When news reports of an evil suicide game circulated online, the headlines claimed that children were receiving a series of challenges that started out innocuously but increasingly became dangerous; these instructions were given anonymously via smartphone or were embedded in YouTube videos. In 2017, there was the Momo challenge. In 2018, there was the Blue Whale game. News stories about teen suicides linked to these online games proliferated in Russia, Mexico, Argentina, England, the U.S., and other countries, and local police shared warnings via Facebook groups. During this time, many parents encountered social media posts about the dangerous social media trend. But journalists who investigated the cases found that teens themselves were responsible for spreading the hoax (Adeane, 2019).

Because propaganda can take the form of news and journalism, we must reflect and question why we believe some things and not others. Philosophers describe this as the practice of epistemology, the study of ignorance, doubt, and the nature of knowledge. There are many types of so-called fake news and six very distinct paradigms for exploring the topic in the classroom. These pedagogical approaches reflect ideological differences among educators whose own beliefs and attitudes about the news inevitably shape the teaching and learning process.

Many Forms of Fake News

Teachers love posters and visual aids. That's why the European Association for Viewer Interests (2017) created the Beyond Fake News poster as a teaching resource to support conversations about different types of misleading information. While educators may use the term "fake news" to attract student interest, the first step in the learning process requires the development of a more nuanced vocabulary about the many types of misleading information content available today in all forms of media. Some key features are presented below.

Sponsored Content

Sponsored content is a form of online advertising that matches the form and function of the platform on which it appears. It's sometimes called native advertising. It looks like a news story or a social media post, but it's an ad that is designed to blend in or look natural by matching the other information on the website page. Another related term is content marketing, which refers to editorial content that has a marketing or propaganda goal.

The practice of disguising ads this way is very profitable for media companies. On many websites, you can find sponsored content that looks like a link to a video, news, or other content. In reality, it is an ad meant to be clicked on. For example, at CNN.com, I scroll down the page and see something that says, "More Stories." There I find a number of boxed images and headlines. One headline down at the bottom reads: "When Jimi Hendrix Opened for The Monkees." This particular content shows up because, while using my browser, I have provided clues that reveal my gender, age, and my interest in the awesome music of the 1960s. When I click on the image, I am taken to another website, one that offers something called "brand storytelling." A variety of phrases or labels for sponsored content may be used, but sometimes you simply have to guess who might be paying for this content to appear. Sponsored content intentionally blurs the line between information, entertainment and persuasion, which helps disguise its real purpose as propaganda.

Beyond Fake News Poster

Partisan News

Partisan news is the term used to describe news and journalism produced in alignment with a particular worldview. Information that reinforces the worldview is emphasized through often compelling true stories, while information that doesn't fit into the ideological frame is omitted. Depending on your point of view, you might see Fox News or MSNBC as partisan journalism. Although partisan journalism has a long history in newspapers around the world, partisan news shows on U.S. radio and television began only after the Fairness Doctrine was overturned in 1987. Today, Tucker Carlson, Rush Limbaugh, Sean Hannity, and Rachel Maddow all present news and current events information from a distinctly partisan point of view.

Conspiracy Theories and Pseudoscience

Conspiracy theories offer simple explanations for complex phenomena, often by blaming a problem on a group of unknown or mysterious others who have intentionally engaged in harmful activities. Conspiracy theories rely on people's tendency to prefer simple explanations and identify villains, and many people also enjoy feeling they have secret knowledge shared only by a few.

When you hear the word "pseudoscience," you might think about creationism, UFOs, astrology, or alternative medicine. Most people think that pseudoscience relies on evidence that is not falsifiable. Others see it as a type of science that rejects conventional authority and expertise. But contrary to popular opinion, philosophers of science explain that there is no hard-and-fast litmus test for identifying pseudoscience. When a large group of people agree on a set of practices for determining what counts as evidence, we call those practices science. When a large group of people rejects the methodologies and evidence base of other scientists, they call it pseudoscience. Social consensus matters in the construction of knowledge in science and in all domains and fields of inquiry. As one scholar puts it, "The boundaries separating science, nonscience, and pseudoscience are much fuzzier and more permeable than . . . most scientists . . . would have us believe" (Pigliucci, 2010, p. iii).

Parody, Satire, Hoaxes, and Memes

Parody, satire, hoaxes, and memes may appear as literary, cultural, social, or political criticism and commentary. These types of propaganda are highly valuable to society because the ability to freely critique authorities is essential to democratic self-governance. Watching *Last Week Tonight* or *The Daily Show with Trevor Noah,* viewers get a mix of parody, satire, and news about current events that is carefully designed to influence beliefs and attitudes through the use of humor. People who create hoaxes have a variety of motives for using deception to trick readers or viewers. One of the most famous hoaxes familiar to high school English teachers is *Go Ask Alice*, a book published in 1971 as the diary of a 15-year-old girl who starts taking LSD, gets sucked into the drug underworld, and ends up dead. Although it sold 5 million copies, it was not a real teen's diary. The copyright actually belonged to a Mormon therapist. As one critic explains, literary hoaxes "expose the fragility of the norms of reading" where concepts of authority and authenticity are flexibly manipulated to accomplish a goal (Menand, 2018, p. 1).

Bots, Trolls, and Sock Puppets

Bots and trolls are forms of propaganda and disinformation that depend on disguise. Bots are computer programs on social media networks like Twitter, Facebook, and YouTube. Bots may be used to identify information on social networks, respond to it, or share it (Wardle, 2017). When a botnet is created (that's the term for a group of bots), it can create an illusion of popularity by amplifying information. The term troll is generally used for humans who disguise their online identity or create multiple fake identities to share, critique, or amplify online content. The term first emerged on electronic bulletin boards in the 1990s. At that time, some people deliberately baited others, verbally provoking them to elicit an emotional response. Today, trolling can be a business, where employees are paid to post comments on articles and influence political debates on social media (Gorwa, 2019). Groups of people who are paid to send messages that divide or disinform are known as a troll army.

Trolls may create multiple identities online to hurl abuse at people or ideas that they dislike. For example, the Turkish government hired 6,000 trolls to organize online lynch mobs against journalists who critiqued the country's leader, Recep Tayyip Erdoğan. Trolls combine propaganda with the power of personalization to attack opponents (Shearlaw, 2016). They trick people into thinking that there is widespread opposition to an idea, when in fact, it's all bought and paid for by one agent. Because they attack opponents in order to shape public opinion, trolls can cause a lot of damage.

A sock puppet is a term for a third-party source who is paid by a propagandist to create information and transmit messages that align directly with the propagandist's interests and goals. University researchers and nonprofit organizations can be sock puppets when they receive funding to communicate messages that support the strategic goals of a funder. If you are wondering where the term came from, consider how a sock puppet is a sock pulled over a hand to create a fake character. When it's used by politicians or businesses, sock puppets create the illusion of public support for particular social issues or products. For example, a car manufacturer might create a fake nonprofit environmental organization to develop a report that mentions that a particular vehicle is energy efficient.

But it's not just corporations who sometimes hide their identity. Governments may use sock puppets, too. In 2014, the government of Norway paid $5 million to a nonprofit organization to produce information designed to influence top officials in the White House. The nonprofit was serving as the sock puppet for the Norwegian government, who wanted to convey ideas to U.S. leaders without being on the record for it (Lipton, Williams, & Confessore, 2014). During World War II, it was called "black propaganda" when the identity of the agent responsible for the message is intentionally disguised, making it difficult or impossible for people to determine the message's actual author and purpose.

Government-Sponsored News

You are probably familiar with RT as a source of news even if you don't know that RT stands for Russia Today. It is state-sponsored news programming funded by the Russian government. Since RT is a global TV news network, it broadcasts in English, Arabic, Spanish, and French from its studios in Moscow, Washington, DC, London, and Paris. It is the most-watched TV news network on YouTube, with more than 10 billion views and 16 million subscribers (Rapid TV News, 2020). As a result of congressional pressure in 2018, YouTube has begun labeling news content funded by governments as part of their commitment to greater transparency. Below every RT video on YouTube, it says, "RT is funded in whole or in part by the Russian government."

RT's YouTube video clips include everything from breaking-news tsunami footage from Asia to stories about Bitcoin, to news about the dangers of transgender sexual reassignment surgery. Watching the live feed, it's easy to see the network's distinct point of view on topics like feminism and civil rights. One afternoon, I watched as, within a span of 15 minutes, the network offered news coverage on disparities in pay for male and females who play professional soccer. There was stridently negative coverage of Budweiser's LGBTQ marketing campaign and a snarky perspective on the controversy in Japan concerning businesses that require female workers to wear high heels. The tone of this news coverage clearly suggested that Western concerns about gender discrimination were just plain silly. If you watch long enough, you'll find that RT even has a political comedy show called *Redacted Tonight* that offers political rants about the failure of the so-called American Dream, delivered by a young comic in ways that might be "highly appealing to an angry 15-year-old boy" (Simon, 2017, p. 1).

Russia Today launched in 2005 as a strategy to improve Russia's image abroad but has now become a strategic tool for President Vladimir Putin's foreign policy. Russia claims that RT is no different from BBC, France 24, or other state-controlled broadcasters. But critics say that under the guise of contributing to freedom of opinion and freedom of the press, they are intentionally mocking and undermining it. One journalist pointed out, "Many Western countries regard RT as the slickly-produced heart of a broad, often covert disinformation campaign designed to sow doubt about democratic institutions and destabilize the West" (Erlanger, 2017, p. 1).

More often than delivering outright lies, RT deals in moral equivalency or what is sometimes called whataboutism. The *Oxford English Dictionary* defines it as "the practice of responding to an accusation or difficult question by making a counteraccusation or raising a different issue." Whataboutism offers a response to perceived hypocrisy or inconsistency, and it's not a new propaganda technique by any means. Ancient Roman orators used the expression *tu quoque*, which is Latin for "you also" (Yagoda, 2018, p. 1). It's a time-honored rhetorical defense: When you are criticized, simply turn the same criticism back against the accuser. When RT is accused of bias, it does not deny it. It simply uses the whataboutism technique to "point the accusing finger back at the West," noting that other news media are just as biased (Dowling, 2017, p. 1). Sadly, there's some merit to this claim. Since the 1950s, the U.S. government has disseminated information and news to people around the world to advance its strategic goals. You may be familiar with the United States Information Agency or the Voice of America, which has been described as the largest public relations firm in the world. After a restructuring process, this government organization is now known as the United States Agency for Global Media. The head of this agency is appointed by the President of the United States. In previous eras, distinguished journalists have held the position and they have been committed to the goal of impartial journalism. But in the summer of 2020, the agency reported that Wuhan, China had successfully limited the spread of coronavirus. President Trump attacked, tweeting that the agency was promoting "foreign propaganda." The head of the agency responded, saying, "We cover stories from all different sides. That's part of the reason we are so trusted by people around the world." A political firestorm erupted and within days, she resigned her position, enabling President Trump to appoint Michael Pack, a documentary filmmaker who has collaborated with Steve Bannon, co-founder of the far-right website, Breitbart News (Ellison, 2020).

Errors in Journalism

Some people have called mistakes in news reporting a type of fake news, because errors can and do contribute to public misunderstanding. Of course, because human communication is imperfect, everyone is prone to experience misunderstanding when interacting with other human beings and their symbolic creations. But there are important structural factors that make journalism uniquely prone to error. Due to budget pressures, the intense time pressure involved in reporting, and the reliance that journalists have on their sources, errors in journalism are inevitable.

Despite practices like fact-checking, journalistic error endures. For example, in just one week in December 2017, the mainstream media made several errors in reporting on President Donald Trump's relationships with Russian government officials. For example, ABC News's Brian Ross reported that Lt. General Michael Flynn was prepared to testify that he had been instructed by then-candidate Donald Trump to initiate contact with Russian officials. But later that day, the source clarified the message, explaining that during the campaign, Trump assigned Flynn and a small circle of other senior advisers to find ways to repair relations with Russia, including opportunities to work jointly against the Islamic State. As punishment for the error, the reporter was suspended for four weeks without pay. That same week, CNN, CBS, and MSNBC all reported on an email that seemed to prove the Trump campaign had advance notice about emails hacked by Wikileaks. As it turned out, the email appeared in Trump's inbox *after* the Wikileaks information was already public (Dilanian & Memoli, 2017). Given that journalistic error is inevitable, encouraging people to distrust journalists simply because they make mistakes is itself a form of propaganda.

LEARNING ACTIVITY

What Journalism Can Do

Many different types of journalism support self-governance in a democratic society.

Activity: Students study a single edition of a particular news publication or broadcast outlet to consider how effectively it serves the community by looking for specific examples of news content. These categories are aligned with ideas from Michael Schudson's (2008) book, *Why Democracy Needs an Unlovable Press*. Students present their examples in a short presentation or create a video or audio story, followed by time for reflection and discussion.

Six or Seven Things Media Can Do for Democracy

1. ***Information:*** Provide fair and full information so citizens can make sound political choices.
2. ***Investigation:*** Investigate concentrated sources of power, particularly governmental power.
3. ***Analysis:*** Provide coherent frameworks of interpretation to help citizens comprehend a complex world.
4. ***Social empathy:*** Tell people about others in their society and their world so that they come to appreciate the viewpoints and lives of other people, especially those less advantaged than themselves.
5. ***Public forum:*** Provide a forum for dialogue among citizens, through pluralistic and interdisciplinary approaches to issues, and serve as a common carrier of the perspectives of varied groups in society.
6. ***Advocacy & mobilization:*** Serve as advocates for political programs and perspectives and/or mobilize people to act in support of these programs, without compromising verification standards and public interest.

For Discussion: As a media consumer, which of these six functions is most important to you and why? Among the six functions, which function was most common? Which was least common? Which of these functions might be seen as a form of propaganda by some readers or viewers?

The Takeaway: Many different types of journalism are valuable in helping fulfill people's needs as citizens in a democracy.

–Adapted from *Journalism, "Fake News" and Disinformation* (UNESCO, 2018)

The Power of Framing

Framing sometimes refers to the way that language, choice of content, and the organization of ideas can be used to shape people's interpretations of people, events, and experiences. As one writer put it, "Frames are rhetorical devices that guide audience thinking. Like rhetoric, framing can be consciously or unconsciously used as a means of persuasion" (Carver, Wiese, & Breivik, 2014, p. 211).

People naturally think that if an issue is in the news frequently, it must be important. It also turns out that there is a first-mover advantage to news and information. Propagandists can shape a news story if they are the first ones to tell it. This is why in 2019, Attorney General William Barr immediately released a four-page summary of the Mueller Report and delayed the release of the full report for nearly one month. Barr's interpretation of the Mueller Report framed it as a win for President Trump by minimizing the evidence of obstruction of justice. Since people did not have access to the actual report, at the time there was no way to see if this interpretation was warranted. Because people could not directly access the special prosecutor's report, the attorney general's interpretation stuck in the public's mind.

But framing by government officials is not always effective when misleading statements are made. Vice President Pence held a coronavirus press briefing in June 2020, saying that the government was effectively "flattening the curve." That day, there were a record-breaking number of new cases reported in the U.S. The gap between the Vice President's verbal statement and the data reported by the Centers for Disease Control and Prevention led people to see Pence's statement as either propaganda or spin (Gearan & Abutaleb, 2020).

Framing is an informal type of social control, one of the many ways to regulate human behavior. It relies on the robust use of language to define social reality. Most people do not understand how language is a form of social control because speaking and listening seem so fluid, flexible, and neutral. But how we think is structured by language in ways that most people are not aware of (Lakoff & Johnson, 2008). For this reason, a major focus of propaganda analysis focuses on examining how word choice can influence human thinking and behavior.

Disinformation expert Joan Donovan has described how reactionary talking points are created through viral sloganeering. White supremacy groups may use catchy phrases like "Jobs Not Mobs" or "It's OK to be white," which became a Twitter hashtag, #IOTBW, that was reported on by news organizations including *The Washington Post* and the *Boston Globe* (Donovan & Friedberg, 2019). Simply by referring to other human beings as pests, animals, reptiles, or parasites, people can be made to feel emotionally distant, fearful, or anxious about others. When the president of the Philippines, Rodrigo Duterte, called drug addicts the "walking dead" and Hungary's Viktor Orbán called migration "a poison," those were efforts to dehumanize people in order to justify policies of oppression. Such language has dangerous implications, as history has proven time and time again. Dehumanizing rhetoric can lead to dehumanizing actions.

It's not only the skillful use of metaphors that shapes people's attitudes and beliefs. Adjectives and nouns can be a powerful form of influence. But most people don't notice how different grammatical tenses of verbs are used in news and journalism. Psychologists have found that simply by tweaking the grammatical form of verbs in political messages, people's impressions of a political candidate's past actions can be altered (Fausey & Matlock, 2011). In one research study, participants were informed about a fictitious politician who was seeking reelection. Participants read about some negative behaviors, including an affair with an assistant and receiving hush money from a prominent constituent. The subjects were randomly assigned to read one of two passages that were identical except for small differences in grammar. The grammatical differences in the sentences are shown here:

> *Last year, Mark* was having *an affair with his assistant and* was taking *money from a prominent constituent.*

> *Last year, Mark* had *an affair with his assistant and* took *money from a prominent constituent.*

Notice that the first sentence uses the past progressive tense (*was* verb + *ing*) while the second sentence uses the simple past (verb + *ed*). All the other content of the articles was the same. When answering questions about whether the candidate would be reelected, those who read the phrase "was having an affair" were more confident that the senator would not be reelected than those who read the sentence using the simple past-tense phrase "had an affair." Those who read sentences in the past progressive tense also gave higher estimates of the amount of money involved in the bribe (Fausey & Matlock, 2011). Why? Without our conscious awareness of it, past progressive verbs focus people's attention on the details of specific actions. They make those actions stand out. To underline the point, I'll just say that strategic and intentional use of verbs *are influencing* people's thoughts, feelings, and beliefs.

English teachers use many different types of learning activities to help students gain awareness of how language is used to frame and shape perceptions of social reality. But you may be surprised to learn that science educators have also explored framing as a way to bring media literacy pedagogy into the science classroom (Jarman & McClune, 2002). After all, news about climate change will depend on the knowledge and background of the reporter, the sources they consult, and the amount of pressure they are under in their newsrooms. Science educators have observed that, in news reports, climate change may be presented as a weather problem, an environmental problem, a political problem, or a business problem.

Two professors from Dublin City University used a class team project to help university students understand how news coverage of climate change is framed in ways that confer legitimacy on people, ideas, and information. They wanted students to understand how the practices of journalists may affect the content of the news they produce. In one lesson, students learned to identify the competition that exists between sources who seek to influence the media agenda on a particular story. Working in teams, college students explored different climate change–related topics that were selected in advance by the instructor. Some examined the release of local temperature data, a local extreme weather event, the publication of a scientific paper from a national or international organization, or other news. Each team tracked and analyzed the amount and type of news media coverage of their chosen event over a one-month period, setting up keyword alert systems to monitor online media coverage (Robbins & Brereton, 2016).

Through careful analysis, students learned to recognize the different frames used to present news about climate change. Within each team, individual students focused on a particular topic. For example, one student focused on language use, while another focused on the reporter's identity, noticing who was a science or environmental correspondent, a feature writer, opinion writer, general news reporter, or a political reporter. Another student looked carefully at which sources were used, noting the pattern of factual information that was presented. Another team member paid special attention to how skeptics or deniers were presented. Students then made a formal oral presentation to the class and composed a written reflection on their learning (Robbins & Brereton, 2016). As a lesson on news framing, such instructional practices are valuable for learners. But this lesson did not focus on the role of propaganda in the news making process. For this, students must learn how public relations professionals influence news and journalism to get publicity for their clients.

LEARNING ACTIVITY

Spot the Genetics Frame

Frames are used in science journalism to describe genetic research. After being introduced to the frames, students get a chance to practice identifying them in a sample of newspaper articles about science.

Activity: The instructor selects a sample of science news about genetics or students search and find examples on their own. Review Table 4.1 to learn to recognize the frames. As they read each article, students color-code and underline phrases or ideas that are relevant to one or more of the frames. After the activity, students discuss the advantages and limitations of each of the five frames in explaining genetics research to the public.

The Takeaway: By learning to recognize frames in science news about genetics, students deepen their knowledge about genetic causation and gene-environment interactions. After this lesson, students should be able to see how the evolutionary frame, in particular, helps people understand the interaction between genes and environment as it relates to cancer, diabetes, obesity, and other health matters.

TABLE 4.1: News Framing in Genetics

GENE FRAME	DESCRIBES THE GENE AS	KEYWORDS OR PHRASES	METAPHORS	EXAMPLES
Symbolic	An abstract representation of inheritance	"It must be in the genes"		"Fashion has always been in my genes"
Deterministic	A definite causal agent	"Gene for," cause, control, culprit, blame, disease gene, responsible, born with, no choice, "genes or environment"	Like a computer program	"Scientists have found the gene for breast cancer"
Relativistic	A predisposing factor	Influence, disease risk, chance, factor, associated with, susceptible to, linked to, contribute, predispose		"Genes double risk of breast cancer"
Evolutionary	A dynamic agent interacting with the environment	Interact, in combination with, expression, genes and environment	Like a switch or tap that can be turned on or off	"Mother's food turns genes on and off"
Materialistic	A discrete physical unit	DNA, chromosome, identify, map, locate, code, protein, mutation	Alphabet, book, map, code, beads on a string	"Genes are digital codes written on DNA molecules"

Source: Carver et al. (2014)

Public Relations as Propaganda

Neither educators nor the general public have a good understanding of how the public relations industry shapes the practice of journalism and influences online media. Many businesses hire professional communicators, usually those who have a background in journalism, to help them make a positive impression on the public and other audiences. Public relations professionals work to influence public opinion by trying to shape and influence the content of daily news. When they aim to influence people in Washington, DC, or other centers of power, people who do this work have job descriptions or titles that include the words "public affairs." Public affairs professionals are paid to develop relationships with important decision makers as a way to influence them in relation to their company's business goals.

The relationships between public relations professionals and journalists has been called transactional journalism. It is a type of mutual backscratching that occurs between reporters and the businesses, government officials, and others who are trying to shape public opinion. As journalists rely on access to people in power, they sometimes give their influential sources what they want in order to maintain the relationship. Generally, this involves offering a particular spin on a particular event. For example, one reporter described how Secretary of State Hillary Clinton's aides got journalists to describe her 2009 speech as "muscular" by making the use of this particular adjective a condition for getting advance access to the speech (Attkisson, 2017). Such transactions are seen as "win-win" by both journalists and PR folks, and they are generally invisible to the public.

A lack of transparency in transactional journalism can raise important questions about press ethics. Propaganda can be unethical when key facts about audience and purpose are hidden or disguised because it hinders the receiver from fully evaluating it (Stanley, 2015). Yet in the practice of public relations, press releases often contain exaggerated claims or disguised points of view. When such techniques are used for issues related to science and medicine, the resulting news coverage is also more likely to also communicate the same exaggerations to the general public. In one study, more than 20% of science news stories were found to overstate the conclusion or causal claim (Schat et al., 2018). Distorted findings about medical research can damage the quality of people's decision making about wearing masks to prevent the spread of virus, vaccination, and other medical treatments. Scholars have long argued that misleading public relations contributes to declining trust in journalism and the medical establishment (Gross, 1994).

But merely demonizing public relations industry does little to promote critical thinking. It's important to understand the tensions, paradoxes, and contradictions that public relations professionals are asked to balance as part of their work. That's why I ask students to read and discuss the work of Ryan Holiday. He calls himself a master manipulator, someone who specifically describes how he uses lies, truth, and half-truths to get bloggers and mainstream journalists to provide his clients with press attention and publicity. In his 2012 book, *Trust Me, I'm Lying*, Holiday describes how he got media coverage for his clients by "trading up the chain." It's also been called source hacking, a strategy used to mask a problematic source in ways that permit its circulation in mainstream media (Kellner, 2003). Since small blogs don't generally fact-check content, Holiday places his work there. After it's published online, the client or his proxies promote the blog heavily through social media to draw attention. Then Holiday reaches out to larger news organizations, persuading them to either promote or debunk the story. When this is published, the message has reached an even larger audience. By exploiting the tendency for larger news organizations to recirculate stories generated by smaller organizations and bloggers, the public relations propaganda goal has been achieved.

Holiday's descent into the madness of manipulative marketing is balanced by the contrition and humanity he eventually displays. After illustrating a variety of techniques for getting attention on behalf of his clients, Holiday devotes the second half of the book to considering the ethical dimensions and consequences of his work. He offers a *mea culpa* to apologize for his actions and explains that he now sees that the cumulative impact of online manipulation is "unreality," noting that by writing the book, he decided, "I not only want to render the tricks useless by posing how they work but I want to opt out of doing them myself" (Holiday, 2012, p. 236). Much harm can result from the manipulation of the online ecosystem. Holiday noted, "If you chase the kind of attention I chased, and use the tactics I have used, there will be blowback" (p. 234).

It can be difficult to recognize how public relations professionals manipulate attention for profit, but when such work causes harm, the outcomes may become newsworthy in and of themselves. Holiday tells the story of one journalist who wreaked havoc by spreading false information about comedian Jon Stewart, who was accused of being sexist. Using anonymous and off-the-record sources, the story was widely circulated and republished by other media outlets. Even after dozens of on-the-record responses from people currently working with Stewart were published, and the story was debunked, the journalist continued to repeat unfounded accusations as established facts. As Marwick and Lewis (2017, p. 39) explain, "By getting the media to cover certain stories, even by debunking them, media manipulators are able to influence the public agenda."

The Partisan Propaganda Feedback Loop

Journalism's financial troubles have helped propaganda to thrive. Because the public seeks to confirm what they already believe more than seek out new information, media owners aim to provide the public with what they will pay attention to. As news organizations struggle to find funding, partisanship offers a business model that works. Perhaps you have seen those annoying YouTube ads for *The Epoch Times*. It's a U.S. based international newspaper that's owned by the Falun Gong religious movement, who also own the performing arts company, Shen Yun. *The Epoch Times* has discovered the profitability of promoting far-right politicians in Europe and the United States and they also advance anti-vaccination conspiracy theories on their YouTube channel.

You may want to blame the Internet for the rise in political partisanship. Indeed, partisanship has accelerated greatly due to the Internet and digital culture. The Drudge Report originated as an email newsletter in 1995 and with 2.5 million subscribers, it is now considered the "wellspring of the conservative media ecosystem" (Pilkington, 2018). YouTubers have also brought political partisanship to the world of entertainment with diverse types of news content. The Young Turks claims to be the "largest online news show" in the world. Hosted by Cenk Uygur and Ana Kasparian, this YouTube show offers a mix of politics and entertainment that has a liberal, progressive partisan edge. The Daily Wire is a politically conservative news and opinion web channel featuring daily podcasts by Ben Shapiro live streamed to YouTube every weekday. Lauren Chen's YouTube channel offers highly conservative commentary on news with a sometimes-feminist twist.

Partisanship can be found in many types of news, entertainment and information. It is specially designed to reinforce the ideological perspectives of the owners and authors, and of the audiences who consume it. Some YouTubers like Steven Crowder or Lauren Southern attract people into far-right online communities through lively and provocative discussions of racial inequality and feminism. Other YouTubers like Stephen Bonnell (known as Destiny) and Natalie Wynn (known as ContraPoints) provide an alternative point of view that speaks directly to the biases of those who are already indoctrinated (Roose, 2019).

Partisanship is not a bogeyman to be feared. It is a fact of life in many parts of the world, where newspapers and television stations are owned or controlled by people who are closely affiliated with political parties or government officials. In European democracies, news media organizations may be aligned right, left or center, and their coverage of controversial issues (like immigration) may vary greatly. For example, the right-wing press may emphasize the dangers and risks of immigration while the left-wing press may debunk myths about immigrants. But in Europe, researchers have not found that increased exposure to partisan news leads to political polarization (European Parliament, 2019).

In the United States, American presidents have long cultivated sympathetic news organizations for support in getting their message to the American public. But the symbiotic relationship between President Trump and Fox News is unprecedented in modern times. Since his election in 2016, Trump has made more than 60 guest appearances on the morning show *Fox & Friends* (Hutzler, 2019). Back in 2011, that's where he launched the birther conspiracy theory, claiming that President Obama was not born in the United States. Donald Trump has shared his great admiration for Fox News many times in speeches and tweets. Many of his cabinet officials and staff moved into the White House after working at Fox News. After they leave, they return to the network.

Over time, the relationship between political elites, news organizations, and audiences can evolve into a partisan propaganda feedback loop. Because the public seeks to confirm their political identity more than they seek truth, people generally stick to a narrow range of information sources. To get the public's attention, political elites align with identity-confirming positions, which then leads media organizations to give more favorable coverage to politicians whose views confirm those ideological positions. As a result of this propaganda feedback loop, researchers have found that partisan news organizations are more likely than mainstream media to include false statements made by both hosts and guests (Benkler, Faris, & Roberts, 2018).

But lest you think this was only a special problem for Fox News, it's clear that the partisan feedback loop also affects mainstream media and the entire news ecosystem. Although *The New York Times* is operating under a nonpartisan model of journalism, their coverage may seem to take on "a partisan flavor" without the news staff actually straying from their focus on journalistic objectivity (Benkler, Faris, & Roberts, 2018, p. 81).

How do teachers introduce the concept of partisanship to their students? One way to support student learning about partisanship is through studying the curated lists and charts that identify the various sources of news and journalism. Such charts and lists have value for learners who are beginning to explore news and journalism. You have probably seen one or more of these charts like the one shown below.

At the Oakland Public Library in California, librarians created a list of resources and teaching materials for the educators in their community. In it, they included the News Quality chart, created by Vanessa Otero, which visually depicts the quality of news sources. The vertical axis locates news sources on a scale from fact-based reporting to inaccurate fabrication. The horizontal axis displays an assessment of the ideological bias of the news organizations. Fox News, *Slate*, and the *Huffington Post* are identified as hyperpartisan, and *The Economist* offers complex analysis with minimal partisan bias. As you can see, CNN is right on the edge between fair and unfair persuasion, and Fox is right on the edge of unfair persuasion and propaganda. Students may appreciate charts like this because they are unfamiliar with so many of the news sources that come across their social media feeds. To many students, Politico, Alternet, The Guardian, and the Daily Caller are just names.

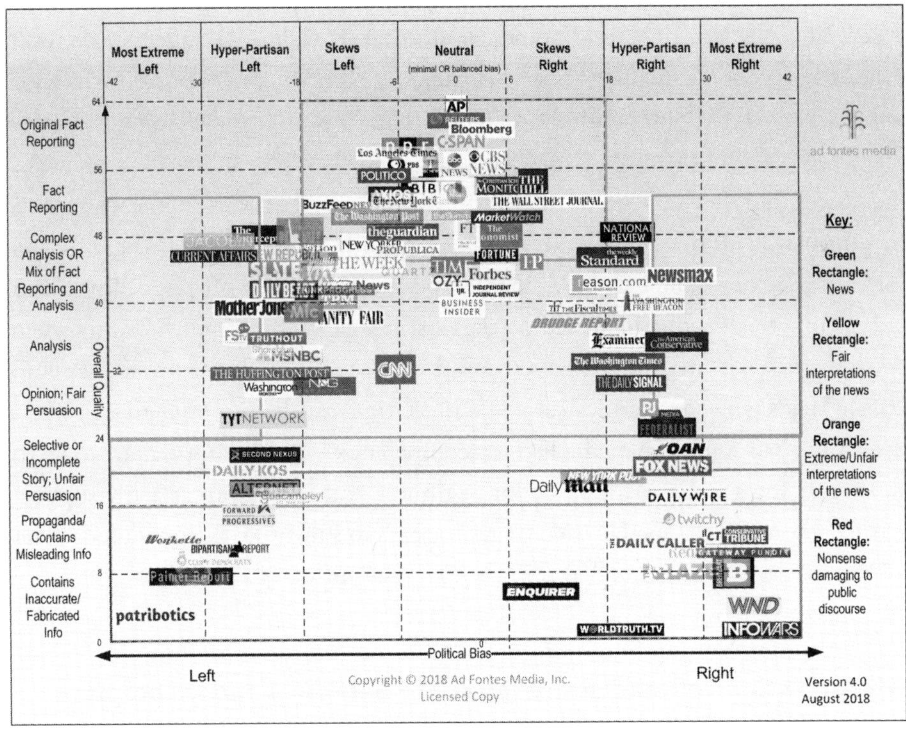

The News Quality Chart by Vanessa Otero

But lists and charts of media bias and fake news websites like this can be time-consuming and challenging to maintain, given the rapidly changing nature of the media ecosystem. When Melissa Zimdars wanted to help her college students critically analyze news, she developed a chart that located news websites on an ideological continuum, identifying sources with tags such as biased, fake, unreliable, or satire. She collected over 1,000 examples of such websites. Today, as she points out, many of these websites no longer exist or have been redirected to other websites.

And let's not forget that such lists and charts represent the particular point of view of the people who created them. After Zimdars's list was publicized, people emailed her outraged that MSNBC was on the list but Fox News Channel wasn't. But MSNBC was not on the list: what was on the list was a fake version of the network called MSNBC.com.co. She's been frustrated that journalists call her list a "fake news list," when she repeatedly points out that most of the websites on the list don't publish intentionally false stories. To help students navigate "a cluttered, complicated and often overwhelming media environment," the list simply encourages students to be "skeptical and rigorous at all times" (Zimdars, 2016, p. 1).

A variety of educational websites have emerged to help younger learners explore partisanship in the news. The AllSides website, which presents news and current events from the left, right, and center, claims that since "media outlets evolve over time," they conduct regular reviews of news content in their "quest to provide unbiased news" (AllSides, 2019). To identify bias, they ask readers to first identify their own bias and then rate an article's bias. Then they look at how everyone rates the article, and they take the average rating using several articles from each source. In October 2018, they identified Vox as Left, noting that the news organization "often frames news and issues as if the Left perspective is the only perspective." But ratings like this may be impacted by the hostile media effect, which occurs when partisans perceive media coverage as unfairly biased against their own side (Perloff, 2015). That's why some critics see some limitations to the use of charts and lists as a strategy for building media literacy competencies. Relying on a chart to learn about bias is a good starting place for beginners, but it may not actually support learner autonomy if it merely encourages learners to substitute their own judgment for that of a trusted intermediary (in the case, the author of the chart).

Interpretations of Media Messages are Selective and Incomplete

The process of selection shapes both how messages are created and how they are consumed. I discovered one of the consequences of this phenomenon more than 30 years ago in research I conducted to measure how people learn from television news. During the 1980s, television news was changing. Due to economic pressures to reach large audiences, sound bites were getting shorter and shorter. Images were getting more and more eye-popping and sensational. As it turns out, I discovered that people don't really learn much from watching TV news. Instead, they monitor the news to make sure that their existing beliefs are still valid. Watching the news, you find that the world is still chaotic and dangerous; politicians are still self-serving and power hungry. For most people, the surveillance function of news consumption far outweighs the learning function (Hobbs, 1985).

The consequences of this phenomenon explain much about the nature of news and journalism, and they require us to take a hard look at our own behavior. You've probably heard about confirmation bias in relation to the issue of fake news. It is the natural human tendency to pay attention to and actively interpret new information as confirming our existing beliefs. When we have a choice to read news that confirms our worldview or challenges it, we almost always choose the former. Some people have described confirmation bias as a problem that needs to be solved.

But cognitive scientists think that confirmation bias developed to maintain our sociability. Agreeing with the group's perception of reality turns out to make you a better group member. From an evolutionary point of view, this aids in your survival. Plus, it simply feels good when your existing worldview is reinforced. Researchers have found that people "experience genuine pleasure—a rush of dopamine—when processing information that supports their beliefs" (Kolbert, 2017, p. 1).

With all the talk about confirmation bias and media partisanship, you might be wondering: Should people learn to intentionally consume a wide variety of news from sources across the ideological spectrum? Many people seem to think the answer is yes. After the 2016 presidential elections, some experts recommended that people consume more diverse news coverage, noting the importance of getting exposure to "a wide array of perspectives in order to ascertain how people of differing viewpoints are thinking about a given issue" (Gable, 2017, p. 1). But is this a valuable and appropriate practice for students, teachers, and citizens?

My response to this question is purely personal. Of course, it's good to be aware of the ways in which news is framed through the lens of partisanship and I do recommend explicit teaching about confirmation bias. But I don't require my students to consume news from "all sides" because I don't find this helpful for myself. I get frustrated, confused (and sometimes infuriated) when I encounter news that presents a distorted view of current events. Watching Tucker Carlson or reading Breitbart seems like a colossal waste of my time. I simply don't want to suggest that my students read or view content that I myself find reprehensible.

I also don't feel the need to convert students or persuade them to change their opinions about the choice of news they use, given that these patterns are usually established in the home and family. Since people feel uncomfortable when exposed to media that pushes back on their world views and perspective, they usually end up avoiding it. For most people, well-meaning suggestions that people consume a "balanced news diet" are simply not viable strategies for supporting the development of people's critical thinking and communication skills. Instead, activating intellectual curiosity is simple and far more effective as a strategy for identifying and addressing partisanship and propaganda in the news.

Rather than consume news from "all sides," I urge students to use news media to gain knowledge on just one event or topic of special interest to them. When students select one current events topic of special interest to them, they gradually become experts on that topic. By deepening focus on one topic, students develop background knowledge that helps them evaluate and analyze information. They may begin with the news media that is familiar to them, but inevitably through this process, they will encounter different points of view as their knowledge grows. Gradually, learners come to recognize the controversies and differences of opinion that exist within and across knowledge communities. On Wikipedia, students can study the Talk page to look "under the hood" of the encyclopedia and discover which elements of a topic are debated and discussed most. Wikipedia editors actively debate what constitutes accurate information. As students gain deeper knowledge, their appetite for complexity expands, and their ability to discriminate between quality sources and junk increases. This naturally leads them to seek out more high-quality perspectives. In this way, consuming news and information becomes a delight and a source of fascination and not merely a chore or assignment. Such practices lead students to appreciate and value (rather than mistrust) quality information and journalism.

LEARNING ACTIVITY

The Listening Protocol

It takes practice for people to learn to discuss controversial topics in respectful ways.

Activity: Establish the following procedure and ground rules for a structured discussion on a controversial news or current event topic where diverse perspectives are presented without criticism or debate. In this protocol, participants must make a genuine effort to learn more about what the other person thinks. Participants ask questions to probe these ideas with respect and curiosity. They should not frame their questions in a way that criticizes, voices skepticism, or subtly advocates a competing view. Students promise to maintain strict confidentiality about the content of ideas expressed during the session. Rules include:

- The first participant has 20 seconds to share a particular belief, using the "I believe . . ." sentence structure.
- The next participant has 20 seconds to ask a probing question about that belief, and the first participant makes a thoughtful 20-second response.
- The moderator then asks a new participant to share an "I believe . . ." statement, inviting a new topic or a different ideological perspective that contrasts with the previous one.
- Time for debriefing enables participants to reflect on the experience and notice how protocols for social interaction may help improve listening skills.

The Takeaway: Exposure to divergent perspectives helps advance new knowledge.

–Adapted from Daniel Sussman, From Partisanship to Pluralism (2017)

News Analysis in High School Social Studies

In one of his earliest books on education, Neil Postman used a metaphor to consider the relationship between culture and education. He argued that culture was like an ecosystem and that education served to balance the inevitably competing ideologies that circulate in culture. Through education, we can "make visible the prevailing biases of a culture" (Postman, 1979, p. 19). When I met Emily Glankler and Emily Pool, I could see how their approach to teaching and learning was aligned with this view of the relationship between culture and education. They have a lot of experience teaching social studies, and they are media literacy educators, too. Glankler teaches social studies at the Griffin School in Austin, Texas, and Pool teaches at Cherry Creek High School in Denver, Colorado. When they present at conferences together, they sometimes call themselves "the Emilys."

Whether they teach a special elective course called Current Events, International Relations, Contemporary Issues, or Discussion Skills, or a regular required course in American or world history, these two educators embed media literacy in their daily teaching of social studies. They are also convinced that current events need to be part of their class for 10 minutes a day. The Emilys recognize that students feel anxiety about discussing current events. Teachers can feel this anxiety, too, of course. But through trial and error, plus a lot of exploration of resources, they have discovered what works for their learners. At the South by Southwest Edu Conference, an annual event held in Austin, Texas, these two teachers shared some best practices developed over the course of their careers.

When the Emilys were in high school, years ago, current events were not a big part of the curriculum. Instead, all the focus was on evaluating primary and secondary source materials. Emily Glankler remembers going to the high school library as a ninth grader, as part of their research project assignment, where school librarians wheeled out a big cart of books, showing the carefully curated sources that students could use for their projects. By the end of high school, librarians were directing them to search library databases for information. From this, Glankler learned that teachers and librarians steer students toward quality sources.

So, when Glankler started teaching about current events in high school, she steered students towards quality news. She showed students a media bias chart that listed mainstream media in the middle and the more ideologically tinged news sources on the outer edges. She explained, "I used to tell my students: stay in the middle, don't go to the edges. But I realized I was making a mistake with that strategy. When we exclude less-reliable sources from the classroom, students don't really learn how to evaluate content."

When all the content that students use in school has been vetted by teachers and librarians, the act of evaluating it becomes an artificial exercise. So Glankler decided to bring unreliable information into the classroom, where she could safely support and guide student inquiry. Her students were already relying on Google for information on all kinds of topics and issues. She explained, "Students are going to experience fake news, so let's teach them how to evaluate it."

Instead of making students believe that some news is biased and other news is not, the Emilys teach students the intellectual value of bias. Much like the term propaganda, the word bias has a negative connotation. Students come into high school thinking that the word is synonymous with words like "untrustworthy" or "inaccurate." When students encounter a message they think is biased, they may tend to disregard the message. But for the Emilys, explicit instruction on evaluating source materials relies on a key media literacy principle: "All media messages are selective and incomplete."

Because the Emilys believe that bias can be intellectually valuable, early in the semester, they replace the term "bias" with a different word: perspective. They help students understand the power of point of view by using a short video created by Alex Cequea, an Austin-based animator. In the YouTube video "Why Facts Don't Convince People," we learn that the human brain responds to social cues better than facts. The video points out that evolution has promoted a tribal perspective among humans: After all, it's safer to agree with your tribe because it prevents social isolation. Our brains protect this worldview: That's why we respond aggressively to information that seems to contradict or threaten our existing beliefs. One of the reasons why fact-checking is not effective for most people is that when they encounter facts that contradict their beliefs, they tend to cling even more tenaciously to the information they believe. When people have strong feelings of group identification, they may also become less empathetic to the perspectives of others outside the group.

Because the Emilys want to build knowledge and understanding, they know that they must help students to explore and learn from multiple perspectives that are different from the ones they get exposed to at home and in their community. They must learn to get comfortable with differences of opinion. Applying this philosophy, they use an instructional strategy that is carefully designed to prevent students from merely expressing their preexisting opinions or debating topics in ways that provoke tension and hostility.

In the first phase of the process, students explore how to identify the point of view in news and information sources through discussions of partisan news. The teacher shows two screenshots of television news, with the logos of the news organizations carefully edited out. Students are encouraged to be "perspective finders," identifying the perspectives offered in the visual content of two news stories. How are these TV news stories approaching the immigration issue? Looking at the two screenshots shown below, students compare the headlines, "In-state tuition for illegal immigrants under fire in growing number of states" and "Trump announces change in asylum rules for migrants." They notice words and phrases like "illegal," "under fire," "change in asylum rules," and "migrants" and discuss the nuances of meaning associated with the use of these terms.

News About Immigration

Students discover that both stories offer valuable information they can learn from. Each news story offers some information and emphasizes some ideas that align with particular social values. As Romanian educator Nicoleta Fotiade (2018) puts it, students should not avoid or dismiss news sources completely just because of the company's owner. "Even very biased sources can offer useful information," she explains.

A close look at the images shows that they have been ever so slightly manipulated by the teachers. The news logos have been removed. Emily Pool explains, "We've learned that we must hide the news organization's logo for this activity to work." Why? When students see the logos, they tend to stop thinking. Their preexisting stereotypes about news organizations interfere with appreciating the valuable perspectives that each news story may have to offer. These teachers want their students evaluate information based on the quality of ideas and information itself, not the journalistic brand.

Some teachers are concerned about bringing so-called fake news into the classroom because they fear that this practice will legitimize it. But as history teachers, the Emilys are confident that students can analyze partisan news and propaganda just the same way that they analyze any primary source documents. When teaching about perceptions of immigrants in 19th-century politics, history teachers commonly use political cartoons from newspapers of the time, often from the rich digital collections of primary source materials from the Library of Congress. Some of these materials illustrate radically different public perceptions of immigration. Glankler explained, "Why would I feel comfortable showing my students a racist political cartoon about Chinese immigrants from the 19th century but not a social media post about a caravan of immigrants who are flying the Honduras flag as they burn the U.S. flag as they march towards the U.S.?"

LEARNING ACTIVITY

Get HIPP to Analyze News

Protocols for analyzing news can be effective in helping learners internalize the practice of critical thinking.

Activity: Select any form of media—a news story, a website, or a primary source document. Use the HIPP model to analyze it by answering these questions:

Historical Context

- **Who** created the source?
- **What** do you know about the author? Where and when was the source produced?
- **What** do you know about the time period in which the document was produced?
- **How** might this information affect the meaning of the source?
- **Why** is the source important?
- **To what** broad historical theme(s) does the source relate?

Intended Audience

- **Who** is the target audience?
- **What** beliefs and knowledge are this group of people likely to possess?

Purpose

- **Why** was this source produced at the time it was produced?
- **How** might this information affect the meaning of the source?

Point of View

- **Who** is the author? Analyze the author's gender, social background, economic status, political affiliation, ethnicity, nationality, religion, and race.
- **What** is the author's point of view?
- **What** point is the source trying to convey?
- **How** does the author's point of view affect his reliability?

The Takeaway: The practice of critical analysis can become internalized when the questioning is used not just for exams and test taking, but to examine the texts and media of everyday life.

–Adapted from College Board AP History Document-Based Analysis (2016)

Teaching the News: Do's and Don'ts

There are some instructional practices that may have more risks than returns. Let's consider the reasons why some teachers and librarians have moved away from certain instructional practices as they aim to build students' media literacy competencies in responding to news and current events:

- ***Maintaining a current events journal.*** Neither Emily Glankler nor Emily Pool recommends using a current events journal, a common assignment in middle school and high school. In such assignments, students write short summaries of news articles, following a particular format. Assignments like this may do more harm than good. According to the Emilys, this type of assignment makes paying attention to news and current events a chore, a form of homework, and something to be dreaded. It is unlikely to inspire students to want to be informed on current events. Such tasks do little to activate intellectual curiosity about the news.

- ***Pro-con classroom debates.*** Current events debates do not promote deeper civic understanding among students. Issues have more than two sides, of course. And when students are positioned to take opposing sides and encouraged to gather evidence, argue their side, and win, this gamelike practice can actually work against the development of genuine understanding and knowledge. As Glankler said, "Debate is not productive because it promotes competition. It is not deliberative" (Glankler & Pool, 2019). When it comes to learning, the goal should not be winning—the focus must be on understanding.
- ***Hoax websites.*** The Emilys don't like to play "the gotcha game" by tricking students with hoax websites like DMHO.org, the Pacific Tree Octopus, or the First Male Pregnancy websites. Instead, they want students to think before they share by knowing about how algorithms work. They point out that when people comment, react to, or share hoax websites, they are helping false ideas to spread. Emily Glankler said, "If you comment on a social media post, you are helping it spread—even if you say, 'This is fake.'"

Teachers and librarians may benefit from being reminded of how our own well-meaning actions may inadvertently influence the information ecosystem. For example, well before the Trump election, many librarians and social studies teachers began using MartinLutherKing.org as a way to warn students about the importance of critically evaluating their information sources. Students were asked to visit the website to learn about Martin Luther King and gather information. The website is simple and clearly designed to appeal to children who are looking for answers for assignments and book reports. "Bring the Dream to life in your town!" the front page reads. "Download flyers to pass out at your school." But students who downloaded these flyers were surprised to find them full of racist white supremacy. For example, King was referred to as a communist and "sexual deviant," and readers were urged to repeal the King holiday. Such learning activities certainly provided an emotional jolt, as students realized easily how they were tricked into gathering information on an African American leader from a white supremacy website. The website does not hide its politics: it states clearly that is hosted by Stormfront on its front page and advises users to "Join (the) MLK Discussion Forum," which links to a Stormfront forum called The Truth About Martin Luther King.

Unfortunately, so many teachers and librarians began to use this hoax MLK page in teaching about website evaluation that Google's algorithm interpreted the hyperlinks as evidence of quality. Many school librarians included links to the MLK hoax on their school library website. As a result, the racist website began to appear at the top of Google search results when people searched for information about Martin Luther King. At the time, many librarians and educators were unaware of how Google algorithms measure website quality by looking at hyperlinks. When Google's public liaison for search investigated why this particular website appeared so prominently in search results, he found that librarians and teachers were inadvertently contributing to increasing the visibility and prominence of this racist website simply by using it as a teaching tool (Collins & Toomey, 2018).

Some librarians and educators may choose to shield their students from "iffy" content, using browser extensions like one provided by the for-profit company News Guard, created by Steven Brill. They sell a browser extension that tells users about the quality of websites by asking journalists to conduct reporting to identify a website's ownership, financing, credibility and transparency. When these tools are employed, users get visual signals of information quality: Breitbart gets a bright red flag and *The New York Times* gets a green flag. But critics say these tools essentially outsource the critical thinking process and do nothing to advance media literacy competencies (Rogow, 2020).

Both students and teachers need time to practice judging the credibility of information sources and forming opinions about issues of public concern. This is not a one-and-done kind of skill. As researchers explain, "In order for youth to make fluent and flexible use of the media literacy skills and strategies they learned, students need lots of practice" (Hodgin & Kahne, 2019, p. 103). In a five-minute daily discussion, students can practice the art of perspective taking on news and current events. Emily Pool sometimes starts class with a question to the whole group about a particular current events topic: "What are all the things you have heard about this topic, regardless of whether you believe it or not?" (Glankler & Pool, 2019). This invites general sharing and gathering of ideas, and it frees students to offer ideas without being associated with or having to defend them. As Pool explains, "Students can share information without isolating themselves from their tribe. Plus, this method does not alienate the students who aren't familiar with the news event or controversy under discussion. There's no penalty for not knowing. Students can learn a lot about current events from their peers."

In the classroom, all opinions are not created equal. Glankler says, "I'm trying to address a social problem we have in society today. Part of the problem is that people think they are entitled to an opinion on everything." Glankler maintains a classroom rule for current events discussions: "You only have a right to an opinion if you have evidence or experience to back it up." If you don't, she says, then ask questions, listen, and learn. When students hear this, they feel a sense of relief. Glankler gives students permission to listen and learn, and they are invited to show that they are participating by asking questions and taking notes. Thus, the Emilys offer four tips for talking about current events:

1. ***Develop a safe classroom environment.*** Know all the students' names. Don't do all the talking. Be humble. Say "I don't know" when you don't know the answer to a question and model the process of finding answers.
2. ***Start with familiar topics*** for which your class has a likelihood of agreement and over time, gradually move towards more controversial issues.
3. ***Engage learners*** with deep philosophical questions with no clear right-or-wrong answer, like "Is violent protest ever appropriate?"
4. ***Do not assume*** that everyone has prior knowledge or assume they know nothing. Let students provide their peers with key facts and information before sharing opinions.

Current events discussions provide opportunities for metacognition to develop. Emily Glankler sometimes asks students to assess their performance after the discussion, reflecting on the question, "How did I do as a participant? Did we have low talkers? People who dominate? Did everyone follow the norms?" She gives students note cards where they are encouraged to write about how they participate in a discussion. One student might write, "I tend to talk a lot," while another might write, "I have ideas, but I don't share them," and another might notice, "There are some people in the room that I just don't listen to." She uses this type of reflection as a way to ask students to identify their own typical patterns when participating in a discussion. Then students are encouraged to set a personal goal for changing some aspect of the way they participate in current events discussions (Glankler & Pool, 2019). In this manner, students can be subtly encouraged to take risks, listen better, ask questions, or suspend judgment. As students begin to take responsibility for their own learning, reflection and metacognition are among the most valuable pedagogies to advance critical thinking about news and information (Hodgin & Kahne, 2019).

LEARNING ACTIVITY

From Credible to Incredible

Organize information on a continuum from most to least credible and explain why you judge certain content to be credible or incredible.

Activity: Choose a topic that's in the news. Working individually or with a partner, create a list of what you already know or have heard about this topic. After making a list of keywords and phrases to use in a search activity, use a search engine to identify content on your topic. After reading some articles and watching some videos, try using different keywords and notice differences in the search results. Experiment with different search engines to see how it may affect their results. By reading the results, you will gain knowledge on this topic that will help with the next stage of the project.

Then revise your search strategy to try to find the most wacky or questionable sources on this same topic. You may need to go deep down in the search engine result list to find this kind of content.

Create to Learn: To document your discoveries, create a PowerPoint slide deck using screen shots to display 10 different sources of information about your topic, ranked in order on a continuum from most credible to least credible. In an oral presentation or a short piece of writing, justify your choices, explaining why you judged certain sources as more or less credible.

For Discussion: How do people decide what is credible? What are some typical features of content that is incredible? How much consensus exists about these judgments?

The Takeaway: Sometimes people make credibility judgments about online content without much conscious awareness. Being asked to explain your reasoning for ranking content helps heighten awareness of how you evaluate information.

–Adapted from Media Education Lab's Assignment: Media Literacy (Hobbs, 1999)

Six Paradigms for Teaching About News and Information

The prevalence of misinformation, disinformation and propaganda in the news has led to the rise of a variety of different paradigms for addressing the challenges posed by these forms of expression. Each approach has embedded theoretical assumptions about learning and teaching.

This book's approach to the study of propaganda is distinctly rooted in media literacy education. Because media literacy educators examine the constructed nature of media representations, they acknowledge that information, news, and journalism is neither a transparent window on reality nor a malevolent or intentionally falsified illusion. Media literacy scholars have long problematized the concept of realism. As Bertolt Brecht once pointed out, much evidence of the "real" is supplied by the media itself. "In learning about the media, then, we are learning about the ways in which the real world has been mediated, about how our understanding and knowledge have been constructed" (Alvarado, Gutch, & Wollen, 1987, p. 117). In addition to considerations of form and content, media literacy education also includes the study of the political and economic forces driving media institutions, messages, and technologies; recognition of the sender's agenda and biases that shape content; awareness of media environments that shape daily life; and producing media for the public good (Fry, 2014, p. 127).

Not everyone finds this particular approach to media literacy education compelling. In carving out the topic of news literacy as distinct from media literacy, Bill Kovach and Tom Rosenstiel perceive a "left-leaning" orientation for media literacy that "teaches how the media in all its forms manipulates us on behalf of commercial and establishment interests" (2010, p. 202). This is why professional journalists coined the term news literacy. They emphasize the positive role of the press in a democratic society, using learning activities designed to help learners feel confident in trusting news reports from mainstream journalistic organizations. Because news literacy educators are generally themselves former journalists, they have been successful in leveraging their networks of colleagues to get publicity and funding for their efforts. Many journalists are sympathetic to news literacy because it positions journalism in a good light, especially at a time when journalism seems under siege by declining revenues. Teachers appreciate news literacy curriculum resources especially if they are not active news consumers themselves. But one study of undergraduate students enrolled in a news literacy course, although students did become more aware of current events and more knowledgeable about journalism, they were "ill-equipped to identify commercial biases or to reflect on ideological and ownership issues related to news" (Ashley, 2019, p. 1156).

There are many different ideological values that underpin the study of so-called "fake news." Among the pedagogical approaches available for examining news and information, six distinct educational paradigms emerge. Table 4.2 describes the six paradigms, which include information literacy, media literacy, news literacy, online civic reasoning, youth participatory politics, and the propaganda model. As you read about these different paradigms, you might see elements from each one that you particularly appreciate or value. I'll describe the six approaches in a bit more detail, and you can identify which approaches align most closely with the needs of your students and your own world view and values.

TABLE 4.2: Paradigms for Learning About News & Journalism

NAME	KEY ASSUMPTIONS	PEDAGOGY
Propaganda Model of News	Structural and economic factors are responsible for the news functioning as a form of propaganda. News is constructed to maintain status quo power relationships between business and government.	Gain knowledge about media ownership and examine the relationship between reporters and sources. Learn how institutionalized enemies are used to marginalize ideas.
Information Literacy	There is a hieracy of information quality. Quality information sources are identifiable through an examination of authority and credibility.	Use effective search strategies to find scholarly and professional sources. Review features of information content including author, source, and genre.
Media Literacy	Media messages are carefully constructed to represent social reality in ways that are selective and incomplete. People interpret messages differently.	Consider the interplay between news media and popular culture sources. Use dialogue and discussion informed by critical questions and an inquiry learning process that includes creating media.

NAME	KEY ASSUMPTIONS	PEDAGOGY
News Literacy	Journalism is identifiable by its reliance on verification, which is why news consumers can trust mainstream media.	Gain knowledge about the professional practices used by journalists to construct news. Recognize key features of quality news.
Online Civic Reasoning	Through the comparison of information across multiple sources, the accuracy of online information can be determined.	Examine the content of digital media and compare and contrast information from various sources to determine the accuracy of information.
Youth Participatory Politics	Direct participation in democratic practices contributes to individual and collective human flourishing.	Collaborate and connect to others through participating in social change initiatives. Make creative work that explicitly responds to the needs of a community and addresses civic and political goals.

Propaganda Model of News

This approach explicitly conceptualizes news as a form of propaganda through a careful examination of the political economy and routines and norms of the press. This approach to media literacy was developed in 1989, when Edward Herman and Noam Chomsky published *Manufacturing Consent: The Political Economy of the Mass Media,* a book that offered an important perspective on the role of the mass media in society. Unlike the traditional story that gets told in schools (i.e., that mass media upholds the practice of self-governance in a democratic society), Herman and Chomsky offered an alternative view. They claimed that the function of the mass media is to deeply inculcate people into social roles that support the existing institutional power structures of the society.

Through consuming media, people are shaped into passive spectators of a political game played by elites because "in a world of concentrated wealth and major conflicts of class interest, to fulfill this role requires systematic propaganda" (Herman & Chomsky, 1989, p. 1). Five practices are used by media organizations to ensure that businesses and corporations get their messages out to the public through news and current events. These include: (1) concentrated media ownership, (2) reliance on advertising revenue, (3) the relationship between reporters and official sources, (4) the use of critics to dismiss or trivialize messages that don't fit with a pro-capitalist world view, and (5) the creation of institutionalized enemies. According to this view, news functions as a form of propaganda because of structural and economic factors that ensure the maintenance of status quo power relationships between business and government (Achbar & Wintonick, 1992).

By focusing on the political economy of the media, this approach emphasizes learning about the business of media industries. Students learn that audiences are the product sold to advertisers and that the news media targets primarily elite audiences (not ordinary citizens) because of their disproportionate influence on decision making. Adherence to a belief in journalistic objectivity is itself a form of propaganda which upholds the institutional power of journalism. Because this system has been made to seem natural, it is "internalized largely without awareness" especially by those who are college-educated (Herman & Chomsky, 1989, p. 302).

Some educators may value this approach because it looks at macrostructural features of the economy to explain how news media perpetuates structural racism and inequality. But other educators may fear that this model increases cynicism by disrupting the long-standing U.S. narrative that news media supports democracy through a free press. Journalism educators may dislike this model because it positions the news media industry as subordinate to (and not independent from) business and political interests. As a pedagogy, this approach may also diminish the significance of personal agency and the social responsibility of both journalists and the public.

Information Literacy

Librarians use an approach that focuses on helping people learn how to identify their information needs and select relevant content that meets those needs. Students learn that academic credibility is constructed by networks of experts who use processes like peer review to determine quality and trustworthiness. Informational content has different levels of authority, and students learn about differences between scholarly, professional, and amateur content. In this sense, information literacy uses hierarchies to help students evaluate the relative quality of information.

Instructional practices are designed to help students find and use quality information sources in library databases. Students learn to use keyword search processes and practice identifying and selecting information (Eisenberg, Lowe, & Spitzer,

2004). This approach is designed to help young people learn to recognize the various genres and forms that information takes. For this reason, some librarians have developed procedures that help learners recognize websites with high-quality or low-quality information. Librarians may (or may not) perceive Wikipedia to be an authoritative source. School librarians may teach students to use the CRAAP Test checklist. The acronym suggests evaluating sources based on currency, relevance, authority, accuracy, and purpose, using questions to help patrons determine whether a source is trustworthy. Since many librarians must teach information literacy skills in a one-shot lesson, this heuristic protocol has some practical advantages. Although such tools have sometimes been criticized for superficiality, academic and school librarians rarely get sufficient time with learners to develop more nuanced approaches to information access and analysis activities.

As trusted neutral stakeholders in a school or community, many librarians shy away from political controversies. During the 2016 election season, school librarians were unlikely to directly address the kinds of fake news that their students encountered via social media. In their quest to valorize library databases and other high-quality information sources, some librarians may be unaware of the ways in which their students were liking, sharing, and learning from information on Instagram, TikTok, and Snapchat. However, others offered workshops with young adults and demonstrated strategies to evaluate and create memes, social media posts, and YouTube videos (Hobbs, Deslauriers, & Steager, 2019).

Media Literacy

As elaborated earlier in this book, the key elements of this approach focus on helping people routinely internalize critical questions that promote an active, engaged, and skeptical stance toward information, entertainment, and persuasion. Media literacy educators highlight the value of noticing omissions as a means to identify a message's potential bias. In the practice of creating media, learners engage in understanding how content choices and textual features shape the practice of meaning making and interpretation. This approach is designed to induce metacognitive reflection that increases people's awareness of the work they perform as both creators and consumers and their role in shaping culture and society (Hobbs, 2019). A key idea is that the interpretation of media messages is a fundamentally social practice. When students share and discuss their interpretations in a group, they also become more aware of how ideas and information are socially constructed through networks of shared meaning (Hoeschsmann & Poyntz, 2012). Educators value this approach because it is aligned with inquiry and project-based learning pedagogies. But some people perceive this approach as too focused on asking questions and making interpretations and not sufficiently focused on critiquing powerful institutions and the inequalities they maintain and reproduce.

News Literacy

This approach focuses on helping people recognize and appreciate quality journalism. Instructional practices are designed to cultivate the habit of reading and viewing the news every day, being aware of current events, and selecting quality journalism from mainstream news media sources. Students learn to distinguish between investigative journalism, straight news reporting, and opinion editorials as they embrace the role of being informed citizens, capable of using quality journalism to make decisions. When students learn about the effort involved in professional news gathering, they appreciate quality journalism and acknowledge the value of journalists in maintaining checks and balances on political power.

News literacy is sometimes described by journalists as addressing the supply-and-demand problem. If education could help restore public trust in journalism at a time when newspapers are little trusted, this might increase the public appetite for quality news and information. In college courses in news literacy, students learn what makes journalism different from other types of information. Under the banner, "This Is Journalism," students see screenshots of National Public Radio, the *Washington Post*, and NBC News. Unlike advertising, publicity, propaganda, entertainment, or raw information, journalism claims to be reliable because of the process of verification, accountability, and independence. Verification involves the identification of an independent individual or organization that is directly accountable for the information provided. Journalists are accountable because they put their name on their work. Students learn that accountability is a distinguishing characteristic of journalism, and instructional materials in news literacy point out, "If a mistake is discovered, a journalist goes through the embarrassment of publishing a correction. What other professions or crafts do this?" (News Literacy Project, 2019).

History and civics teachers may like the fact that the news literacy approach celebrates the First Amendment, positioning mainstream media as serving a public interest function in upholding democracy. Critics may be troubled by the lack of reflexivity and self-awareness about the blind spots in contemporary journalism, including its focus on crime, conflict and sensationalism, horse-race political campaign coverage, the rise of the blogosphere, the ongoing financial struggles of local newspapers and TV stations, hyperpartisanship in news, and the role of public relations and public affairs professionals in shaping the news agenda. Philosophers strenuously reject claims by journalists that their method of truth-seeking is superior to other ways of knowing.

Online Civic Reasoning

The term online civic reasoning emerged from a test developed by education researchers at the Stanford History Education Project who study methods of teaching history. When students are asked to search for, evaluate, and verify social and political information online, they are invited to ask: Who is behind the information? What is the evidence? What do other sources say? Students are encouraged to verify arguments by consulting multiple sources because this is the practice used by professional fact-checkers (Wineburg & McGrew, 2017). Education technology experts call it lateral reading, the practice of looking at many different websites to see what other authoritative sources have said about a particular topic. The take-away idea: truth is more likely to be found in the examination of a network of related content than from a single website (Caulfield, 2018).

Online civic reasoning aims to deepen the ordinary ways that readers make sense of online information and news. In judging the credibility of online content, users generally rely on shortcuts. Most people judge the quality of a website by its placement in a list of search engine results, believing the top result is the best result. They may also look at the visual design and judge that a pleasing, modern site design is evidence of quality (Flanagin & Metzger, 2007). As scholars point out, "If being attractive and typo-free are all that is required for a website to convince users it is trustworthy, those users are likely to be repeatedly deceived" (McGrew et al., 2018, p. 166).

Teachers generally like that online civic reasoning relies on easily-scorable worksheets and assessments. The instructional method is an extension of the pedagogy of primary source documents as they are typically used in history classes. Some educators reject the idea that young people need to learn to think and behave like fact-checkers, who use technical tools to inspect manipulated images and video and spot patterns across data points. They see lateral reading as an oversimplified framing of the more complex practice of deep inquiry on a subject, where assessing credibility, authority, and expertise involves a full immersion in multiple perspectives and points of view.

Youth Participatory Politics

The term participatory politics describes peer-centered actions that involve a combination of voice and influence on issues of public concern. Today, people may seek out and analyze information from a variety of sources; they may engage in both online and face-to-face dialogue about the issues. They may share content with members of a network, create original content, and rally others to help accomplish civic or political goals (Kahne, Middaugh, & Allen, 2015). These processes can be a powerful antidote to apathy and cynicism. This approach is rooted in issues of social justice and in empowerment as a process of democratic self-governance.

Youth participatory politics encourages young people to get interested in the political process by using "any media necessary" to get their message across, including print media, radio, public action, and other tactics (Jenkins et al., 2016). Rather than see young people either as helpless victims or dupes of powerful interests, it acknowledges that online networks now structure how youth engage and interact with both people and information. It emphasizes how some young people may choose to be civically engaged as a dimension of their identity or personal lifestyle. It can be truly thrilling for educators to see how students use communication to take up forms of social and civic action that are personally meaningful to them. Teachers may appreciate how youth participatory politics focuses on community engagement in real world issues. But some educators worry about whether and how this work connects to the curriculum they are required to teach. Others see potential risks of indoctrination resulting from the increasing politicization of education as teachers and other mentors bring their identities as activists into the classroom.

As this chapter comes to a close, I trust that you recognize the potential value and the limitations of all six of these approaches to teaching about news, information, partisanship, and propaganda. There's simply no one right way to develop digital and media literacy competencies. With 60 million students in K–12 schools and 16 million students in colleges and universities, each of these approaches is likely to support certain learners in certain contexts. Each approach is infused with differing assumptions and ideologies about the epistemology of information, journalism, media, and education. It's probably good for young people to be exposed to all of these different ways of thinking about news, information and propaganda. Such diversity is a source of strength for the educators who are passionate about this work.

You may consider how your own views about news, partisanship and propaganda align with the ideologies depicted in this chapter. Ideally, educators may choose to use a variety of these approaches flexibly in response to the needs of the students, the curriculum, and the learning context. One scholar explained, "Only by loosening our grip on our own ideologies can we position ourselves to challenge our students' ideologies" (Lynch, 2009, p. 730).

Indeed, teaching about news can be a Rorschach test of sorts for the political beliefs and values of educators themselves. Teaching and learning inevitably includes a particular ideology, reflecting ideas about what we value. Different paradigms enable different insights about news, journalism, culture, and democracy as they intersect with issues like access, power, social justice, equity, fairness, and opportunity. The practice of reflection helps educators consider how their values and their instructional practices align with the needs of learners and society. One of the reasons why media literacy education is so demanding is that it is a deeply contextual process that requires educators to continually modify and adapt their practice to the realities of an ever-changing world.

Whether we like it or not, students of all ages encounter bigoted, dehumanizing, and manipulative propaganda that is an increasingly dangerous part of media culture today. As we'll see next, exploring the potential harms of propaganda can be risky, but it also creates opportunities for learners to develop resilience, reasoning, and problem-solving competencies that advance intellectual curiosity, support lifelong learning, and nurture civic engagement.

5

The Dark Side of Propaganda

Lies, Hate Speech, and Terrorism

Although propaganda can be used a weapon, it is legally protected in the United States

Among the many surreal incidents of the 2016 U.S. presidential election was a protest event that occurred outside the Islamic Da'wah Center in downtown Houston. A group that called itself the Heart of Texas had organized to protest what they said was the Islamization of Texas. When a reporter arrived, he found 10 protesters on one side of the street, with T-shirts reading "White Power" and a banner reading "White Lives Matter." One protester was carrying an AR-15 rifle (as it is legal to openly carry weapons in the state of Texas). On the other side of the street were 50 counterprotesters, organized by the Save Islamic Knowledge Facebook group.

What the reporter did not know at the time was that both groups were organized by Internet trolls. This example was cited in Special Prosecutor Robert Mueller's indictment of Russians who tampered with the U.S. presidential election (Glenn, 2018). In 2016, Russians used both propaganda and hacking to disrupt the presidential election process. During the 2016 presidential campaign, Russian trolls created convincing pro-Trump social media posts designed to appeal to churchgoers and military families. Leaked emails suggested that Clinton was secretly pro-Wall Street. Social media propaganda played a role in suppressing voter turnout in 2016, communication experts acknowledge (Mayer, 2018). Although many American Facebook users in the Houston area saw the posts promoting this protest event on their social media feeds, only a few people showed up to actually participate. At the time, no one was aware that the accounts promoting the event were Russian trolls operating out of St. Petersburg and paid for by the Russian government. The social media posts created the impression that many people from the local area would be going to the protest. People were tricked into believing that there was strong local support.

Propaganda is only one of many forms of potentially dangerous expression that people encounter online. Harassment, revenge pornography, sexual predators, racism, gossip, hate speech, and threats flourish. Today, the unchecked dissemination of lies and falsehoods on social media is doing real damage to the democratic process. Dangerous propaganda also comes from the voices of our political leaders. When President Trump treated the coronavirus pandemic as a political and cultural problem, and not a public health crisis, his words and actions contributed to sickness and death (Sorkin, 2020).

Propaganda has caused significant harm to individuals and society throughout history. When used to promote lies, hate, and intolerance, propaganda can be a potent form of information warfare. Attacks on opponents with language, images, and other symbols can lead to physical violence. A variety of stakeholders weaponize social media as a means to manipulate public opinion. After all, the capacity to spread ideas and reach audiences is no longer limited by access to expensive, centralized infrastructure. Instead, a user can reach millions by attracting and holding attention on just a few digital platforms: Facebook (which owns Instagram), Google (which owns YouTube), and Twitter. Indeed, the technological features of the platforms, their legal context and business model, and the behaviors of social media users are well aligned to support the viral spread of propaganda.

People create and share harmful and dangerous propaganda for a lot of different reasons. Some are seeking to promote social, cultural, or political change. Some want to inflict harm on others, while others are just having a bit of irresponsible, reckless fun. Alt-right extremists have a strong need for attention and they have discovered how to get that attention by tearing down social institutions, including and especially the press (Marantz, 2019).

Around the world, creating and disseminating harmful speech can be a criminal act that can get you fired, jailed, or even killed. Most liberal democracies have rules that prohibit hate speech. But in the United States, tolerance and freedom of speech are so valued that there are few restrictions on problematic propaganda. In the United States, hate speech is legally protected by the First Amendment. And laws that protect Internet service providers have been described as "the First Amendment on steroids" (Kosseff, 2019, p. 212). When the U.S. Supreme Court reinforced this position in a 2017 ruling, it seemed as if freedom of speech is considered an end in itself, not a means to promote the democratic process of self-governance. The First Amendment shields and absolves propagandists from taking responsibility for their expressions and actions. When claims of free speech are used to mute criticism or bypass social responsibility for speech and actions, the deeper purpose of freedom of expression is degraded.

In this chapter, I begin by considering the sometimes subversive pleasures of propaganda and then identify how a culture of distrust emerges when hateful propaganda flourishes. We consider the relationship between intolerance, hate speech, disinformation, conspiracy theories, and, finally, terrorism. You'll get a chance to evaluate some potential regulatory solutions to consider whether and how content moderation and platform regulation may help alleviate potential dangers. Harmful propaganda is a vast and complicated subject, so here I primarily consider strategies for addressing it productively as a subject of inquiry in the high school and college classroom.

Propaganda and Pleasure

The dark side of propaganda is fueled by our own fascination with it. We experience a mixture of feelings when encountering potentially harmful propaganda, including excitement, discomfort, disgust, and even the raw pleasure of encountering content that taps into our secret or unacknowledged beliefs, fears, and desires. Watching a world leader expressing obviously false information while ridiculing members of his own political party can be a riveting form of entertainment. CNN media critic Brian Stelter (2018) has observed how President Trump's behavior can be addictively fascinating as he challenges the media's traditional norms about reality by mixing intentional lies and deception with distorted worldviews and misinformation. It's hard to look away. When *The New York Times* reporter Farhad Manjoo (2017) tried to avoid all Trump-related news for a seven-day period, he found Trump was simply impossible to ignore. Whether Trump news is negative or positive, its amplification through our relationships and conversations makes it inescapable.

Propagandists know the power of shock value, repetition, and simplicity as a way to desensitize people to reasoning, information, and the logical presentation of ideas. Going down the rabbit hole of the Internet, you can step into an upside-down world where everything you thought was true seems to be wrong. On TikTok, young men shame other men by calling them "simps" if they engage in basic acts of kindness towards women. In certain parts of online society, abusive power relationships and racist, radical voices can seem sensible. Conspiracy theories can seem to be based on irrefutable evidence. It can be fun to read (and write) content that is politically incorrect. For the bored, the underemployed, or the disillusioned, online behavior that breaks social taboos around sexism, racism, and misogyny may feel exciting, countercultural, and invigorating.

Propagandists can activate a roller-coaster ride of strong emotions that may include a potent mix of kindness and pride, anger and revulsion, delight and disgust. When Frankfurt School cultural critics were trying to make sense of the rise of Nazism in the 1930s, they considered the pleasure principle developed by Sigmund Freud. This theory posits that, in seeking to maximize pleasure and reduce pain, people sublimate their envy of those in power to accept the will of a powerful leader. Subordinating self-interest to collective interest is thus experienced as pleasure. Considering this phenomenon in relation to the rise of fascism, Walter Benjamin observed that the appeal of propaganda's spectacles enable people to even perceive war as a form of entertainment, writing that "humanity's self-alienation has reached such a degree that it can experience its own destruction as an aesthetic pleasure of the first order" (1969, p. 242).

Many forms of media and culture set up conflict between different emotions, creating friction that people can experience as bliss (Barthes, 1957). The relentless juxtaposition of different messages creates an emotional thrill, according to Neil Postman (1986), author of *Amusing Ourselves to Death*. He called it the "Now This!" effect. Today, news is made up of small packages of information presented in quick succession in newspapers, radio, and television. Online, we encounter an endless array of little boxes with attention-getting headlines and images. As viewers and readers, we don't stay on a subject for very long, and we expect to move quickly from one topic to another. Even within a single YouTube video, the "Now This!" formula can be exploited. For example, if you watch an Islamic State propaganda video, you may see a handsome, strong-looking fighter delivering toys to small children. In the very next shot, you'll see a group of fighters marching a group of Syrian men to their execution. When Fox News broadcast a graphic, 22-minute ISIS propaganda video of the murder of a Jordanian pilot, it featured the captured pilot, doused in fuel, inside a cage. An ISIS member then lights the pilot on fire. Critics said that Fox News aided ISIS by helping this horrifying form of propaganda to spread (Ohlheiser & Booth, 2015). Jihadist propaganda clearly taps into people's deep attraction to media that provokes, shocks, and angers them (Cottee, 2017). Flooded with strong feelings caused by the juxtaposition of images, there is simply no time for authentic reflection, careful thought, or serious study (Postman, 1986).

Because it provides emotional stimulation by reducing complexity, Jacques Ellul argued that people actually crave propaganda. It's simply too difficult for the average person to sort out the "incoherent, absurd and irrational" elements of news and information circulating in the world (Ellul, 1973, p. 145). With journalism constantly spewing decontextualized facts at people, propaganda can provide a coherent structure for making sense of events. That's because the expression of emotion and opinion can seem more authentic than the expression of facts. Feelings can put facts in context. Writing 20 years before the rise of talk radio, Ellul also noticed that people like to express opinions because it gives them a feeling of participating and belonging. In a world replete with social inequalities, propaganda gives people "justification for otherwise useless feelings of anger and resentment" (Wollaeger, 2013, p. 284).

Because online content appears to users as a continual scroll of boxed images, text, and hyperlinks, users don't easily discriminate between user-generated content, sponsored content, news, and disinformation. In both mass media and social media, the seamless mix of entertainment, information, and persuasion can be difficult to evaluate. Indeed, the ambiguity of online content can inspire people to share it. Consider the case of KONY2012. When Jason Russell created a 30-minute YouTube video about the Ugandan warlord Joseph Kony and his army of child soldiers, it became the most viral video of all time, reaching 100 million views in just seven days. One reason the video was so widely shared was that people weren't really sure what type of message it was. Was KONY2012 a work of art, journalism, or activism? People gained insight into the meaning of the text from seeing how people they trusted responded to it (Hobbs, 2012).

Through online sharing, we engage in collective interpretation. We use the reactions and other cues provided by our family and friends to figure out what the story really means. And because online platforms dominate the way messages circulate in culture, these forms of collective interpretation *become* the public sphere (Tufecki, 2017).

Yet when you're online, it can feel like quite a private experience. That's why people have less inhibition about watching violent pornography, a neo-Nazi video, an animal getting crushed to death by a person in high heels, or a video of a policeman killing an unarmed African American man. Although these messages may be received by thousands or even millions, they are delivered privately to individual screens. The phenomenon of online disinhibition occurs when people feel reduced levels of guilt and shame about viewing emotionally arousing content that they wouldn't want their families, coworkers, and friends to know they use. Socially unacceptable behavior can be transformed into a kind of entertainment (Hobbs & Grafe, 2015). Today, people around the world may experience emotional thrills from the most malignant propaganda.

Propaganda can also create feelings of status and belonging. If you create or share content that resonates with others, you can feel like an insider. You can belong to the group. If you know the latest slang and in-jokes on a particular website or message board, you can take advantage of your insider status and make fun of outsiders who are newbies to the subculture. This can feel empowering. Schadenfreude is enacted in such Internet subcultures, where creating harmful propaganda and disruption strengthens social bonds. The troll mantra is, "I did it for the lulz"—loosely translated, for the laughs (expressed as the plural of LOL, which stands for "laugh out loud"). People find many stupid forms of playful hate to be entertaining on channels like 8chan and 4chan. For some adolescent boys, spending time there is a type of manly rite of passage, just the same way that watching the 1978 horror film *Faces of Death* was for an earlier generation. But it's not just a youth phenomenon. One scholar pointed out how it "operates in part through the internalization of authority by promoting strategic forms of group identification" (Wollaeger, 2013, p. 294). The seemingly private and individualized nature of online communities may inspire anyone to become mean-spirited. Indeed, online communities that do not use robust content moderation quickly become places where hate speech proliferates (Marwick & Lewis, 2017).

Lies as Propaganda

Lying, as a form of social power, is woven into the fabric of our humanity. Lies are false statements that take the form of an assertion of objective fact, made knowingly by the speaker. Small lies, of course, occur in many social situations when the speaker and the listener share an understanding that concealing or distorting the truth is preferable to truth-telling. But in general, lying reduces trust and profoundly damages relationships, introducing societal risks that propagandists throughout history have sought to avoid. That's why most experts acknowledge that propaganda is most effective when it's built with credible information, regardless of whether that information is actually true or false. Credible lies enable the powerful to maintain their power.

Propagandists make a choice whether to use truth, half-truth, or lies as means to accomplish their goals. Politicians, business leaders and activists make these decisions every day. But journalists have struggled to document the scope and volume of Donald Trump's obvious lies and inaccurate statements. The *Washington Post* reported that in his first two years in office, President Trump made 8,158 false or misleading claims, with more than 6,000 in the president's second year. They even created an interactive infographic and searchable database, updated daily, that documents each false or misleading statement. For example, Trump repeated one particular claim about Democrats' support for immigration 123 times as of May 2019, saying:

> *Their entire party has been taken over by far-left radicals who want to nullify and erase American borders. They want open borders. They want open borders. They want people to pour in, and they think that's going to be votes ultimately for them. Democrats want to allow totally unlimited, uncontrolled and unchecked migration, all paid for by you, the American taxpayer.*

All these statements are obvious lies designed to demonize opponents. As the *Washington Post* points out, Democrats do not advocate for illegal immigration. They have repeatedly put forth immigration bills that include both a solution for the children of undocumented immigrants raised in the United States (the DREAMers) and new border security measures (Fact Checker, 2019).

Such lies have been called common knowledge lies. These are false assertions that do not depend on special knowledge available only to the speaker. This type of lie occurs when "the speaker not only knows the statement is false, but she knows her listeners also know that she knows the statement is false; it is thus common knowledge that the statement is false" (Hahl, Kim, & Zuckerman Sivan, 2018, p. 5). Such lies are the specialty of bullshit artists who publicly challenge truth as a social norm.

Such obvious lies grab people's attention because they are a brazen display of power. They break through the clutter of everyday life. People who rely on sensation seeking as a source of personal identity may not be highly concerned about

Trump's sensational lies if his vision of what's wrong with America resonates with theirs. But the scope and scale of Trump's lies do remind some of "the big lie." This term comes from Adolf Hitler, who, in *Mein Kampf*, explained it as "a fact which is known to all expert liars in this world and to all who conspire together in the art of lying." Ordinary people are more likely to be persuaded by a big lie than a small one. Statements that contain colossal untruths are basically more effective than small lies.

Why are big lies so persuasive? According to Hitler, everybody tells small lies in little matters, but most people "would be ashamed to resort to large-scale falsehoods." Most people simply don't believe that others have "the impudence to distort the truth so infamously" (Langer, 1972, p. 1). The philosophy of the big lie was aligned with Hitler's other general principles about strategic political communication. When the U.S. government researchers examined Hitler's communication style, they observed that his primary rules were these:

> *Never allow the public to cool off; never admit a fault or wrong; never concede that there may be some good in your enemy; never leave room for alternatives; never accept blame; concentrate on one enemy at a time and blame him for everything that goes wrong; people will believe a big lie sooner than a little one; and if you repeat it frequently enough people will sooner or later believe it. (Langer, 1972, p. 1)*

When one group in society does not feel they are being served by the political establishment, the bold lying of a political demagogue might be appealing. After all, people are more than willing to break social norms that no longer feel legitimate. Through public rallies and the constant use of social media, Trump reaches his audience directly, without any filters, seeming to be an authentic champion who is willing to break social and political norms for the benefit of his constituency. His use of common knowledge lies may thus be seen as "gestures of symbolic protest" towards an illegitimate establishment (Hahl, Kim, & Zuckerman Sivan, 2018, p. 9).

Our culture is awash in another powerful type of expression that can be conceptualized as a special type of lying—fiction. Fiction writers throughout history have known that simplified narrative storylines provide an emotional clarity that can be more satisfying to audiences than messy, complicated reality. A quote widely attributed to Mark Twain claims, "Never let truth get in the way of a good story." For his fans, Trump's lies are just part of the stories he tells, which may feel "truer than the truth." This may help explain why all the fact-checking in the world does not interfere with the attention-getting qualities of Trump's latest surprising action, statement, or tweet (Grosz, 2019, p. 1).

Fighting Global Disinformation with Media Literacy

Today, disinformation is global, and so is media literacy education. Between 2006 and 2017, scholars and practitioners from more than 7,100 institutions around the world downloaded scholarly articles from the *Journal of Media Literacy Education*, the official journal of the National Association for Media Literacy Education. Users from 195 countries made 200,000 downloads of the 240 articles in the collection. Nearly 1,000 groups and organizations are active in media literacy education and research across the 28 member states of the European Union (European Audiovisual Observatory, 2016). Since 2010, scholars, educators, journalists, and librarians in eastern European countries have been active in media literacy as library organizations like the International Federation of Library Associations and Institutions and UNESCO began to collaborate on media and information literacy (Carlsson & Culver, 2013).

Propaganda has a long history in eastern Europe, where disinformation and conspiracy theories have long been used to maintain power and buttress an ideology (Pomerantsev, 2019). But media literacy education came to Ukraine in a very unique way at a dramatic moment in its history. When the Kremlin greatly increased its disinformation and propaganda in Ukraine in 2013, in the months before the Maidan Revolution, it threatened to upend the country's political stability.

About 30% of residents of Ukraine speak Russian, and the people who lived in Crimea were being specially targeted with messages designed to stir up fear that they would be treated as second-class citizens. In this political environment, lies and half-truths played on people's fears, confusion, national identities, and patriotic feelings, creating high levels of uncertainty, confusion, and doubt about news and journalism (Susman-Peña & Vogt, 2017). Because newspapers and television stations are controlled by oligarchs with business ties in Russia, reporting on Crimea tended to align with these economic and political interests. Thus, people received competing messages from at least four different ideologies: the Kremlin, Ukraine's political parties, the oligarch-controlled media, and western Europe and the rest of the world. This made it difficult for ordinary people to sort out what to believe.

When Russia annexed the peninsula in 2014, the world was shocked. Crimea was invaded by Russian forces in a process quite different than the techniques it had used in the past in Hungary, Czechoslovakia, and Afghanistan. To observers, it seemed more of an infiltration than an invasion, with subtle use of unmarked police forces and no visible violence (Mankoff, 2014). Today, Crimea is controlled and governed by the Russian Federation, even though it is internationally recognized as part of Ukraine. Today, there is both an information war and a military war ongoing between the two countries.

To address the problem of information warfare, journalism professionals in Ukraine created a fact-checking organization called StopFake by creating a database of fake news that has appeared in Ukrainian and global media. This enabled them to trace the evolution of Russian propaganda and identify core narratives that are part of its foreign policy strategy. Common themes were identified, including claims that Ukraine is a Western-backed junta, a fascist state, or a failed state. Pushing the idea of territorial disintegration legitimized the Crimea annexation, of course. Some propaganda took the form of conspiracy theories by proposing that war in Ukraine was actually conducted by the United States, NATO, and private contractors from the West (Grynko, 2019).

The Ukrainian government responded with censorship, expelling many Russian journalists, banning Russian channels from cable TV, and even blocking Russian social media and Internet resources. But an alternative strategy was also developed, with financial support from the government of Canada to IREX, a nonprofit organization that supports global development and education. In 2015, they implemented Learn to Discern (L2D), a media literacy program developed in partnership with local organizations including the Academy of Ukrainian Press and StopFake.

The L2D program was designed as a means to counter highly sophisticated Russian disinformation campaigns. The approach uses the classic media literacy instructional process of asking critical questions to help citizens recognize and resist disinformation, propaganda, and hate speech. Using a combination of discussion and lecture activities, videos, and interactive games, the program tries to help people internalize a set of practical skills. The program reached more than 15,000 adults of all ages and professional backgrounds over two years. Research conducted a year after the program ended found that participants had a 24% increase in the ability to distinguish trustworthy news from fake news, a 22% increase in cross-checking the information in the news they consumed, and a 26% increase in confidence in analyzing news (Murrock, Amulya, Druckman, & Liubyva, 2018).

With support from the education minister in Ukraine, classroom teachers in 50 high schools are now teaching media literacy using the L2D curriculum. Key elements of the program include a focus on teaching critical analysis skills, rather than telling people what kinds of media messages are credible or not. Small-group discussions involving the analysis of media build people's trust in the power of conversations and peer-to-peer learning. Because the program has a practical focus and makes flexible use of current events news, participants see it as immediately relevant to their lives. Some people who participated in this media literacy education experience described a powerful affective impact, saying, "I'll never watch TV news or read online news the same way!" This profound sense of personal transformation may even lead some students and educators to become activists for media literacy education.

LEARNING ACTIVITY

Analyze Global Propaganda and Create a Screencast Video

The careful examination of global propaganda can activate intellectual curiosity.

Activity: Find an example of an ad or a public service announcement that was created in a foreign country. Many of these use little spoken language and others have English subtitles. Review examples from the Mind Over Media online gallery (www.mindovermedia.gallery). Working with a partner, select an ad and discuss it using the five critical questions of media literacy to structure your inquiry:

1. ***Who*** is the author and what is the purpose of this message?
2. ***What*** techniques are used to attract and hold attention?
3. ***What*** lifestyles, values, and points of view are presented?
4. ***How*** might different people interpret this message differently?
5. ***What*** is omitted?

Create to Learn: Gather additional information on the country and the topic of your example using the Internet and library research. To address these questions, you will need to gather additional information using the Internet and library research. After answering the questions, learners then create a screencast. A screencast is a video created by capturing the image and sound from a computer screen. First, collect screenshot images of key elements of the commercial using only the images needed to make your ideas clear to the target audience and then compose a simple script where the critical questions and answers are presented. Using a free screencast production tool like QuickTime or Screencast-0-Matic, record and perform an oral response to the questions as you display a sequence of visual images. The doctrine of fair use (part of the Copyright Act of 1976) provides important protections for comment and criticism and other transformative uses of copyrighted material. As critical commentary, a screencast that analyzes global propaganda would likely be considered a fair use under U.S. law, which would mean that from a copyright standpoint it should be legally shareable with public audiences.

The Takeaway: A screencast analysis video creates an "aha" experience for learners. They gain new insight on both the content and the form of propaganda while increasing their intellectual curiosity about social and political issues around the world.

–Adapted from Mind Over Media: Analyzing Contemporary Propaganda (Media Education Lab, 2018)

From Intolerance to Hate Speech

Attacking opponents is an effective way to gain power, and those who spew hate seem to be rising in visibility around the world. Even as rates of poverty are declining and gender equality is increasing, xenophobia, racism, and intolerance are on the rise, and "the human rights agenda is losing ground," according to UN

Secretary-General António Guterres, who shared insights on the state of global human rights at the United Nations Human Rights Council. He said, "Hate speech is a menace to democratic values, social stability, and peace. It spreads like wildfire through social media, the internet, and conspiracy theories" (McHangama, 2018, p. 1).

More and more colleges and universities are revoking athletic scholarships and even offers of admission when they discover evidence of racist and sexist social media posts shared on social media. Young people have created Google spreadsheets to document racist behavior, using screenshots and videos to identify those involved (Levin, 2020). On college campuses, the number of white supremacist propaganda efforts reached an all-time high in 2019, with the distribution of racist, anti-Semitic, and anti-LGBTQ fliers, stickers, banners, and posters averaging more than seven incidents per day, more than doubling in just one year (Anti-Defamation League, 2020). Researchers who document white supremacist activities and anti-Semitism are finding that neo-Nazi groups are rapidly increasing in the United States.

There's no clear consensus among educators about the most effective pedagogical strategies for introducing the topics of intolerance and hate speech in either K–12 or higher education contexts. At the Teaching Tolerance website, the most common educational practice is the case study, where students examine and discuss a specific hypothetical or real situation. Such discussions can be meaningful and productive. Media literacy educators also use popular children's film and media to unpack issues like discrimination, prejudice, stereotyping, intolerance, and scapegoating. For example, some educators have used *The Boxtrolls*, a 2014 animated children's film created by Anthony Stacchi and Graham Annable, which features an extended family of quirky boxtrolls who live below the streets of the city. There, they lovingly raise an orphaned human boy named Eggs. When educators engaged in serious talk with young children about the film, they noticed how the film creates complex opportunities to talk about "how categories of 'otherness' are socially created and how that leads to social exclusion, myth building, labelling and the maintenance of group stereotypes that may even justify the ruthless extermination of 'unpopular' or stigmatised others" (Odrowaz-Coates, 2016, p. 82).

Hate and intolerance include a wide range of behaviors that must be examined holistically on a continuum that includes the following elements:

1. ***Intolerance***, unwillingness to accept views, beliefs, or behavior that differ from one's own.

2. ***Bullying***, interpersonal behavior and expression directed at an individual that involves a real or perceived power imbalance. Making threats, spreading rumors, and excluding someone from a group on purpose are types of bullying.
3. ***Online harassment*** is interpersonal expression or threats directed at an individual that undermine a person's safety, health, morals, or reputation.
4. ***Hate speech***, abusive or threatening speech or writing that expresses prejudice against a particular group, especially on the basis of race, religion, or sexual orientation.
5. ***Dangerous speech***, any form of expression that can increase the risk that its audience will condone or participate in violence against members of another group.

The chart below shows the relationship between mild and severe forms of hate and intolerance. On the left hand side, there are terms for harmful speech that targets a group, including potentially criminal acts of hate speech and dangerous speech. On the right hand side, you find terms generally applied when hate is aimed towards specific individuals. Although many teens and young people have experience with these forms of online intolerance, they don't always understand how these concepts are interconnected.

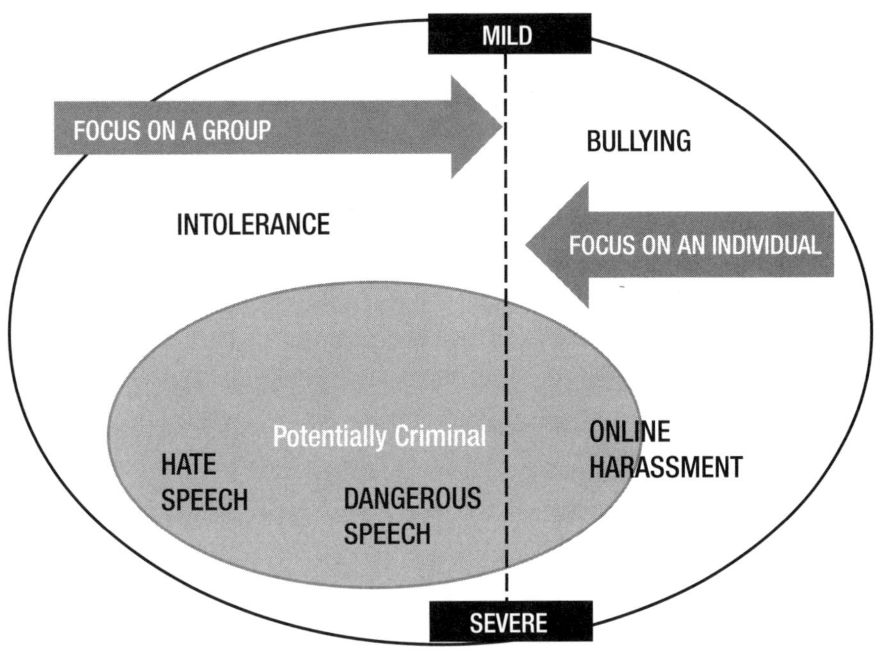

LEARNING ACTIVITY

Examining White Supremacy Rhetoric

The study of white nationalist hate-group rhetoric enables students to reflect on people's assumptions about racism, hatred, and free speech. It forces learners to confront head-on the big lie of racial superiority and to consider the importance of denouncing racism in all its forms.

Activity: Find out what students already know about white nationalism. After distributing sticky notes to students, say words like "white supremacy," "Ku Klux Klan," and "alt-right" aloud and ask students to write down the knowledge, thoughts, and feelings that come to mind when hearing those terms. Students post their notes on a designated wall. Teams of students work together to arrange the notes to find patterns and report what they find. Gaps in knowledge and misunderstandings can then be identified and remediated.

Analyze a Website: Display the website of the National Policy Institute, which is an alt-right hate group founded by Richard Spencer. Avoid using ridicule to comment on the website. One expert explains, "Despite the seeming ridiculousness of some hate-group rhetoric and imagery, the teacher should never treat the material lightly" (Morgan, 2001, p. 1). After students have time to examine the website on their own, ask them to pick out key phrases or ideas that they noticed and encourage them to analyze the visual symbolism and language use.

Generate Questions: What questions come to mind? After learners generate a list of questions, take time to organize them into two lists to distinguish between (1) factual questions that can be answered through research, and (2) values questions where discussion is needed. Choose one factual question and one values question to explore in more detail and model the research process before opening up class discussion.

Listen and Discuss: Play an audio recording of an interview with Richard Spencer by Al Letson, an African American journalist, in a 23-minute episode of the Reveal podcast titled "A Frank Conversation with a White Nationalist."

Questions for Discussion: After listening to the podcast, invite students to share their opinions and address the following questions:

1. **What** was the most interesting part of the interview for you? What was most troubling?
2. **How** is "identity politics" described in this podcast?
3. **What** are some key features of the rhetoric of hate that Spencer promotes?

The Takeaway: White supremacy can be expressed through both overt and covert messages that use language and imagery to spread hate. Messages that advance messages of racial superiority can be countered with a questioning process and dialogue that promotes a spirit of genuine inquiry and understanding.

–Adapted from the work of Kathryn Leslie and Malcolm Cawthorne (Wertheimer, 2017)

Online harassment and hate speech in schools have been on the rise for several years. In a special report developed by *Education Week* in collaboration with ProPublica, researchers identified 472 incidents of hate speech in schools between January 2015 and December 2017. Most involved Black and Latino students, as well as Jewish or Muslim students. Swastikas, the n-word, "Build the wall," and variations on "Go back to Mexico" were the most common forms of expression. In this particular survey, the largest number of reports occurred on a single day in K–12 schools: November 9, 2016—the day after the 2016 presidential election (Vara-Orta, 2018).

In U.S. schools, racism may be boldly expressed or merely ferment under the surface. Hate speech at school does not occur only among students. Teachers and support staff also sometimes engage in hate speech and bigotry. At one New Jersey high school with a predominantly Latino student population, a white male teacher called Mexican immigrants "pigs" and "lazy" on the day after the election in 2016. Researchers have found that hate speech and bigoted ideas coming from a teacher can traumatize students in ways that affect their academic performance (Vara-Orta, 2018).

In the United States, hate crime is defined as criminal behavior that is motivated by an offender's bias against a race, religion, disability, sexual orientation, ethnicity, gender, or gender identity. Only in very limited ways can hate speech be subject to prosecution. The Supreme Court has held that the First Amendment protects even speech that threatens action against a particular group unless the speech incites or produces "imminent lawless action" or "is likely to incite or produce such action" (*Brandenburg vs Ohio*, 1969). The clear and present danger test is two-pronged: you have to look at both the words spoken and the likely result of those spoken words under the circumstances. If someone shouts "Let's kill the Muslims" to an angry mob outside a mosque, and the mob then attacks the mosque and people are hurt or killed, the speaker could be prosecuted and found liable for the deaths and injuries. But if a speaker shouts those words standing on a Fifth Avenue sidewalk, such statements are most likely protected by the First Amendment.

Concerns about civility and intolerance on American college campuses have led to the development of speech codes in response to efforts by Holocaust deniers, white supremacists, and others to gain a platform on college campuses to share their ideas. These actions may inhibit learning and perpetuate hate by using the rhetoric of free speech (including ideas about the need to tolerate intolerance) to perpetuate a system of social dominance that subordinates members of marginalized social groups (Chamlee-Wright, 2018). Students and faculty have expressed increasing discomfort with speakers who come to campus to express extreme nationalist right-wing views. Extremist groups including the Traditionalist Worker Party, Identity Evropa, American Renaissance, and Vanguard America have specifically targeted college campuses. More than 25 protest incidents have occurred on college campuses since the 2016 presidential election, which have incurred substantial financial costs for the universities involved (Bell, 2019). For example, police security costs for a college event featuring conservative political commentator Ben Shapiro exceeded $600,000, which led university officials to reconsider the practice of allowing students to select speakers for public lecture series (*Wall Street Journal*, 2018). Some campus protests have led to violence and even death. The organizers of the 2017 Unite the Right rally in Charlottesville, Virginia were protesting the removal of a statue of Robert E. Lee from a local city park. The clash that occurred between extremists and counter protestors led to the death of Heather Heyer, who was killed when a white supremacist drove his car into protestors.

Some propagandists exploit hateful provocation for fame and fortune. At the University of California–Berkeley, college students protested in 2016 over a planned lecture by Milo Yiannopoulos, an alt-right demagogue who calls feminism a "mean, vindictive, spiteful, nasty, man-hating philosophy." For a time, Yiannopoulous relied on ridicule as an alt-right culture warrior–propagandist, noting, "Wrap the truth in a good joke and you're unbeatable" (*Wall Street Journal*, 2018, p. 1).

Facebook has modified its policies since 2015 to accommodate the uniquely hateful discourse of President Donald Trump. But only when advertisers like Starbucks and Patagonia began to boycott Facebook has the social media platform begun to take action in response to public complaints. In 2020, Reddit banned a pro-Trump group and Twitch temporarily suspended a Trump political campaign account. But social media companies that "de-platform" controversial speakers or speech by denying them access to a venue in which to express their opinion is a far-from-perfect solution to the problem of hate speech. Even after Alex Jones of Infowars was banned from YouTube, Facebook, Twitter, Apple, Spotify and Google, his many conspiracy videos were uploaded to YouTube by proxy accounts. One critic explained, "Taking down some high-profile extremists looks good for public relations purposes, but countless other shrill voices surely remain" because attempts by social media platforms to silence hate speech is an unwinnable game of whack-a-mole (McCall, 2019).

Can the subject of hate speech be meaningfully addressed in the classroom with younger students, those who are in middle school or high school? To answer this question, we turn to the Hacking Hate project developed by Hans Martens and his colleagues at European Schoolnet. They developed a study of European adolescents as part of the Social and Emotional Learning for Mutual Awareness (SELMA, 2019), a curriculum initiative that uses principles of social and emotional learning, media literacy, and citizenship education. Researchers conducted survey research and focus groups with teens ages 11–16 in Denmark, Germany, the United Kingdom, and Greece. Nearly 60% of participants had experienced some form of online hate speech; fewer than one in three said that their teachers (or any other educator) talked with them about hate speech. Researchers found that although many teens have experienced online hate speech, they have a limited understanding of its nature, causes, and consequences. For example, most students were unaware that hate speech typically goes beyond feelings of dislike and might lead to abusive, harassing, or insulting conduct, including physical violence. For learners, the term "hate speech" was sometimes interchangeably used with other terms like revenge porn, catfishing, stalking, gossip, and chain letters. When asked about the possible consequences of hate speech, European teens generally mentioned the problem of desensitization. One German student said, "Hate comments have become normal and people think as individuals they can't change anything about it." Other teens recognized that hate speech leads to polarization that divides people (SELMA, 2019, p. 74).

The European educators who helped to develop the SELMA project don't think educators should respond to the problem of online hate speech by telling kids not to use social media or activating guilt and shame by making them feel bad for enjoying digital media or sharing private information. Instead, they believe that learning experiences can help people to critically and creatively engage with the problem of online hate speech and its possible solutions (SELMA, 2019). They created a tool kit of engaging activities designed to build bridges between home and school. By combining media literacy competencies with social and emotional learning, these lessons explore forms of online hate as behavior that is interconnected with the social and cultural contexts in which it takes place.

There is a curious paradox in the relationship between tolerance and intolerance that's important to consider. This problem was first explored by Karl Popper in his 1945 book *The Open Society*. In it, he claimed that "in order to maintain a tolerant society, the society must be intolerant of intolerance" (Popper, 1945/2012). As Popper saw it, any society that tolerates the intolerant is destined to eventually see itself destroyed by the intolerant. Writing in the immediate aftermath of the Third Reich as a European Jew who escaped from Germany to England and then to New Zealand, Popper saw firsthand how fascism cynically exploited liberal tolerance in ways that enabled persecution, violence, and eventually genocide.

The paradox of tolerance is sometimes used to explain why freedom of expression is not absolute and why it must be carefully balanced against other human rights. In many European countries, for example, it's widely understood that a tolerant society must protect its own existence by limiting intolerance. Too much free speech can be destructive to individuals and society. As one legal scholar explains, "The argument that denigrating speech leads to violence is something that Europeans, who have seen the dangers of extremism, understand and Americans do not" (Bell, 2019, p. 315).

In the United States, respect for the dangers of "too much free speech" never took hold. American legal and political scholars generally believe that conflict between ideas is part of the process of democracy. They do not want the government to regulate the free expression of ideas. Their argument is that more speech is the best antidote to hate speech. Enlightenment thinkers emphasized how people have to engage in the exploration and analysis of all ideas—even truly evil ones—in order to reach their own conclusions about which ideas have value and significance. The philosopher John Stuart Mill pointed out that we must tolerate even the ideas we hate because sometimes even hateful ideas can be valuable, by helping people clarify or revise their views in ways that advance knowledge. Through the conflict and clash of ideas, we may come closer to the truth.

But intolerance and hate speech can escalate into political polarization, discrimination, hostility, and violence. So, what's to be done? When faced with intolerance, lies, and hate, public criticism and expressions of disgust can be important. When thousands of protesters marched after the murder of George Floyd by Minneapolis police, they signaled the urgent need to eliminate racial discrimination in policing. Such public displays of disapproval may promote tolerance while limiting the potential harms that come from the free expression of ideas.

LEARNING ACTIVITY

Facing a Culture of Hate

This activity is designed to help students understand hate speech and consider the different ways the media represent it.

Discuss Media Coverage of Hate Crimes Against Disabled People

Severely disabled girl left cowering under table following sickening attack on mom at McDonald's

Heartbroken mum describes how children mocked her disabled daughter in supermarket...and one mum even labelled little girl 'disgusting'

Disabled children hate crime reports increasing

Mum's horror as children start abusing her disabled daughter in supermarket – and their mother joins in

Activity: Read and Reflect. Learners should be encouraged to review the news photo and read the headlines of a story about the harassment of a young child with a facial disability. Study the language used in the headlines and make inferences about the emotions and motives of those involved in the stories: the target or victim(s), perpetrators, reporters, law enforcement, and other involved parties.

For Discussion:

- **What** feelings might the people involved in these events have experienced? Can you think of a time when you felt the same way?
- **What** similarities and differences do you notice about the different headlines?
- Does the way an incident is reported change how you feel about it? **Why or why not**?
- **What** could people who are targeted or affected by hate do as a result of their experience?
- **Who else** could take action, and what form could this take?

The Takeaway: Multiperspectival thinking about hate speech and hate crime requires both media literacy competencies and socio-emotional sensitivity. News headlines about people with disabilities can be constructed in ways that promote discrimination or help to create empathy.

–From the SELMA (2019) Hacking Hate Curriculum

Platform or Publisher?

To understand the dark side of propaganda that can be found online, learners need to understand the technological, political, economic, and regulatory environment that enables it. Jaron Lanier explains that when the Internet was new, there was a debate about how to regulate it. The lack of regulation, which helped the Internet to grow, led to what Lanier calls "an explosion of cruel nonsense." Many Silicon

Valley companies financially benefit from online content that "clogs conversations and minds so that both truth and considered opinion become irrelevant" (Lanier, 2018, p. 1).

How should such forms of media be regulated? As we are beginning to understand the ways in which social media is transforming society, scholars, policy makers, and regulators are now debating whether social media are platforms or publishers. The term platform is used to describe a software application that offers any user the ability to upload content. The term publisher is used for companies that offer a curated selection of bundled media content to audiences. Publishers use editorial judgment before sharing content, while platforms use content moderation after its publication. Publishers are liable for the content they publish. That means that they can be sued for libel and defamation if particular content causes harm or damage to individuals or institutions.

Google, Facebook, and Twitter are platforms because they distribute other people's content without editorial oversight. Users of platforms can easily upload content. Content moderation is used to exclude some content or decrease its visibility after it has been posted online. Some content moderation involves human judgment, while other types are the result of algorithms. From a business point of view, platforms attract a large number of users because they enable the free distribution of content. But the public still lacks a solid understanding of the pros and cons of content moderation and editorial judgment.

Platforms have a unique legal advantage over publishers. In the vast majority of cases, they cannot be sued for the harms that online speech and expression may inflict. Under Section 230 of the U.S. Communications Decency Act, no social media platform operator can be held liable for the contents of a user post. This immunity is known as a safe harbor. The Section 230 safe harbor clause explains why services like 4chan and 8chan can avoid liability for the harmful content that's on those websites. But this immunity has some limitations. If the platform operator edits or even just reviews the contents of a user post, and someone sues the platform operator based on the contents of that post, then the Section 230 safe harbor may not apply. This is not to say that the operators of social media platforms have to let anyone upload anything that they want without any regulation at all. It is perfectly legitimate for a social media platform to have certain rules that are enforced by content moderators. For example, Facebook has a "no nudity" policy. They also ban the sale of alcohol and tobacco between users. But moderating other kinds of written content, such as hate speech, can be much more challenging. The chart below shows how regulatory policies shape and control media content. Publishers use editorial judgment in deciding what to include in a publication. They are protected by the First Amendment, but they are also liable if the content they publish is false and damages someone's reputation. Platforms use content moderation to remove or restrict potentially harmful content after it has been published. Section 230 shields platform companies from liability, giving them a significant competitive advantage over publishers. These two different forms of control influence how people may experience harmful propaganda.

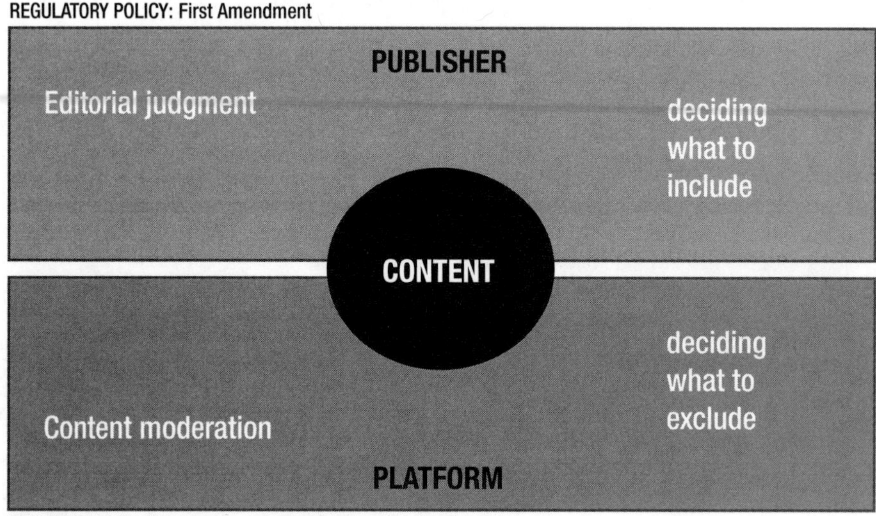

Given the tension between free speech and real-world harm, letting platform companies regulate propaganda and hate speech has risks. In many cases, women who have been the victims of vile, sexist words and images have no legal recourse because of Section 230 immunity. Some critics think tech platforms like Facebook and Google have too much power. When governments ask these companies to control hate speech and propaganda, that simply expands their power. Before long, the technology will enable "machine-speed, real-time moderation of everything we say online" (Lichfield, 2018, p. 1). For a tech company to draw these lines is "extremely problematic," said Jonas Kaiser, a Harvard University expert on online extremism. "It puts social networks in the position to make judgment calls that are traditionally the job of the courts" (Fisher, 2018, p. 1).

Reporters have found that Facebook's hate-speech rules favor elites and governments over grassroots activists and racial minorities (Angwin & Grassegger, 2017). Moreover, Facebook's content moderation policies are not transparent.

When journalists have examined these policies, there are many apparent contradictions and inconsistencies that reflect the biases of the people responsible for creating the rules. For example, Facebook policies have limited how users can comment on religion in India. The guidelines change frequently in response to particular conflicts and political actions across the globe. The company maintains lists of banned groups, political parties, and associations around the world, but representatives of some of those groups have now been elected to the European Union parliament (Fisher, 2018). According to a ProPublica report, the Facebook list of banned groups does not include Holocaust denial and white supremacist sites. Plus, while Facebook removes content that calls for violence and dehumanizing generalizations against migrants, they do not remove content that calls for their exclusion from society or offers degrading generalizations that are not dehumanizing. For example, migrants can be referred to as "filthy" but not called "filth" (Angwin & Grassegger, 2017). In making these kinds of subjective determinations about content moderation, Facebook is primarily responsive to the needs of those in power, as it does not want governments around the world to block its service to their citizens.

After the Christchurch massacre in New Zealand, where the gunman live-streamed his mass killings to his Facebook account, governments around the world called for the company to do a better job of policing the content posted on its platform. They passed laws to censor harmful propaganda that promotes violence. In Australia, social media executives can be imprisoned if their platform streams real-world violence, including murder, attempted murder, torture, rape and terrorism. Even Mark Zuckerberg has voiced support for governments to pass laws that regulate online speech. The company has aimed for greater transparency about its efforts to decrease hate speech, noting that it had removed four million hate-speech posts during the first three months of 2019, with more than 65% of them detected through artificial intelligence (Conger, 2019).

When protests turned to violence after the murder of George Floyd by Minneapolis police, President Trump posted a tweet, saying, "When the looting starts, the shooting starts." More than 5,000 Facebook employees denounced the company's decision to exempt President Trump from their policy to remove language that incites or facilitates serious violence (Dwoskin, Timberg & Romm, 2020). To many, it seemed as if both Twitter and Facebook were giving special protection to President Trump, who has asked Congress to eliminate the Section 230 safe harbor clause. Platform companies may be motivated to protect powerful politicians to avoid losing important legal privileges.

Around the world, calls for platform regulation are growing. As propaganda, harassment, hate speech, sexually explicit and graphically violent images, self-harm, and extremism have risen, an increasing number of stakeholders see the need for improvements in social media platform regulation. Some combination of industry self-regulation and government regulation will be needed. Most policy makers believe that communication industry laws should be revised to include public service obligations, including:

- ***Transparency obligations.*** Social media platform operators should be required to report data about how they moderate content to the public or to a regulatory agency, providing lists of the types of content they remove.
- ***Minimum standards for moderation.*** Laws should establish minimum response times to remove dangerous content or offer mechanisms for people to complain if they feel content has been removed unfairly.

Some Internet policy experts believe that a new law should also mandate that platforms provide financial support for organizations and digital literacy programs that help users navigate online harassment, hate speech, and disinformation (Gillespie, 2018). Such a law would make it more likely that all American children and young people can learn about contemporary propaganda in the context of their formal K–12 education.

LEARNING ACTIVITY

Content Moderation Policies

Practice your skills of content moderation by taking two quizzes created by journalists and based on real scenarios as well as Facebook's own content moderation guidelines. Reflect on platform policies that limit online content by role-playing the job of content moderator. After taking the two quizzes, discuss the questions below.

- ***The Cleaners Quiz:*** *Be a Facebook Censor.* Created by *Independent Lens*, this 11-item quiz invites you to make judgments about whether to ignore or delete different kinds of controversial content (PBS, 2018).

- ***What Does Facebook Consider Hate Speech?*** Created by *The New York Times*, this six-item quiz examines how definitions of hate speech can be challenging to enforce without cultural and historic context (Carlsen & Haque, 2017).

For Discussion:

- **What** was the most surprising thing you learned by taking these quizzes?
- **What** is the overall impression or feeling that you get after taking each quiz?
- **What** similarities and differences did you notice in how these quizzes were designed?
- **Which** quiz did you prefer and why?
- **What** questions are raised in your mind after completing this activity?

The Takeaway: Defining online hate is challenging because of the nuances of meaning and interpretation embedded in all forms of human expression. But the particular content and design features of online quizzes can also lead people to be more or less optimistic about the potential value of regulating hate speech through content moderation.

Teaching About Disinformation

The word "disinformation" has become well known as a result of its association with Russian election meddling in 2016, which included personalized propaganda targeting millions of Americans along with hacking into the computer networks of the Democratic National Committee and the creation of fake Facebook groups. Disinformation is defined as intentionally false information designed to manipulate public opinion. After Russian intelligence services interfered with the American presidential election, experts noted that such coordinated state efforts to disseminate false or misleading information have long been part of spycraft. Disinformation is linked to the Soviet concept of active measures, which is the term used for a variety of techniques designed to strategically undermine opposition governments while strengthening allies (Jack, 2017).

Disinformation can be profitable. Many of the wacky news sites that publish unsourced, unverifiable, or fabricated stories are not really motivated by politics. They are simply money-making ventures, "whose owners were driven less by politics than by the prospect of profit from clicks" (Jack, 2017, p. 3). While some forms of disinformation are explicitly designed to deceive people, others offer a mix of true and false information with a particular ideological agenda attached. Disinformation takes many forms, and it may be spread by "techno-libertarians, white nationalists, Men's Rights advocates, trolls, anti-feminists, anti-immigration activists, and bored young people" who leverage social media to express their ideas, opinions, and beliefs (Marwick & Lewis, 2017, p. 3). These voices may offer anti-establishment perspectives on mainstream society and challenge status quo norms of equality. They may advocate for a particular politician or dismiss them all as worthless.

Disinformation, like propaganda, is in the eye of the beholder. As one scholar notes, "Whether a given story or piece of content is labeled as misinformation or disinformation can depend as much on a speaker's intent as on the professional standards of who is evaluating it" (Jack, 2017, p. 3). Educators may wonder how (or whether) they will explain the history of 2016 Russian election interference to future generations. Some California legislators want to make sure that when schools update their history textbooks, they include a lesson about how Russian hackers interfered with the presidential election. In 2018, California Assemblyman Marc Levine asked the state to adopt new high school history curricula, noting that high school students need to learn about that threat because it was an overt attack on American democracy. In 2019, Senator Amy Klobuchar introduced the Digital Citizenship and Media Literacy Act. If passed by Congress, this law would authorize $20 million to advance media literacy education as a means to address the problem of disinformation and propaganda (Klobuchar, 2019). But educators still don't yet know exactly how to best examine the topic of disinformation with young learners. It will take considerable trial and error to figure out what works, because American educators' own ideas about politics will certainly affect how and what they teach their students.

Could playing a video game help people better understand digital disinformation and propaganda? A Dutch organization called DROG created the Get Bad News game in 2017. This interactive media experience that helps people recognize and resist online disinformation. Players are invited to be the creators of fake news, using techniques and strategies to spread online misinformation. For example, players are shown a short text or image (such as a meme or article headline) and can react to it in a variety of ways. When they behave as propagandists, they get more followers and credibility. Too much blatant lying or ridiculous manipulation causes them to lose credibility and followers. The goal of the game is to gather as many followers as possible without losing too much credibility. By playing the game, learners can explore the following concepts:

- ***Impersonation.*** When you use a social media account that mimics the appearance of a communicator with high credibility through a fake news blog, your work looks like a real news website and your content gets shared widely.
- ***Emotion.*** By adding emotional content to your website, you earn followers. For example, choosing to share information about scientists studying genetically modified food gets you no points, but attacking scientists by making a meme that compares scientists to an image of Hannibal Lecter from *The Silence of the Lambs* gets you hundreds of new followers. Anger and fear seem to be the emotions that increase the number of followers.
- ***Polarization.*** When you amplify existing grievances to make them seem more important than they really are, you can attract attention. For example, when a political issue like crime is polarized, bots retweet the message, and polarization increases. Controversy increases the reach of a message. Then as real users interact with bots, the conflict accelerates.
- ***Conspiracy.*** In this part of the online learning experience, users discover that sharing a message that's too weird, banal, or bizarre decreases credibility and leads to the loss of followers. Users also discover that promoting a well-crafted lie can cause people to lose trust in social and political institutions. They also learn how simply casting doubt on an official narrative can increase the number of their followers.
- ***Discredit.*** When confronted with a fact-checker who debunks a conspiracy theory you have been promoting, you can try to discredit the critic,

thus deflecting attention from the facts. Attacking a critic both increases controversy and adds followers.

- ***Trolling.*** In the final phase of the game, users are invited to stir up a controversy about a plane crash. They discover that if they act respectfully toward the victims of the crash, their followers urge them to investigate the matter more fully. Users have the chance to fabricate images through Photoshop or pretend to be a grieving family member. Eventually, users have so many followers that their post automatically attracts interest from mainstream news sites, and the story takes on a life of its own as it begins to be retransmitted by journalists (DROG, 2017).

In an experimental study of users who played the game, researchers found that it was effective in reducing the perceived reliability of misinformation (Roozenbeek & van der Linden, 2019). Such hands-on, experiential learning may provide learners with a better understanding of the many techniques used to intentionally mislead and deceive. But there may be some downsides to such games. Because it teaches students how to create disinformation, the game may serve to normalize disinformation and make it look like harmless entertainment. Indeed, my students had so much fun playing the game, competing with each other to get a high score, that I worried it might be teaching them how to be disinformation experts. I wondered whether the playful spirit of the game with its competition for points interfered with thoughtful ethical reflection about the real-world consequences of spreading false and harmful messages.

LEARNING ACTIVITY

Disinformation Games

When students pretend to be disinformation specialists, they may gain a deeper understanding of how it works.

Activity: Play Get Bad News, an online game (www.getbadnews.com). It takes about 20 minutes to complete the six badges of the disinformation game (DROG, 2017). Learners can play the game in one classroom period or as a homework activity. After playing, consider these questions for reflective writing and discussion.

For Discussion:

1. **How** did it feel to take on the role of a person spreading disinformation?
2. **What** did you notice about how your feelings changed during the course of the game?
3. **How** realistic was this game, in your opinion?
4. **How** could these disinformation practices damage American elections?
5. **What** are some other real-world consequences of spreading the kinds of messages that the game encouraged you to share?

The Takeaway: Disinformation can be hard to recognize but it has some distinctive features. When disinformation is used in American elections, it may diminish people's trust in the fairness of the election process.

Teaching the Conspiracies

Conspiracy theories are growing in popularity, but they are still more or less taboo in many American schools. But creative high school teachers have discovered that some students can learn to enjoy writing research papers when they get a chance to explore conspiracy theories through inquiry learning pedagogies. For many students (and teachers) in the U.S., the research paper assignment is not a favorite activity. John Bradford, an English teacher at Creekview High School in Canton, Georgia, uses the topic of conspiracy theories in his elective class on argumentative and persuasive writing, and his students happily write research papers to discover what is known about a conspiracy theory that interests them. With support from the school librarian, students find three debatable points to write about, including merits and limitations of the conspiracy theory in question. They write a carefully structured eight-paragraph essay, organizing sentences into paragraphs and including properly formatted MLA-style citations.

Bradford got the idea for the unit after watching the Oliver Stone film *JFK*. As part of the unit, students begin by listening to the *War of the Worlds* broadcast from 1938, when Orson Welles and the Mercury Theater of the Air tricked listeners into believing that aliens had landed in New Jersey. They discuss how people can be vulnerable to false information when it's presented in ways that make it seem credible. They then watch the famous BBC April Fool's Day hoax, "Spaghetti Story," a three-minute segment from 1957 where a British narrator explains the importance of the spaghetti harvest as we see Swiss women harvesting spaghetti from trees. Students learn that back in the 1950s, British people were not familiar with spaghetti, which was considered an exotic delicacy. For many viewers, then and now, the black-and-white documentary video, with its voice-of-God male British narrator, shows spaghetti actually growing on trees in a wholly believable way.

Bradford knows that students value the opportunity to choose a conspiracy theory of interest to them. Students debate their topics after finding pro and con sources and evaluating the quality of those sources. Students have examined faked moon landings, the Martin Luther King assassination, and the 9/11 attacks on the World Trade Center. The teacher sets some limits, however: he doesn't let students research celebrity deaths or racist conspiracy theories.

Conspiracy theories are a type of disinformation that embodies the idea that a group of people make secret agreements and take actions to accomplish malevolent goals. Conspiracy theories fundamentally proclaim that nothing happens by accident, nothing is as it seems, and everything is connected (Barkun, 2013). While some conspiracy theories have credible evidence both for and against them (like the question of who killed John F. Kennedy), Bradford encourages his students to let credible sources influence their thinking. He explained that students find it challenging to evaluate media sources. Students explored and discussed concepts like evidence, source, authority, and expertise. Bradford noted, "On the Internet, anyone can put up anything and make it look slick and professional. But my students learn to look for bias and investigate the sources of information because they're motivated and engaged—they want to learn more" (Hobbs, 2017c, p. 21).

The practice of identifying credible sources can be a bit sticky, Bradford admits. He notes that in his very conservative Southern town, simply "telling students that the *Washington Post* and *The New York Times* are more credible than the *National Inquirer* is not always accepted." He is cautious about how he describes sources like Fox News and MSNBC. Where he teaches, some parents are angry that their children are not allowed to quote from the Bible when writing academic research papers (Hobbs, 2017c). Still, he's gotten no pushback from parents or school administrators about his lessons. Students like the conspiracy theory assignment because they get to explore a topic of interest. Plus, due to the nature of the genre, their writing has real drama, tension, and conflict in it. They learn to see sources of authority as constructed and contextual, recognizing that expertise is evaluated differently by members of a knowledge community. School leaders like the overall message of the assignment: make sure that the information sources you choose to believe are based on reasoning and evidence.

It takes courage for an educator to include genuine inquiry learning in the classroom because you never know what kind of information and ideas your students will find. In a world where teachers feel the strong need to protect students, this can seem odd. But such instructional practices are good preparation for the world outside the classroom. Today, students need many such opportunities in school to make sense of the wide range of messages that are part of the contemporary information ecosystem. Conspiracy theories are particularly useful in helping students understand the social construction of expertise, where even people with PhDs may publish nonsense in "sketchy online journals willing to publish anything for a fee," in a type of information laundering that enables information to travel from "propagandist to bot to veteran conspiracy theorist to authoritative spokesperson to Hannity to news articles from respected sources" (Ellis, 2018, p. 1).

Today, a generalized mistrust of authority seems a logical stance for many people who are troubled by the complexity of the world's problems. Concerns about digital privacy, algorithms used by search engines, and even controversies about medicine and health are sometimes framed using the tropes and formulas of conspiracy. In times of anxiety and insecurity, conspiracy theories can be reassuring. They offer a clear identification of evil by simplifying the world into villains and victims. Conspiracy theories rely on the us-versus-them paradigm. Perhaps that is why conspiracy theories are "sticky." People who believe in a conspiracy may receive social reinforcement from other like-minded individuals through online echo chambers (Sunstein, 2016).

As the coronavirus pandemic wreaks havoc on people in the U.S. and around the world, belief in conspiracy theories can seriously damage public health. Survey research shows that only half of African Americans are likely to get a COVID-19 vaccine when it becomes available (Gramlich & Funk, 2020). Distrust of the health care system is widespread in part because of a historical record of discrimination and mistreatment, including the infamous Tuskegee syphilis study, which was once considered to be a conspiracy theory. When it was proved true in the 1970s, it was a stunning revelation that rocked the medical world and disrupted the African American community's trust in the health care system. When a conspiracy theory is believed to be true, it can be difficult to displace. The less control you have over your life, the more likely you are to believe in conspiracy theories. People who believe one conspiracy theory are more likely to believe others. Researchers who have studied medical conspiracy theories find that 37% of Americans agreed that the Food and Drug Administration is intentionally suppressing natural cures for cancer because of pressure from drug companies. People who believe in medical conspiracies are less willing to follow traditional medical advice, such as using sunscreen or vaccines, and are more likely to use alternative treatments like supplements (Oliver & Wood, 2014). Not surprisingly, both liberals and conservatives are equally susceptible to conspiracy theories. Fortunately, education seems to be a mitigating factor. Educational background is associated with reduced belief in conspiracy theories, with 42% of people without a high school diploma believing multiple conspiracy theories as compared with 23% of those with postgraduate degrees (Uscinski & Parent, 2014).

Conspiracy theories have social power that can influence people's behavior. In one experimental research study, some subjects were shown a conspiracy theory video claiming that climate change was a hoax while others saw an informational video on another topic. Those who saw the climate change hoax video were significantly less likely to think there is widespread scientific agreement on human-caused climate change. They were less likely to say they would sign a petition to help reduce global warming, less likely to give money to a political candidate, and less likely to use energy efficiency as a selection criterion when buying a light bulb or household appliance (Jolley & Douglas, 2014).

Given how contagious conspiracy theories are, educators acknowledge that there are some risks to teaching about them. Screening conspiracy theory videos in the classroom does create a risk of validating them. Some students may find them persuasive. There may not be enough time in class to examine evidence in depth. On some topics, there's simply too much junk information online and not enough quality information for students to sort through in a class period or two. For other topics, it can be a little too easy to trivialize stupid or silly conspiracy theories, reinforcing us-versus-them thinking by positioning believers as dumb or gullible. But precisely because this powerful form of propaganda has become increasingly prominent in our culture today, students need opportunities to discuss and unpack the ideas and emotions that are embedded in conspiracy theories. They need to analyze and reflect upon their appeal. Tackling the topic of conspiracy theories in the classroom may involve some unpredictability and risk, but it is a risk worth taking.

LEARNING ACTIVITY

Autocomplete Conspiracy

Students learn to recognize and reflect on how conspiracy theories use mystery to capture imagination, leading people to the conclusion that powerful forces are secretly controlling information and society. They discover the power of questioning as a means to advance intellectual curiosity and gain knowledge.

View and Discuss: View a YouTube video titled "Google Censors Anti-Hillary Search Results." The video was created by Mark Dice, a noted conspiracy theorist. The three-minute video demonstrates how, in contrast to other search engines, Google autocomplete results do not include references to Hillary Clinton's health.

Annotate and Inquire: To carefully analyze the video's presentation of information and evidence, instructors may want to scaffold student learning by first having them use a video annotation tool like Video Ant (www.ant.umn.edu). It allows learners to "talk back to video," slowing down their interpretation and encouraging them to notice and observe how the video has been constructed. Students can be invited to analyze how specific elements of spoken language, text on screen, facial expressions, images, or music or sound are used to convey meaning in audiovisual texts. Then students can work individually or with a partner to accomplish these tasks:

1. **Make a list** of all the background knowledge needed to understand the message. What does an ordinary viewer need to know in order for this video to make sense?
2. **Generate a list** of further questions raised by viewing. What questions did this video raise for you?
3. **Revise** one of your questions so that it could be tested using the scientific method.

For Discussion

- **Why** does Google make adjustments to the algorithm for autocomplete?
- **How** may Mark Dice's own previous usage of the Google search engine have influenced the results he received? Would others conducting the same search at the same time receive the same results? Why or why not?
- **Is "bias"** the right term for the phenomenon Dice describes? Why or why not?

The Takeaway: To analyze fact claims, background knowledge is needed. Making a list of the types of background knowledge required to interpret claims ignites intellectual curiosity as learners recognize gaps in their own knowledge. When people generate questions that they really want to learn about, nothing can stop them.

When Terror Strikes

Terrorism has been called "propaganda of the deed." Terrorists use the power of violence as a form of communication to accomplish political goals. Defined as the use of violence against noncombatants in order to achieve a political objective, terrorism inspires fear that aims to force political change. History shows that terrorism has long been a part of political discourse. Many different types of political and ideological movements have used terrorism to attempt to achieve their goals. Terrorists may be anarchists, or they may belong to nationalist or separatist groups seeking to be liberated from oppressive powers in their country. They may be fighting capitalism or fighting on behalf of their religion. They may be a minority group seeking equal rights. They may even be "lone wolf" terrorists who want to feel part of a virtual community of hatred (Post, McGinnis & Moody, 2014). As a political strategy, terrorists offer a relentless combination of words and deeds to affect the hearts and minds of target audiences all around the world.

But terrorism is also part of American culture and has been since well before the period of Reconstruction. White supremacists in the United States have long used terrorism to silence and marginalize African Americans through lynching, land grabs, and other forms of violence. In 1921, the Tulsa race massacre took the lives of 300 people in the Greenwood District, a neighborhood known as "Black Wall Street," where white people looted and burned nearly 40 city blocks. Bodies were buried in unmarked graves and no one was prosecuted for the murders.

White supremacists have been using the Internet since the very early 1980s, when Don Black launched the Stormfront website. Over 40 years, it has amassed a user base of over 100,000 people. When Dylann Roof shot and killed 12 people at close range in an African American church in Charleston, South Carolina, his racial manifesto and postings at Stormfront drew renewed attention and led to increases in the number of donations (Harmon & Bowdish, 2018).

Clear evidence shows that domestic white terrorists engage in a type of online learning. The man who opened fire in an El Paso Walmart in 2019 wrote that he drew some inspiration from the white nationalist terrorist attack in Christchurch, New Zealand. Other terrorists have learned from a massacre at a Pittsburgh synagogue in 2018. Investigative journalism found that "at least a third of white extremist killers since 2011 were inspired by others who perpetrated similar attacks, professed a reverence for them or showed an interest in their tactics" (Editorial Board, 2019).

How do American teachers teach about local, national, and global terrorism? Many educators may be experiencing compassion fatigue as the number of school shootings and terrorist massacres has scaled up in recent years. People who work with traumatized people can experience compassion fatigue when they notice feelings of reduced empathy toward the suffering of others. But emotional exhaustion can also occur from exposure to media. Media professionals may experience a sense of alienation and despair that they inadvertently spread to their audiences. Communications scholars have observed that because war, disease, famine, and death are an ever-present part of our media ecosystem, journalists themselves are desensitized to trauma, leading them to "search for ever more sensational tidbits to retain the attention of their audience" (Moeller, 1999, p. 2).

Both direct and mediated exposure to terrorism can significantly impact a person's mental health. For example, the tragic legacy of the September 11, 2001 attacks on New York City, Washington, DC, and Pennsylvania continue to affect people's lives. A large proportion of people who lived in proximity to the World Trade Center experienced symptoms of post-traumatic stress disorder. Studies have been conducted on firefighters and rescue workers, children, and even those who simply watched TV news reports of the attacks. After the September 11 attacks, a nationally representative survey of Americans found that 44% reported substantial stress reactions from indirect exposure to the event through print and television media reports. Severe stress reactions were correlated with the number of hours that people watched television news coverage of the event (Neria, DiGrande, & Adams, 2011).

Compassion fatigue is reaching crisis levels in the United States. Many adults have become desensitized to violent events, paying less and less attention to major disasters that unfold through the news media. But as we learned from public response to police brutality towards African Americans, sustained protests can be an effective form of activist propaganda that stimulates public policy. After young protesters responded to the massacre at Parkland High School, 11 states changed their gun policies to limit firearms (Beckett, 2019). For this reason, when terror strikes, teachers should take time to talk about the relationship between feelings, information, and civic and political action as part of the democratic process.

LEARNING ACTIVITY

Sharing Livestream Video: Should It Be a Crime?

Discuss whether or not terrorist video live streams should be censored by government or platforms.

Activity: In the Christchurch shooting in 2019, 50 people were murdered in a New Zealand mosque. This horrible terrorist act was the work of a "self-described fascist hoping to pull viewers into his deranged hate-ravaged point-of-view, immortalizing the captured images of terror on his victims' faces at the second their stolen lives flashed before them" (Niman, 2019, p. 1).

The video was shared and spread by people online. At the time of the murders, fewer than 200 people watched the stream live. But some people recorded and posted the video to 8chan, a social message board website that hosts offensive content banned on many mainstream platforms. Immediately, millions of people then began trying to re-upload the video to Facebook, which blocked more than 1.2 million attempts, taking down more than 300,000 copies of the video (Graham-McLay, 2019).

In New Zealand, it is a crime to possess material that depicts extreme violence and terrorism. Although the country has freedom of expression, they have a human rights law that forbids incitement of racial disharmony. Although hate speech is legal in New Zealand, public officials have determined that media content and publications that are deliberately constructed to inspire murder should be censored.

Read and Discuss: Read the article by Issie Lapowsky, "Why Tech Didn't Stop the New Zealand Attack From Going Viral" in *Wired* magazine. After reading, discuss these questions:

- **What** are some of the technical challenges to removing harmful live-stream video?
- **What** are some of the different reasons why some people tried to copy and share the mosque shooting video?
- **What** are the advantages and disadvantages of the New Zealand law that penalizes people for possessing and distributing media content containing extreme violence and terrorism?
- **Should** the United States consider passing a law like this? Why or why not?

The Takeaway: Terrorism and political violence are forms of propaganda that destroy people's lives. There are good arguments for limiting live-stream video by governments, but there are risks to such regulation as well.

Extremist Propaganda in the Classroom

Educators must give some careful thought to the question of when, whether, and how to critically analyze extremist propaganda with high school and college students. Media literacy educators find much value in having structured, teacher-guided conversations about controversial and difficult content that is highly relevant to contemporary culture. When teachers select examples of videos to screen or memes to discuss and analyze, robust classroom dialogue can be stimulated. Learners benefit from opportunities to share and unpack the feelings and ideas that such content may evoke.

Deliberative dialogue about extreme propaganda can also help model the practice of addressing controversial issues in ways that make visible the power of empathy. Deliberative dialogue builds on the colonial town meeting tradition where individuals share opinions with each other in a democratic manner. It is a type of public interaction in which small groups of diverse individuals exchange and weigh ideas and opinions about a particular issue of public importance. Sharing personal experience and knowledge, people may or may not come to consensus, but they deepen their understanding of the complexities of the issue and come to an informed opinion about it. Grassroots social movements, and especially nonviolent campaigns, use deliberative dialogue plus symbolic displays of unity. Through learning and discussion opportunities, people work through differences of opinion and develop effective strategies for coordinating their actions (Levine, 2018).

When discussing and deliberating on issues of public importance, it may or may not be appropriate to display examples of extreme propaganda in the classroom. Whether we like it or not, because propaganda activates strong emotions, people's critical analysis competencies can be bypassed. There is a risk of unintentionally increasing (rather than decreasing) political polarization in the classroom. There is even the possibility that the use of extreme forms of propaganda in the classroom may normalize and desensitize students to certain truly harmful views.

The concept of the "oxygen of amplification" may apply when educators use extreme forms of propaganda for teaching and learning purposes. It's not only social media sharing and journalists who help to make extremist messages more visible. Teachers can also extend the visibility of extremist content, even when their use of such content takes an explicitly critical stance. In addressing how news media coverage can make trolls stronger, one scholar notes, "Amplification makes particular stories, communities, and bad actors bigger—more visible, more influential—than they would have been otherwise" (Phillips, 2018, p. 5).

But ignoring extreme forms of political propaganda can also be educationally irresponsible. As Phillips explains, "The bigoted, dehumanizing, and manipulative messages emanating from extremist corners of the internet" are impossible, "and maybe even unethical, to ignore" (2018, p. 6). To educate people about the difficult cultural realities of contemporary democracy today, some forms of extreme propaganda simply need to be seen and discussed to be understood. For example, I can describe how an alt-right political party in Finland created a comic-book superhero narrative to influence the 2019 election, but until you see the video, you can't really understand the power of the phenomenon itself.

Using a combination of live action and animation, the fictional narrative of "Ketutus" is a six-minute film that features journalists taking bribes and dark-skinned foreigners preying on women and children. In the story, a corrupt group of elites hold all the power and wealth in the country, inspiring the wrath of the common man. He takes the form of a monster who violently repels the evil politicians. It was created by the True Finns political party, which paid movie theaters across the country to air the political video as a movie trailer in the weeks before the election. The propaganda was designed to cultivate anger toward elected government officials.

The cartoon video depicts the use of political violence: in the story, we see the monster attacking the driver of the political elites as a means to effect change. Violence is presented as a justified form of political action. So when a left-wing political candidate, Suldan Said Ahmed, a Helsinki political activist of Somalian descent, was attacked before the election at a subway station in Helsinki, some people wondered if that particular political violence was inspired by the True Finns' propaganda video (Uutiset, 2019). The ensuing controversy was covered in the news media, which oxygenated the issue, helping to increase the visibility of the propaganda message and enabling it to reach an even wider audience.

Using extreme propaganda from a foreign country can be an effective way to engage learners in dialogue. A teacher might feel it's safer to use examples of foreign propaganda than more homegrown and local forms of political propaganda. Students may simply find it easier to establish a certain critical distance from it. Because contextual knowledge is needed to interpret it, unfamiliar but provocative foreign propaganda may also activate students' intellectual curiosity. Students may be inspired to want to learn more about the cultural, political, social, and economic context in which the propaganda was produced.

But teachers should avoid using propaganda in a superficial or casual way, as way to merely grab students' attention or as a form of entertainment. Teachers may use small portions of extremist propaganda for purposes of illustration when time for dialogue and discussion is truly limited. Personally, in my teaching, I avoid screening extremist propaganda merely for its shock value or sensational appeal. Also, I don't use foreign extremist propaganda when I don't have time for critical questions or inquiry learning, as simply displaying the propaganda for illustrative purposes may create or reinforce damaging cultural stereotypes.

LEARNING ACTIVITY

Examining Anti-immigrant Political Propaganda

View and discuss political propaganda circulated by the True Finns party, an extreme right-wing group in Finland.

Part 1. View and Ask Questions: As you view the Finnish political campaign video about Ketutus, pause at key moments and give students time to generate a list of questions that come to mind. Each question can be written on a note card. Small groups can then gather up note cards and organize them into two piles. One pile should consist of questions that can be answered through library and Internet research, and one pile should consist of questions that require discussion and the sharing of ideas.

For homework, students select one fact-based question to explore more deeply and return to their small group to share what they learned. Then each group should select one or more of the value-based questions to discuss. Each group summarizes key ideas raised in their discussion, sharing with the whole class. This activity helps build contextual background knowledge that is needed in order to interpret and evaluate propaganda.

Part 2. Spot the Hateful Ideologies: Introduce the four themes below and then watch the video again, pausing at key moments to identify the presence of these ideologies.

Creating the Outsider. An Insider-Outsider frame is established by identifying a target group (or multiple groups) designated as the Outsider. In hateful ideologies, the Outsider must be portrayed as being both inferior and threatening, to establish the need to take action against them. Distorted histories and interpretations of past and current events implicitly suggest that violence is necessary to preserve the status and purity of the group.

Constructing a Glorious Past. Hateful ideologies often suggest that the Insider Group has lost its direction and forgotten its once-glorious past. Sometimes, this problem is portrayed as being the fault of some former members of the Insider group who were fooled or subverted by the Outsiders. Destroying the Outsider is needed to restore this glorious past.

Claiming Victimhood. Hateful ideologies may position the Insiders as victims themselves. Insiders are shown as having experienced suffering or obstacles. Outsiders are never depicted as victims.

Divine Right or Natural Law. Insider superiority is depicted as natural, and this special status is sometimes granted by God. Insiders who fight and defeat Outsiders are promised a special status, and even if defeated, they can claim the identity of being martyrs for a noble cause.

The Takeaway: It can sometimes be easier to spot how hateful ideologies are used in global media than in more familiar fare. A vigilant and inquiring mindset is needed when encountering extremist political propaganda.

–Adapted from Media Smarts, Facing Online Hate Tutorial (ND)

Advancing or Hijacking Dialogue

As we have seen in this chapter, the pleasure, shock, and dark drama of propaganda and hate speech are among the reasons why its visibility has grown. News media coverage causes it to spread even further. Back in 1994, when the Internet was in its infancy, Douglas Rushkoff recognized the power of memes, noting how they are transmitted from one human to many through media. He used a biological metaphor, noting that a media virus might be "an event, invention, technology, system of thought, musical riff, visual image, scientific theory, sex scandal, clothing style, or even a pop hero." By clinging to the "nooks and crannies in popular culture," these media viruses become noticed. As people pay attention to them, they "inject hidden agendas into the data stream in the form of ideological code," and they infiltrate our understanding of social reality (Rushkoff, 1994, p. 10).

Activists use the power of violent language to attract attention to their ideas. As part of his attention-seeking behavior, Milo Yiannopoulos, a critic who specializes in making racist and misogynistic statements about women and people of color, told at least two news outlets that he wanted vigilantes to start shooting journalists. He texted the message, "I can't wait for vigilante squads to start gunning journalists down on sight" to a reporter for the *New York Observer*. The news outlet wrote about the incident, of course, giving Yiannopoulos even more attention for his radical views.

Mocking or satirical threats of this type are sometimes called "shitposting." The term first circulated on Reddit when participants noted that some users did not adhere to expectations that they make constructive posts that added useful information to a forum. Frequently these posts were offensive and intentionally designed to aggravate other users. Deliberate, mean-spirited efforts had the result of hijacking dialogue. When applied to politics, shitposting can be dangerous propaganda, indeed. Many other countries have laws designed to minimize the potential harms of hate speech and dangerous propaganda but in the U.S., playful hate like this is a form of legally protected free speech.

Teachers who explore dark propaganda in the classroom must make careful choices about the kinds of examples that they screen and discuss in class, being aware of the potential of their own pedagogy to inadvertently amplify hateful ideas. But educators also cannot ignore the bigoted, dehumanizing, playful but manipulative messages that are part of media culture today. Indeed, it can be argued that it would be unethical not to examine these new forms of hate speech circulating online. Educators can model the spirit of inquiry, respect, empathy and tolerance toward others.

Students need help to deepen their respect for and appreciation of the role of citizens in a pluralistic democracy where self-governance empowers us. Exploring controversial issues in the classroom is more important than ever today, and it can help learners develop the capacity for both resilience and resistance, competencies increasingly required of all of us. In Chapter 6, we'll consider how propaganda can be used to promote human dignity, inspire civic activism for social welfare, and help in the development of self-governing citizens.

6

Beneficial Propaganda

Art, Activism, and Elections

In the marketplace of ideas, propaganda is an essential component of the democratic process

It's dawn on the Santa Monica Pier, and as morning arrives we see people gathering on the pier to watch a strange display: It's a giant black screen with a couple of life-size skeletons who are hugging and kissing. Soon, two people come out from behind the screen, as we see an attractive young lesbian couple, who smile at the crowd and wave as the screen reads, "Love has no gender."

Then we see other dancing skeletons and soon we discover an African American woman and Asian man, who hug and kiss as the screen reads, "Love has no race." Then, two small skeletons dance adorably, and soon we meet a 10-year-old girl and her younger sister, a little girl with Down syndrome. As they smile and hold hands, the screen reads, "Love has no disability." We see a hearing-impaired family talking about the event in sign language. Next, we see three skeletons dancing, and soon two gay African American men and their young son come out, who smile and wave at the crowd. Then follows a visual montage that includes an older couple, a Christian minister and a woman in an Indian sari, a Jew and an Arab. It's a montage of voices who speak phrases like, "My heart doesn't see race," "Love has no age limit," "We are neighbors and best friends," and "Our family is no less than any other family." The tag line reads: "Rethink bias at lovehasnolabels.com."

Filmed on Valentine's Day in 2015, this award-winning public service announcement was designed as an antidote to living in divisive times. The image shown below captures a sense of the compelling and heart-warming PSA. With hate crime on the rise and many groups feeling marginalized and unsafe, the Ad Council's campaign is designed to make prejudice unfashionable. The Ad Council created this public service advertising in coordination with brand partners PepsiCo, Unilever, the Southern Poverty Law Center, and the Bank of America. With nearly 160 million views on broadcast television and 60 million views on YouTube, it is one of the most popular community activism campaigns ever (Nudd, 2016).

Love Has No Labels Campaign

You may be wondering: What does an Ad Council PSA have to do with art, activism, and democracy? Initially, it may not seem like this particular campaign is fundamentally tied to democratic practice and a focus on elections, governments, and laws. But political ideas that influence democratic decision making can be embedded in many forms of media that may not, at first glance, appear to be political. In the case of the Ad Council PSA, the idea of equality is the emotional heart of this message. And since the protection of basic individual human rights is fundamental to democracy, this is a form of political propaganda. It positions the viewer as "one of us," as members of the great human community with a need for love and belonging. This PSA reinforces equality as a core value of American culture through a combination of entertainment and persuasion that emphasizes our shared human heritage. Democracy relies on pluralism and respect for diversity because the dangers of the tyranny of the majority are well known. The social value of equality must be reinforced through culture through the establishment of ethics, norms, and customs (Dasandi & Taylor, 2018).

In this chapter, we consider propaganda as a necessary and beneficial dimension of democracy. All forms of social, political, and cultural activism require it. To move people to action, people use a combination of feelings and ideas, putting their values and beliefs into the marketplace of ideas. Civic engagement takes new forms in an era of hashtag activism, but artistic expression has always been used as a form of propaganda. By examining how political campaign experts and social change activists navigate the ethical dimensions of creating messages that inspire and influence, I will show how propaganda is fundamentally tied to the universal urge to make a difference in the world.

Beneficial Propaganda

Yes, I'll admit it: The phrase "beneficial propaganda" seems strange. My students have described the peculiar feeling they get when I first use the term. The meme shown below was created by one of my students to capture this feeling. At the beginning of the semester, they ask, "How could propaganda possibly be beneficial?" When I remind them of the genre of PSAs, they immediately understand that propaganda can be designed for social good. Public service announcements may warn us not to text and drive, urge us to get a colonoscopy, or help increase awareness of how prejudices and stereotypes limit our social relationships. This type of propaganda might point out the benefits of drinking milk—or urge us to stop drinking it. But propaganda cannot always be so easily recognizable as good or bad. Individuals must evaluate propaganda for themselves to determine if it is beneficial or harmful. Your judgment will depend on your existing knowledge, opinions, and beliefs.

After hearing the term "beneficial propaganda," learners immediately ask a question like, "Beneficial to whom?" Of course, propaganda is created by authors who feel the message they created is beneficial. Otherwise, why would someone expend all the effort it takes to create it? Consider the most negative, nasty political campaign ad you've ever seen in your life and recognize that, in the minds of the political consultants who created it, it served a valuable purpose in strategically attracting attention and influencing potential voters.

Clearly, in thinking about the potential benefits and harms of propaganda, values come into play. When we evaluate a message to determine whether or not it is beneficial, we may consider its relevance to (1) the author who created it; (2) ourselves; (3) our family, neighborhood, or community; or (4) the larger society, culture, and even the world. We may think of immediate or longer-term potential benefits, risks, or harms.

Because such evaluation is a form of judgment where people apply specific criteria to consider the value of propaganda, the social context will play a key role in the interpretations and conclusions made. Of course, to analyze the benefits and harms of propaganda, careful consideration of the author, message, audience, purpose, and context is also needed. When students learn to use explicit criteria for evaluating propaganda, they immediately see the advantages of such reasoning over judgments made quickly, intuitively, and without a formal reasoning process.

Artistic and literary propaganda has long been an important part of culture and society, because, as one writer put it, "Ever since the Stone Age, self-reinforcing myths have served to unite human collectives" (Harari, 2018, p. 238). Fictional stories and myths that inspire people can induce them to follow a powerful leader or act together as members of a tribe. Patriotism is cultivated through symbolic expression designed to strengthen feelings of national identity. During World War I, a large number of famous writers and poets publicized their patriotism by participating in the construction of pro-war propaganda, including Rudyard Kipling, H. G. Wells, and Arthur Conan Doyle. Painters, illustrators, sculptors, and other artists were sent to the front to make artwork that depicted the hostility in virtuous, noble ways. Such work was widely understood as beneficial. The war was framed as a life-or-death struggle that would require enormous sacrifice on the part of ordinary people, and politicians took note of how patriotism surged during wartime as government censorship enabled exaggerated and distorted depictions of warfare. For example, throughout the Great War, the public knew little of the real nature of trench warfare because of the overt secrecy and suppression of information (Haste, 1995).

Many people are unaware that America's leading producer of public service announcements, the Ad Council, was started as a means to spread war propaganda in 1941, when the U.S. entered World War II. Your grandparents were persuaded by Kate Smith to buy war bonds. Some readers may be old enough to remember the Crying Indian campaign in the early 1970s, beginning with Earth Day in 1971. Others may recall Nancy Reagan's Just Say No antidrug campaign in 1982. Some readers may remember that in 2006, the TV Boss campaign helped parents understand how to use parental controls on their digital devices. In 2009, Michelle Obama launched the Let's Move campaign to address childhood obesity. More recently, Melania Trump has urged attention to issues including well-being, online safety, and opioid abuse with her Be Best campaign.

Ad Council PSAs are funded by a large group of advertisers who make a financial commitment to support the design and creative production of the ads. The most effective public service campaigns control when, where, and how often audiences are exposed to PSA messages by paying for airtime. Although some PSAs are played for free by broadcasters as part of their public service obligation, many radio and television stations may simply use PSAs as "filler" when they don't have paid advertisers for particular time slots. Therefore, the visibility of PSAs tends to fluctuate with the health of the economy.

Around the world, beneficial propaganda may be created by governments, insurance companies, or civil society organizations. Many forms of beneficial propaganda are messages that raise awareness, inspiring and motivating people to take action. In 2017, director David Lynch created a powerful PSA to call attention to the plight of war veterans as part of his foundation's effort to encourage at-risk populations to practice transcendental meditation as a source of healing. The ad depicts scenes from the battlefield—a helicopter in flight, guns shooting, bombs dropping, and buildings exploding. Viewers are immersed in these battle scenes by disturbing and fearsome sounds. But then viewers are invited to really listen to the soundtrack, and the ad cuts to everyday scenes from ordinary life. We hear the same sounds, but now we see an alarm clock going off, a fan swirling, a machine washer spinning, balloons, popcorn popping, and fireworks bursting. We learn that the ordinary noises of life can be traumatic triggers for veterans of war. Through the creative use of sound and image, the ad succeeds in raising awareness of and sympathy for the plight of returning war veterans. Was this PSA effective? We don't know for sure. Researchers who have studied the impact of PSAs have found it challenging to assess their relative impact. Sometimes small differences in the message content or format may have differential impact on target audiences (DeJong, 2017).

LEARNING ACTIVITY

Analyze a Documentary

Consider the 30-minute documentary From One Second to the Next, *a short film directed by Werner Herzog and sponsored by AT&T, the telecommunications company. The short documentary film explores the impact on individuals affected by accidents where texting while driving was involved. The film activates a wide range of emotions as viewers are invited to identify with the victims, family members, and even the perpetrators.*

Activity: Use a digital video annotation tool that enables teachers to upload a video from YouTube to a platform where learners can view, pause, and annotate by inserting a comment that is displayed at a particular point in the film. Learners can read the comments of others and reply to them. The image below displays a screenshot from the digital video annotation platform VideoAnt, created by the educational technologists at the University of Minnesota.

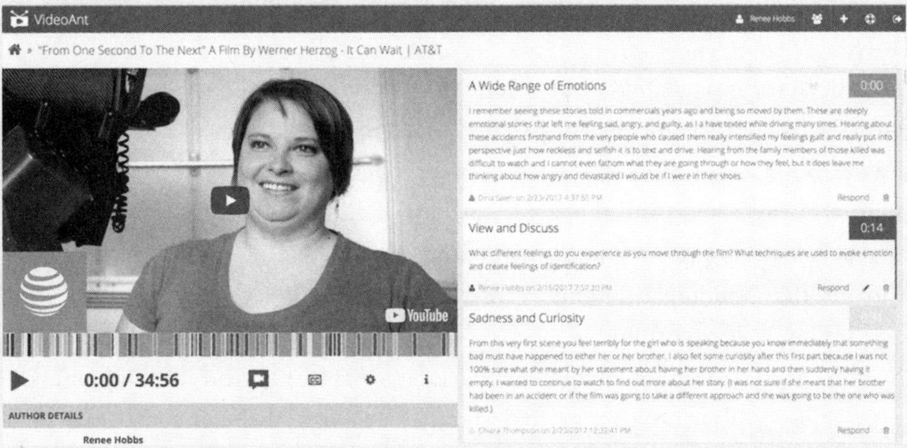

View and Analyze: Examine a documentary that is a form of positive propaganda about texting and driving. As you watch, notice the different feelings you experience and try to identify the specific language, image, sound, and editing techniques used to activate these feelings. Compose annotations that capture your observations, feelings, and ideas. Then read the comments of others and respond to their ideas.

Questions to Discuss:

- **How** have your beliefs and attitudes about texting and driving changed?
- **Which** moments in the stories were emotionally powerful for you? Why?
- **How** does the experience of digital annotation support critical thinking about media?

The Takeaway: Video annotation can help slow down the viewing process to help people notice how carefully documentaries are constructed using a strategic combination of images, language, sound, and editing. Documentary film can perform a propaganda function when it forges deep connections between feelings, ideas, and behaviors.

Feelings as Information

Film documentaries activate our emotions by positioning us not just as spectators but as active participants in some shared social reality. Propaganda, like storytelling, works by creating a kind of communal groupthink (Harari, 2018). That's why some academics and educators are suspicious of all forms of language and media that stimulate strong emotions. This reflects a long-standing tradition in Western thought that positions emotions as inferior to thinking. Yet whether we like it or not, feelings rule over thinking in many ways. When people's feelings are activated by propaganda, the emotional intensity tends to displace critical thinking; it takes extra effort to develop a reasoned response. Although this can sometimes be a problem, it's also clear that feelings and emotions are a powerful type of information that affects decision making.

The shared experience of emotion actually helps people achieve social consensus, which is critical to understanding the power of propaganda. When such feelings are activated, people arrive at quicker judgments, especially in the context of social relationships like family and group decision making. Emotions influence public policy and jury-based decisions. Because people use their emotions in decision making, they sometimes experience feelings first, and then form attitudes, judgments, and opinions that align with their feelings. Political campaign consultants may take advantage of this phenomenon. Researchers have also found that when people experience positive emotions after viewing ads, this can also increase intellectual curiosity, increasing their interest in searching for additional information (Hasford, Hardesty, & Kidwell, 2015).

Propagandists have long recognized the value of feelings as information. During the Cold War, as concerns about nuclear war intensified, experts in civil defense recognized the need to manage the emotions of the American public (who were thought to be prone to panic). In helping people "learn to live with the bomb," emotions were understood not as merely private and individual experiences. They were seen as cultural practices that could be shaped and transformed through stories, practical advice, and emotional support (Oakes, 1995). By persuading people that self-protection was possible through the use of fictional stories of people surviving a nuclear blast, feelings of panic were transformed. As a result, a large number of Americans came to accept the belief that the unpredictable dangers of nuclear war could be overcome through knowledge and preparation.

Many educators are well aware of the links between feeling, thinking and social consensus. After all, the relationship between learning, emotion, and the body is interwoven with the notion of learning itself. Emotions are vital to managing social interactions and social relationships. As Lev Vygotsky pointed nearly 100 years ago, human social and cultural functioning is the foundation for much of human reasoning. As researchers explain it, "Without adequate access to emotional, social, and moral feedback, in effect the important elements of culture, learning cannot inform real-world functioning as effectively" (Immordino-Yang & Damasio, 2007, p. 2).

In a sense, we only really think deeply about the things we care about emotionally. Good teachers leverage emotions in the classroom to produce deep understanding and help real-world skills transfer from the classroom to the culture. For example, history teachers may use powerful visual images of injustice, like pictures of lynchings, to activate strong feelings that help students remember historical ideas (Berry, Schmied, & Schrock, 2008). Science teachers may activate fear when they explain how millions of tons of carbon are released into the atmosphere every day by power plants and factories alone (Climate Reality Project, 2019). But managing emotion in the classroom can sometimes require significant effort. English teachers may choose to not to use a particular work of canonical literature in the classroom if teaching that text causes them too much emotional pain (Nguyen,

2018). Because people learn through experience how to make sense of their emotional reactions, emotion-laden interpretations and inferences that occur in schools form a central dimension of how we learn (Cavanagh, 2016).

People choose some products over others as a result of experiencing short bursts of feeling from exposure to the hundreds of advertising messages they receive in a single day. Most advertising is devoted to cultivating brand preferences based largely on the creation of associations between products and feelings. By linking products to feelings, advertising "manages to make the brand part of your identity," creating a "product cult, whose loyalists cannot be influenced by mere information" (Wu, 2016, p. 79). The reason why McDonald's spends so much money to advertise their products is that they want to be always "top of mind" for their target audiences. This phenomenon is called affect transfer, and it is rooted in the understanding that people make decisions using information gleaned from a network of short-term memories (Pinkleton, Austin, & Fujioka, 2001).

The study of propaganda gives educators a chance to talk with students about the interplay between feeling and thinking, social relationships and civic action. Feelings are important: They activate perceptions and beliefs that are then integrated into a person's overall understanding of self, others, and the world. As Pham (2004, p. 368) points out, "Intelligent decisionmakers need the ability to interpret their feelings." Understanding feelings as a type of information can actually help learners understand themselves in the social contexts of their lives. As they explore power of propaganda, an increase in emotional awareness may also help in making better life decisions.

LEARNING ACTIVITY

How Propaganda Activates Emotions

Analyze how propaganda activates a wide range of emotions in an attempt to influence public opinion.

Activity: Select one example of propaganda from the Mind Over Media website (www.mindovermedia.gallery) that activates strong emotion. On the website, rate the example and then read the comments of other people who may have interpreted it. Then use the Internet and library research to learn more about the example you have selected. Develop your analysis by considering some critical questions:

- ***Reality Check:*** What is accurate and inaccurate about the content of a media message?
- ***Private Gain or Public Good:*** Consider who is benefitting financially (or in other ways) from the distribution of this media message.
- ***What's Left Out?*** Noticing omitted information helps to identify the point of view of a media message.
- ***Values Check:*** How does this media message align with or contradict your own values?
- ***Read Between the Lines:*** What ideas are implied but not stated directly in the media message?
- ***Stereotype Alert:*** Consider the ways that stereotypes are used to influence your emotions.
- ***Solutions Too Easy:*** How does the media message attract your attention by simplifying ideas?
- ***Record/Save for Later:*** Decide upon the overall worth and value of the message.

Create to Learn: Reflect on the power of emotions to influence people's attitudes and behavior. To share your ideas, you may want to compose a blog post or create a short video using a free online platform or a video editing tool of your choice.

The Takeaway: Critically analyzing propaganda that activates strong emotions can increase emotional awareness and cultivate intellectual curiosity.

Exploring Art and Activism as Pedagogy

The aesthetic qualities of media and their function as culture are linked to the process of social struggle, according to some critics and scholars who see media and technologies as instruments of both creative expression and political activism (Kellner, 1991). Activists have long used art to address social and political issues including taxation, sweatshops, wage inequality, and corporate welfare (Harold, 2007). Culture jamming is a form of media activism that emphasizes the intentional distortion of advertising messages as a way to highlight its function as propaganda. For example, in 2002, an activist worked with colleagues to create the Billionaires for Bush campaign, splicing together a donkey and elephant to create a logo and using Photoshop to morph photos of George W. Bush and Al Gore into a single image. As part of their fake campaign, they developed slogans like the following:

- Free the Forbes 400;
- Corporations are people too;
- We're paying for America's free elections so you don't have to;
- We don't care whom you vote for, we've already bought them.

As a form of social critique, this form of culture jamming was highly effective. They even created bumper stickers, buttons, a series of posters, and a website. They developed mock radio ads which they sent to radio stations across the country (Boyd, 2016). Through memes and memorable graphics, the activists created a interest group around the theme of reclaiming America from the uber-wealthy.

To explore the connections between art and activism, Michael Kirby, an art educator at Lanier Middle School in Houston, Texas, gave each of his students a small piece of paper with an individual message. Phrases included such examples as "No cell phone," "Road construction ahead," and "Hunting prohibited." Without revealing which message had been received, students were told to design a sign or logo to communicate the words they had been assigned. After all the images were displayed, students interpreted the images, noticing whether or not the signs they designed communicated the intended message to classmates. The activity helped students learn that a logo should clearly communicate its meaning to target audiences who may have different cultural backgrounds and life experiences. In another activity, students tried to guess the name of a company based only on hearing its slogan. The teacher used both recent and older slogans from to help students understand how companies construct a public image. The teacher was surprised that students had no trouble correctly linking a slogan to its company, even including slogans that were circulated way back in the 1990s.

Practices like détournement can also be used to alter our perception and interpretation of the everyday cultural environment, helping to see media messages with fresh eyes. Essentially, the idea goes like this: to understand how a text works, you must change it, alter it, or play around with it. Artists and educators can inspire people to offer a critical commentary on propaganda to discover or unveil its overt or hidden agenda (Harold, 2007). In one project, students identified a social issue like global warming or rising levels of obesity, and then remixed a logo and slogan using image manipulation software. Students were able to explore the consequences of corporate behavior while gaining knowledge about graphic design principles used in propaganda (Chung & Kirby, 2009).

Reading and writing practices can also benefit from activities that help people become less susceptible to manipulation by acquiring a critical disposition "that is cognizant of the possible worlds that are created through textual manipulations" (Teo, 2014, p. 542). For example, when academically high-achieving students in Singapore participated in a reading and writing program that was designed to raise their critical awareness of ideological meanings, they first watched a series of ads and YouTube videos and looked at various websites. They then discussed questions like these:

- **Who** is the target reader of the text? How can you tell?
- **Whose** perspective is the text written from?
- **Whose** voice or perspective is represented in the text and whose is not? How do you know?
- **What** do you think the text is trying to make target readers think or believe?
- **Who** benefits from such texts and who does not?

Then students were asked to select one of the texts and rewrite it in order to lay bare its inherent stereotypes and assumptions. After these projects were reviewed and discussed, students wrote reflective essays, where these prompts were provided:

- **What** have you learned about the role that words and images play in shaping or framing our expectations and interpretations of the meaning in texts?
- **To what extent** has the way you look at everyday texts changed as a result of this program?
- **Can this** be applied even to the textbooks you use in school? Why or why not? (Teo, 2014)

Exploring propaganda using practices like this can challenge students' unexamined attitudes and beliefs, helping them "understand how power works on them, through them, and for them in the service of constructing and deepening their roles as engaged thinkers and critical citizens" (Giroux, 1996, p. 53). At the university level, scholars and students have used video détournement to illustrate and problematize claims connected to public debates about education, including issues of control by teacher unions, charter schools, and standardized tests. As part of a learning experience, preservice teachers got to create their own video productions, using the presentation of conflicting news sound bites and a series of text slides to present a critical perspective on the challenges of public education in the 21st century (French & Campbell, 2019).

Art has always been linked in one way or the other to the practice of activism and propaganda. When art and activism are combined, they may increase people's receptivity to examining and critiquing society. In delivering an important speech at the annual conference of the National Association for the Advancement of Colored People (NAACP) in 1926, the African American intellectual W. E. B. Du Bois distinguished between beneficial propaganda, where art truthfully portrays African American society, and negative propaganda, which offers harmful and misleading stereotypes (Malloci, 2018). Building upon this theme in a freshman writing course at Wellesley College that was part of a blended learning initiative called Art or Propaganda?, Erin Royston Battat and her students examined political art of the 1930s. Students created digital humanities projects that showcased their research on works from the college's art museum.

Each student chose a work of art to study, researched its historical context and critical reception, and wrote an original essay. For example, in one student project, a lithograph by Prentiss Hottel Taylor titled *Scottsboro Limited* was analyzed. The student showed how the image depicts the Scottsboro Boys as Christlike heroic victims by portraying rays of light shooting out from their bodies and telephone poles as a type of cross (Battat, n.d.). The powerful emotional tone in this art induces feelings of sympathy for the victims, and the title of the work makes it clear the artist is commenting on the infamous legal case of African American teenagers wrongly accused of sexual assault.

Art educators also want students to understand how "art is often the glue that solidifies and unifies people under one cause" (Christenson, 2017, p. 1). Posters, poetry, musical concerts, dramatic performances, photography, and films can all call attention to problems in society that need to be addressed. But students do not merely learn to appreciate the power of art as beneficial propaganda. As students become aware of the vast array of social problems in the world, they can be inspired to make a difference through using the power of art to express both emotions and ideas.

In one lesson on nonprofit logo design, each student was asked to find a cause they feel passionate about. They studied how other artists have explored this topic and created a plan for a nonprofit organization to focus on the issues. They created that organization's name and mission statement and then developed a logo design. When the logos were complete and the mission statement had been written, they presented their work to the class in order to spread awareness. In these sessions, students also experienced the classical art-school critique, because, as Christenson pointed out, "With every activist struggle, there is an opposing force of resistance" (2017, p. 1). Students responded to feedback to try to better understand the thinking of those who disagreed with them.

The Marketplace of Ideas and the Public Sphere

To understand the vital role of propaganda in a democracy, we must understand public opinion, which can be defined as the aggregation of many people's views and interests regarding political issues, leaders, institutions, and current events. Jürgen Habermas coined a related term, the public sphere, in describing how the rise in access to books, newspapers, and journals created the need for spaces for political discussion, which included parliaments, political clubs, literary salons, public assemblies, pubs and coffeehouses, and meeting halls. As people participated in these gathering spaces, public opinion coalesced through consensus and gradually became a new form of political power. Access to opportunities to share information and communicate with others enabled ordinary people to unify their voices and achieve political strength through consensus-building. Propaganda is a vital dimension of this work. Consensus-building accelerated with the Gutenberg revolution because, as historian Paul Starr puts it, "Publications weave invisible threads of connection among their readers," as readers participate in a community that becomes a public that "extends beyond the limits of a local, face-to-face community" (2004, p. 24).

But consensus-building begins long before children learn to read and write. During childhood, opinions about politics first develop in the context of family socialization, where parents have absorbed political preferences from their own families and communities. Religious beliefs may shape political ideologies. Of course, people may also form opinions using self-interest as it intersects with underlying personal values and community norms. But in general, people do not independently form their political beliefs; instead, they look to trusted thought leaders, including parents, friends, co-workers, ministers and community leaders.

Some have even claimed that public opinion is a fiction of sorts, as people form preferences about political issues merely in response to whatever informational choices are offered and available at a particular moment in time. Thus, the ability to manipulate the specific timing of how people get access to information represents "the knowledge of how to create consent" (Lippmann, 1922/1997, p. 1). President Donald Trump understands that belief in lies and disinformation may also have an "advantage over truth when it comes to uniting people" because it signals a profound kind of loyalty that is required for people to stick together in times of crisis (Harari, 2018, p. 244). For these reasons, democratic processes are subject to greater levels of manipulation by those who seek to shape public opinion (Lowi, Ginsberg, Shepsle, & Ansolabehere, 2018).

All governments attempt to manipulate their citizens' beliefs through the use of propaganda. President Trump has repeatedly claimed that the legal investigations being conducted into his abuses of power and potential criminal behavior are a "coup." As we learned earlier, the choice of words is a powerful form of propaganda. A coup denotes a violent, illegal, and sudden overthrow of a government by a political faction, military, or dictator. By using this word, Trump characterized both the Mueller investigation and the congressional impeachment process as an illegal attempt to violently overthrow the government. And because coups are generally defeated through violence, his followers are encouraged "to be outraged at his critics, to literally be filled with anger and rage at them. In stirring this rage, Trump implicitly sanctions violence and retribution against his critics" (Ott, 2019, p. 1).

Political leaders may also use propaganda to project a national image that aligns with specific policy goals. In countries like China and Russia, where politicians can control the media messages that their people receive through censorship, a single message can be repeated over and over. But in Western democracies, such control is impossible. So instead, people face a torrent of information, delivered to their TV sets, newspapers, and social media platforms. Some of it is accurate, important, and of high quality. Some of it is distorted, irrelevant, silly, or just plain wrong. People must sort out the value and quality of particular messages for themselves in the marketplace of ideas.

Critically examining the value of many competing ideas is at the heart of the rationale for democratic self-governance. The marketplace of ideas underpins the First Amendment's emphasis on unregulated freedom of expression, and it also explains why propaganda is plentiful in democratic societies. In Europe, before the rise of printing, censorship was the norm as only a small number of people could afford manuscript books, which were tightly controlled by monarchies and the church. In fighting the corruption of the Catholic Church, Martin Luther questioned the power of the papacy to control ideas about spirituality, which opened a generation up to the value of independent thinking. In the 1600s, increased trade in books as commodities created cross-national distribution networks with better roads and postal systems. Printers aligned themselves to government interests as a matter of survival. But because printed books were regulated and censored by governments, many writers felt they had more freedom by sharing handwritten newsletters with individuals and groups. Over time, newspapers emerged to share information, and some of them acquired independence from the government (Starr, 2004). Soon a veritable flood of printed matter offered competing perspectives on the political issues of the day, and for many, it was a liberating experience. For monarchies and governments, it was a nightmare. They punished activists, authors and publishers whose views did not align with the centers of power in order to restrict the flow of ideas and information.

That's when the idea of government censorship was first attacked in principle by John Milton in an essay titled "Areopagitica." Instead of restricting access to ideas, Milton argued that a work should not be censored by the government. People should be free to examine and refute the ideas only after their publication, not before. He believed that "being learned" involved reading books of all sorts, even including books with false ideas. Milton argued that since every person has reason, free will, and conscience, they have the capacity to judge ideas for themselves. Milton believed that the mind is not corrupted simply by encountering falsehood. He claimed that when faced with the widest range of ideas, people will choose true ideas over false ones. As the power of this idea developed during the Enlightenment, the Western world experienced enormous optimism about the potential of widespread access to ideas and information. Eventually, social pressure grew to enable widespread support for literacy, libraries, schooling and formal education for all.

But after reading about the dark power of propaganda in Chapter 5, you may question whether the marketplace of ideas theory still holds. The 20th century has amply shown us that people are not nearly so rational as the Enlightenment thinkers assumed. Just as in an actual marketplace, products that are cheap and fast are considered good. We are particularly vulnerable to messages that activate emotion, simplify information, attack opponents, or appeal to our deepest hopes, fears, and dreams. The marketplace of ideas is flooded with pleasant and unquestioned falsehoods that people prefer over complex and difficult truths. Because people are socialized by their families into a class-based cultural and economic environment, our beliefs and values are constructed through various forms of groupthink and social pressure. The quality of content in the marketplace of ideas is inevitably shaped by the formation of communities that coalesce around shared values, where the need to belong dominates. For these reasons, truths that contradict conventional wisdom may not gain much traction among the public (Wonnell, 1985).

Autocrats and dictators recognize the limitations of democratic institutions that require people to be engaged and active participants. Too many choices in the marketplace can be exhausting. For people who are disillusioned with the burdens, responsibilities, and limitations of making choices in a crowded marketplace, follow-the-leader is an alternative strategy for forming personal opinions. By asking people to follow the leader, politicians essentially simplify the need for independent decision-making by activating positive feelings of respect for authority, loyalty, and self-sacrifice. When political power is condensed into one authority figure, some people find this more orderly and comforting than the chaos of deliberative dialogue and consensus in the wide-open marketplace of ideas (Mometrix Academy, 2018).

Authoritarianism and totalitarianism are systems of government that explicitly reject the premise of the marketplace of ideas. People continue to debate the conditions under which autocratic leadership may flourish. Some claim that it has been fueled by systematic efforts to spread disinformation that impairs the process of consensus formation. Others say that it is merely a reaction to the ineffectiveness of democratic pluralism when it comes to economic growth (Dasandi & Taylor, 2018). Some note that Asian countries including Singapore and South Korea achieved exceptionally high rates of economic development under authoritarian leadership where speech and expression are far more limited than in the United States. In developing countries where violence has occurred as part of the democratic political process, autocratic leadership may actually seem more stable and traditional than the rough-and-tumble process of democracy. For these reasons, it is easy to see how countries like China and Russia might stand to benefit from declining levels of global public trust in the marketplace of ideas.

Election Propaganda

The term of art for election propaganda is spin, which encompasses all the forms of political communication, including publicity, news management, public address, and even "bullshit." While some people use the term to refer to damage control or lying, in general, the term spin is more neutral: it is a bias or slant on information, intended to create a favorable impression or to control the interpretation of information. The term emerged during the Reagan years, in the presidential debates of 1984 and 1988, when political campaign aides began to regularly use the term to describe their work in providing commentary on the candidates' performance after the debates (Greenberg, 2016).

Most of what Americans know about the process of election campaigns comes from fiction films or behind-the-scenes documentaries about the political communication process. Many high school civics teachers use *Wag the Dog*, the 1997 film satire directed by Barry Levinson (and based on a novel by Larry Beinhart) that explores the relationship between media and politics (Rock, n.d.). In the film, after a president gets caught up in a scandal, his spin doctor fabricates a war and creates all kinds of other distractions to help win reelection. Students generally enjoy the likable characters and the absurdity of the plot, and teachers use the film to discuss issues like the role of the president's press secretary, the trustworthiness of television news, and how wars and conflict unite the citizenry. Many educators believe that using film in the classroom helps make abstract political concepts more concrete and relatable (Goble & Goble, 2016).

History and civics teachers may devote some time to the study of political advertising. In the early 1990s, many teachers videotaped local political ads off the air on VHS tapes at home, which they would bring into class, where students would complete a worksheet as they viewed each ad. In one resource published by the Organization of American Historians, a worksheet asked students to view a TV ad and then name the politician, the political party he or she was affiliated with, the office he or she was running for, and the reasons given in the ad to vote for the candidate, or the reasons given to vote against an opponent (Burson, 1992). Filling out such worksheets certainly builds students' familiarity with the names and positions of various politicians. But watching a set of political TV ads from past elections and getting a mini-lecture from the teacher on the particular controversies of each election does not build critical thinking skills.

Still, in studying election propaganda in the history classroom, this type of worksheet view-and-chart type activity seems to be a long-standing instructional practice. In a lesson plan from *The New York Times* Learning Network, students view political ads selected by the teacher (Schulten & Gonchar, 2016). After viewing, students respond to questions like this:

- What do you see in the commercial? Describe images or text.
- What do you hear in the commercial? Describe voices, music, background sound effects.
- What do you think the commercial producers want you to feel or think? What makes you say this?
- Do you think the ad is effective? Why or why not?

These questions encourage students to look carefully at exactly how the message has been constructed. By slowing down the process of interpretation through close analysis, such activities create space for reasoning and reflection. Such questions invite an examination of the political nature of representation, "looking at what is included and excluded, and at how these things are put together, in order to make claims about the world" (Buckingham, 2019, p. 1).

Another common strategy for teaching about media and politics involves the historical analysis of political campaigns of the past and the identification of classical rhetorical techniques (Iyengar, 2016). For example, students might be asked to look at examples of political ads and identify examples of cherry-picking, when candidates selectively present facts and quotes that support a certain position; the nondenial denial, when a seemingly straightforward denial is not really a denial; or burying the story, releasing unfavorable news at a time when it is believed that the media will focus on other news (Ronald Reagan Presidential Foundation, 2016).

Today, new tools are available to help students learn to critically analyze political campaign advertising. The Facebook Ad Library enables people around the world to see the actual ads that politicians use to target potential voters. Students can see how particular messages are crafted for younger and older voters, for example. They can see how political messages change over the course of a particular campaign and can track how much candidates spend on Facebook advertising. This database enables educators to incorporate inquiry learning and data literacy competencies into the study of political propaganda.

Then there's the Political TV Archive, a searchable, viewable, and shareable online archive of political TV ads. Users can see where and when a particular ad aired and see evidence from fact-checkers about the informational content of individual ads. Because the website includes data about when, where, and how many times political ads aired on TV in key markets, the project was useful to reporters during the 2016 election to analyze how campaigns and outside groups were targeting messages to voters in different locations. The website collected nearly 3,000 ads from the 2016 election and also tracked instances when candidate debate sound bites appeared in TV news shows (Donnelly, 2016).

Kristina Frank, a social studies teacher at Eagle Ridge Middle School, asks students to analyze four political campaign commercials in order to understand the role of political parties in the election process. As students watch political ads from two different time periods, they put themselves in the position of the campaign staff member. Then they analyze the ads from the perspective of a voter. Finally, students create their own campaign commercials for an upcoming presidential election (Frank, 2012). To create memorable political propaganda, political consultants point out that it has to grab and hold people's attention—and be something that people want to talk about (*PBS News Hour*, 2016). As election propaganda becomes even more algorithmically personalized learners how the data we supply through platforms like Google and Facebook is shaping political messages we receive online.

LEARNING ACTIVITY

Exploring Movies About American Elections

Through entertainment, popular films depict the use of propaganda as part of the election process and offer divergent ideologies about self-governance and the public good.

Activity: Students select a fiction or non-fiction movie from a list of choices below and they watch it at home. Then they write a review summarizing the movie, explaining how it relates to civic concepts and ideas explored in class and discussing these films with their peers.

Write a Review: In the review, students (a) explain what they liked or disliked about the film, and (b) describe what they learned about politics and media from viewing. Then they (c) generate three questions that they found themselves wondering about while viewing. Students also (d) make a recommendation about whether or other students in the class should see it. Finally, students share their reviews with peers in small jigsaw-style groups and discuss common themes found in all films about American elections.

Dramas and Comedies:

- ***The Campaign.*** Directed by Jay Roach, this 2012 satire uses every political stereotype available to tell the story of two politicians from North Carolina as their campaigns progress to election day.
- ***Milk.*** Directed by Gus Van Sant, this 2008 drama examines the life and political career of Harvey Milk, California's first openly gay politician to be elected to public office.
- ***Recount.*** This 2008 television film from HBO explores the history of the 2000 Bush v Gore Presidential election and stars Kevin Spacey and Laura Dern.
- ***The Contender.*** Directed by Rod Lurie, this 2000 political drama tells the story of a president who nominates a woman to be a replacement vice president and the dirty tricks and backroom deals that result.

- ***Election.*** Directed by Alexander Payne, this 1999 farce gives a disturbing but hilarious look at the democratic process at work in a high school government election as a teacher sabotages a student who is running for student body president.
- ***Bulworth.*** Directed by Warren Beatty, this 1998 comedy features a politician who gets fed up with the campaign process and starts to tell the truth.

Documentaries:

- ***Caucus.*** Directed by A. J. Schnack, this 2013 documentary captures the modern political process through the experiences of eight Republicans who participated in the Iowa Caucus.
- ***Street Fight.*** Directed by Marshall Curry, this 2005 documentary follows Cory Booker's efforts to fight political corruption in his campaign to become mayor of Newark, New Jersey.
- ***Dark Money.*** Directed by Kimberly Reed, this 2018 documentary examines the consequences of the 2010 Citizens United Supreme Court ruling on the people of Montana, showing how political campaign financing negatively impacts people's actual lives.

The Takeaway: Fiction and nonfiction films about the U.S. political campaign process embed divergent ideologies about the practice of democracy and the role of propaganda as a means to influence public opinion.

Fact-Checking the Elections and Beyond

Fact-checking has been hailed as one of the most important tools to reign in the power of political propaganda, and such efforts are especially important at election time. Indeed, if we look at the history of political fact-checking, it was clearly conceptualized as a form of media literacy for the general public. When Kathleen Hall Jamieson, a communications scholar at the University of Pennsylvania, first began a process of fact-checking political campaign advertising in 2004, she offered information about the claims and evidence used in political advertising along with a rhetorical analysis of the strategy used to persuade.

Such efforts to deconstruct and analyze the rhetoric of political campaign advertising helped Americans understand how politicians tapped into the deepest hopes, fears, and dreams of American voters at a time when the political campaign process was changing. Kathleen Hall Jamieson regularly appeared on the PBS TV show *Bill Moyers Journal* to deconstruct political ads, offering media literacy education to the general public. In one episode, Jamieson analyzed the political campaign ad that served as the biographical introduction to Barack Obama, who was previously unknown to the public (Moyers, 2008).

Fact-checking can support the practice of media literacy for both students and the larger public. In 2007, Jamieson's book with Brooks Jackson, *UnSpun: Finding Facts in a World of Disinformation*, offered easy-to-remember advice to readers on how to protect themselves from election propaganda, including "If it's scary, be wary" and "Beware the blame game." They saw fact-checking as an antidote to the problem of spin. Their organization, FactCheck, has been active for 15 years, with a strong focus on presidential candidates in presidential election years and on top Senate races in midterm elections. They review transcripts of the Sunday talk shows on the major networks and cable stations, TV ads for all federal elections as well as remarks given by the president, including every speech and press conference. When they find a statement that may be inaccurate or misleading, they reach out to the person or organization that is being fact-checked, asking the person or organization making the claim to provide evidence to support it. If the material does not support the claim or if no evidence is provided, they conduct research on their own, using primary sources of information from government and nonpartisan groups.

This approach to fact-checking helps to reduce the level of deception and confusion in U.S. politics, of course. But the selection of which facts to check can itself introduce a form of bias. As Bill Adair of PolitiFact explains, fact-checkers cannot possibly check all claims. Researchers compared how three fact-checking organizations covered topics including climate change, racism, and national debt. They found that PolitiFact published 16 checks relating to the influence of racism during the two-year period of the study while Fact Checker and FactCheck published none. On the topic of the national debt, PolitiFact devoted 89% of its checks to assertions that the debt is problematic, while Fact Checker devoted 63% of its checks to assertions that the debt is not problematic. Thus, the decisions that fact-checkers make about what to evaluate "provide implicit information to citizens about what is important and what is suspicious" (Marietta, Barker, & Bowser, 2015, p. 587).

Today, more than 50 organizations around the world provide fact-checking of news and political communication, including organizations that range from the Associated Press, to Snopes. These organizations use a variety of rating features to make information accessible to audiences, but these techniques may introduce another form of bias. For example, PolitiFact uses its Truth-O-Meter to designate levels of accuracy in a factual statement, ranging from true to mostly true, half true, mostly false, and false. They reserve the category of "pants on fire" for the most ridiculously false statements. The *Washington Post* uses a different metaphor, giving statements one to four Pinocchios depending upon the degree of inaccuracy.

Researchers who study the reliability of fact-checking of presidential campaign ads have found general consistency between the three leading organizations (Amazeen, 2015). When there are disagreements, they tend to center on judgments about how much context is needed to interpret a claim. For example, FactCheck and the *Washington Post*'s Fact Checker disagreed on a statement from a Romney ad called "Dear Daughter," which included the claim, "The poverty rate for women—the highest in 17 years." FactCheck indicated that the poverty statistics for women stated in the ad were cited correctly, but Fact Checker indicated that the numbers deserved some context and offered evidence that the high rate of female poverty was not unique to the Obama administration (Amazeen, 2015, p. 14). As a result of differences in interpretation that are inherent to the fact-checking process, some have claimed that the fact-checkers themselves can be partisan (Uscinski & Butler, 2013).

Politicians have exploited the appeal of fact-checking for propaganda purposes. When the UK Conservative Party changed their Twitter account to make it look like a real fact-checking site during the election debate between Conservative Prime Minister Boris Johnson and Labour Party leader Jeremy Corbyn, they used the name FactCheckUK along with a logo quite similar to those used by fact-checkers worldwide. But the tweets were political spin, pure and simple. They were an intentional effort to mislead people. Around the world, politicians have sometimes claimed to be fact-checkers. Senator Elizabeth Warren created Fact Squad as part of her campaign for president. Even the Mexican government has launched its own fact-checking operation (Tardaguila, Funke, & Benkelman, 2019).

The most challenging question for fact-checkers is whether their work makes a difference in the minds of voters. Because of confirmation bias, people tend to selectively recall fact-checks that align with their preexisting ideological beliefs. As it turns out, the major impact of fact-checking is that it can influence politicians themselves, who fear reputational damage. The threat of fact-checking serves as a deterrent. In one experiment, researchers sent some legislators reminders that they are vulnerable to fact-checking while others were not contacted. Those who did not get the reminder were more likely to receive a negative PolitiFact rating or have the accuracy of their statements questioned publicly as compared with legislators who got the reminder (Nyhan & Reifler, 2015). The greatest value of fact-checking may be in keeping politicians honest.

Media, Money, and Politics

Facts certainly matter when it comes to understanding the role of money in the political process. Experts predict that in the 2020 election, political media spending will far exceed $6 billion. Nearly half of the expected funds will be spent on the presidential election (Advertising Analytics and Cross Screen Media, 2020). The 2020 presidential election is particularly noteworthy for the truly staggering level of spending by Michael Bloomberg, who spent more than $230 million on online and TV advertising in the first few months of 2020 (Schaul, Uhrmacher, & Narayanswamy, 2020). In June 2020, Joe Biden and Donald Trump set an all-time record for political campaign fundraising, gaining more than $270 million for their presidential campaigns in just one month (Goldmacher, 2020).

Why do politicians spend so much? Compared to other democratic countries, American elections are far longer and costlier. In many countries around the world, governments place strict limits on spending. In Great Britain, for instance, TV ads are banned, and political parties can spend no more than $29.5 million in the year before the election. In Canada, each political candidate for the country's Parliament spent under $100,000 during the 2015 election (Ingraham, 2017).

TV and digital propaganda make American political campaigns expensive. Of course, connecting with voters involves spending time and money. At a minimum, a political candidate needs to set up and run a website and hold rallies or appear at events that the media will cover. Although volunteers can be valuable for many tasks, staffers are needed to coordinate them. But the big money is needed to create and place political advertising on television, the Internet, and social media. Emotionally compelling and visible propaganda can make a difference in the political campaign process. The effectiveness of these messages can help define the candidate's priorities, connect to voters' values and needs, and attack opponents.

Giving money to a political campaign is a form of political expression that is protected by the First Amendment. When the Supreme Court ruled in 2010 in a case called *Citizens United v. Federal Election Commission,* they had a chance to limit the role of money in politics. But instead, the Supreme Court claimed that big campaign contributions are a form of political speech protected by the First Amendment. The high court also protected corporations (and labor unions) with the same rights as individuals under the law. This case empowered wealthy individuals, businesses, and other groups to use money to influence elections with more freedom than they had before. Most experts believe that this legal decision has dramatically increased the level of political corruption in the United States, where wealthy people give money to politicians in exchange for political favors of all kinds. Plus, access to unlimited campaign funds for negative advertising contributes to public cynicism about politics, since Super PACs do not have to take responsibility for what they say (Edsall, 2018).

It's a timeless issue that the critic George Seldes warned about long ago. In a book about recognizing propaganda, he urged readers to always look for the economic interest behind political communication. He pointed out, "If you look for the social-economic motive you will not have to wait for history to tell you what was propaganda and what was truth" (Seldes, 1942, p. 71). The role of money in influencing public opinion is not confined to politics and elections, of course. It would be wise for educators to make sure that all learners get a chance to explore the economics of propaganda as they consider Seldes's sage advice.

LEARNING ACTIVITY

The Economics of Political Campaigns

No other country on earth spends as much money on political campaigning as the United States. Every American needs to understand how campaign finance laws ensure that expensive propaganda is a ubiquitous part of the election process.

Activity: Watch the Crash Course video titled Political Campaign Basics for an overview of campaign finance law. Then select one of the following key terms or court cases to research further:

Federal Election Campaign Act
McCain-Feingold Act
Buckley v. Valeo
Citizens United v. FEC
Super PACs
Soft money
527 organization
Van Hollen v. FEC
McCutcheon v. FEC
American Tradition Partnership, Inc. v. Bullock

Search and Learn: Use keyword search to identify one or two useful sources about one of these terms or court cases. Working under deadline pressure, write down three to five bullet points of key information, explaining ideas in your own words.

For Discussion: In a group discussion, use what you learned as you consider these questions:

- ***How*** is giving money to political campaigns related to freedom of speech?
- ***Who*** does campaign financing benefit? Why? Who is harmed? Why?
- ***Why*** would a corporation be motivated to spend large sums of money to support a certain candidate?
- ***What*** are some benefits and risks associated with this practice?
- ***How*** do legal challenges to campaign finance affect the political process?

The Takeaway: Campaign finance regulation is the major way that the American public can control how money and interest groups influence the political process.

–Adapted from *PBS NewsHour* (2016) Lesson Plans

Polling as Propaganda

Throughout this chapter, it's become obvious that public opinion is an essential factor in the political process and that propaganda is the mechanism by which public opinion is shaped. In the United States, the horse race tradition offers a near-continuous stream of public opinion data to inform people who's ahead and who's behind in a political campaign. Because the mass media carry out polls constantly throughout the election process, there is often far more news coverage on who's ahead and who's behind than on the issues, policies, and political agendas of the candidates themselves. As a result, voters learn little about a candidate's policy goals, qualifications, or knowledge (E. Johnson, 2019).

Many people tend to think about opinion polling as merely a way to measure public opinion, but this is only part of the story. Polls do not just measure public opinion: They also help to construct it. When we answer questions, we figure out what we think about a particular topic. Many times, the very act of responding to a quiz or poll makes implicit beliefs and attitudes become explicit. It's one of the reasons why quizzes and polls are so popular online. Taking a quiz helps people clarify their opinions and preferences.

Propaganda enters into public opinion polling with the practice known as push polling. You may have been a victim of a push poll if you have received a phone call that starts off sounding like a neutral opinion survey, but then the interviewer starts to provide negative information about a particular candidate. They are called push polls because "the objective is not to find out what you think, it's to signal what you ought to think" (Funt, 2018, p. 1). In one vivid case that occurred in 2016, Nolan Dalla described a phone call he received where, suddenly, the interviewer started offering hypothetical information about Bernie Sanders, saying, "What if I were to tell you the Washington Post said that Bernie Sanders' campaign promises would cost more than $20 trillion and would raise everyone's taxes—would you now be 'more likely' or 'less likely' to vote for Sanders, or has your opinion remained unchanged?" (Dalla, 2016, p. 1). Push polls are a little-known form of election propaganda. Candidates use them to test ideas to see what information might cause voters to change their minds about a candidate. These types of polls attempt to persuade people by suggesting opinions to them, in the guise of questions. From this, they can learn which ideas and information will be most likely to change people's attitudes. Push polls may even explore how rumors and falsehoods can influence people's attitudes. For this reason, they are usually done by phone (not online), since this makes them harder to trace. Not surprisingly, some research has shown that political consultants have mixed opinions about the ethics of push polls, with only one in four considering push polls ethical (Nelson, Dulio, & Medvic, 2002).

Since his election, President Trump has actively used push polls to encourage the American public to be suspicious of journalism. As news about Russian interference in the election was revealed and as an increasing number of Trump associates were found guilty of financial fraud and other crimes, Trump sought to sour the American public on those responsible for reporting the news. In July 2018, Donald Trump and the Republican National Committee began running a survey, called the Media Accountability Survey, by asking these questions:

- **Do you believe** that the media purposely tries to divide Republicans in order to help elect Democrats?
- **Do you believe** that the media has been too quick to spread false stories about our movement?
- **Do you believe** the media disdains conservatives?
- **Do you believe** the media dislikes Americans of faith?

Loaded questions like these are written in a way that embeds a point of view in the question. These questions encourage the respondent to give an answer that may not accurately reflect his or her opinion. Such questions seek to shape opinions rather than merely gather them. The opening letter, signed by Donald Trump, even asked, "Why is the mainstream media's opinion any more important than yours?" In urging supporters to take the survey, Trump left no doubt about the goal: "To show the media that the American people are fed up with the Fake News Machine" (Funt, 2018).

Push polls are a form of propaganda that spreads negative information about political opponents as a means to influence public opinion. For this reason, they are sometimes used in local elections, too. In some states, when a political campaign makes public reference to a poll it has conducted or commissioned, it is obligated to provide details of the poll questions. In upstate New York, a push poll was meant to spread some unflattering ideas about a politician as a way to influence the election results. Starting with the question, "If the election were held today, who would you vote for?" voters were then asked if their position would change if they knew the politician had (a) raised taxes, (b) not spent money on road repairs, or (c) hired a rapist for a key position in the local county administration (G. Kelly, 2019). Regardless of the truth or falsity of the items, such a question would be highly likely to activate the local mutter brigade, spreading gossip and rumor in ways that could directly damage a candidate's chance of getting elected.

LEARNING ACTIVITY

Create a Public Opinion Poll

Public opinion polls do more than measure public opinion. They may also serve as a form of propaganda by subtly influencing people's views on matters of public concern.

Activity: In this civic action project, students create, analyze, and share data about the opinions of people in their school or community.

Steps in the Process: First, decide what sample of people you will gather data from. Will you focus on family members, students, teachers, or people in the community? Decide what general topics of interest you want to measure. Will you explore people's attitudes about the coming election? Will you assess people's attitudes about systemic racism, climate change, the economy, the cost of higher education, or other issues?

In the classroom, whole-class collaboration is an ideal way to develop a polling project. Students work in teams or groups to design, create, distribute, and analyze opinion data. This way, the work can be spread out over a period of time. The groups proceed in sequential order:

- ***Design group:*** The task of this group is to create and share a list of proposed questions of different types (multiple choice, scaled, or open-ended responses). The design group gets feedback from the whole class before selecting the 10 most important questions.

- ***Creation group:*** This team searches for free online survey tools to produce an online survey. They pilot test the online survey with the class and accept feedback to improve their work.
- ***Sampling group:*** This team figures out how to reach the target audience. They may create posters with QR codes, meet with teachers to have the survey distributed in classes, or organize to get the link sent out to a community sample of respondents. They must ensure that they receive at least 100 responses.
- ***Analysis group:*** This team starts work after the surveys have been completed. They review the evidence and develop charts and graphs to report the results of the survey, making an oral presentation, infographic, or video to share the findings.

Share and Discuss: After the data is presented, it's time for discussion and debriefing. This is the most important part of the learning activity. Discuss some of the questions below:

- **What** was the most predictable finding from the survey results? The most surprising evidence?
- **Which** question was the most difficult to answer and why?
- **How** did the format of the questions shape the responses received?
- **Were there any** loaded questions in this survey? Loaded questions are written in a way that forces the respondent into an answer that doesn't accurately reflect his or her opinion.
- **What** were the strengths of this survey? What were the weaknesses or limitations?
- **Which** questions might have been interpreted in different ways by some participants?
- **How** might the survey findings be useful? Who might value this information?
- **Could** any of the survey results be used as a form of propaganda?

- **What** future actions could be taken as a result of the information gained?
- **How** confident are you that these findings are reliable (i.e., that the evidence would be the same even if a larger group of people were surveyed)?

The Takeaway: Surveys and polls involve human choice, judgment, and reasoning. The information that results from surveys and polls is a selective and incomplete representation of people's beliefs and attitudes.

–Adapted from *Growing Voters* by Jo-Anne Hart (2016)

Social Media, Civic Action, and Agency

Media literacy education supports civic engagement and fosters respect for democratic political practices, which is one of the reasons why it is growing in visibility all around the world. After the series of rebellions and uprisings across the Islamic world inspired by the 2011 protests in Tunisia, people were very hopeful about the potential power of networked social movements as a form of citizen action. The term hashtag activism was used to describe how people were using the Internet and social media to identify shared interests. Hashtags have been used to advance numerous social movements, including Black Lives Matter, Occupy Wall Street, Me Too, and Time to Impeach.

As a result of digital activism, anyone can join political dialogues. Symbolic actions online can be a powerful way to influence the people you interact with, depending on the context. For example, when some Facebook users protested discrimination against gay people by changing their profile image, they signaled their political beliefs to the people in their social networks (Tufecki, 2017). Today, personal and collective actions intersect to help change social norms that ultimately change law and policy (Bennett & Segerberg, 2016). Activist propaganda can help to shift social norms through increasing consensus. Stimulating strong emotions, simplifying information, responding to audience values, and critiquing opponents are essential elements of the activist's playbook.

To understand the rise of social media propaganda in the context of 21st-century democracies, some trends are worth pointing out. People today tend to merely scan the media for a small subset of issues of greatest concern to them. No one has the time to stay current on all the political, social, and economic issues. Increasingly, political participation occurs in online communities where people signal their affiliations on one or two topics of special interest using liking and sharing of social media posts. People are selective in the issues that matter most to them. In deciding whether to take any form of political action, people calculate the intensity of their feelings, the likelihood of the action having an impact, and the potential benefit of the action to society (Zuckerman, 2016). People who are exposed to online propaganda on a topic of interest to them may participate in forms of civic action (like emailing a member of Congress or participating in a peaceful protest) if it's not unduly burdensome.

Propagandists can also use digital advertising techniques to specifically tailor political messages to particular individuals (Katz, 2019). Online political microtargeting involves creating carefully crafted messages targeted at narrow categories of voters based on tracking and collecting evidence of people's online behavior. Microtargeting lets politicians match a particular policy issue to the interests of the targeted voter. Naturally, college students might receive different messages than families with young children or older people retired from the workforce. Getting geographically personalized attention online can feel flattering, and the personalization of messaging also helps connect with the voters' emotions on social or political issues.

Personalization can also take the form of personal attacks on social media users who express their political opinions on Facebook, Instagram, or Twitter. Microtargeting is inherently manipulative when it is used to suppress voter turnout, as it was in 2016 when the Trump campaign targeted African American voters with anti-Clinton ads. Because only those who are targeted see such posts, they are called dark posts. When a political party highlights different issues for each voter, this can lead to a lack of transparency about a politician's position on a variety of policy issues (Zuiderveen Borgesius et al., 2018).

Attacks can be used to divide and conquer groups of like-minded people. When people experience harassment and abuse on social media, they can be intimidated and silenced. The many complications of politics can overwhelm people, leading them to see political elections largely as a spectator sport, to be watched rather than played. Interest-based political action can be even more difficult for ordinary people to understand, as stakeholders seek to change society through legal actions and court rulings in state or federal court. For these reasons, efforts to teach about social media and civic engagement are often centered around thinking in new ways about the concept of agency. When people feel a sense of agency, they are willing to take risks in pursuit of their goals. Formal and informal learning activities both contribute to political socialization, helping young people "to recognize personal, corporate and political agendas" and be "empowered to speak out on behalf of the missing voices and omitted perspectives in our communities" (Hobbs, 2010, p. 17).

Teachers can facilitate creative learning processes where, using social media, students can discover their civic voice. One example of this is the work of Paul Mihailidis and his colleagues at the Salzburg Academy on Media and Global Change. Working in collaboration with undergraduate students and faculty from many countries, they have been exploring how to use social media, multimedia storytelling, and cross-national research that positions teaching and learning about media as an act of civic engagement. In the summer program, which is located at the grand Austrian baronial manor where *The Sound of Music* was filmed, students begin by reflecting on their personal identity and gradually move from "me" stories to "we" stories as they examine causes and issues that matter to them. When students begin the learning experience, they "often do not appreciate the potential power of their own thoughts and words" (Mihailidis & Gerodimos, 2016, p. 384). Discovering how to use the power of emotion and symbolic expression can be powerful and life changing for young citizens.

Such work has never been more important. Walter Lippmann, a critic and public intellectual of the early 20th century, was convinced that education was the best long-term, authentic solution to the role of propaganda in democratic societies. In the final pages of his book, *Public Opinion*, written in 1922, he urged educators to prepare students for dealing fully with the contemporary world in which they live, by "teaching the pupil the habit of examining the sources" of information and developing "a habit of introspection about the imagery evoked by printed words." The educator can help students see their own culpability in the dissemination of propaganda, learning to recognize "the enormous mischief and casual cruelty of our prejudices" (Lippmann, 1922/1997, p. 256). These important ideas are at the heart of the practice of media literacy education.

Teaching About Election Propaganda

When it comes to civic education, we naturally expect there to be reasonable disagreement among people with diverse points of view. As Robert Kunzman (2018, p. 4) points out, "Helping students recognize reasonable disagreement is a key step toward mutual understanding and productive deliberation."

Teaching during a tumultuous presidential election can be "a priceless pedagogical opportunity" offering "a gold mine of historical, international, and theoretical comparisons," according to Ted G. Jelen, the late professor of political science at the University of Nevada–Las Vegas. During the 2016 presidential election, some political science faculty found it necessary to weave references to different political traditions, such as fascism, into their lectures (Schmidt, 2016, p. 1). Others taught about the election in the usual way: for example, Jo-Anne Hart (2016) described a simulation activity where students take on the roles of the political prep team for two political candidates, media consultants for the political parties, and journalists who conduct interviews with the prep team and media consultants. But for many, the 2016 election posed a "vexing problem" because even the scholarly experts on American politics could not come to agreement about the best ways to teach about it (Schmidt, 2016).

It was not just college faculty in disciplines including history, political science, and communication studies who struggled with how to teach about election propaganda. Many social studies and English teachers in middle schools and high schools across the United States struggled with teaching the 2016 presidential campaign. How could the widespread distribution of Trump's vulgar comments taped during an *Access Hollywood* interview be ignored? During the 2018 midterm elections, what could a teacher have said about then–Attorney General Jeff Sessions, who joined in a chant of the anti–Hillary Clinton rallying cry, "Lock her up!" at a conference for conservative high school students? In that speech, Sessions claimed that "some schools are doing everything they can to create a generation of sanctimonious, sensitive, supercilious snowflakes" (Mikelionis, 2018, p. 1).

Katherine Schulten of *The New York Times* Learning Network encouraged teachers to lead discussions on questions like, "What makes a good leader and how do leaders come to power?" Students and teachers viewed and discussed videos like "Can a Divided America Heal?" and wrote research papers on understanding what divides the United States in regard to race, gender, politics, and economics. Still other educators asked students to write a letter to the president-elect, expressing their hopes and dreams for the United States and "letting Mr. Trump know the kind of president we hope he will be" (Schulten & Gonchar, 2016).

Educators are themselves citizens who express and share their political views as part of their own personal and professional identity. When political science professor Kathleen Iannello shared with students her objections to Mr. Trump during the lead-up to the 2016 election, she wanted people to know about it, writing an op-ed for the *Philadelphia Inquirer.* She believes that the Trump presidency was a threat to everything liberal arts colleges stand for. She wrote, "It is a disservice to students to attempt to provide balance when I know that balance is an offense to the truth" (Schmidt, 2016, p. 1).

But many other educators were much more hesitant about teaching the election in 2016. A number of college faculty stayed clear of any discussions about the election. For example, David O'Connell, an assistant professor of political science at Pennsylvania's Dickinson College, said, "I never comment on the appropriateness of any candidate for office," and he believes "staying neutral and objective makes me better as a teacher and makes me better as a scholar" (Schmidt, 2016, p. 1). Other educators made the decision to stay quiet because they experienced events both at home and at school that led them to believe that talk about the elections would simply be unproductive. After all, well before the 2016 U.S. presidential election, political polarization was evident as both Republicans and Democrats had strong perceptions that the opposing party's policies were so misguided that they "threaten[ed] the nation's well-being" (Pew Research Center, 2014, p. 1).

To work around these issues, some teachers approached the elections using creative strategies that foregrounded the role of expressive communication, including literature as a means to promote reflection on leadership and social responsibility. Henry Cody Miller teaches ninth grade English language arts at P. K. Yonge Developmental Research School, the University of Florida's affiliated K–12 laboratory school. He enjoys helping students make connections between literature and current events. During the 2016 primary campaign, he integrated discussions of politics into their literature circles, where students were reading and discussing young adult novels like *If You Could Be Mine*, *Sunrise Over Fallujah*, and *Never Fall Down* as well as classic works including *Lord of the Flies* and *The Things They Carried.*

Students need practice to learn to recognize how political issues pervade everyday life. In one class, students were challenged to keep track of political issues that were embedded in the media they used and the stories they were reading, including subjects like war, the military, refugees, same-sex couples, and the representation of immigrants and Muslims. Students then read the presidential candidates' websites and recorded where each stood on these issues. Then each student selected a character from the book they were reading and cast ballots as if the character was voting, using evidence from the text to explain their choice. For example, a student who read *Lord of the Flies* pointed out how Simon's instinct to care might motivate him to vote for Bernie Sanders, while Jack's more aggressive nature would inspire him to vote for Donald Trump. According to the teacher, students benefited from thinking deeply about how a candidate thinks, feels, and acts, as these factors influence the way the candidate would govern. As Miller explained:

> *Using literature to teach about candidates' views satisfies the need to have students critically engage with the media and with political ideologies while adhering to state and administrative mandates such as the Common Core State Standards. During my classroom activity, students referenced the text, made interpretative statements and defended their ideas based on textual evidence. (2016, p. 1)*

But for every teacher like Henry Cody Miller, many more found themselves opting out of teaching and learning activities focused on the U.S. presidential election in 2016. In an informal survey of K–12 teachers conducted by Teaching Tolerance, many educators voiced their concerns about maintaining their own objectivity and their ability to manage classroom discussion. For example, in response to the statement "I am hesitant to teach about the 2016 presidential election," 43% of K–12 educators agreed. High school teachers were not as hesitant as elementary teachers, but some teachers avoided discussing the campaign altogether. One elementary teacher, who in previous years enjoyed offering her young students a lesson on the election, decided that the 2016 campaign was off limits. She explained, "Not sure what's worse—the candidates or what they stand for!!" (Southern Poverty Law Center, 2016, p. 1).

As I have discussed earlier, for some teachers, there can be career consequences for talking about controversial news, politics, and current events in the classroom. Immediately after the election, a Bay-area high school history teacher at Mountain View/Los Altos High School was placed on paid leave after a parent complained that the teacher drew parallels between Donald Trump and Adolf Hitler. Frank Navarro, the teacher, who served as a Mandel Fellow for the U.S. Holocaust Memorial Museum in 1997, had explained to students that Hitler's strategic efforts to scapegoat Jews and communists had remarkable parallels to Trump's comments on Latinos, Blacks, and Muslims (Sanchez, 2016).

When educators feel like their own political views differ from those of the community and parents, they may be less likely to engage in learning activities about controversial issues. In some communities, talking about elections in school can create tension between parents and school leaders. Teachers may get clear signals from their school leaders, who suggest that students have their political discussions at home. A study published in the *American Educational Research Journal* found that many teachers wanted to talk with students about the election and related issues but were also afraid of backlash. Many felt they shouldn't, or couldn't, share their political affiliations or feelings, due to the idea of maintaining political neutrality in the classroom (Dunn, Sondel, & Baggett, 2018). In another study that investigated how two eighth-grade teachers handled the 2016 presidential election, researchers found that both teachers maintained neutral positions on the candidates during the weeks and months before the election. After the election, however, one of the teachers showed her disdain for Donald Trump in the context of classroom learning (Anderson & Zyhowski, 2018).

Indeed, the period immediately after the election of 2016 was tumultuous in many American schools. In the Teaching Tolerance survey of more than 10,000 teachers, counselors, and administrators, 90% reported that school climate was negatively affected by heightened anxiety after the election, especially from marginalized students, including immigrants, Muslims, African Americans, and LGBTQ students. Participants reported derogatory language directed at these students, and students were targeting each other based on which candidate they'd supported. Thousands of educators described specific incidents of bigotry and harassment that were inspired by election rhetoric, with swastika graffiti, assaults on students and teachers, property damage, fights, and threats of violence among the most commonly reported. The report authors pointed out that because of the heightened emotion, half of the teachers who participated in the survey felt hesitant to discuss the election in class. In some cases, school principals even told teachers to refrain from discussing the election (Southern Poverty Law Center, 2016). While understandable, such shortsighted strategies do real harm by failing to prepare a generation of students for citizenship in a democratic society.

Educator Stances on Political Self-Expression

Teacher reluctance to examine controversial political issues is not new. Researchers who have studied teacher political neutrality in the context of social studies education find different nuances in the stances taken by reflective practitioners. One major distinction has been found between teachers who withhold their political views from students and those who freely express their views. Kelly (1986) makes the following typology in identifying teachers' attitudes about their own political self-expression in the classroom:

- ***Neutrality:*** Teachers avoid controversial topics even though they are aware that talking about controversies has educational value for learners.
- ***Neutral impartiality:*** Teachers encourage students to express opposing viewpoints and promote critical student dialogue on controversial issues but withhold their own views on the issues.
- ***Committed impartiality:*** Teachers express their views on political issues yet welcome opposing viewpoints, value diverse perspectives, and use evidence and reasoning to evaluate the integrity of political positions.
- ***Partiality:*** Teachers make clear their particular positions on political issues, sometimes stifling dissenting information or oversimplifying complex issues.

Each of these stances has merit in some contexts, but for most educators, deciding between neutral impartiality and committed impartiality is not easy.

Withholding political views may be a wise and appropriate choice for some educators. In their book *The Case for Contention*, Jonathan Zimmerman and Emily Robertson (2017) explore teachers' anxieties about discussing controversial issues in the classroom and the important balancing act that considers the interests of children, parents, educators, and the state. Their important work synthesizes some of the key reasons why so many teachers adopt the stance of neutrality and avoid discussing controversial issues. When asking high school teachers about which Supreme Court cases deserve attention in American high schools, Diana Hess (2004) found that virtually all teachers mentioned their inability to teach the case that established the legal right to abortion, *Roe v. Wade* (1973). Teachers acknowledged it was a landmark case and that the issue of abortion rights is still very much an important, relevant, and controversial issue in the United States. Although some believed that even a mention of the topic would cause a community-wide uproar, more often, teachers described how their own views led them to believe that they could not approach the issue fairly.

Sometimes teachers' avoidance of political discourse is the result of their strong views about an issue, not the absence of political engagement. This is a meaningful insight. For this reason, Hess decided to split the concept of impartiality into two parts: denial and avoidance. She uses the following terms to describe teachers' attitudes:

- ***Denial:*** Teachers don't perceive a particular issue as controversial and teach it as if it were not controversial.
- ***Avoidance:*** Teachers recognize a controversial political issue and do not address it because they do not think they can teach it fairly.
- ***Balance:*** Teachers recognize that an issue is controversial and aim toward balance to ensure that various positions are represented using reasoning and evidence.
- ***Privilege:*** Teachers recognize that a political issue is controversial but identify a clearly preferred position and encourage students to adopt that position.

I like features of both of these models which I display below. Depending on the particular topic, educators may have different stances towards addressing controversial issues in the classroom.

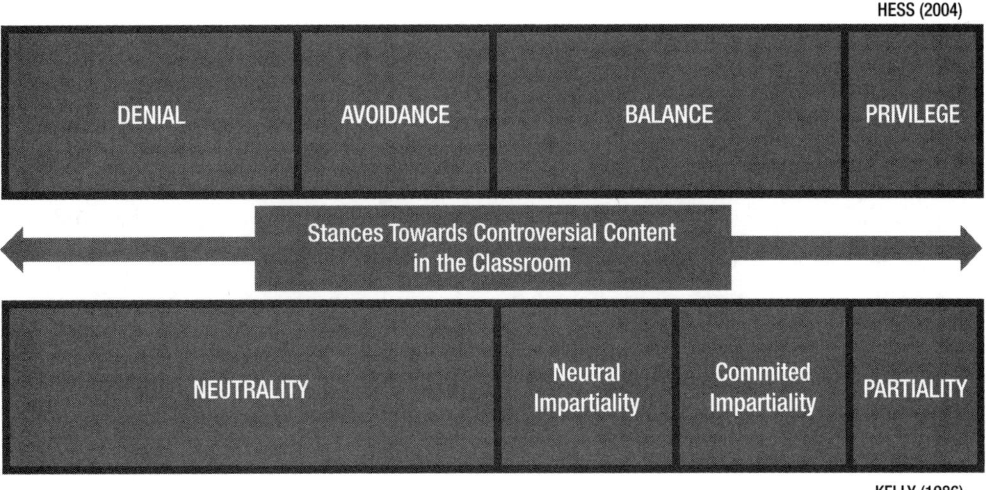

Teachers make decisions about how to address controversial issues situationally and in relation to the needs of their students and their learning objectives. Different social and political issues might cause educators to adopt different stances. Educators should reflect on their own reasoning processes involved in making these decisions. You might first consider the reasons for maintaining neutrality on a particular topic or issue. Decisions to avoid controversial issues (or denying that some topics even are controversial) have consequences. You can next decide whether withholding or sharing your views on a particular controversial issue is appropriate, depending on the issue itself, the learners, and the learning context. And finally, you can decide whether or not to identify a clearly preferred position and encourage students to adopt that position. For certain topics and issues, you can and should be an advocate. Sometimes, this is a valid and morally justifiable position to take.

Either-or Pedagogies

Three dichotomies can be productively examined and reflected upon through the study of propaganda that is rooted in politics and activism:

- Fact versus Opinion
- Reason versus Emotion
- Authority versus Authenticity

Each of these distinctions offers a world of complexity and nuance. If fact-checking organizations struggle mightily with determining the accuracy of facts, consider the plight of elementary teachers who must address the distinction between fact and opinion with the youngest learners. Educators sometimes simplify the distinction out of basic respect for the developmental needs of the child. In some elementary classrooms, there is a poster hanging on the wall that defines facts as "something that is true about a subject and can be tested or proven" and opinions as "what someone thinks, feels or believes." In the children's book *The Sad Little Fact,* Jonah Winter and Pete Oswald address the topic of fake news for children ages 3–7. The little fact is a blue circle with big eyes who faces big bad Authorities who bury all the facts deep underground, then release a bunch of lies that resemble the facts. Fortunately, a group of hard-working Fact Finders dig up the real facts, saving the day.

Across the K–12 spectrum, the Common Core requires students to learn to distinguish between fact, opinion, and reasoned argument. Sometimes, these distinctions are taught in a superficial manner. Educators may set up rigid hierarchies between facts and opinions, implying that facts are strong and opinions are weak. There are hundreds of teacher-created worksheets online that make students read sentences and then determine whether a particular statement is a fact or an opinion. The teacher merely marks student responses as correct or incorrect with little opportunity for discussion and reasoning. Students are forced to distinguish between facts and opinions as if the distinction were a matter as simple as sorting socks and underwear.

But according to philosophers, either-or dichotomies like this may neglect the important intersections between fact and opinion. Unfortunately, if students internalize either-or thinking about facts and opinions, they may end up categorizing all expressions of value as mere opinions. For example, a statement like "It's wrong to kill people" could be categorized as merely an opinion. You can see the potential danger of such superficial approaches that trivialize complex moral reasoning with either-or dichotomies.

Of course, when handled with care, either-or framing can sometimes be effective in helping learners discover the middle ground, where reality lies. This is especially important because issues of value are embedded in each of these three binaries about the nature of knowledge. Each can be explored through a practice of moral reasoning, which uses the practice of critical analysis to analyze specific events to determine what is right or wrong. Sadly, most people don't engage in moral reasoning. Instead they approach moral situations using emotions, social pressure, or the desire to conform (Ethics Unwrapped, 2019). To address the nuances of facts versus opinion in the context of teaching and learning, one scholar recommends we add these ideas to our lessons:

- Fact are things that are true, while opinions are things we believe.
- Some of our beliefs are true. Others are not.
- Some of our beliefs are backed by evidence. Others are not.
- Value claims are like any other claims: some of our values are morally right; others are morally wrong (McBrayer, 2015, p. 1).

Educators want students to acknowledge the value of facts as well as the provisional nature of information (and much expert knowledge). As any expert will tell you, facts change. Facts are our best approximations of the truth at a particular point in time (Pigliucci, 2010). When considering the middle ground, "[t]he hard work lies not in recognizing that at least some moral claims are true but in carefully thinking through our evidence for which of the many competing moral claims is correct" (McBrayer, 2015, p.1).

Let's also briefly consider the reason-versus-emotion dichotomy. Some teachers emphasize the distinction between reason and emotion as if the two ways of knowing were hierarchical and in opposition. Some educators, through their actions, may imply that thinking is good, feeling is bad. But you've already come to understand how propaganda activates emotions as a form of information upon which we can reflect. The careful study of propaganda provides plentiful opportunity to examine how emotional response is a vital part of our humanity. As this chapter has revealed, "the theatricality and combativeness of spin are more likely to draw in citizens than are antiseptic or Olympian statements that purport to tell citizens all they need to know" (Greenberg, 2016, p. 9).

Finally, the tension between authority versus authenticity illuminates an epistemological paradox of our times. We live in a world packed with scientific experts on every topic under the sun, and yet we seem to value the point of view of the high-visibility athlete, celebrity, or musician whose character we most admire. Consider how the political views of actors and musicians like Taylor Swift, Katy Perry, Leonardo DiCaprio, Jenny McCarthy, Shonda Rhimes, or Kanye West have influence on their fans. To understand the concept of authenticity, educators should explore with their students how the political opinions of celebrities have special meaning and influence in contemporary culture. Many educators can relate to this phenomenon. You may remember learning about current events and politics from comedian Jon Stewart, whose comedy news show aired on Comedy Central. Some people learned more from Stewart than from the official news stories on the broadcast networks. Many people make intuitive judgments about people's trustworthiness based on their perceived levels of similarity, independence, and autonomy. Jon Stewart's character (including his use of comedy and his display of emotion) seemed forthright and honest.

The ancient Greeks used the term *ethos* to describe this important kind of influence based on identity. Today, the term authenticity captures the sense of how aspects of a person's character can serve a propaganda function. As one scholar puts it, "Being authentic now is related to staying true to our inner selves rather than to accepting the social position into which we are born" (Sánchez-Arce, 2007, p. 140). While experts ask for our trust in their evidence, information and reasoning, celebrities inspire our trust in their identities.

However, when the appeal of a person's identity becomes a metric for establishing the trustworthiness of ideas and information, this form of social power can be easily exploited. Celebrities may ask audiences to trust them, to follow them, no matter what. In mirroring the political opinions of a valued celebrity, people may experience the pleasure of belonging, feeling like a member of a tribe. But history has shown the dangers of such hero worship.

In democratic societies, propaganda in art, activism, and elections is part and parcel of how people influence each other in order to be part of a shared social story, where people are integrated into society and all have a meaningful role to play. As a propagandist, your own identity may fuel your creativity and motivate your interest in sharing your unique human experience. You may choose to create and share propaganda that relates to your identity as a new immigrant, a new father, or as a person who loves the mountains. Propaganda is a vital part of the marketplace of ideas because people seek to promote emotionally-resonant media that articulates their deepest passions about human experience and our limited time and place on the earth. Access to competing, diverse, and multiple propagandas can help people embed their lives in something bigger and more meaningful than merely themselves. As we will see, next, entertainment and education can serve as forms of socially meaningful propaganda, offering stories that bind us together across the generations.

7

Entertainment and Education as Propaganda

Because propaganda is in the eye of the beholder, it can be recognized in culture and education

It was a goofy comedy film featuring a dumb-and-dumber pair of bumblers who succeed in assassinating a controversial world leader. In 2014, the themes of entertainment and propaganda were fully entwined in the controversy surrounding *The Interview*, a film by Seth Rogen and Evan Goldberg. The movie features two cable tabloid TV reporters who discover that North Korean dictator Kim Jong-un is a fan. In their quest for fame and fortune in TV journalism, they land an interview with him, but as they prepare to travel to Pyongyang, their plans change when the CIA asks them to use a fast-acting poison to commit a political assassination.

The film depicts some of the propaganda about the glorious leader that the North Korean people themselves must endure. As the comedy narrative develops, the pair of American journalists face a slew of ridiculous North Korean villains. Improbably, in the end, they are successful in killing the North Korean leader. The *Time* film critic Richard Corliss noted, "In its parade of ribald gags and infantile preoccupation with body parts . . . *The Interview* displays all the mindless excesses that repressive regimes condemn in Hollywood movies" (2014, p. 1).

Political assassination as comedy did not seem so funny to those who see the

United States as the greatest threat to world peace. Six months before the film's planned debut, the North Korean government threatened action against the United States if the movie was released. As if to prove their threat, the computer systems of Columbia's parent company, Sony Pictures, were hacked, and thousands of emails, including salary information on all employees, were released on the Internet. This type of punishment can be an effective form of coercion. The group claiming responsibility also threatened terrorist attacks against American cinemas that showed the film. As a result, only a few brave distributors offered screenings. However, the controversy of the terrorist threat and the hacking incident increased press coverage, which amplified public curiosity about the movie. The company made some edits to placate the North Koreans and released the film for video streaming. As a result, they were able to recoup their production costs. For these reasons, *The Interview* is generally considered one of the most controversial films of all time (D'Addario, 2014).

In years past, the North Korean government maintained an effective blackout of all foreign entertainment and information, but they have not been able to maintain this level of tight control in recent years. The rise of thumb drives and cell phones now makes it possible for North Korean people to more easily access pop culture from around the world through a robust local black market. Shows like *Sex and the City, Desperate Housewives, Friends,* and *The Mentalist,* as well as DVDs of American professional wrestling are all available in North Korea. Journalists have even had discussions with ordinary North Koreans about films like *Argo, Frozen,* and *Casino Royale.* Researchers who have studied the attitudes of North Koreans who have defected to South Korea found "a clear correlation between exposure to foreign media and more positive beliefs about the US, South Korea, and the outside world overall, along with a surprisingly strong trust of global media" (Lerner, 2015, p. 55). By offering ideas about the world beyond North Korea to the people who live there, even the most innocuous of Hollywood romantic comedies is serving a propaganda function. For those few North Korean young people who manage to immigrate to South Korea, media literacy education plays an important role in helping them adjust to a culture saturated with media and technology (Yoon, 2010).

The strong, simple narratives of entertainment and education shape our understanding of the world and our place in it. Entertainment and education offer up stories that embody a range of values and principles, including freedom, equal rights, patriotism, respect for power, or the belief that might makes right. True and fictional stories offer up ideas about the qualities of being a hero, a villain, and a victim. Movies, literature, art, drama, and history may all function as propaganda, embodying cultural values and status quo norms in ways that may advance critical autonomy or result in indoctrination.

In this chapter, I explore strategies for teaching and learning about propaganda in the publishing industry, in art and literature, Hollywood films, and in public architecture, monuments, and memorials. As we will see, in the eye of the beholder, propaganda embodies all aspects of culture and education. Depending on your point of view, you may find propaganda in pop culture or in public education. This chapter may fascinate or frustrate you because the institutions of both entertainment and education are implicated in the generational transmission of ideologies. Of course, these two institutions don't primarily function to deliver propaganda. Just because something reaches a large audience does not automatically make it propaganda. Weather forecasts reach a large audience, and they aren't intentionally designed as propaganda. But they may take on that function in the eye of the beholder, for example in certain debates about climate change. As Jonathan Auerbach and Russ Castronovo explain, "Propaganda entails propagation, but not everything that propagates is propaganda." As we will find in the pages ahead, those who are most deeply involved in "teaching, preaching, selling, publicizing and other analogous rhetorical modes" have often deeply resisted their close "proximity to propaganda" (Auerbach & Castronovo, 2013a, pp. 5, 7).

By unpacking the differences between indoctrination and education and uncovering how propaganda uses the timeless features of good storytelling to shape attitudes, values, and behavior, we'll consider how propaganda in popular culture, literature, art, and education responds to the human condition. Entertainment and education propaganda can be used to call into question the social inequalities of daily life or reproduce the ideological values and interests of the powerful.

LEARNING ACTIVITY

Violence, Discrimination, and Tolerance in Video Games

Video games have embedded ideologies that need to be recognized and questioned.

Activity: After students analyze two different video games that feature immigrants, they create a video game to embody or illustrate their understanding of human rights laws in Europe. First, students compare and contrast two video games that depict the experiences of refugees and immigrants. Then they consider how different media representations of violence may shape people's ideas about human rights. Finally, they create a prototype for a new video game that represents the complex experiences of refugees and immigrants in their country (Ranieri, 2019).

Steps in the Process: In the first phase of the lesson, students play an educational video game titled *Against All Odds*, which was produced by the UN refugee agency (UNHCR). In this game, users have the vicarious experience of being a refugee. They experience questioning and persecution from governmental authorities, and then negotiate the process of getting out of the country across a border. They claim asylum and then face the challenges of integrating into an unfamiliar society. Then students play a second video game, *Grand Theft Auto IV*, an action-adventure game developed by Rockstar North, an entertainment company. Here the player takes on the role of an immigrant from Eastern Europe who comes to the U.S. to escape a dangerous Russian mafia boss but gets drawn into criminal activities. Students answer the questions below to consider the similarities and differences in the two different representations of refugees in video games.

TABLE 7.1: Compare, Contrast, and Discuss Video Games

QUESTION	*GRAND THEFT AUTO IV*	*AGAINST ALL ODDS*
Is this video game intended to be realistic? What are the features that make the video game realistic and/or unrealistic? Does the video game claim to tell the truth about migration? How does it try to seem authentic?		

QUESTION	GRAND THEFT AUTO IV	AGAINST ALL ODDS
How does the video game represent particular social groups? Are those representations accurate? Does the video game support particular views about migration and violence? How does it put across moral or political values?		
How does the video game affect your view of particular social groups or issues such as migration and violence?		

The Takeaway: Some video games have embedded political messages about immigration and immigrants. It is important to recognize, critique and challenge harmful media representations that promote fear. People can create alternative representations of the lives of immigrants that are rooted in respect and empathy.

–Developed by Maria Ranieri and Francesco Fabbro, MEET Tolerance (Ranieri, 2019)

Entertainment Values as Propaganda

When D. W. Griffith released *The Birth of a Nation* in 1915, it was the first feature-length motion picture in history and a masterpiece of entertainment propaganda, telling the history of the Civil War, Reconstruction, and the rise of the Ku Klux Klan. The pure spectacle of the film romanticized the KKK by expressing the idea of racist vigilante justice. A box-office smash, it offered a representation of history that reflected the dominant historical interpretation of the era. But its explicit racism aroused people to riot in several cities and the film was condemned by African American leaders (Lehr, 2014).

Because people don't think of entertainment as a form of propaganda, it is not easy to recognize. When entertainment media embody ideas, values, and points of view that you agree with and see as normal, you won't even notice it. Of course, you may recognize how some films and shows activate different values. For example, you might notice that television shows like *Duck Dynasty* and *The Big Bang Theory* celebrate the values of family, companionship, and respect for diversity, while *Game of Thrones* and *House of Cards* demonstrate the consequences of selfishness, greed, and the lust for power. While these programs all offer entertainment value to audiences, most people need practice to learn to identify ideological messages in entertainment.

Some conservative critics are vocal about what they perceive to be the liberal values of Hollywood media professionals. In writing a book about values in television titled *Primetime Propaganda,* conservative pundit Ben Shapiro interviewed a variety of Hollywood executives who readily acknowledged that "the world of popular culture increasingly reflects a shared reality in which the Republican Party is either absent or anathema" (Chait, 2012, p. 1). As a result, some conservatives have expressed anger about the routine presentation of liberal values they see espoused in movies, music, and popular culture.

Indeed, conservatives have struggled with Hollywood's perceived liberal bias for many years. During the Great Depression, when Frank Capra and other filmmakers were making films about liberal politicians fighting against corrupt business interests, other films like *Gabriel Over the White House,* created in 1933, suggested that political leaders might need to transform America into a fascist dictatorship in order to address the many problems faced by Americans who were out of work (Greenfield, 2018).

During the 1970s, TV networks were competing for viewers' attention by using more overt depictions of nudity, sexuality, and violence. Many people around the country got angry. Public pressure ramped up as thousands of citizens reached out to the Federal Communications Commission to try to stop it. They asked Congress to increase regulation of the television industry. The TV industry developed the Family Viewing Hour as a compromise, agreeing to broadcast shows that were appropriate for parents and young children for two hours each evening. But Hollywood writers and producers hated the idea of censorship and fought the policy; by 1976, the Family Viewing Hour was ruled unconstitutional, a violation of the First Amendment. Still, networks generally reserved the 8 p.m. hour for family-friendly television. In 1987 when Fox launched as a new national TV network, it began to compete head-on for viewers, placing *Married . . . With Children* at 8 p.m. during its first season. The actor Ed O'Neill played the leading role of Al Bundy, a white lower-middle-class man who was sexist and mean. His unrealistic, farcical performance featured raunchy and crude comedy about erections, vibrators, and pornography. It was the kind of outrageous TV that made people either laugh or cringe.

To many conservatives across the country, the program represented families in ways that valorized stupidity and selfishness. The activist Terry Rakolta launched an organization called Americans for Responsible Television and wrote to advertisers, asking them to boycott the show. When it turned out that the controversy actually increased the size of show's audience, Fox made the small gesture of moving the show to 8:30 p.m., where it reached 17 million viewers each week (Seymour & Byrd, 1990).

Even today, Americans perceive that some values depicted on television are not aligned with their own. Perhaps you hate *The Real Housewives* franchise, with its profuse deployment of shame, humiliation and gender stereotypes. In 2018, hundreds of angry parents wrote letters to PBS after learning that an episode of the children's cartoon *Arthur* featured a gay marriage. Here is a sample letter from the PBS website, where letters from the public are archived:

> *I was very saddened to hear that my favorite children's program,* Arthur, *has a new episode where Mr. Ratburn comes out as gay and marries another man. Why do we feel the need to indoctrinate children at such a young age into the LGTB agenda? I do not understand why we cannot allow our children to grow up & understand sexuality (after they have already gone through puberty themselves) before subjecting them to lifestyle choices they might not understand (nor need to at a young age), some of which may conflict with their families' religious beliefs. Please do not politicize such a wholesome, non-controversial program for young children. I am disappointed that PBS is falling into this trap. Keep children's programing* [sic] *for children. They'll be force-fed this ideology from elsewhere at a later age but many of us parents count on PBS to deliver high quality educational programing with no political agenda. Sincerely, a disappointed mom of three Arthur fans and a high school teacher. (Corporation for Public Broadcasting, 2019)*

Although this parent sees clear evidence that the show is a form of propaganda, the creator of *Arthur*, Marc Brown, was surprised by this interpretation. He did not see this episode as intentionally designed to shape public opinion or influence attitudes or behaviors. Marc Brown explained that his decision to include a same-sex wedding on the show was born out of his interest in making viewers from all walks of life feel represented. He said, "We want children to be educated so they can see there's not just one type of family" (Wong, 2019, p. 1). But his story was interpreted as propaganda by some viewers, nonetheless.

You might wonder whether or why Hollywood has liberal values, given the scope and power of the entertainment industry. The industry itself is a vast profit sector as the nation's second-largest global exporter (the largest U.S. export product is military hardware). The question of Hollywood's liberal bias has generated a lot of controversy among scholars in the field of communication and media studies for more than 40 years. Some ideas on the matter seem particularly naive, as in the essay titled "Why Is Hollywood so Liberal?," where a scholar argues that because actors must develop empathy for characters they might not necessarily like, "the emotional requirements of acting are conducive to progressive politics" (Gross, 2018, p. 1). But back in the 1990s, research was conducted to try to quantify the liberalism of Hollywood producers, writers, and celebrities. Most of this research consisted of interviews with people in the industry, and it was funded by right-wing conservative groups. One exception to this trend was Herbert Gans, a distinguished social scientist, who pointed out that Hollywood liberalism was the result of commercial rather than ideological biases. He wrote:

> *Unlike, say, the supermarket business, which must reflect the demands and wishes of the general public, entertainment caters to a set of specific and fickle audiences, and has to be, virtually by definition, deviant, daring, and even oppositional to the values of these audiences. Popular movies and TV programs are not about everyday marriage but about passionate or violent affairs; they do not deal with car theft but with murder; they ignore life in the suburbs for life in the Mafia. If Hollywood product reflected the attitudes of the general public, the result would be documentaries which only social scientists would watch, or entertainment so mild as to turn away even the youthful audience for G-rated films. (Gans, 1993, p. 151)*

Deviance and transgression grab audience attention. In considering the preponderance of books, movies, and television programming that focus on crime and criminality, scholars have noted the continuing appeal of the outrageous as the central idea of our time, where stories about characters breaking the rules and crossing boundaries is a principal source of entertainment (Penfold-Mounce, 2010).

It is not necessary to claim a direct causal relationship between depictions of criminality in news and entertainment and crime and violence in the real world to acknowledge that both news reporting and crime dramas affect legal institutions and government policies. But although crime stories may help audiences understand the criminal justice system, transgressive depictions of human criminal behavior are first and foremost designed to maximize profit by reaching the largest possible audience. The depiction of taboo behavior, illicit pleasures, chaos, and debauchery can be riveting to the attention, providing an adrenaline rush of thrills that can be addictively satisfying.

Today, conservative perspectives are commonly included in contemporary Hollywood film and television productions. Clint Eastwood has directed films that present hard-working white people who struggle with scary, gun-toting Mexican criminals and other bad hombres. Shows like *NCIS*, one of the longest-running and most popular television crime dramas, emphasize virtues like loyalty, obedience, and self-sacrifice. Shows like CBS's *SEAL Team*, NBC's *The Brave,* and the CW's *Valor* offer romantic and heroic depictions of the U.S. military, veterans, and the heartland.

The long-running reality show, *Cops,* presented a socially conservative image of policing. After its cancellation in 2020, a review of 846 episodes revealed that the show presented a world that is much more dangerous than real life. It misrepresented crime by people of color and exploited poor people and drug addicts. It also depicted the police as being much more successful than they are in real life (Blake, 2020).

Inevitably, commercial entertainment serves a propaganda function because stories articulate ideologies. To consider the entertainment function of propaganda, the ideas we have previously discussed about intentional manipulation must be set aside. Instead, we must consider the operations of mass culture from a sociopolitical perspective, using the power of literary and cultural interpretation as a guide (Barthes, 1957). When considering the institutions of entertainment and education, "propaganda can be understood in relation to ideology as an attempt to influence public opinion through the transmission of ideas and values" (Taylor, 1998, as quoted in Papazian, 2013, p. 68). By seeing reality represented through potent symbols that activate strong emotions, audiences may come to feel connected to a particular set of cultural values and the web of meanings that underpin them. Even though films, music, and TV shows are created primarily for commercial profit-making purposes, they may serve a propaganda function without having been intentionally designed as propaganda.

Storytelling as Ideology

Both entertainment and education propaganda deliver their persuasive messages when people are not really expecting them. For this reason, social theorists have conceptualized entertainment and education as the most powerful propaganda genres of all. Jacques Ellul used the term sociological propaganda to refer to cultural activities that express behaviors and lifestyles as an ideology.. Functioning as "a sort of persuasion from within," Ellul writes that "when an American producer makes a film, he has certain definite ideas he wants to express, which are not intended to be propaganda. Rather, the propaganda element is in the American way of life with which he is permeated and which he expresses in his film without realizing it" (Ellul, 1973, p. 64).

A wide range of seemingly ordinary cultural practices reinforce ideology in subtle ways, which is why sociological propaganda is generally seen as nonpolitical. It is woven into the fabric of everyday life, often by means of stories. As every parent and educator knows, the power of storytelling has long been seen as valuable in providing moral lessons for children. Ever since the rise of children's literature during the Victorian era, critics have observed its positive function as a type of propaganda that aims to be both entertaining and educational. In Britain, children's literature has offered moral messages, social codes, and ways of thinking ever since the 1740s, when writers experimented with short fictional stories designed to teach ethical lessons. In one story, "The History of Miss Polly Friendly," a little girl accidentally breaks a set of china. She hides the pieces, but when the problem is blamed on a servant, the little girl admits her fault. Due to her exemplary moral character, she grows up to be the Lady Mayor of the town (Grenby, 2014).

Some 19th-century children's picture books depicted horrific consequences for children who disobey parents. For example, Heinrich Hoffman's 1845 German children's book, *Shockheaded Peter*, includes the stories of a boy who wasted away after refusing his soup and another kid whose thumb was cut off after he sucked on it (Laskow, 2017). In Nazi Germany, children's books and toys communicated cultural values, too. Anti-Semitic messages of hate were woven into children's stories to cultivate us-versus-them thinking at an early age. For example, the notorious 1938 children's picture book *The Poisonous Mushroom* explains, "Just as it is often hard to tell a toadstool from an edible mushroom, so too is it often very hard to recognize the Jew as a swindler and criminal" (USHMM, 2007). Because children's literature is double-voiced, speaking to both children and adults simultaneously, specialists in children's literature acknowledge that it can function as a form of propaganda and be highly effective in promoting ideological messages (Reynolds, 2011).

In the broadest sense, many forms of storytelling and mythmaking serve a propaganda function. Narratives give people a sense of meaning and purpose to life. They offer moral guidance, a guide to living, and insight into the complexities of human experience. Joseph Campbell (1949) identified the monomyth as a narrative arc common to stories and myths around the world. In it, circumstances cause an ordinary person to embark on a journey in order to face a challenge that causes some significant transformation or change. Just as heroes may help people stay optimistic in the face of human fallibility, antiheroes remind us that the world is falling apart (Kettmann, 2013).

One example of the hero's journey as propaganda is the genre of captivity narratives, stories about the experiences of white colonial settlers who were kidnapped by Native Americans. They are among the earliest forms of literature created in the United States. After the second-generation Puritan settler Mary Rowlandson was taken captive in Lancaster, Massachusetts in 1676, her ordeal was recounted in a book. Stories like this were among the best-sellers of their time. These tales served to warn people about the dangers around them. They reinforced prejudice against Native people and also fueled anti-Catholic sentiment against French settlers who traded with them (Smith, 2011). Such literature serves as a form of propaganda because "existing economic, political and sociological factors progressively allow an ideology to penetrate individuals or masses" (Ellul, 1973, p. 63).

Leaders in the culture industries have long understood books, theater, and art to be an enduring form of propaganda. The distinguished publisher W. W. Norton himself once observed how ironic it was that the book that most influenced the war, *Mein Kampf,* was written "by a man who hated some books enough to burn and ban them." The royalties Hitler received from that book made him for a time the top-selling author in the world (Hench, 2016, p. 68). And of course, the Third Reich's Ministry of Popular Enlightenment and Propaganda, led by Joseph Goebbels, controlled virtually every kind of storytelling and cultural expression: book, newspaper, and magazine publishing, radio and musical recordings, movies, museums, theater, and art galleries, not to mention the regulation of state holidays and the curriculum of schools, colleges, and universities. Even tourism became a propaganda effort controlled by the Nazis (Zeman, 1995).

The American publishing and film industries actively used storytelling as a form of positive propaganda during and after World War II, when, during the period of de-Nazification, they continued to be active. After the war, American publishers led an effort to distribute fiction and nonfiction books all across Europe, where they were intentionally used as a form of propaganda designed to restore calm. Millions of translated American and English books were distributed throughout Europe and the rest of the world as a means to "disinfect" the minds of those affected by Nazi values. Such books were not specifically written as propaganda, of course. They were ordinary books that satisfied the need of Europeans who were starving for literature after the ravages of the war came to an end. But the choice of books to be imported to Germany was overseen by the U.S. government. Books with anti-Semitic passages were rejected, as well as books that depicted Americans as money-grubbers (Hench, 2016).

Nazi Film Propaganda

Movies are the most powerful form of propaganda ever created, according to Nazi propagandist Joseph Goebbels. During the Third Reich, many films were produced with the aim of distracting people, and Nazi ideology was often presented in a subtle way. In 1936, Goebbels outlawed film criticism and mandated that journalists could only describe films, not critique them. In 1937, the Nazis banned foreign films and nationalized the entire film industry. People in the film industry were sent to Nazi film school to learn how to make films harmonious with Nazi ideology. Censors (called National Film Dramaturgists) reviewed film projects from inception to release. And while the Nazis never nationalized the local cinemas, they required theaters to show a newsreel and a documentary before the main fiction film at every regular film showing (O'Brien, 2004).

Many people are not familiar with the entertainment propaganda produced in Nazi Germany beyond Leni Riefenstahl's epic film, *Triumph of the Will.* But students benefit from getting some exposure to how narrative stories conveyed Nazi ideology. Through drama, some Nazi propaganda films rely on the power of reversal, depicting their enemies as the perpetrators of the same types of violence that they themselves actually used against Jews, Poles, Romanis, homosexuals, political enemies, and more. For example, in one powerful Nazi drama called *Homecoming*, the narrative offers a compelling rationale for the invasion of Poland, justifying this aggressive action to the German people. In this film, Polish children mercilessly taunt, bully, and abuse a young German girl. As one critic notes, "The Polish characters are hatefully portrayed. It's hard not to hate them when you watch it." As the dramatic action rises, Polish people actually imprison Germans in places that look like concentration camps. Polish people are presented as senseless and brutal killers who want to exterminate Germans. When the German army marches into Poland, the filmmaker makes it seem like a rescue action (Moeller, 2015). The narrative literally rewrites historical fact to justify German aggression.

During the Third Reich, more than 1,000 such films were made between 1933 and 1945. The Allies banned 300 of these films after the war, and more than 40 are still banned from public view today, stored in a special building at the Federal Film Archive in Hoppegarten, Germany. In the 2015 documentary *Forbidden Films,* filmmaker Felix Moeller examines the question of whether Nazi propaganda films should still be banned. More than 70 years after these films were created, is a ban still needed?

After my students view *Forbidden Films,* I ask them to respond to this important question. Inevitably, they respond in different ways. One student believed that restrictions were a good idea, noting that these films should only be "shown in controlled environments where context can be explained before or after viewing." He does not believe that people under the age of 18 should view them, noting that "these films can have extremely manipulative effects on young minds." Another student disagreed, noting that the films should be shown in schools to make sure people understand how propaganda is transmitted through entertainment. She wrote, "This question immediately made me think of the quote, 'Those who do not learn history are doomed to repeat it.' These films must be shown to serve as educational examples of the thinking and attitudes that enforced Nazi ideas for years."

I experienced the power of these forbidden films firsthand. After viewing and discussing the *Forbidden Films* documentary, I previewed the 1940 fiction film *Jud Süß* as I considered whether or not to use it in the classroom. Previewing is an essential practice for the educator. Educators should never screen film or video in the classroom that they have not watched beforehand. *Jud Süß* is considered the most anti-Semitic film of all time. It is a costume drama, set in the 17th century, featuring a Jewish villain, Süß, who pretends to be a Christian. He ingratiates himself with the Duke of Württemberg. As the drama unfolds, we see how Süß's actions cause harm. The villain rapes and murders with impunity and impoverishes the entire community with his greedy financial manipulations. But because he disguises his true motives, the trusting Germans do not suspect him.

Watching the film on my laptop at home with my husband via a streaming service, we were both astonished by its dramatic quality: it was an impressive historical drama that activated strong emotions by offering up creepy but fascinating characters that you simply love to hate. In the end, of course, the villain is punished for his misdeeds as order is restored. After viewing the film, I reflected on the roller-coaster of feelings that were activated by this vividly presented drama. I was repulsed by the hateful stereotypes but acknowledged the entertainment value of the movie. I ultimately decided not to infect my students with this still-dangerous form of entertainment propaganda.

LEARNING ACTIVITY

War Drama as Propaganda

Examine how historical drama is carefully constructed to express an ideology.

Activity: Select one of these two war dramas to view and discuss. Preview the questions below before viewing.

- ***Dunkirk.*** This 2017 drama about World War II, directed by Christopher Nolan, shows how 333,000 British and French forces were safely evacuated from the beach using every naval and civilian vessel that could be found.
- ***Lincoln.*** Directed by Steven Spielberg, this 2012 historical drama tells the story of the conclusion of the Civil War by examining the last four months of Lincoln's life.

Questions for Discussion: Discuss your response to these questions with a partner or in a small group:

1. ***What*** is the story about? Who are the main characters? What are the important conflicts that occur in the film?
2. ***How*** was shot framing, camera angles, camera movement, color, editing choice, or length of shot used by the filmmakers to express an emotion or convey an idea?
3. ***Describe*** two moments, images, or bits of dialogue from the film that stand out in your mind. Discuss why those images impressed you. What key ideas and values were presented in those moments?

4. ***Describe*** an event or a character portrayal in the film that, on the whole, accurately reflects the historical reality it aims to represent. What makes this event or portrayal seem historically accurate?
5. ***Describe*** a lesson from this film that viewers can apply to their own lives.
6. ***How*** might this film function as propaganda for some viewers?

The Takeaway: Historical drama creates a powerful illusion of reality that can serve as a form of propaganda by presenting an ideology in ways that shape people's emotions, knowledge, and attitudes about the past.

–Adapted from Teach With Movies (2016)

Movies as War Propaganda

Filmmakers have long depicted war in ways that may either glorify it or demonize it, depending on the tenor of the times. When Dalton Trumbo's *Johnny Got His Gun* was released in 1971, this powerful antiwar film resonated with a generation of young people fighting to end the Vietnam War. The story of one ordinary soldier who is severely injured in World War I indicts the system that "sent all the young men away to kill each other." It presents the mental torture of a war veteran, the story of a soldier hit by a bomb blast, who lost his arms, his legs, and most of his face "and handled it, strange to say, in a way that's not so much antiwar as pro-life" (Ebert, 1971, p. 1). The film's sensitive treatment of a vulnerable war veteran managed to appeal to both antiwar protesters and right-to-life activists (who were outraged that abortion was beginning to be decriminalized at the state level).

While antiwar films are easily recognized as propaganda, films whose story lines feature military conflict may also serve a propaganda function. Movies that feature the military may offer a variety of narratives that promote an ideology that justifies war. Such films often advance the key themes of American exceptionalism, which is the political philosophy that the United States of America has a special role to play in the world, as it was founded on the principles of individual liberty, private property rights, and equal justice for all. In examining the ideological biases of the entertainment industry, one critic notes, "Hollywood is like any other major institution: It reflects and reinforces its society's assumptions, its economic systems, and its audience's most deeply held beliefs" (Isquith, 2013, p. 1).

It is in the interest of the U.S. military to ensure that the American public has a positive impression about the armed services, so it's no surprise that the military has long collaborated with Hollywood producers. In their self-published 2017 book, *National Security Cinema*, Matthew Alford and Tom Secker document the relationship between the military and entertainment industries and point out how many Hollywood films embody the ideological premise that U.S. military supremacy is fundamentally benevolent. The authors gather data from government reports to examine the Pentagon's involvement in film production projects. Alford and his colleague, who runs a website called Spy Culture, are known to the U.S. government as "vexatious requesters" (Secker, 2017). This term is used to describe people who make a very large number of requests to federal agencies under the Freedom of Information Act. Using information gained this way, Secker and Alford have documented the relationship between Hollywood and the military, finding examples of collaboration in over 900 movies and TV shows since 2005 (Alford & Secker, 2017). For example, from the Department of Defense, Alford and Secker learned that the U.S. military enthusiastically helped Michael Bay with the *Transformers* film franchise, which features 12 different types of Air Force equipment and plenty of troops in uniform.

It makes sense that the U.S. military would want some control over the content of the movies they support, in exchange for supplying filmmakers with access to expensive military equipment, locations, and personnel. The military provides support for filmmakers whose stories they approve and withholds support from film projects that do not depict the military in a flattering light. As a result, films like *Avatar*, *Meet the Parents*, and *The Terminator* have been shaped in part by the U.S. Department of Defense.

Consider the role of the CIA in the film depiction of the hunt for Osama bin Laden, the man who masterminded the September 11 attacks. The CIA was involved in the 2012 thriller directed by Kathryn Bigelow, *Zero Dark Thirty*. Filmmakers wanted to depict the raid that resulted in the killing of bin Laden as a model of coordination between the Pentagon and the CIA. The conclusion of the film re-creates the U.S. Navy SEALs' helicopter assault on the hideout. The film was a critical and commercial success, but it was recognized as pro-American propaganda by some viewers. When I saw the film, it brought back some awful memories of watching TV news. I remembered how shocked I felt when learning that U.S. commandos had killed Osama bin Laden in 2011. Watching the TV news about the event, I found myself feeling really uncomfortable with all the public jubilation. Bin Laden was not armed at the time of his death. He was not captured and put on trial. He was simply murdered in an extrajudicial killing. At the time, the United States called bin Laden an "enemy combatant," but this label was itself a propaganda term, created by President George W. Bush to permit U.S. military authorities to detain people indefinitely, denying them the rights and protections afforded under the Geneva Convention (Hunt, 2011).

Watching the Hollywood film about this event, perhaps it was easier for me to notice the propaganda function of *Zero Dark Thirty* because it offered a filmic interpretation of a historical event that stood in stark opposition to my own prior knowledge and beliefs about the event depicted. Other viewers who did not see the bin Laden killing as problematic might not perceive that the film serves a propaganda function, because propaganda is in the eye of the beholder.

Around the world, the film was interpreted in very different ways. In Pakistan, cinema owners refused to screen the film because they resented how the film depicts U.S. forces conducting the military operation without the Pakistani government's authorization. To them, such depictions are humiliating. In Europe, people objected to the depiction of the fake vaccination program set up by the CIA to get DNA samples from relatives of bin Laden, noting that "the scene had the dangerous effect of reinforcing mistrust of Western nongovernmental organizations working to eradicate disease in the region, and several polio workers have been murdered in the country since the film's release, thus escalating violence in the area" (Shaw & Jenkins, 2017, p. 100).

The film made counterterrorism look heroic, that's for certain. Because of its realism, many viewers may not have recognized how the film seems to justify torture. The film's depictions of the bin Laden raid look a lot like documentary footage. But even some members of Congress had concerns about the film. Senate Intelligence Committee members Dianne Feinstein, Carl Levin, and John McCain were so angry about the film that they sent a letter to the president of Sony Pictures, suggesting that the depiction of torture as useful was grossly inaccurate and misleading (Daunt, 2012). To them, it seemed as if *Zero Dark Thirty* was aiming to distort history and erase public memories of the 2004 torture and prisoner of war abuses at Abu Ghraib prison in Baghdad, Iraq.

LEARNING ACTIVITY

Compare and Contrast Historical Films About Feminism

Compare and contrast two historical dramas about how women used propaganda and politics to win the right to vote.

Activity: Watch two historical dramas about suffragettes from different cultures and time periods and then create a Venn diagram to compare the similarities and differences between the films. You may want to watch both films together, but this activity also works well if each partner watches one of the two films.

- ***Suffragette***, directed by Sarah Gavron (2015), tells the story of British women in 1912 who used political violence to win the right to vote.
- ***The Divine Order***, directed by Petra Volpe (2017), tells the story of a group Swiss women who organized to win the right to vote in 1971.

Questions for Discussion: Talk through these questions with a partner as you develop ideas by analyzing the two films.

- ***Audience Response.*** What did you notice about your own emotional response to each film? What scenes evoked the strongest and most visceral emotions for you?
- ***Characters.*** In each film, who is the hero? How does the hero change over the course of the film? Which characters are presented as villains? Which characters are depicted as victims? Who are the helpers? How does the filmmaker help viewers identify and recognize the heroes, villains, helpers, and victims?
- ***Plot.*** In each film, what different types of conflicts between characters are depicted? How are these conflicts resolved?
- ***Composition.*** What is the most memorable moment in each film? What dialogue was particularly powerful or compelling? What location shown in each film did you like best and why?

- ***Representation.*** What does each filmmaker do to convey a sense of realism? How realistic or unrealistic does it seem?
- ***Ideology.*** What political and social issues are debated in each film? How do these ideas relate to what's happening in the world today?
- ***Questions.*** What questions did you find yourself wondering about after viewing each film? What topics would you like to learn more about?

Create to Learn: After the discussion, synthesize the main ideas by creating a Venn diagram, using short phrases or bullet points to document the similarities and differences between the two films. Represent your findings as an infographic, using headlines, language, images, and graphic design to compose an attractive digital display.

The Takeaway: Storytelling techniques embody ideologies that influence people's knowledge, attitudes, feelings, and beliefs about both historical and contemporary injustices and inequalities.

Art, Literature, and Propaganda

Among the most well-known American children's authors is Theodor Geisel, better known as Dr. Seuss, famous for *The Cat in the Hat* and other books. When asked about his own favorite among his many works, he identified *The Lorax*, the story of the creature who speaks for the trees. Geisel began working on the book in 1969 when he learned that the highly polluted Cuyahoga River in Ohio had burst into flames. Although *The Lorax* is a children's picture book about the need for people to protect the environment, it generated major controversy because of opposition from the timber industry. The book was included on the American Library Association's Banned Books Week list after community activists made several attempts to ban it. One group even took out a full-page newspaper advertisement claiming that "our kids are being brainwashed" (Wolfe, 2008, p. 5).

Clearly, art and literature may function as propaganda by intertwining aesthetics, ideology, and subjective human experience. Visual propaganda probably began with cave painting and it has continued since then. During medieval times, geographers made beautifully illustrated maps that served as a kind of visual propaganda for the city-states they depicted. Depictions of grandiose palaces, city walls, harbors, and streets prepared visitors to accept the authority of the ruling power. One scholar points out that maps are never value-free images; they are not in themselves either true or false. As media, maps use specific signs, symbols, and styles of representation as a way of "conceiving, articulating, and structuring the human world" in ways that serve the interest of the powerful in society (Harley, 2009, p. 129).

In a way, it is inevitable that poets, writers, sculptors, photographers, filmmakers, and painters all "reflect the social conditions of their day" given that art "is an instrument of social influence" (Ewers, 1943, p. 80). The complex relationship between art and propaganda has been debated and discussed by critics and literary scholars for generations, going back to the Enlightenment. But recognizing when art becomes propaganda is an essential life skill, and it's woefully neglected in our education system today.

Educators might not like to think of the literature that is read in American high schools as a form of propaganda, but it is. In many school districts, students have little choice in what they read. Students are required to study "the highly valued, high-cultural texts that have traditionally acted as arbiters of literary value" (Mukherjee, 2011, p. 1). Even though there are more than 15,000 school districts across the United States, students in Michigan read nearly the same works of literature over the course of four years as students in Alaska or Louisiana. That's because many educators, parents, and community leaders are deeply socialized to accept the centrality of the literary canon, which consists of works of literature that "grapple with difficult, timeless questions about love, life and death" (Korbey, 2019, p. 1). As adolescent reading competencies have declined, some literacy educators and librarians have encouraged students to select for themselves the texts they want to read, because when students read books they have personally chosen, their reading stamina may improve. But this practice is far from normative in American public schools, where school districts and curriculum specialists control the choices of literature and media texts.

What American kids read in school is, of course, quite different than what teens read in the schools of the United Kingdom, France, Italy, or Germany. Each country has a different set of texts that have been selected because they embody or reflect certain civic and cultural values. The works of art and literature that have been deemed worthy of remembering are the ones educators feel compelled to transmit to the next generation. According to some scholars and educators, works by authors including Shakespeare and Mark Twain have cultural authority. Required reading helps preserve the value of literature over time, because the transmission of cultural heritage is one function of education (Dewey, 1910). Defenders of the literary canon say it is flexible, adaptable, and open to enormous variation, while critics observe how works selected for the canon generally reflect "ideological conformity with dominant political and intellectual regimes" (Mukherjee, 2011, p. 1). British cultural studies scholar Raymond Williams observed how such lists function as propaganda by maintaining the class structure of society, with wealthy people at the top.

But as power shifts in society, the canon shifts, too. In the early 1990s, multicultural literature was incorporated into English language arts instruction in order to more accurately reflect the culture and values of ethnic groups and women. In 2000, the term culturally responsive pedagogy was coined to describe instructional practices that include respect for student differences, the inclusion of real-world issues into the classroom, and the use of students' culture to shape curriculum and instruction. However, a review of state teaching standards shows that only a few stated explicitly acknowledge these competencies (Muñiz, 2019).

Orwell's Legacy

Many American and British students get their first formal exposure to the study of propaganda while reading *Animal Farm* by George Orwell, written in 1949. This book is read as early as seventh grade in some American schools. Many teachers perceive the book as useful for teaching and learning purposes because it is short, entertaining, and quite accessible for students who dislike or struggle with reading.

The book entered the literary canon in the 1950s, only a short time after its publication, in part because it enabled British and American teachers to offer easy critiques of communism through the study of literature. Orwell's liberal anticommunist ideology promoted the values of the "free world" against Stalinism. During the Cold War, some students were even provided with Cliffs Notes summaries that offered detailed correspondences between events in Russian history and the fable's characters and events. One teacher who wrote about his experience teaching the novel to high school students noticed that much of the excitement of the reading experience revolved around an "aha!" experience that occurred when the young readers realized that the book was "an allegory with a serious subtext" (Rodden, 1991, p. 507).

Today's educators may be tempted to compare the elaborate schemes of Napoleon the pig ruler not to Stalin's totalitarianism but to President Donald Trump's own authoritarian impulses, lies, and emotion-laden statements. A wide range of comparisons could be productively explored. For example, in *Animal Farm*, Orwell shows us how leaders lie to maintain their power and how they get surrogates to lie on their behalf. One critic has observed how Trump's phrasing even mirrors the statements of Orwell's self-aggrandizing leaders. In *Animal Farm*, the pig called Squealer insists, "No one believes more firmly than Comrade Napoleon that all animals are equal." Trump uses this sentence structure often:

- There's been nobody tougher on Russia than President Donald Trump;
- No one respects women more than me;
- I am the least racist person you'll ever meet;
- No one reads the Bible more than me;
- Nobody knows more about trade than me;
- There's nobody that's done so much for equality as I have (Cain, 2018).

In *Animal Farm*, Orwell presented "the telltale signs of totalitarianism in the clearest and simplest terms, in order to make sure the populace would steer clear of electing any such ruler in the future" (Cain, 2018, p. 1).

Because teachers continually find creative ways to deepen students' learning, some have explored the power of simulations to illustrate the process by which authoritarian leadership develops. Pauline Hawkins, a high school English teacher, uses a simulation activity when teaching Orwell's *Animal Farm*. At the beginning of one class, she sternly tells the students they have rebelled against her authority in the classroom. She gives them a list of five things they have to accomplish before they can start functioning as a literature class:

1. Develop a motto or rallying song.
2. Come up with a new name for the class.
3. Write commandments (at least four) for this new classroom.
4. Create a plan to maintain the purpose of this group as that of a literature class.
5. Begin functioning as one.

Then she sits at the back of the room for the rest of the period and watches what students do. Hawkins refuses to acknowledge students' questions that are directed to her. Every time, she explained in a blog post, a single male student or a group of boys become the leader. Every class attempts to accomplish the goals listed on the board. One year, a student jumped up to be the leader, but never once did he speak directly to the class. He had clearly read George Orwell's book carefully. He asked another student to come up to the front of the room and then he spoke to this other boy, who then spoke to the class. Through his chief propagandist, the rules were communicated, and the other students followed these rules. The teacher sat at the back of the room, thrilled and terrified at the same time.

As part of the debriefing, students consider the meaning and significance of their own participation in the classroom game. Then Hawkins asks students to respond to this writing prompt: "Pick one leader or one follower from the book and analyze how that character destroys freedom and equality on the farm." One of her students wrote about Benjamin, the donkey, noting that "it is the followers, not the leaders, who hold the key to maintaining freedom and equality in any civilization" (Hawkins, 2013, p. 1). What a powerful insight these lucky students received from this simulation experience!

LEARNING ACTIVITY

Teaching *Nineteen Eighty-Four*

This classic novel depicts a dystopia where the government has created its own reality. In this society, many important facts go unrecorded and unremembered. Instead of politics and history, sports, sex, crime, and astrology entertain the masses.

Activity: As you read *Nineteen Eighty-Four* by George Orwell, reflect on these questions.

- **What** is power, and how is it gained and used?
- **What** does it mean to abuse power? What can citizens do if power is abused by a ruling group or government?

- **Can** individuals change society? Can changing language change people's thoughts?
- **How** do governments balance the rights of individuals with the common good?
- **Why** do some individuals take a stand against oppression while others choose not to participate?

Create to Learn: Work with a partner to create a short podcast where you interview each other to answer one or more of these questions, using examples and ideas from the novel in your discussion.

The Takeaway: People who choose to reject absurd or harmful propaganda may face challenges from both the powerful and the powerless.

—Adapted from Teaching Orwell and *1984* with *The New York Times*

The Many Forms of Science Propaganda

When more than 350,000 American science teachers received pamphlets, a DVD, and a book titled *Why Scientists Disagree About Global Warming*, the materials looked important. Created by the official-sounding Nongovernmental International Panel on Climate Change, the book challenges the scientific consensus that climate change is real and human-made. These curriculum resources were funded by the Heartland Institute, whose mission is to discover, develop, and promote free-market solutions to social and economic problems.

For many teachers, attractive and well-designed free resources are like a gift from heaven. While some educators devote considerable energy to developing their own curriculum, others use what's already in the building or what arrives in the mail. Some may even scramble to find appropriate resources by relying on Teachers Pay Teachers or Pinterest, harvesting worksheets and lesson plans created by peers.

But even those teachers who work diligently to acquire knowledge on their subjects through genuine inquiry are sometimes challenged to find high-quality resources. For example, the glossy materials distributed to teachers through the Heartland Institute state that concern over climate change is unwarranted and that there is no scientific or economic reason to restrict the use of fossil fuels. When it comes to climate science education, there is a glut of materials developed by the energy industry that are misleading or outdated. The Climate Literacy and Energy Awareness Network (supported by the U.S. government's National Oceanic and Atmospheric Administration) reviewed more than 30,000 free online educational resources and found only 700 of them accurately represent the scientific consensus about climate change (Associated Press, 2019, p. 1). That means the vast majority of curriculum materials available online are not suitable for teaching and learning purposes. One sixth grade teacher attended a training session sponsored by the Oklahoma Energy Resource Bureau, which is funded by the oil and gas industry. The illustrated lesson plans featured a character who has a nightmare about "everything that would be missing from his life if there were no petroleum products, from his toothbrush to his school bus" (Associated Press, 2019, p. 1). In the teacher's opinion, the materials were "borderline propaganda" because they portrayed petroleum as absolutely essential to one's personal life with no mention of the danger that mass petroleum use poses to our climate. Perhaps this is not surprising, since in Oklahoma, state education standards make no mention of climate change, so teachers interested in exploring the subject with students are on their own.

In deciding what resources to use in the classroom, teachers generally choose curriculum materials that align with their own knowledge, attitudes, and beliefs. In 2016, a survey of U.S. science teachers found that 31% believe that global warming is still up for debate. One in 10 told students that climate change is a natural phenomenon. Five percent of science teachers simply didn't mention the subject in the classroom at all (Plutzer et al., 2016). All in all, only half of American science teachers taught that climate change is caused by humans putting 50 billion tons of carbon into the atmosphere each year (Branch, 2019).

Because teachers' attitudes about science affect how they teach, the National Research Council developed the Next Generation Science Standards in order to emphasize the critical thinking and communication skills that students need for postsecondary success and citizenship in a world fueled by innovations in science and technology. For example, by the end of grade five, students should know that if Earth's global mean temperature continues to rise, the lives of humans and other organisms will be affected in many different ways. By the end of grade eight, students should recognize that human activities, such as the release of greenhouse gases from burning fossil fuels, are major factors in the current rise in global warming. By the end of grade 12, students should recognize how global climate models are used to understand the process of climate change. In gaining this knowledge, students must be able to pose questions and retrieve and comprehend information presented in a variety of forms. They need to evaluate the credibility and accuracy of information sources, integrating information from texts, flowcharts, and diagrams to form an overall understanding. They must be able to explain ideas using language and images, using reasoning, evidence, and skillful organization (NGSS, 2013).

With or without good curriculum resources, teaching about climate change can be tricky in some communities if colleagues, parents, or community leaders perceive the subject to be "too political." One science teacher at a high school in Pennsylvania describes the emotional stress of having a teaching colleague who tells students that climate change is a hoax (Associated Press, 2019). Cultivating doubt is one of the main strategies used by climate change deniers. The media scholar and critic danah boyd once noted, "Contemporary propaganda isn't about convincing someone to believe something, but convincing them to doubt what they think they know" (2018, p. 1).

Humor as a Propaganda Weapon

Science propaganda can be misleading—and hilarious. Today, anti-vaxxer parents have taken to creating compelling social media posts that promote not vaccinating children. But their critics have also taken aim at those parents using the playful power of the meme. Appropriating classic meme templates, they point out the lack of scientific evidence behind claims that vaccinations cause autism. Other critics have used satire and parody to attack the anti-vaxxer community. After a measles outbreak in Oregon, a Portland-based marketing firm created a satirical anti-vaccination lifestyle blog, with sales from merchandise going toward a vaccination advocacy campaign. The website, called Unvaccinated Life, includes fictional opinion posts with titles like "Putting the Me in Measles." They also sell branded merchandise like T-shirts with the phrase "Unvaccination Is Contagious." Although it was intended as satire, when the site first went live, anti-vaxxer readers frequently misunderstood the website as sincere. The marketing director could see from the comments that many readers did not get the joke, so the company now includes a disclaimer explaining that the website is satire (Gormley, 2019, p. 1).

The spirit of playful propaganda goes far beyond the critics of anti-vaxxers, however. Today, political elites, journalists, and mass media voices are not the only perspectives heard when it comes to politics. Members of special interest groups, educators, and ordinary citizens respond to and comment upon current events, presidential campaigns, and other news, engaging across multiple platforms asynchronously and in real time. Political propaganda is becoming a playful type of sport for participants of all stripes. The equipment needed to play the game is simple: access to the Internet, creativity, and a bit of chutzpah.

Speaking of entertainment, consider the power of Donald Trump's political rallies. By bringing people together in large public spaces, Trump's extemporaneous performances often feature his quite entertaining impersonations of political opponents. His rallies offer the spectacle of Trump as the big boss, a character that his fans enjoyed during his time on the popular TV show *The Apprentice*. In his speeches at rallies, Trump reduces his opponents to laughable caricatures by using goofy names, accompanied by exaggerated body language and gestures. You may remember how, while on the campaign trail, Trump used wrist and facial movements to humiliate a reporter with a disability. Researchers who studied 27 hours of video from Trump's political rallies found many examples of this type of behavior, noting that his gestures mirror the style used by stand-up comedians. The histrionic facial expressions, rolling eyes, sarcasm, anti–political correctness, staged rituals of masculinity, and the name-calling and bullying of opponents demonstrates a classic comedy style where "insults and gestures are produced in excess and often coordinated to enhance comedic effect" (Hall, Goldstein, & Ingram, 2016, p. 79). This unconventional political style is a form of entertainment that aligns with the norms of reality TV, which is itself a staged parody of reality.

For many people, humor is an important entry point into political discourse and debate. Since the dawn of the Enlightenment, humor has been recognized as a subtle and powerful means of social control while also functioning as a force for resistance. Parody, satire, hoaxes, and political humor can function as propaganda, especially when such messages oversimplify information and attack opponents. Irreverent wit, sarcasm, and playful use of memes are common civic practices online. During American political elections, researchers found that parody and joke accounts were highly retweeted and generated substantial interaction (Davis, Love, & Killen, 2018).

Entertainment propaganda can be effective in shifting public opinion, especially in the absence of other information. Communication scholars have shown the many ways that comedy journalism shows like *The Daily Show*, *The Colbert Report*, or *Last Week Tonight with John Oliver* tackle the subject of climate change

(Feldman, 2013). In one study, researchers showed either a climate change comedy clip or a control video clip to participants. Watching the comedy clip increased subjects' confidence that climate change is happening and their perception that scientists agreed on the issue. The shift in attitude was strongest among people who reported the lowest levels of interest in the topic beforehand (Brewer & McKnight, 2017).

For people without prior knowledge, comedy journalism can be truly educational. Plus, many people are likely to agree with an idea if it's presented satirically, because humor's pleasurable appeal leads people to bypass critical thinking in responding to it. By arousing emotions using humor, entertainers can deliver propaganda that may not be scrutinized as carefully as other genres.

Scare Tactics and Official Knowledge

Some opponents of climate change education try to scare people about the pedagogy of teaching climate change in schools. Consider the work of David Horowitz, who aims to protect "traditional American values" against adversaries on the left, through the Freedom Center, his conservative nonprofit organization. Horowitz has been complaining about immigrants, Muslims, and climate change scientists for decades, and his organization has long supported the work of Steve Bannon, Kellyanne Conway, and many others from the Trump administration.

In a typical news story on their website, the Horowitz School for Political Warfare warned about intergenerational learning strategies being used to teach about climate change. One headline read, "Government Experiment Brainwashes Children to Manipulate Conservative Parents." The May 2019 article describes a scientific article, published in *Nature*, that examines a study of child-to-parent learning in which researchers designed an experiment to test the viability of a set of lessons designed for middle school children to encourage them to talk with their parents about climate change. Researchers found that parents of children in the treatment group expressed higher levels of climate change concern than parents in the control group. They concluded that intergenerational learning may be a valuable educational practice.

The Horowitz Center described this particular research project as a dangerous form of propaganda. In a blog post on the subject, the Horowitz Center writer punched up the words "experiment" and "treatment," making a particular form of educational outreach seem quite dangerous. The idea that scientists are secretly manipulating vulnerable children attracts people's attention, and it has the elements of a classic conspiracy theory. According to the Horowitz Center, sinister scientists are trying to manipulate the children of conservative parents to believe in climate change using techniques reminiscent of the Soviet KGB during the Cold War (Greenfield, 2019).

But when the scare tactics and hype are removed, there is still a valid point to be made: intergenerational approaches to climate change education may be a form of education propaganda if children are encouraged to inform their parents as a means to change their attitudes. Whether you see this action as beneficial or harmful propaganda will depend on your pre-existing knowledge, beliefs, and attitudes.

Some climate science education propaganda takes the form of impressive-looking reports published by a think tank, which is a type of research organization that addresses topics relevant to social policy, economics, military, technology, and culture. They may be funded by governments, corporations, or advocacy groups. They often create formal-looking documents that show no sign of being propaganda. Both conservative and progressive think tanks may deliver official-looking propaganda in the form of institutional research. Think tanks exist because, at the start of the 20th century, rich business leaders decided that they could offer advice to the U.S. government. They set up shop in Washington, DC, and began exploring topics of interest. You may remember from a previous chapter that the Rockefeller Foundation even got interested in conducting research on propaganda way back in the 1930s.

Because millionaires provided a permanent endowment for these institutions, some think tanks and foundations are truly independent of political influence. But many rely on ongoing, annual fundraising. Some think tanks are dependent on federal government funding and others are highly partisan advocacy organizations with an explicit ideological and political agenda. For example, the Family Research Council and American College of Pediatricians are opposed to LGBTQ rights. Anti-immigration think tanks include the Federation for American Immigration Reform, the Center for Immigration Studies, and NumbersUSA (Ellis, 2016). Left-wing progressive think tanks include the Institute for Policy Studies and the Economic Policy Institute. There are now even think tanks dedicated to white supremacy, like the National Policy Institute and the New Century Foundation.

But many think tanks that claim to be nonpartisan blur the lines between research and advocacy. Consider a think tank's simple practice of journalistic framing, as in the 2016 report from the Cato Institute titled, "Lukewarming: The New Climate Science That Changes Everything." This report argues that "global warming is not hot—it's lukewarm." Now that is a catchy phrase, indeed. In the report, they say that the impact of global warming has been exaggerated by climate science advocates whose work is itself a form of propaganda. The Cato Institute's message backs away from climate change denial—because the scientific evidence makes that impossible to believe anymore. Instead, the Cato Institute has skillfully adjusted their argument in order to minimize and trivialize climate science by critiquing scientists' zeal about the urgent need to address the issue. They merely claim that scientists are out for their own selfish interests in overstating the problem. It's another case of propaganda in the eye of the beholder.

Because the political, ideological, and financial biases of think tanks are generally not disclosed, these organizations can sometimes mislead policy makers, experts, and the general public into believing that the information they provide comes from neutral, disinterested experts. Think tanks and foundations now shape many dimensions of scholarly discourse in a wide number of fields. More research is needed to understand the role of think tanks and foundations in shaping public discourse and influencing policy. Unfortunately, in some fields, the visibility and reputational prominence of foundations and think tanks may erode the autonomy and independence of scholarly experts.

Back in the classroom, science teachers are worried because of the growing desire of politicians to legally control how educators teach about both climate change and evolution. In several states, laws have been proposed to offer guidance to public school teachers who want to teach "diverse" (read: nonscientific) views on these scientific issues. After Alabama passed a new law that requires students to learn about climate change and evolution (for the first time) as part of an overhaul of the state's science education standards, lawmakers in the state issued a joint resolution acknowledging the controversy. They urged teachers to behave respectfully toward parents who deny climate change and evolution (Worth, 2018, p. 1).

Fortunately, in some places, students themselves are leading the charge for climate change. The most well-known climate change activist is Greta Thunberg, who at age 15, first went to the Swedish Parliament holding a sign that read, "School Strike for Climate." After speaking at the United Nations Climate Change Conference in 2018, she inspired other high school students around the world to hold school strikes to call attention to the urgent need for regulation (Gessen, 2018). In Portland, Oregon, after students came forward with their concerns about climate change, the local school board passed a resolution that climate change and climate justice would be integrated into the curriculum at all levels. High school students at Portland's Roosevelt High School have benefited from a strong media literacy and journalism education program for years (Madison, 2015). In 2018, these high school students organized a youth summit on climate change, reflecting the spirit of youth participatory politics that is cultivated by students and high school faculty alike. Students at Roosevelt High have also learned how to make advocacy documentaries on topics that interest them, which inspires their civic engagement. In 2019, student activists pressured the superintendent to allocate $200,000 to climate justice education, using the money to hire a full-time coordinator and establish a stand-alone course in climate justice in all the city's high schools (Seely, 2019).

In different cultures, different propaganda education strategies are used to address the problem of climate change. When people in China struggled with what they called "fog," they took to wearing smog-repellent face masks on days when particulate levels were high. Then they started distributing photos showing the scope of pollution that people experience. Then they made documentaries about the problem. But people did not criticize the government or demand action. Instead they focused on carefully documenting the coughing, hacking, and general bad health that people experienced from breathing highly polluted air. They framed their concerns as a public health issue. Over time, people started to use the term "smog" instead of "fog," and then the government finally began to monitor and report measures of particulate matter in the air. Since then, the country has made sweeping changes to curb pollution in its most populous cities, and China even signed the Paris climate accord in 2016, promising to increase the use of renewable energy (Mina, 2019).

Data Literacy and Trust

Given that data can be seen as the currency of the 21st century, it is not surprising that a variety of actors are trying to influence and shape it for personal gain. In earlier chapters, we've learned how data on our online behavior is used to provide personalized advertising, information, and entertainment, even as it entails risks to privacy, data breaches, and other potential harms. As data is being used for overt and covert propaganda purposes, some educators, librarians, and scientists around the world are calling for data literacy, which is defined as the knowledge and skills needed to use, analyze, interpret, and create data. This form of education includes attention to topics including artificial intelligence, machine learning, algorithms, data analytics, and user interface metrics.

Data literacy starts at the outset with issues of representation. Data represent observations of physical and social reality—which are aspects of people's lived experience. Thus, the quality of data is important. Just looking at a chart or graph without knowing how the underlying data was collected or analyzed can leave people vulnerable to manipulation. When it is trustworthy, scientific data can paint a picture of the world on which people can act. To decide what data to trust, people must take into account the reputation of the data creators, the reliability of the instruments used to gather data, the soundness of underlying theoretical frameworks, and the completeness, accuracy, and validity of the data (Koltay, 2017).

We tend to think of scientific data as neutral and unbiased. But historians have revealed the long-standing relationship between the U.S. government and private scientific groups, showing how the process of developing scientific consensus has been deeply rooted in politics for most of the 20th century (Wolfe, 2018). For example, since he came into office, President Trump has been actively contemptuous of environmental regulation. He has used Twitter to depict the Environmental Protection Agency (EPA) and other federal agencies as part of what he calls the deep state, which refers to a supposed secret government inside the government, a covert network of people in pursuit of their own agenda and goals. To limit the EPA, the Trump administration even changed their policies for data collection by specifying how scientific assessments may use computer-generated climate models. The impact of climate change will be modeled only through the year 2040, rather than to 2100 as previously (Davenport & Landler, 2019). As a result of changing the scientific model, official U.S. government data on climate now amounts to a half-truth, giving a misleading picture of the future impact of carbon emissions. Changing this policy intentionally reduced the quality of the data to minimize its value. Data are always selective and incomplete, of course, but this example reveals an intentional strategy to make data function as propaganda.

How do people come to recognize what forms of data can be trusted or distrusted? In a complex society, people do not have time to fact-check every claim or assertion they encounter in the news, social media, or online. Certainly, I do not have the inclination to second-guess my sources of information when data is presented in the context of news about social and political issues. I simply don't have the time. In my work and everyday life, I must make decisions about who and what to trust. For this reason, students and teachers both need opportunities to reflect on the question: How do you decide who you can you trust?

Since ancient times, philosophers have been wondering about this question. In his book *Nonsense on Stilts*, the philosopher Massimo Pigliucci (2010) points out why trusting experts is important even though expertise is an imperfect mechanism to find truth. As people develop expertise, they generally display habits of mind that are useful for citizenship in general, becoming less rigid and more flexible, introspective, and responsive. But expertise is also narrow and specific to a particular domain of knowledge: You can't be an expert in everything. As Pigliucci notes, "The only way to assess whether an expert is in fact an expert is to be an expert oneself" (2010, p. 269).

It's not merely a matter of gaining independence in deciding which experts deserve to be trusted and respected. Decisions about who to trust are social practices, made in the context of a tribe or community. Since expertise does not transfer across all subject matters and domains, people need to cultivate a variety of experts on all sorts of different topics and issues. Walter Lippmann called these people thought leaders and recognized that they play an important role in negotiating social consensus. For example, among my friends, I rely on Mary E. for her Midwest baking expertise, but when it comes to scrumptious salads, Mary O.'s flavorful suggestions can be counted upon. Likewise, some people depend on my expertise in media literacy education, but this does not make me an expert in finance, physics, or special education.

Through community engagement and skillful use of social media, we can extend networks of relational trust. We are lucky to be able to form relationships with all kinds of thought leaders using personal learning networks. Through cultivating these relationships, we can learn whose ideas can be trusted and who is less trustworthy. As people gain broad knowledge and experience in gathering information from diverse sources, they become better at judging both the authenticity and the authority of various sources. Still, trust in experts only goes so far. Expertise does not guarantee truth. Science is a human process that is limited by the available evidence, our emotional reactions, and our cognitive capacities. That's why the ability to recognize, understand, analyze, resist, and even create propaganda is essential for lifelong learning.

Textbook Propaganda

For most of the 20th century, education scholars recognized that that schooling serves as an instrument of nationalism, noting that "teachers and administrators have often followed unwittingly the lines laid down for them by social forces which they did not understand or perhaps even discern" (Counts, 1927, p. 147). Studies that have compared the representation of historical events in textbooks from Germany, France, and England reveal national bias in the treatment of historical topics. These depictions can foster prejudice and perpetuate myths of national identity that may inflame hatred. As one scholar points out, "School history is a kind of official history" (Low-Beer, 2003, p. 5), where the content of the curriculum is decided by governments.

In autocratic regimes, rulers make decisions about what to teach. In democratic societies, these decisions are up for debate, and activist stakeholders emerge to support or contest a particular approach or strategy. For example, some political conservatives have taken issue with how recent history is described in textbooks like *We the People*, published by Pearson Education. They see bias against political conservatives, President Trump and his administration, and Americans of faith. They also object to descriptions of institutionalized racism in the United States. For example, one critic disparaged the textbook for its description of the rise of the Black Lives Matter movement in the aftermath of the Ferguson, Missouri, shooting. This statement appears in the textbook: "The nearly all-white police force was seen as an occupying army in the mostly African-American town." The textbook also refers to the number of white males in President Trump's cabinet and his "not-very-hidden racism," leading one critic to interpret the textbook as "overt political propaganda being scooped into the most capable students' minds under the guise of education" (Pullman, 2018, p. 1).

Clearly, propaganda is in the eye of the beholder. For this reason, the specific content of American history textbooks has long been contentious. Fights over textbook content began in the early part of the 20th century. In the American South, for example, activists promoted a false version of U.S. history, one that minimized slavery's central role in the Civil War. They depicted the Confederacy as a heroic cause and the South as a victim of Northern aggression. To get these types of messages into the curriculum, activist efforts were required.

One such activist was named Mildred Lewis Rutherford. She was a well-educated Southern belle who became the historian of the United Daughters of the Confederacy. In what is sometimes called the Lost Cause version of Confederate history, multiple generations of Americans learned that, in the Southern states, slaves were well treated by their masters and better off than in their "savage life in Africa." In these American history textbooks, African Americans were depicted as "faithful servers . . . who sang and danced for the amusement of the home circle" (Huffman, 2019, p. 1). This group ensured that Confederate flags and portraits of Confederate leaders were displayed in the states' public schools.

As the self-appointed spin doctor for the Confederacy, Rutherford led the charge to erect Confederate monuments and memorials in many cities and towns across the South. She also created a list of standards for history textbooks in 1919, titled, "A Measuring Rod to Test Textbooks and Reference Books in Schools, Colleges and Libraries." This simple set of rules for textbooks included a blacklist of textbooks that did not embrace the Lost Cause ideology. In North Carolina and other states, this list was used in statewide campaigns to pressure state superintendents to ban certain books. Gradually, these efforts led to the development of state textbook commissions, which took the process of selecting school textbooks away from local school boards. American textbook publishers had to include the Lost Cause dogma in order to sell books to school districts in the Southern states. As a result, generations of Americans grew up with school textbooks that included false ideas about the cause of the Civil War.

Fortunately, this form of education propaganda was disrupted by the efforts of another education activist, the historian James Loewen. When the state of Mississippi voted to reject their textbook in 1975, Loewen and his colleague Charles Sallis decided to fight back. With the help of the NAACP Legal Defense and Education Fund, they sued the state of Mississippi in federal court. The state had selected a textbook that placed blame for the harsh punishment of slaves on Black overseers. The textbook portrayed the Ku Klux Klan as a fraternal club and did not mention racial violence such as lynchings. By contrast, the textbook written by Loewen and Sallis, titled *Conflict and Change*, included details of lynchings, segregation, and violence against civil rights protesters. It even included photographs of white people standing over the burning body of a Black lynching victim. In 1980, the history professors won their lawsuit, and the state of Mississippi was forced to include *Conflict and Change* on the approved list of textbooks. In making the legal decision, Judge Orma Smith observed that some members of the state's seven-member rating committee testified they had turned the book down six years earlier because they felt it stressed Black history too much and because they didn't like the picture of the lynching (Rich, 1980). Notes one scholar, "It was the first time that state endorsed a textbook that veered from the Lost Cause narrative" (Huffman, 2019, p. 1).

Of particular concern to Loewen is the rise and spread of misinformation in the Trump era. When Loewen released a new edition of his famous book about bias in history textbooks titled *Lies My Teacher Told Me: Everything Your Teacher Got Wrong*, he observed the new challenges raised by the presidency of Donald Trump, who has made it clear from the start of his administration that facts do not get in the way of his interpretation of reality. He critiques the faulty thinking embedded in the term "alternative facts," first used by Trump advisor Kellyanne Conway in 2017 during a television interview about the size of the inauguration crowd. The Trump administration's claims about the number of people attending the inauguration were inconsistent with the available evidence (Ford, 2017). To Loewen, a fact is something that can be proven with evidence, such as a photograph, a document, or a firsthand account. To illustrate this point, in the new edition, Loewen includes photos that compare the number of participants who attended the Obama and Trump inaugurations (Loewen, 2018, p. xvi).

LEARNING ACTIVITY

Memorials and Monuments as Propaganda

Study monuments and memorials in your community to see how they express an ideology that may function as propaganda.

Activity: Media literacy education can occur *en plein air*. Walk around a part of your city or town where you can see local architecture, monuments, and memorials and take photos of them. There are many forms of public art in nearly every city, town, and village. Students can do this independently or in small groups. They can collect photos of examples from their community and region. Then, students conduct research to learn more about the history of the monuments and critically analyze their depiction of history.

Questions for Discussion:

- **What** specific events and people are being remembered and honored in the public art, monument or memorial?
- **What** messages, key ideas, and information are expressed?
- **What** feelings and thoughts come to mind when you see it?
- **Who** supported or financed this work? Why was it placed in that location?
- **Was** there any controversy or opposition to the public art, monument or memorial during or after its construction?
- Do you view this monument or memorial differently than people did when it was planned and built? **Why or why not?**

- Were other groups involved in the events depicted or represented in the public art, monument, or memorial–for instance, women, people of color, or working people? **Why or why not?**

Create to Learn: Students create some kind of media to creatively communicate what they learned through observation, discussion, and research. Perhaps they will reenact a story about one of the characters related to the event depicted in a monument. Or they may choose to create a simple website with additional information about the memorial that students found during their research. Alternatively, they may design and plan for a new or updated memorial to be located on the site of the original.

The Takeaway: Monuments and memorials are forms of public art that may serve a propaganda function by depicting people and historical events in ways that support the interests of those who created it.

–Adapted from *Teaching Tolerance* toolkit, Set in Stone

The Ethics of Propaganda

Now that we understand the vast scope of propaganda in entertainment and education, it's easy to appreciate the tension between those who see propaganda as inherently problematic or even immoral and those who have a more neutral or even a positive perspective. Propaganda is a concept that fully acknowledges the power of language and symbols to shape perceptions and beliefs. As such, it is a peaceful means of gaining social power and influence. At the turn of the 20th century, U.S. government propaganda was understood as a way to refute misinformation and build a sense of national unity on the side of compassion and truth (Greenberg, 2016). For some, propaganda was seen "as a tool . . . no more moral or immoral than a pump handle" (Lasswell, 1948, p. 545).

To examine the ethics of propaganda, we must consider its truthfulness or falsity, its intentionality and strategic purpose, and its stance towards the target audience. Some philosophers consider how to distinguish between beneficial and harmful propaganda by considering how propaganda may promote flawed ideologies (like the belief that wealthy people are superior to others). By appealing to human status needs in order to advance an ideology, these problematic beliefs "unreflectively guide us through the social world" (Stanley, 2015, p. 184). Other philosophers see propaganda as a type of media message (in any genre or form) that inherently reduces human agency or aims to limit the freedom of the target audience to accept or reject a particular message or ideology.

When propaganda is indifferent to truth, it becomes ethically suspect. What does it mean to be indifferent to truth? Think of it this way: Propagandists may use truth when it works to their advantage, just as they may use lies and half-truths when they work to achieve a goal. Propagandists may use truth for the wrong reasons, according to Walter Cunningham, author of *The Idea of Propaganda*. When truth and truthfulness are treated as nothing more than a strategic communication tool, the practice of reasoning and critical analysis can be disfigured (Cunningham, 2002).

Applying ethical reasoning can help people carefully consider the potential consequences of their communication, behaviors, and actions, which have the power to change the world—for good or for evil. Ethics is a social practice rooted "in dialogue and reciprocal participation in a common life" (Marlin, 2013, p. 353). For this reason, exploring the ethics of propaganda provides a space for reflective thinking. Reflecting on the issue of the morality of propaganda, Jacques Ellul acknowledged that, in Germany under the Nazis, propaganda was total, with violence the means used to enforce it. For this reason, even small acts of resistance were acts of courage that are important to commemorate. But when there are many different forms of propaganda and they are diverse, plentiful, and respectful of human freedom, then propaganda is not coercive and does not limit human freedom (Ellul, 1981).

Clearly, we cannot evaluate whether propaganda is beneficial or harmful without appreciating the significance of the interpretive frames that are constructed by culture and society. We are not wholly independent in how we evaluate propaganda, as we are situated within our particular time and place in culture. This shapes how individuals interpret the potential benefits and harms of propaganda. Certain types of media messages may be indifferent to truth, for example, when their primary purpose is to entertain. However, when propaganda that is designed to inform becomes indifferent to truth, it is not only ethically flawed, it may become downright harmful.

Some people see deception as the key feature that makes propaganda unethical, seeing propaganda as a type of lying. Propaganda is pragmatic: it uses "myths, stories, symbols, group loyalties, group-oriented appeal to the people, popular enthusiasms, visual imagery, and any techniques of persuasion that are psychologically effective" (Walton, 1997, p. 409). Propagandists deliberately replace the messy, ambiguous complexities of the real world with a simplified vision of reality. This kind of deception, even when done for aesthetic or business purposes, is why some scholars claim that propaganda is pseudocommunication, because it does not effectively distinguish between reality, representation, simulation, and falsehood (Moran, 1979).

All forms of human communication use metaphors and symbols to arouse mental responses and activate powerful emotions in their audiences. Propaganda may provide people with feelings of empowerment, give them a sense of self-worth, or offer a cure for loneliness. When propaganda is repeated over and over, it may serve as a form of social glue that binds us to others. For this reason, we may be attracted to propaganda that aligns with socially sanctioned beliefs and values.

Fortunately, as media literacy educators insist, audiences have a good deal of conscious control over their interpretations. We can take epistemic responsibility for the meanings we produce. As Jacques Ellul insists, people are not victimized by propaganda. Propaganda requires the willingness of the listener, reader, or viewer to participate in the meaning-making process. Propaganda does not work without our active participation (Ellul, 1973, p. 155).

While some people think of propaganda as inferior, biased speech, media literacy educators emphasize that all forms of expression and communication are biased, because they were created by humans. As a result, propaganda is fundamentally a form of communication behavior, with a particular point of view, rooted in a particular political, economic, and cultural context. For this reason, it's simply not possible to make a blanket statement of whether propaganda is ethical or unethical. Case-by-case reasoning that includes deep examination of the cultural context and situation is essential. Sometimes propaganda is deeply ethical. Other times, it is profoundly unethical. Considering the full context and situation can help people distinguish between ethical and unethical propaganda.

When used in responsible ways, propaganda can help address social problems and improve society. Activating sympathy and other strong emotions can change minds: Such messages can be both true and sincere. Tapping into people's deepest hopes, dreams, and fears is not inherently unethical or manipulative—it's profoundly human.

Because moral principles and values govern the actions and decisions of individuals and groups, propaganda can be valuable for exploring ethical reasoning through the consideration of means and ends. To explore the ethics of propaganda with my students, I ask them to simply consider the relationship between the communicator, the subject, and the audience. Each has obligations to the other; each has expectations for how the other should behave and act. Balancing and negotiating competing loyalties requires practice. Filmmakers have a primary ethical obligation to the ideas, events, and subjects they depict. A leading scholar of documentary film has offered his insights on the ethics of propaganda, noting the filmmaker's need to respect the dignity of subjects and viewers alike. Bill Nichols points out the inherent power imbalance between a filmmaker and the subjects. This power imbalance can be easily abused. He writes, "Subjects who are dependent on the filmmaker to have their story told—subjects, that is, who occupy the lower social strata generally and who can most readily be cast into the position of victim—are most vulnerable to misrepresentation and abuse" (Nichols, 2019, p. 1). Filmmakers must also respect their audiences as well. Filmmakers are obliged to provide accurate information and evidence, even while evoking feelings that go beyond the reach of reason.

But filmmaking inevitably involves creating unreal realities, forms of misrepresentation that may threaten this ethical obligation. For example, filmmakers may use reenactment to illustrate an event that occurred when no camera was present. They may present footage from one time period or place as if it came from another time and place. For example, in *Triumph of the Will,* Leni Riefenstahl combined shots from different times and places to give the illusion of one continuous event. She manipulated image and sound to create what she considered to be a "higher truth." Certainly, she had the right to create this impression, but in evaluating propaganda, viewers cannot examine only the techniques of production. They must consider the filmmaker's purpose, goals, and moral values in deciding whether the work has integrity.

Ethical reasoning about advocacy documentaries can be an important form of propaganda education. Today, Americans are most likely to experience advocacy films through the work of Participant Media. Founded by eBay billionaire Jeff Skoll, Participant Media is a media company dedicated to entertainment that brings social awareness and engages audiences to participate in positive social change. Many people are familiar with the climate change documentary film starring Al Gore, *An Inconvenient Truth,* which earned $50 million and won an Oscar for best documentary in 2006. Other films include *Food, Inc.*, the 2009 documentary about agribusiness directed by Robert Kenner, and *The Help*, the 2011 civil rights drama directed by Tate Taylor about a white woman who writes a book about the daily life of Black maids and the families they support. Participant Media produces content "that combines the power of a good story well told with opportunities for real world impact around the most pressing global issues of our time" (Participant Media, 2018, p. 1).

Remember the point made earlier about propaganda being in the eye of the beholder. Some forms of film can be emotionally powerful and inspiring and yet still be interpreted as harmful propaganda by those who encounter them. In 2017, Participant Media produced *Wonder*, a family drama about a boy named Auggie coping with facial birth defects. This film made $306 million at the box office, and Participant executives were proud of the way it delivered an inspirational, emotional message about compassion for people with disabilities. Jonathan King, Participant's president of narrative film and television, said, "Kids watch the movie, they internalize that message, it helps to change lives" (Barnes, 2019, p. 1). The film's focus on empathy appealed to many educators, parents, and children. Certainly, the film led to greater public awareness of disabilities that affect the formation of the skull and face.

But critics questioned the representation of disability in *Wonder*. Ariel Henley, a writer who herself has a craniofacial disability like the child portrayed in the film, recognized a number of choices made by the filmmakers that seemed unintentionally insensitive. The film's writer had little familiarity with the topic: She was inspired to write *Wonder* after her 3-year-old son started crying at the sight of a young girl with a facial difference. Henley is concerned that the filmmakers chose not to cast a child actor with the disability in the role. Instead, the actor they selected wore an elaborate prosthesis mask. She notes that by depicting the family as wealthy, the story omitted reference to the significant financial burdens of having a child with a facial difference. In the film, Auggie is a victim of bullying and the film's emphasis on his relentless kindness to his tormentors was appealing. But Henley writes that this representation is a "particularly fraught suggestion for individuals living with disfigurement" because it creates expectations that people with disabilities must "tolerate those who won't tolerate," putting the burden on the disabled person "to educate a society whose impulse is to be cruel" (Henley, 2017, p. 1). Some disability educators have even called the film "inspiration porn." Still, many teachers and students across the country were profoundly moved by the antibullying message of the film. The popularity of the film led to numerous school-wide and community reading programs across the country where children and adults had meaningful discussions about kindness, bullying, responsibility, overcoming challenges, and friendship (Barack, 2017). Clearly, good arguments can be made that the film is both beneficial and harmful propaganda.

Education Versus Indoctrination

You can now see the importance of multiperspectival thinking as it helps us analyze and evaluate propaganda in all its many forms. Because ideas can be dangerous, philosophers, scholars, artists, and educators have debated the dangers of propaganda and indoctrination since the Enlightenment. Indoctrination may occur when educators promote the uncritical, universal acceptance of certain ideas and shun all evidence and points of view that do not align with those ideas.

In many parts of the world, education is intentionally designed as a form of indoctrination to create patriotic and obedient citizens. In China, students have been required to learn about the philosophy of dialectical materialism for decades. Recently, President Xi Jinping has stepped up the levels of indoctrination, describing his desire for students to absorb the doctrine of the Chinese Communist Party by explaining, "Children should memorize the core socialist values by heart, have them melt in their hearts, and carve them into their brains." The Ministry of Education has established 10 Centers of Xi Jingping Thought on college campuses as well as an ideological team of missionaries to spread Xi Jingping Thought "to the very nerve endings" of students (Taber, 2018). By equating love of country with the love for the Chinese Communist Party and Chinese socialism, this type of nationalistic education is a classic form of political indoctrination through education. Such education also exists in Hong Kong, but it has never been as strident or as all-encompassing (Leung, 2004). Mainland Chinese officials have long blamed Hong Kong's social and political activism on the lack of effective political indoctrination (which is often called patriotic education or moral education). In 2019, when hundreds of thousands of protesters erupted to fight an unpopular bill that expanded police authority to extradite citizens of Hong Kong to be tried in mainland China, government spokesmen placed the blame on the education system (Sun, 2019).

In the past, the words "indoctrination" and "education" were once synonymous, with Webster's 1913 dictionary defining indoctrination as "instruction in the rudiments and principles of any science or system of belief" (Gooblar, 2019, p. 1). Today, indoctrination generally refers to the use of academic authority to promote uncritical acceptance of a particular belief or set of beliefs. Let me be clear:

Education is not indoctrination when it activates critical thinking and encourages the exploration of multiple perspectives and points of view. These practices open up learners to the possibility of creating new knowledge through the exploration of diverse views, using evidence, reasoning, and argument.

Occasionally, educators have been accused of indoctrination for pushing a particular ideological viewpoint upon learners. Those who teach about media and communication are not immune from this critique. Teaching about who owns mass media is a common topic in some media literacy courses at the college level, and faculty may emphasize the evils of big business and the dangers of economic monopolies. Examination of issues of representation and media stereotypes involves dissecting gender and racial stereotypes to uncover how they perpetuate inequality. These are common topics for media literacy educators in both high schools and universities.

When teachers examine media representations, they may run the risk of indoctrination if they espouse beliefs that position students as helpless against media influence. Students can experience strong and uncomfortable emotions when familiar texts from their childhood are analyzed for gender or racial stereotypes. Some students may even complain when their professor asks them to critically analyze Disney animation or another media text that is treasured and beloved (Greenwood, 2020). In one study of two high school teachers who examined race, class, and gender representations in the media with their students, a teacher introduced students to critical media theory. The teacher wanted students to understand how patriarchal oppression, femininity, and masculinity are cultural constructs that perpetuate gender inequality. Among the learning activities in this class, students screened and analyzed the Disney animated films *Toy Story* and *Pocahontas.* When one young student objected to the teacher's interpretations of one of the films, the teacher told the student, "You don't notice that because you have been brainwashed" (Friesem, 2018, p. 140).

Telling students that they are defenseless dupes of mass media ideology is not wise pedagogy, that's for certain. But because the teacher's opinion was presented as the only accurate interpretation, a classic pedagogical contradiction was revealed: although teachers claim to want open discussion, they may experience discomfort when students express ideas that do not conform with their own ideological worldviews. As the researcher points out, "Although the teachers noted that there can be different interpretations of media texts, they appeared to be concerned that young people might express 'wrong' ideas" (Friesem, 2018, p. 144).

Of course, teachers are human and make mistakes. Sometimes, in their well-meaning zeal to pull back the curtain on media ideologies, teachers can inadvertently constrict students' ability to learn to think for themselves by creating new sorts of "right" answers that are expected to be parroted back to the teacher (Buckingham, 2019). Even when teachers ask students to create their own media messages by making videos, they may inadvertently risk limiting student voice in ways that directly benefit certain cultural or educational institutions (and their funders) and diminish the personal autonomy of the learner (Bach, 2010). Teachers need to be reflective practitioners as they aim to advance student autonomy and cultivate multiperspectival thinking.

Campus Indoctrination

You don't have to search very far to find examples of education propaganda on college campuses. Beginning in 2004, the Chinese government launched the first Confucius Institute at the University of Maryland. Today, there are more than 100 of them on college campuses across the United States. The Chinese government funds Confucius Institutes and provides Chinese teachers to teach language classes. There are also more than 500 Confucius Classrooms in elementary, middle, and high schools in the United States.

Such efforts have been defined as a positive type of propaganda called public diplomacy, which is the ability to influence global policy through appealing to people's hearts and minds. Public diplomacy from the United States has been often credited with winning the Cold War, as organizations such as Radio Free Europe/Radio Liberty, the Voice of America, and the United States Information Agency communicated the ideals of democracy, individual rights, and the free market (Nye, 2018). Through establishing the Confucius Institute program, the Chinese government is attempting to change the global impression that China is an economic and security threat. The Communist Party's Propaganda Office controls the Chinese Ministry of Education, which is affiliated with the Confucius Institute headquarters, known as Hanban. U.S. schools that contract with Hanban receive between $100,000 and $200,000 in start-up costs, around 3,000 books and other materials, and the services of a Chinese director at no cost to the school. At many underfunded state universities, support from the Chinese government makes it possible to offer courses in Chinese language and culture that might not be available otherwise.

But these resources come with strings attached. In Confucius Institute programs at U.S. universities, topics like the independence of Taiwan or the 1989

Tiananmen Square massacre are strictly off limits. That's why some see the Confucius program as compromising the academic freedom of American universities. Not only does the Chinese government approve all teachers, events, and speakers for Confucius Institute events, but the Chinese teachers who participate in the program sign contracts pledging they will not damage the national interests of China.

Backlash toward Confucius Institutes emerged in 2014 when more than 100 faculty members at the University of Chicago signed a petition saying that the Confucius Institute was incompatible with the values of the university. A documentary film on the Confucius Institutes in Canada, *In the Name of Confucius*, tells the story of Sonia Zhao, whose experience teaching Chinese at McMaster University in Canada contributed to the termination of the Confucius Institute at that institution in 2013. One scholar notes that the expansion of China's presence in schools in the U.S. and other countries is taking place "at the same time that China itself is intensifying its crackdown on dissent, tightening its censorship of the Internet, and publishing prohibitions on what it calls 'false ideological trends,' which include promoting what the propaganda machinery calls 'Western values' " (Bernstein, 2017, p. 1). In 2019, the Senate Homeland Security and Governmental Affairs Committee issued a report on these efforts, finding that China has spent nearly $200 million in efforts to indoctrinate American students by painting a sympathetic portrait of the Chinese communist government. The Senate report states that such efforts "attempt to export China's censorship of political debate and prevent discussion of potentially politically sensitive topics" (U.S. Senate Permanent Subcommittee on Investigations, 2019, p. 1).

There are plenty of other, less visible ways in which the higher education community faces concerns about indoctrination. I will admit that I occasionally experienced it while an undergraduate student myself. Many of my professors were hostile toward business, and I was overtly discouraged from pursuing a career outside academia. As a literature major, a film/video major, and a book lover, I longed for a guest speaker from the film or publishing industry to visit the class so that I could learn about the media business. In both direct and subtle ways, I got the clear message that to enter the world of business was to sell one's soul to the devil. Faculty were not intending to indoctrinate me against capitalism. They were simply offering a worldview that represented their best understanding of the contemporary world. But when I became a young assistant professor teaching media studies to business students, I took responsibility for my own learning and confronted my own unquestioned beliefs about capitalism.

Protesting educational policies can be a form of propaganda that anyone can use for any purpose. In some local communities in Tennessee, parents and school board members voiced concern about "alleged Islamic indoctrination" in the public schools. In wealthy Williamson county, outside of Nashville, seventh grade students study world geography, which includes a week-long unit on the Islamic world. Perceiving a pro-Islamic bias to the curriculum, one school board member questioned whether it's right to test students on the tenets of Islam. School leaders in Williamson County insist that there was no bias toward Islam in the curriculum. Back in 2009, *The New York Times* columnist Paul Krugman also wondered about the rise of righteous protest against global education. He observed that residents protesting the school district's geography curriculum were inspired by the 912 Project, a conservative activist group organized by former Fox News commentator Glenn Beck. This group orchestrated campaigns to grab headlines through disrupting local government meetings. Their efforts were extensively promoted by Fox News, and the group was identified as one of the many fake grassroots organizations that lobbied against the Obama administration's health care reform (Center for Media and Democracy, 2009).

In conservative communities, librarians have long faced criticism for their selection of library books. In the 1980s, book censorship was rampant as efforts to remove certain titles from school and public libraries increased measurably. During this time, public libraries were targeted by conservative Christian groups who identified literature they felt was pornographic. A Georgia state law against displaying lewd and lascivious books and pictures where minors might see them caused one department store chain to stop ordering any new books. In 1982, the Supreme Court ruled in a case that concerned a school district on Long Island, New York, that removed nine books from its libraries and curriculum, including Bernard Malamud's *The Fixer* and Kurt Vonnegut's *Slaughterhouse-Five*. A committee of the school board believed that the books were "anti-American, anti-Christian, anti-Semitic and just plain filthy." The Supreme Court ruled that local school boards "may not remove books from school library shelves simply because they dislike the ideas contained in those books" (*Island Trees School District v. Pico*, 1982, p. 1).

Protest about political indoctrination in schools is an evergreen issue, it seems. During the summer of 2020, President Trump took up the topic at a Fourth of July speech at Mt. Rushmore. He criticized efforts to remove Confederate monuments and referred to it as "cancel culture," a new type of totalitarianism. He claimed that the Black Lives Matter protests were the result of "extreme indoctrination and bias in education, journalism and cultural institutions," saying, "Children are taught in school to hate their own country" (U.S. White House, 2020).

Claims about left-wing educators poisoning the minds of learners have also attracted the interests of lawmakers. In 2017, the Horowitz School for Political Warfare proposed an ethical code for K–12 teachers that would specifically restrict teachers from engaging in political advocacy. Republicans in Pennsylvania and Arizona have already taken up actions to try to make this code a state law. If enacted, the law would empower the state government to fire teachers who discuss politics, religion, or racial issues in classroom settings. The bill would forbid public school teachers from endorsing, supporting, or opposing candidates or incumbents for local, state, and federal offices while in the classroom. On the job, teachers could not discuss enacted or pending legislation, regulations, executive orders, or court cases involving any level or branch of government. This proposed law would prohibit "any controversial issue that is not germane to the topic of the course or academic subject," where a controversial issue is defined as "a point in a political party platform" (Birkinbuel, 2019, p. 1). This proposal would certainly silence legitimate freedom of expression and could be used as a weapon in ways that would deepen political polarization. It would make civic education impossible. Fortunately, it's likely that, if such laws ever were enacted into legislation, they would be overturned and declared unconstitutional by the courts.

The Dangers of Righteousness

Political attacks on educators can have far-reaching consequences, both in the United States and around the world. What starts as propaganda can lead to dangerous action. As history has shown, demagogues promote hate for purposes of war and mass murder. In Turkey, only months after President Recep Tayyip Erdoğan strengthened his power after the attempted coup in Istanbul in 2016, my Turkish friend and Media Education Lab colleague Sait Tuzel was arrested and imprisoned, spending one year in jail. This purge, as it was called, was the result of a power struggle between secular and Islamist factions in Turkey. Some people were sent to jail for simply signing a petition, a peace declaration calling for a halt to military operations to limit civilian casualties in the fight between Turkish security forces and Kurdish rebels. Others were simply caught in the crosshairs of academic politics. My friend Sait was not alone: More than 180,000 teachers, journalists, judges, college professors, and teachers were fired from their jobs or arrested between 2016 and 2018. That's about 10% of all public employees. After nearly a year, he was finally released from prison, but his passport was withheld and he has been prohibited from working in higher education.

After the Turkish government used emergency rule as a way of eliminating enemies, real and imagined, they justified the action using propaganda. The victims were a whole generation of educators, scholars and intellectuals who were trying to create a democratic civil society that could "bring forth generations even more democratic than themselves" through building a fair judicial system, a free press, human rights, and women's rights (Hansen, 2019, p. 1). After the purge, Turkish ministers of education hastily rewrote the textbooks. They shortened the history of Ataturk, the founder of the modern nation of Turkey, to just one paragraph, and they added the story of the attempted coup in 2016 and its aftermath, giving it a full three pages. Turkish education ministers used the school textbook to tell students and teachers what to think and what to believe.

Not to be outdone, the media industry added entertainment propaganda to the mix. Just before the April referendums that would increase and centralize Erdoğan's political power in 2017, a flattering film titled *The Chief* was released that portrays young Erdoğan as a budding hero, whose generosity and courage were evident even in his youth. The famous Turkish soap opera actor who portrayed Erdoğan dismissed allegations that the release of the film was timed to help Erdoğan win the political referendum (Deutsche Welle, 2017).

Among the most negative consequences of indoctrination that I have seen with my own eyes is the one I fear the most: self-righteousness. Consistent exposure to indoctrination can produce self-righteous people who are extremely confident in the superiority of their beliefs. Over the years, I've met plenty of smug people, from all walks of life, who are so very convinced of the truth of their ideas that they are not willing to engage with people whose views differ from their own. After all, if you're deeply convinced of a certain reality, why would you be curious about knowledge that may challenge that reality? These people often have strong opinions about subjects that they know almost nothing about. They feel superior to others who do not share their same ideological beliefs. Others are proud of their ignorance or their biases, seeing them as an asset or a cultural trait. Many are simply too busy grazing the surface of superficial content to focus their attention enough to reflect for even a moment on the limits of their knowledge and understanding. When possessed by a deep sense of righteousness, people may intentionally limit their own learning (Taylor, 2017).

Although indoctrination can be a systemic phenomenon that is not merely a matter of the individual relationship between an instructor and a student, educators can minimize the possibility that indoctrination might occur through modeling humility (Gooblar, 2019). To cultivate lifelong learning, people need to practice both the art of asking questions and the process of developing, expressing, and sharing ideas, information, and opinions, contributing their powerful voices to address the important problems all around us. For this reason, students and teachers both need frequent and regular opportunities to reflect deeply on the socially constructed nature of knowledge, including information, education, entertainment, and persuasion.

Epilogue

Inquiry as a form of learning involves careful consideration of the interplay between the human heart, mind, hands, and spirit. Inquiry is so fundamental to learning and literacy that for more than 20 years I have defined media literacy as the process of "asking critical questions about what you watch, see, listen to and read" (Hobbs, 1998, p. 28). Inquiry learning practices lead towards truth. As one scholar points out, "If we didn't value true beliefs, we wouldn't value these sorts of activities; and we value these sorts of activities because we think they will, more often than not, lead us to believing truly rather than falsely" (Lynch, 2005, p. 14).

Inquiry learning requires curiosity, humility and tolerance for complexity. Intellectual humility is simply knowing you have blind spots and acting as if you might be wrong. When you recognize that a particular personal belief may be fallible, you are attentive to the basis of your beliefs. Scholars disagree about whether intellectual humility is a trait (part of your personality) or a state (a way that you behave or act). But they generally agree that intellectual humility involves recognizing and owning one's position in the culture and noticing how it limits the pursuit of knowledge, truth, and understanding. Such a mindset keeps people alert to their biases, open-minded and willing and eager to engage with and learn from others (Leary, 2018).

Intellectual humility is liberating. I rely on my students and colleagues to challenge my thinking, to contribute to the learning environment through asking questions and sharing knowledge themselves. When students ask a question that I don't know the answer to a question, I answer by saying, "I don't know." My favorite questions to my students are "How do you know that?" and "Why do you believe that?" I find ways to acknowledge and thank students who turn these same questions back on me. I emphasize the practice of basing opinions and ideas on argument and evidence, but I acknowledge the power of feelings and emotions. I support my students in learning to express themselves courageously, fearlessly, and with humility.

As part of the search for meaning and truth, teaching and learning about propaganda involves risk and vulnerability. Exposure to harmful propaganda has the potential to activate anger, resentment, cynicism, apathy, disillusionment, and despair. It may lead people to make bad decisions because of its powerful emotional pull and the comfort we experience when presented with simple solutions. Because propagandists attack opponents in order to accomplish their goal, there's more than enough blame to go around. But in a cultural climate filled with fear and suspicion, we must be courageous and brave. We must truly honor multiple perspectives and points of view, as these help us come closer to truth.

Skeptics who are reading this book may be questioning whether education can even be part of the solution. After all, schools are institutions of the government. Teachers are overworked and underpaid. And to be honest, skepticism and critical thinking may only go so far. Indeed, some scholars even wonder whether media literacy education has inadvertently contributed to the epistemological anxieties of the age, given that its practitioners insist on asking questions about the constructed nature of knowledge (Boyd, 2017).

But these fears fade from view when intellectual curiosity, humility, and respect for multiple perspectives are at the heart of the practice of teaching and learning. As lifelong learners who seek to live in a democratic society, we are not merely consumers, but we also actively contribute to the marketplace of ideas. We make commitments about which ideas to value, course. But we can aim to be open-minded and humble in our encounters with those whose interpretations differ from ours. We can learn to not just tolerate complexity, but to embrace it.

Teaching and learning about propaganda are rooted in the value of inquiry in pursuit of truth in its broadest and most complex sense. Through relevant and engaging learning activities that explore the nature of contemporary propaganda, I've shown in the book the myriad ways that learners can pay careful attention to the content and format of messages, gather information from many sources, examine the quality of evidence, ask questions, and use reasoning to make their thoughts, feelings, and interpretations transparent to others. People create propaganda to share their vision of a better world; in doing so, they address civic issues that matter to them as they explore solutions for the many problems that our global society faces today. The learning activities presented in this book illustrate the value of making deep connections between the classroom and the culture.

Fifty years ago, Jacques Ellul maintained that a heightened awareness of propaganda was ultimately the only way to be free from its powerful pull. I am passionate about teaching about propaganda, but I am also totally willing to revise my ideas when I get new information and new perspectives. That's what a commitment to intellectual curiosity, humility, and multiperspectival thinking requires.

With all the unreal realities of contemporary information, entertainment, and persuasion, it takes effort to sort out truth from lies, knowing that we can never really be certain which is which. As I have shown in this book, our culture has a variety of misconceptions about truth and the nature of knowledge that interfere with our ability to make sense of propaganda. One of the biggest misconceptions is that truth requires certainty. Of course, our experience of the world is never pure and direct since it is "modified by the structures and habits of our own minds" (Lynch, 2005, p. 24), so certainty is out of the question. But "we can still treat truth as a goal of inquiry even if we can never be certain of reaching it" (p. 28). In technology and business circles, this thinking strategy has been described as "strong opinions, weakly held."

The implications of these ideas for teaching and learning and for citizenship and democracy are formidable. One scholar puts it this way:

> *Many conflicts in society stem from disagreements about values, politics, religion, cultural practices, and other topics. These conflicts become intractable when people are unable or unwilling to consider the possibility that their personal views might be, if not incorrect, at least no better overall than other perspectives. In increasingly heterogeneous societies, higher intellectual humility should promote compromise solutions for the good of all. (Leary, 2018, p. 14)*

The urge to find common ground through multiperspectival thinking, humility, and compromise will be increasingly important as we seek to reduce political polarization and find peaceful solutions to the many challenges that face our global society today. It's the only sane way forward.

Propaganda education gives learners the chance to examine how the activation of strong emotion may help people to better recognize and clarify shared cultural values. In responding to propaganda, people of all ages can reflect on the power of emotion, to learn how to talk with each other about how (and why) media messages make us feel. Critically analyzing the emotions we experience together will help cultivate a shared sense of responsibility for our communities.

To navigate the world of everyday propaganda, skepticism, truth-seeking, and empathy must be inseparable. With skepticism, we accept uncertainty as part of truth. With truth-seeking, we are alert to the need to analyze messages, even when those in power tell us otherwise. With empathy, we use an ethic of care in our encounters with others, informed by our own limitations and weaknesses. Cultivating intellectual curiosity and humility through deepening our respect for multiple perspectives and points of view may offer a key to the practice of lifelong learning in a world saturated with propaganda and persuasion.

Acknowledgments

My curiosity about propaganda emerged as a result of an opportunity provided to me by the staff of the United States Holocaust Memorial Museum (USHMM) in 2007 when they were organizing education outreach activities for *State of Deception*, a special exhibit on the history of Nazi propaganda. In working with JoAnna Wasserman, Sarah Ogilvie, David Klevan, and others to build connections between the past, present, and future of propaganda, I began to conceptualize the study of propaganda within the context of media literacy education.

As part of this work, I had many opportunities to talk about historical and contemporary propaganda with many people across the country. Early on, high school and college educators in Philadelphia, St. Louis, Washington, DC, and Chicago offered insights that informed my work. Steven Luckert, a curator of the USHMM permanent exhibition, offered his wisdom at several points during my journey into this complex subject. As part of this learning process, I held my own in heated public debates about whether or not news and journalism could be a form of propaganda. From the distinguished historian Habib Kazdaghli in Tunisia, I learned how history teachers in North Africa conceptualize both historic and contemporary propaganda. Thanks to support from public affairs professionals in the U.S. State Department, I gave workshops and interacted with journalists and educators in Brazil, Germany, and Italy. Special thanks to Munich Consul General Meghan Gregonis for her support of the Propaganda and Disinformation Lab project in Germany. In meetings with media literacy educators in Croatia, Belgium, Italy, Poland, Germany, China, Finland, and Brazil, I gained insights on how to teach today's students about propaganda. I also received valued information from those working in diplomacy and public service, advertising, public relations, social media, and activism who offered their ideas about the role of contemporary propaganda in public life.

The opportunity to help with the creation of the Mind Over Media platform was a significant catalyst for the development of this book. When grants from the European Commission and the Evens Foundation enabled me to bring this unique form of online learning to educators in six countries in eastern and western Europe, my learning was accelerated greatly. Thanks to Sally Reynolds, Paolo Cesarini, Tim Verbist, Joanna Krawczyk, and Eva Van Passel, who provided support for this initiative. I am particularly grateful to my international colleagues Igor Kanižaj, Nicoleta Fotiade, Sonja Hernesniemi, Maja Dobiasz, Bert Pieters, Maria Ranieri, and Silke Grufe, whose expertise in media literacy informed my thinking.

Finally, I would like to thank all those who read and commented on early drafts of this book as it developed, including Frank Baker, Michael RobbGrieco, Yonty Friesem, Samantha Stanley, Frank Romanelli, Christian Seyferth-Zapf, and Silke Grafe. At Norton, editor Carol Chambers Collins offered valuable suggestions to improve the manuscript and copyeditor Karen Fisher improved my prose. Mariah Eppes, Sara McBride Tuohy, Kevin Olsen, Megan Bedell, and Kelly Auricchio worked their magic to help readers find the book. But any mistakes, limitations, weaknesses, or omissions you may find in this book are my responsibility. The scope and depth of this project has been humbling. But it has made me even more dedicated to advance media literacy education as a means to empower people with the competencies, skills, and sense of social responsibility needed to use media and technology wisely.

List of Learning Activities

Chapter 4. **Teaching Fake News**

Chapter 5. **The Dark Side of Propaganda: Lies, Hate Speech, and Terrorism**

Chapter 6. **Beneficial Propaganda: Art, Activism, and Elections**

Chapter 7. Entertainment and Education Propaganda

References

Achbar, M., & Wintonick, P. (1992). *Manufacturing consent* [Motion picture]. United States Zeitgeist.

Adeane, A. (2019, January 13). Blue whale? What is the truth behind an online "suicide challenge"? BBC News. Retrieved from https://www.bbc.com/news/blogs-trending-46505722

Advertising Analytics and Cross Screen Media (2020). 2020 Political Spending Projections. Retrieved from https://www.politico.com/f/?id=0000016b-b029-d027-a97f-f6a95aca0000

Alford, M. & Rozbicka, P. (2018, May 24). Childish Gambino shows pop music can be powerfully political despite censorship. *The Independent.* Retrieved from https://www.independent.co.uk/arts-entertainment/music/childish-gambino-donald-glover-this-is-america-politics-music-censorship-america-a8363561.html

Alford, M., & Secker, T. (2017). *National security cinema.* Drum Roll Books.

Ali, L. (2018, November 16). Why the P word—propaganda—might be best for what we're seeing on our TV screens. *Los Angeles Times.* Retrieved from https://www.latimes.com/entertainment/tv/la-et-st-propaganda-fake-news-tv-culture-20181116-story.html

Alkousaa, R. (2017, June 26). Delaware school cuts professor over post on North Korea captive. Reuters. Retrieved from https://www.reuters.com/article/us-usa-northkorea-detainee-professor/delaware-school-cuts-professor-over-post-on-north-korea-captive-idUSKBN19H2DP

AllSides. (2019). How AllSides rates media bias: Our methods. Retrieved from https://www.allsides.com/media-bias/media-bias-rating-methods

Alvarado, M., Gutch, R., & Wollen, T. (1987). *Learning the media: An introduction to media teaching.* London: Macmillan.

Amazeen, M. (2015). Revisiting the epistemology of fact-checking. *Critical Review, 27*(1), 1–22.

Amoako, A. (2018, May 8). Why the dancing makes 'This is America' so uncomfortable to watch. *The Atlantic.* Retrieved from https://www.theatlantic.com/entertainment/archive/2018/05/this-is-america-childish-gambino-donald-glover-kinesthetic-empathy-dance/559928/

Anderson, J. A., & Ploghoft, M. E. (1980). Receivership skills: The television experience. *Annals of the International Communication Association*, *4*(1), 293–307.

Anderson, D., & Zyhowski, J. (2018). Teaching Trump: A case study of two teachers and the election of 2016. *Social Studies, 109*(2), 101–111.

Angwin, J., & Grassegger, H. (2017, June 28). Facebook's secret censorship rules protect white men from hate speech but not black children. ProPublica. Retrieved from https://www.propublica.org/article/facebook-hate-speech-censorship-internal-documents-algorithms

Anti-Defamation League (2020, February 11). White supremacists double down on propaganda in 2019. Retrieved from https://www.adl.org/blog/white-supremacists-double-down-on-propaganda-in-2019

App Annie (2019). Audience exclusivity in Snapchat. Retrieved from https://assets.ctfassets.net/inb32lme5009/27edQB34n5kbcvAiZw8b79/74d412309835f3e870f975bd5d4ef00c/Snapchat_Audience_Exclusivity.pdf

Ashley, S. (2019). News literacies. In R. Hobbs & P. Mihailidis (Eds.), *The international encyclopedia of media literacy* (pp. 1150–1160). Hoboken, NJ: Wiley-Blackwell.

Associated Press. (2019, May 15). Teachers searching for climate change info find propaganda. *New York Post.* Retrieved from https://nypost.com/2019/05/15/teachers-searching-for-climate-change-info-find-propaganda/

Astor, M. (2020, June 17). Why protest movements are 'civil' only in retrospect. *The New York Times*, A11.

Attkisson, S. (2017). *The smear.* New York: Harper Collins.

Auerbach, J., & Castronovo, R. (2013a). Introduction: Thirteen propositions about propaganda. In J. Auerbach & R. Castronovo (Eds.), *The Oxford handbook of propaganda studies* (pp. 1–16). New York: Oxford University Press.

Auerbach, J., & Castronovo, R. (Eds.). (2013b). *The Oxford handbook of propaganda studies.* New York: Oxford University Press.

Axelrod, A. (2009). *Selling the Great War: The making of American propaganda.* New York: St. Martin's.

Ayer, D. (Director). (2014). *Fury* [Motion picture]. United States: Columbia Pictures.

Bach, A. J. (2010). *Youth media literacy practices: The possibilities and complexities of creating and distributing non-commercial public media in a private and commercial world* (Unpublished doctoral dissertation). Graduate School of Education, University of Pennsylvania.

Baker, F. (2017, October 31). We're not the only ones who want kids' attention. MiddleWeb. Retrieved from https://www.middleweb.com/36205/were-not-the-only-ones-who-want-kids-attention/

Barack, L. (2017, November 11). Critics question the representation of disability in "Wonder." *School Library Journal.* Retrieved from https://www.slj.com/?detailStory=critics-question-representation-disability-wonder

Barkun, M. (2013). *A culture of conspiracy: Apocalyptic visions in contemporary America.* Berkeley: University of California Press.

Barnes, B. (2019, February 22). Oscars provide state for Participant Media's comeback story. *The New York Times.* Retrieved from https://www.nytimes.com/2019/02/22/business/media/participant-media-oscars.html

Barthes, R. (2012). *Mythologies.* New York: Hill and Wang. (Original work published 1957)

Battat, E. R. (n.d.). Art or propaganda? Blended Learning Initiative. Wellesley College. Retrieved from https://www.wellesley.edu/lts/bli/projects/battat

Beckett, L. (2019, February 14). Parkland one year on: What victories have gun control advocates seen? *The Guardian.* Retrieved from https://www.theguardian.com/us-news/2019/feb/14/parkland-school-shooting-anniversary-gun-control-victories

Bell, J. (2019). The resistance & the stubborn but unsurprising persistence of hate and extremism in the United States. *Indiana Journal of Global Legal Studies, 26*(1), 305–315.

Benjamin, W. (1969). The work of art in the age of mechanical reproduction. In *Illuminations* (pp. 217–251). New York: Schocken.

Benkler, Y., Faris, R., & Roberts, H. (2018). *Network propaganda: Manipulation, disinformation, and radicalization in American politics.* New York: Oxford University Press.

Bennett, W. L., & Segerberg, A. (2016). The logic of connective action: Digital media and the personalization of contentious politics. In E. Gordon & P. Mihailidis (Eds.), *Civic media: Technology, design, practice* (pp. 77–106). Cambridge, MA: MIT Press.

Bernays, E. (1929). Are we victims of propaganda? A debate. Everett Dean Martin and Edward L. Bernays. *Forum Magazine.* Edward L. Bernays Papers, Library of Congress. Retrieved from http://memory.loc.gov/cgi-bin/query/h?ammem/coolbib:@field(NUMBER+@band(amrlm+me20))

Bernays, E. (2005/1928). *Propaganda.* Brooklyn: Ig.

Bernstein, R. (2017, April 28). Should the Chinese government be in American classrooms? *New York Review of Books.* Retrieved from https://www.nybooks.com/daily/2017/04/28/should-the-chinese-government-be-in-american-classrooms/

Berry, C., Schmied, L. A., & Schrock, J. C. (2008). The role of emotion in teaching and learning history: A scholarship of teaching exploration. *History Teacher, 41*(4), 437–452.

Big Think. (2018, December 9). Why you should tolerate intolerable ideas. Nadine Strossen [Video]. Retrieved from https://youtu.be/PDwb_5BYm6YBirkenbuel, R. (2019, January 3). Arizona lawmaker's bill mirrors anti-Muslim hate group language. *Newsweek.* Retrieved from https://www.newsweek.com/arizona-lawmakers-bill-mirrors-anti-muslim-hate-group-language-1278732

Blake, M. (2020, June 11). After 32 'egregious and cruel' seasons, Cops was cancelled. This podcast explains why. *Los Angeles Times.* Retrieved from https://www.latimes

.com/entertainment-arts/tv/story/2020-06-11/running-from-cops-live-pd-canceled-podcast -police

Bowers, P. (1980). Paul and religious propaganda in the first century. *Novum Testamentum, 22*(4), 316–323.

Boyd, A. (2016). Interview with Andrew Boyd. Center for Artistic Activism. Retrieved from https://c4aa.org/2016/03/andrew-boyd/#undefined

Boyd, D. (2017, January 5). Did media literacy backfire? Data and Society. Retrieved from https://points.datasociety.net/did-media-literacy-backfire-7418c084d88d

Boyd, D. (2018, June 20). The messy fourth estate. Medium. Retrieved from https://medium.com/s/trustissues/the-messy-fourth-estate-a42c1586b657

Branch, G. (2019). Science teachers in the hot seat. *American Educator, 43*(4), 14–17.

Brandenberg v. Ohio. (1969). 395 US 444. Supreme Court of the United States.

Brandom, R. (2019, March 5). Deepfake propaganda is not a real problem. The Verge. Retrieved from https://www.theverge.com/2019/3/5/18251736/deepfake-propaganda -misinformation-troll-video-hoax

Brayton, S. & Casey, N. (2019). Not tolerating intolerance: Unpacking critical pedagogy in classrooms and conferences. In A. Baer, E. Stern Cahoy and R. Schroeder (Eds.), *Libraries promoting reflective dialogue in a time of political polarization* (pp. 171–186). Chicago: ACRL Press.

Brewer, P., & McKnight, J. (2017). "A statistically representative climate change debate": Satirical television news, scientific consensus, and public perceptions of global warming. *Atlantic Journal of Communication, 25*(3), 166–180.

Brown, J. (1991). *Television "critical viewing skills" education.* New Brunswick, NJ: Erlbaum.

Bruce, D. (2019). Reflection. In R. Hobbs & P. Mihailidis (Eds.), *The international encyclopedia of media literacy* (pp. 1279–1284). Hoboken, NJ: Wiley-Blackwell. doi:10.1002/9781118978238.ieml0195

Buchanan, T. K. (2017). Mindfulness and meditation in education. *Young Children, 72*(3), 69–74.

Buckingham, D. (2019). *The media education manifesto.* New York: Wiley.

Burson, G. (1992). Analyzing political television advertisements. *OAH Magazine of History, 6*(4), 66. https://doi.org/10.1093/maghis/6.4.66

Cain, C. (2018, May 24). George Orwell's "Animal Farm": Guide to the rise of authoritarianism in the Donald Trump era? *Salon.* Retrieved from https://www.salon .com/2018/05/24/george-orwells-animal-farm-guide-to-the-rise-of-authoritarianism -in-the-donald-trump-era/

Campbell, J. (1949). *The hero with a thousand faces.* Princeton, NJ: Princeton University Press.

Carlsen, A. & Haque, F. (2017, October 13). What does Facebook consider hate speech? Take our quiz. *The New York Times.* Retrieved from https://www.nytimes.com/interactive/2017/10/13/technology/facebook-hate-speech-quiz.html

Carlsson, U., & Culver, S. H. (2013). *Media and information literacy and intercultural dialogue.* Gothenburg, Sweden: Nordicom.

Carver, R., Wiese, E., & Breivik, J. (2014). Frame analysis in science education: A classroom activity for promoting media literacy and learning about genetic causation. *International Journal of Science Education, Part B, 4*(3), 211–239.

Casey, R. (1944). The story of propaganda. G.I. Roundtable series. American Historical Association. Retrieved from https://www.historians.org/about-aha-and-membership/aha-history-and-archives/gi-roundtable-series/pamphlets/em-2-what-is-propaganda-(1944)/the-story-of-propaganda

Caulfield, M. (2018). Web strategies for student fact checkers. PressBooks. Retrieved from https://webliteracy.pressbooks.com/front-matter/web-strategies-for-student-fact-checkers/

Cavanagh, S. R. (2016). *The spark of learning: Energizing the college classroom with the science of emotion.* Morgantown: West Virginia University Press.

Center for Media and Democracy. (2009). The 912 Project. Sourcewatch. Retrieved from https://www.sourcewatch.org/index.php?title=Talk:The_912_Project

Chait, J. (2012, August 17). The vast left-wing conspiracy is on your screen. *New York Magazine.* Retrieved from http://nymag.com/news/features/chait-liberal-movies-tv-2012-8/

Chamlee-Wright, E. (2018). Governing campus speech: A bottom-up approach. *Society, 55*(5), 392–402. doi:10.1007/s12115-018-0279-1

Chen, Y., Conroy, N. J., & Rubin, V. L. (2015, November). Misleading online content: Recognizing clickbait as false news. In *Proceedings of the 2015 ACM workshop on multimodal deception detection* (pp. 15–19). ACM.

Cherow-O'Leary, R. (2014). Creating critical viewers. *Journal of Media Literacy Education, 6*(2), 87–92.

Christenson, M. (2017). The perfect project to teach your students about art and activism. Art of Education University. Retrieved from https://theartofeducation.edu/2017/02/02/perfect-project-teach-students-art-activism/

Chung, S. K., & Kirby, M. (2009). Media literacy art education: Logos, culture jamming, and activism. *Art Education, 62*(1), 34–39. doi:10.1080/00043125.2009.11519002

Climate Reality Project. (2019). Climate 101. Retrieved from https://www.climaterealityproject.org/climate-101

College Board (2016). AP United States History Scoring Guidelines. Retrieved from https://secure-media.collegeboard.org/digitalServices/pdf/ap/apcentral/ap16_us_history_q1dbq.pdf

Collins, B., & Toomey, M. (2018, January 13). MartinLutherKing.org is owned by neo-Nazis. *Daily Beast.* Retrieved from https://www.thedailybeast.com/martinlutherkingorg-is-owned-by-neo-nazis?ref=scroll

Confessore, N., Dance, G. J., Harris, R., & Hansen, M. (2018). The follower factory. *The*

New York Times. Retrieved from https://www.nytimes.com/interactive/2018/01/27/technology/social-media-bots.html

Conger, K. (2019, May 24). Hate content is targeted for removal by Facebook. *The New York Times,* B3.

Conick, H. (2018). How to win friends and influence millions. American Marketing Association. Retrieved from https://medium.com/ama-marketing-news/how-to-win-friends-and-influence-millions-the-rules-of-influencer-marketing-d56f81d5d881

Coppins, M. (2020, March). The billion dollar disinformation campaign to re-elect the President. *The Atlantic.* Retrieved from https://www.theatlantic.com/magazine/archive/2020/03/the-2020-disinformation-war/605530/

Corliss, R. (2014, December 17). Review: *The Interview,* the movie you almost never got to see. *Time.* Retrieved from http://time.com/3636016/the-interview-movie-review-canceled-sony-hack/?xid=time_readnext

Corporation for Public Broadcasting (2019). Your feedback. Retrieved from https://www.cpb.org/your-feedback

Cottee, S. (2017, October 5). Why do we want to watch gory jihadist propaganda videos? *The New York Times.* Retrieved from https://www.nytimes.com/2017/10/05/opinion/islamic-state-propaganda-videos.html

Counts, G. (1927). Nationalistic propaganda in school textbooks. *School Review, 35*(2), 147–149.

Cunningham, S. (2002). *The idea of propaganda: A reconstruction.* Westport, CT: Greenwood.

D'Addario, D. (2014, December 17). The most controversial films of all time. *Time.* Retrieved from https://time.com/3637680/most-controversial-films/

Dalla, N. (2016, February 5). I just got "push-polled" by Hillary Clinton's Nevada campaign. Retrieved from https://www.nolandalla.com/i-just-got-push-polled-by-hillary-clintons-nevada-campaign/

Dasandi, N., & Taylor, M. (2018). *Is democracy failing?* London: Thames and Hudson.

Daunt, T. (2012). Senators call Zero Dark Thirty grossly inaccurate in letter to Sony Pictures. Hollywood Reporter. Retrieved from https://www.hollywoodreporter.com/news/senators-call-zero-dark-thirty-405613

Davenport, C., & Landler, M. (2019, May 27). Trump administration hardens its attack on climate science. *The New York Times.* Retrieved from https://www.nytimes.com/2019/05/27/us/politics/trump-climate-science.html

Davis, C. (2018, June 29). Forcing cards: How to identify divisive internet content before sharing. *Memphis Flyer.* Retrieved from https://www.memphisflyer.com/FlyontheWallBlog/archives/2018/06/29/forcing-cards-how-to-identify-divisive-internet-propaganda-before-sharing

Davis, J., Love, T., & Killen, G. (2018). Seriously funny: The political work of humor on social media. *New Media and Society, 20*(10), 3898–3916.

Deal, D., Flores-Koulish, S., & Sears, J. (2010). Media literacy teacher talk: Interpretation, value, and implementation. *Journal of Media Literacy Education, 1*(2), 121–131.

DeJong, W. (2017, July 27). Public service announcements and exposure to health and risk messages. *Oxford Research Encyclopedia of Communication.* Retrieved from https://oxfordre.com/communication/view/10.1093/acrefore/9780190228613.001.0001/acrefore-9780190228613-e-334

Deutsche Welle. (2017, March 3). Actor denies that Erdogan film is propaganda. Retrieved from https://www.dw.com/en/actor-denies-that-erdogan-film-is-propaganda/a-37804563

Dewey, J. (1910). *How we think.* Boston: Heath.

Dilanian, K., & Memoli, M. (2017, December 8). Trumps got emails offering documents after WikiLeaks made them public. NBC News. Retrieved from https://www.nbcnews.com/politics/politics-news/trumps-trump-jr-received-email-offering-hacked-wikileaks-documents-last-n827716

Dodd, P. (2018, September 13). Learning how to pay attention. *Comment.* Retrieved from https://www.cardus.ca/comment/article/learning-how-to-pay-attention/#

Donnelly, K. (2016, April 7). Ten engaging ways educators can use the Political TV Ad Archive. Political TV Ad Archive. Retrieved from https://politicaladarchive.org/ten-engaging-ways-educators-can-use-the-political-tv-ad-archive/

Donovan, J., & Friedberg, B. (2019). Source hacking: Media manipulation in practice. Data&Society. https://datasociety.net/output/source-hacking-media-manipulation-in-practice.

Dowling, T. (2017, November 29). 24-hour Putin people: My week watching Kremlin "propaganda channel" RT. *The Guardian.* Retrieved from https://www.theguardian.com/media/2017/nov/29/24-hour-putin-people-my-week-watching-kremlin-propaganda-channel-rt-russia-today

Doyle, R. (2016). *Banned and challenged books.* Chicago: American Library Association.

DROG. (2017). Get bad news. https://getbadnews.com/#intro

Du Bois, W. E. B. (1926). Criteria of Negro art. *Crisis, 32*(6), 290–297.

Dunn, A. Sondel, B., & Baggett, H. (2018). "I don't want to come off as pushing an agenda": How contexts shaped teachers' pedagogy in the days after the 2016 U.S. presidential election. *American Educational Research Journal, 56*(2), 444–576. doi:10.3102/0002831218794892

Dwoskin, E., Timberg, C & Romm, T. (2020, June 28). Zuckerberg once wanted to sanction Trump. Then Facebook wrote rules that accommodated him. *Washington Post.* Retrieved from https://www.washingtonpost.com/technology/2020/06/28/facebook-zuckerberg-trump-hate/

Ebert, R. (1971, January 1). Johnny got his gun. Review. Retrieved from https://www.rogerebert.com/reviews/johnny-got-his-gun-1971

Editorial Board. (2019, August 4). We have a white nationalist terrorist problem. *The New*

York Times. Retrieved from https://www.nytimes.com/2019/08/04/opinion/mass-shootings-domestic-terrorism.html

Edsall, T. (2018, December 6). After Citizens United, a vicious cycle of corruption. *The New York Times*. Retrieved from https://www.nytimes.com/2018/12/06/opinion/citizens-united-corruption-pacs.html

Eisenberg, M. B., Lowe, C. A., & Spitzer, K. L. (2004). *Information literacy: Essential skills for the information age*. Westport, CT: Greenwood.

Elder, K. A. (2018). Propaganda for kids: Comparing IS-produced propaganda to depictions of propaganda in the Hunger Games and Harry Potter film series. *International Journal of Communication*, *12*, 19.

Elliott, S. (2010, April 26). In a world of ads, teaching the young how to read them. *The New York Times*. Retrieved from https://www.nytimes.com/2010/04/27/business/media/27adco.html

Ellis, E. (2016, October 16). How the alt-right grew from an obscure racist cabal. *Wired*. Retrieved from https://www.wired.com/2016/10/alt-right-grew-obscure-racist-cabal/

Ellis, E. (2018, October 5). Online conspiracy theories: The Wired guide. *Wired*. Retrieved from https://www.wired.com/story/wired-guide-to-conspiracy-theories/

Ellison, S. (2020, June 19). How Trump's obsession with media and loyalty coalesced in a battle for Voice of America. *Washington Post*. Retrieved from https://www.washingtonpost.com/lifestyle/media/how-trumps-obsessions-with-media-and-loyalty-coalesced-in-a-battle-for-voice-of-america/2020/06/19/f57dcfe0-b1b1-11ea-8758-bfd1d045525a_story.html

Ellul, J. (1973). *Propaganda*. New York: Knopf.

Ellul, J. (1981). The ethics of propaganda: Propaganda, innocence and amorality. *Communication* 6, 159–175.

Erlanger, S. (2017, March 8). Russia's RT network: Is it more BBC or KGB? *The New York Times*. Retrieved from https://www.nytimes.com/2017/03/08/world/europe/russias-rt-network-is-it-more-bbc-or-kgb.html

Ethics Unwrapped. (2019). Moral reasoning. University of Texas, McCombs School of Business. Retrieved from https://ethicsunwrapped.utexas.edu/glossary/moral-reasoning

European Association for Viewer Interests. (2017). Beyond fake news. Retrieved from https://eavi.eu/wp-content/uploads/2017/07/beyond-fake-news_COLOUR_WEB.pdf

European Audiovisual Observatory. (2016). *Mapping of media literacy practices and actions in EU-28*. Strasbourg, France: Author. Retrieved from https://www.medieraadet.dk/files/docs/2018-02/Media%20literacy%20mapping%20report%20-%20EN%20-%20FINAL.pdf.pdf

European Parliament (2019, March). Polarisation and the news media in Europe. Panel for the Future of Science and Technology, Scientific Foresight Project. Retrieved from https://reutersinstitute.politics.ox.ac.uk/sites/default/files/2019-03/Polarisation_and_the_news_media_in_Europe.pdf

Ewers, J. K. (1943). Literature and propaganda. *Australian Quarterly, 15*(2), 68–81.

Fact Checker. (2019, May 28). In 828 days, President Trump has made 10,111 false or misleading claims. *Washington Post.* Retrieved from https://www.washingtonpost.com/graphics/politics/trump-claims-database/?utm_term=.ba8589bbc117

Fausey, C. M., & Matlock, T. (2011). Can grammar win elections? *Political Psychology, 32*(4), 563–574.

Federal Trade Commission. (2010). Admongo. Retrieved from https://www.consumer.ftc.gov/Admongo

Feldman, L. (2013). Cloudy with a chance of heat balls: The portrayal of global warming on *The Daily Show* and *The Colbert Report. International Journal of Communication, 7,* 430–451.

Fishbein, M., Hall-Jamieson, K., Zimmer, E., Von Haeften, I., & Nabi, R. (2002). Avoiding the boomerang: Testing the relative effectiveness of antidrug public service announcements before a national campaign. *American Journal of Public Health, 92*(2), 238–245.

Fisher, M. (2018, December 27). Inside Facebook's secret rulebook for global political speech. *The New York Times.* Retrieved from https://www.nytimes.com/2018/12/27/world/facebook-moderators.html

Fishkin, R. (2018, October 9). We analyzed every Twitter account following Donald Trump: 61% are bots, spam, inactive, or propaganda. SparkToro. Retrieved from https://sparktoro.com/blog/we-analyzed-every-twitter-account-following-donald-trump-61-are-bots-spam-inactive-or-propaganda/

Flanagan, C. (2017, May). How late-night comedy fueled the rise of Trump. *The Atlantic.* https://www.theatlantic.com/magazine/archive/2017/05/how-late-night-comedy-alienated-conservatives-made-liberals-smug-and-fueled-the-rise-of-trump/521472/

Flanagin, A., & Metzger, M. (2007). The role of site features, user attributes, and information verification behaviors on the perceived credibility of web-based information. *New Media and Society, 9*(2), 319–342.

Fleming, D. (2019). Fear of persuasion in the English Language Arts. *College English, 81*(6), 508-541.

Ford, M. (2017, January 21). Trump's press secretary falsely claims: Largest audience to ever witness an inauguration, period. *The Atlantic.* Retrieved from https://www.theatlantic.com/politics/archive/2017/01/inauguration-crowd-size/514058/

Fotiade, N. (2018, September 13). Online propaganda, youth radicalisation and extreme violence. Mind Over Media. Retrieved from https://mindovermediasite.wordpress.com/2018/09/13/online-propaganda-youth-radicalisation-and-extreme-violence/

Fox News (2019, November 9). US government warns of potential Russian, Chinese and Iranian election interference ahead of 2020. Retrieved from https://video.foxnews.com/v/6102192694001#sp=show-clips

Frank, K. (2012). Analyzing political campaign commercials. Loudoun County Public Schools, Teaching American History Project. Retrieved from http://chnm.gmu.edu/tah-loudoun/blog/lessons/analyzing-political-campaign-commercials/

Freedman, K., & Stuhr, P. (2004). Curriculum change for the 21st century: Visual culture in art education. In E. Eisner & M. Day (Eds.), *Handbook of research and policy in art education* (pp. 815–828). Mahwah, NJ: Erlbaum.

Freire, P., & Macedo, D. (2005). *Literacy: Reading the word and the world.* New York: Routledge.

French, S. D., & Campbell, J. (2019). Media literacy and American education: An exploration with détournement. *Journal of Media Literacy Education, 11*(1), 75–96.

Friesem, E. (2018). "Too much of a good thing?" How teachers' enthusiasm may lead to protectionism in exploring media and gender. *Journal of Media Literacy Education, 10*(1), 134–147.

Fry, K. (2014). What are we really teaching? Outline for an activist media literacy education. In B. De Abreu & P. Mihailidis (Eds.), *Media literacy education in action* (pp. 125–137). New York: Routledge.

Funt, P. (2018, July 18). Trump's 27 loaded questions. Cagle Post. Retrieved from https://www.cagle.com/peter-funt/2018/07/trumps-27-loaded-questions

Gable, J. (2017). Unbiased news or a balanced news diet: What do we really want? *Perspectives Blog.* AllSides. Retrieved from https://www.allsides.com/blog/unbiased-news-or-balanced-news-diet-what-do-we-really-want

Gans, H. (1993). Hollywood entertainment: Commerce or ideology? *Social Science Quarterly, 74*(1), 150–153.

Gazette Extra. (2018, October 6). Our view: Keep propaganda out of the classroom. Retrieved from https://www.gazettextra.com/opinion/our_views/our-views-keep-propaganda-out-of-the-classroom/article_cc63c57a-0618-5201-a9cc-68c441496005.html

Gearan, A. & Abutaleb, Y. (2020, June 26). Pence tries to put positive spin on pandemic despite surging cases in South and West. *Washington Post.* Retrieved from https://www.washingtonpost.com/politics/pence-puts-positive-spin-on-surging-coronavirus-cases-in-south-west/2020/06/26/70a1dfa2-b7c7-11ea-a510-55bf26485c93_story.html

Genota, L. (2018, September 11). Why generation Z learners prefer YouTube lessons over printed books. *Ed Week.* Retrieved from https://www.edweek.org/ew/articles/2018/09/12/why-generation-z-learners-prefer-youtube-lessons.html

Gessen, M. (2018, October 2). The 15-year-old climate change activist who is demanding a new kind of politics. *The New Yorker.* Retrieved from https://www.newyorker.com/news/our-columnists/the-fifteen-year-old-climate-activist-who-is-demanding-a-new-kind-of-politics

Gessen, M. (2019, June 4). What HBO's "Chernobyl" got right, and what it got terribly wrong. *The New Yorker.* Retrieved from https://www.newyorker.com/news/our-columnists/what-hbos-chernobyl-got-right-and-what-it-got-terribly-wrong

Gillespie, T. (2018). *Custodians of the internet.* New Haven, CT: Yale University Press.

Giroux, H. (1996). *Fugitive cultures.* New York: Routledge.

Glander, T. (2000). *Origins of mass communications research during the American Cold War: Educational effects and contemporary implications.* New York: Routledge.

Glenn, M. (2018, February 20). A Houston protest organized by Russian trolls. *Houston Chronicle.* Retrieved from https://www.houstonchronicle.com/local/gray-matters/article/A-Houston-protest-organized-by-Russian-trolls-12625481.php

Goble, P., & Goble, R. R. (2016). *Making curriculum pop: Developing literacies in all content areas.* New York: Free Spirit Publishing.

Goldmacher, S. (2020, July 3). Biden outraises Trump as millions pour in for both. *The New York Times*, A16.

Gooblar, D. (2019, February 19). What is "indoctrination"? And how do we avoid it in class? *Chronicle of Higher Education.* Retrieved from https://www.chronicle.com/article/What-Is-Indoctrination-/245729

Gormley, S. (2019, March 11). A Portland marketing company created a fake anti-vaccination lifestyle blog. *Willamette Week.* Retrieved from https://www.wweek.com/culture/2019/03/11/a-portland-marketing-company-created-a-fake-anti-vaccination-lifestyle-blog/

Gorwa, R. (2019). Poland: Unpacking the system of social media manipulation. In S. Wooley & P. Howard (Eds.), *Computational propaganda: Political parties, politicians and political manipulation on social media* (pp. 86–103). New York: Oxford University Press.

Gottwig, B. R. (2013). The impact of high school principal's technology leadership on the sustainability of corporate sponsored information communication technology curriculum. Dissertation, University of Montana.

Graham-McLay, C. (2019, March 21). Spreading the mosque shooting video is a crime in NewZealand. *The New York Times.* Retrieved from https://www.nytimes.com/2019/03/21/world/asia/new-zealand-attacks-social-media.html

Gramlich, J. & Funk, C. (2020, June 4). Black Americans face higher COVID-19 risks. Pew Research Center. Retrieved from https://www.pewresearch.org/fact-tank/2020/06/04/black-americans-face-higher-covid-19-risks-are-more-hesitant-to-trust-medical-scientists-get-vaccinated/

Greenberg, D. (2016). *Republic of spin: An inside history of the American presidency.* New York: Norton.

Greenfield, D. (2019, May 17). Government experiment brainwashes children to manipulate conservative parents. Frontpage. Retrieved from https://www.frontpagemag.com/fpm/273776/government-experiment-brainwashes-children-daniel-greenfield

Greenfield, J. (2018). The Hollywood hit movie that urged FDR to become a fascist. Politico. Retrieved from https://www.politico.com/magazine/story/2018/03/25/gabriel-over-the-white-house-fdr-inauguration-217349

Greenwood, V. (2020). *Navigating media literacy: A pedagogical tour of Disneyland.* New York: Myers Education Press.

Grenby, M. (2014). Moral and instructive children's literature. British Library. Retrieved from https://www.bl.uk/romantics-and-victorians/articles/moral-and-instructive-childrens-literature

Griner, D. (2016, May 2). How Jet Blue achieved the impossible: Getting passengers to love it when babies cry. *Adweek.* Retrieved from https://www.adweek.com/creativity/how-jetblue-achieved-impossible-getting-passengers-love-it-when-babies-cry-171179/

Gross, A. G. (1994). The roles of rhetoric in the public understanding of science. *Public Understanding of Science, 3,* 3–22. doi:10.1088/0963-6625/3/1/001

Gross, N. (2018, January 27). Why is Hollywood so liberal? *The New York Times.* Retrieved from https://www.nytimes.com/2018/01/27/opinion/sunday/hollywood-liberal.html

Grosz, S. (2019, January 9). The real reason Donald Trump lies. *Financial Times.* Retrieved from https://www.ft.com/content/b752121c-127a-11e9-a581-4ff78404524

Grynko, A. (2019, March 29). Ukrainian outlets Vesti and Strana.ua on elections in Ukraine: Fake narratives, heroes and antiheroes. Stop Fake. https://www.stopfake.org/en/ukrainian-outlets-vesti-and-strana-ua-on-presidential-elections-in-ukraine-fake-narratives-heroes-and-antiheroes/

Hahl, O., Kim, M., & Zuckerman Sivan, E. W. (2018). The authentic appeal of the lying demagogue: Proclaiming the deeper truth about political illegitimacy. *American Sociological Review,* 83(1), 1–33.

Hall, K., Goldstein, D. M., & Ingram, M. B. (2016). The hands of Donald Trump: Entertainment, gesture, spectacle. *HAU: Journal of Ethnographic Theory, 6*(2), 71–100.

Hamblin, J. (2014, November 11). It's everywhere, the clickbait. *The Atlantic.* Retrieved from https://www.theatlantic.com/entertainment/archive/2014/11/clickbait-what-is/382545/

Hansen, S. (2019, July 24). The era of people like you is over: How Turkey purged its intellectuals. *The New York Times Magazine.* Retrieved from https://www.nytimes.com/2019/07/24/magazine/the-era-of-people-like-you-is-over-how-turkey-purged-its-intellectuals.html

Harari, Y. (2018). *21 lessons for the 21st century.* New York: Spiegel & Grau.

Harley, J. B. (2009). Maps, knowledge, and power. In G. Henderson & M. Waterstone (Eds.), *Geographic thought: A praxis perspective* (pp. 129–148). London: Routledge.

Harmon, C., & Bowdish, R. (2018). *The terror argument: Modern advocacy and propaganda.* Washington, DC: Brookings Institution.

Harold, C. (2007). *Our space: Resisting the corporate control of culture.* Minneapolis: University of Minnesota Press.

Hart, J. (2016). Growing Voters. Retrieved from http://www.growingvoters.org

Hasford, J., Hardesty, D. M., & Kidwell, B. (2015). More than a feeling: Emotional contagion effects in persuasive communication. *Journal of Marketing Research, 52*(6), 836–847.

Haste, C. (1995). The machinery of propaganda. In R. Jackall (Ed.), *Propaganda* (pp. 105–136). New York: New York University Press.

Hawkins, P. (2013, November 30). Animal Farm lessons. Retrieved from https://paulinehawkins.com/2013/11/30/animal-farm-lessons/

Hayik, R. (2011). Critical visual analysis of multicultural sketches. *English Teaching: Practice and Critique, 10*(1), 95–118.

He, H. (2019). Media literacy education and second language acquisition. In R. Hobbs & P. Mihailidis (Eds.), *The international encyclopedia of media literacy* (pp. 817–823). Hoboken, NJ: Wiley-Blackwell.

Heim, J. (2020, January 17). National Archives exhibit blurs images critical of President Trump. *Washington Post.*

Heins, M., & Cho, C. (2003). Media literacy: An alternative to censorship. New York: Free Expression Policy Project. Retrieved from http://bit.ly/2MN5JJI

Hench, J. (2016). *Books as weapons: Propaganda, publishing and the battle for global markets in the era of World War II.* Ithaca, NY: Cornell University Press.

Henley, A. (2017, December 21). *Wonder* is a "feel-good" movie that needed more realism. *The Atlantic.* Retrieved from https://www.theatlantic.com/entertainment/archive/2017/12/wonder-is-a-feel-good-movie-that-needed-more-realism/548828/

Henning, T. (n.d.). Argument, persuasion or propaganda? Analyzing World War II posters. ReadWriteThink. Retrieved from http://www.readwritethink.org/classroom-resources/lesson-plans/argument-persuasion-propaganda-analyzing-829.html

Herman, E., & Chomsky, N. (1989). *Manufacturing consent: The political economy of the mass media.* New York: Pantheon.

Hess, D. E. (2004). Controversies about controversial issues in democratic education. *PS: Political Science and Politics, 37*(2), 257–261.

Hitlin, P., & Rainie, L. (2019, January 16). Facebook algorithms and personal data. Pew Research Center. https://www.pewinternet.org/2019/01/16/facebook-algorithms-and-personal-data/

Hobbs, R. (1985). *Visual verbal synchrony and television news: Decreasing the knowledge gap.* (Unpublished doctoral dissertation). Harvard Graduate School of Education.

Hobbs, R. (1998). The seven great debates in the media literacy movement. *Journal of Communication, 48*(1), 16–32.

Hobbs, R. (1994). *Know TV.* Bethesda, MD: Discovery Communications.

Hobbs, R. (1999). *Assignment: Media literacy.* Maryland State Department of Education and Discovery Communications. Retrieved from https://mediaeducationlab.com/assignment-media-literacy

Hobbs, R. (2010). *Digital and media literacy: A plan of action.* Washington, DC: Aspen Institute and the John S. and James L. Knight Foundation.

Hobbs, R. (2012). The blurring of art, journalism, and advocacy: Confronting 21st century propaganda in a world of online journalism. *I/S: A Journal of Law and Policy for the Information Society, 8*(3), 625–637.

Hobbs, R. (2017a). *Create to learn.* Malden, MA: Wiley.

Hobbs, R. (2017b). Teaching and learning in a post-truth world. *Educational Leadership, 75*(3), 26–31.

Hobbs, R. (2017c). Teach the conspiracies. *Knowledge Quest, 46*(1), 16–24.

Hobbs, R. (2019). Media literacy foundations. In R. Hobbs & P. Mihailidis (Eds.), *The international encyclopedia of media literacy* (pp. 851–870). Boston: Wiley-Blackwell and the International Communication Association.

Hobbs, R. (2020). Propaganda in an age of algorithmic personalization: Expanding literacy research and practice. *Reading Research Quarterly, 55*(3), 421–533.

Hobbs, R., Deslauriers, L., & Steager, P. (2019). *The library screen scene: Film and media literacy in schools, colleges and communities.* New York: Oxford University Press.

Hobbs, R., & Grafe, S. (2015). YouTube pranking across cultures. *First Monday.* Retrieved from https://firstmonday.org/ojs/index.php/fm/article/view/5981

Hobbs, R., He, H., & RobbGrieco, M. (2015). Seeing, believing, and learning to be skeptical: Supporting language learning through advertising analysis activities. *TESOL Journal, 6*(3), 447–475.

Hobbs, R., & McGee, S. (2014). Teaching about propaganda: An examination of the historical roots of media literacy. *Journal of Media Literacy Education, 6*(2), 5.

Hobbs, R., & Mihailidis, M. (Eds.) (2019). *The international encyclopedia of media literacy* Boston: Wiley Blackwell and the International Communication Association.

Hobbs, R., & Moore, D. C. (2013). *Discovering media literacy.* Thousand Oaks, CA: Corwin/Sage.

Hobbs, R., Seyferth-Zapf, C. & Grafe, S. (2018). Using virtual exchange to advance media literacy competencies through analysis of contemporary propaganda, *Journal of Media Literacy Education, 10*(2), 152–168.

Hobbs, R., & Tuzel, S. (2017). Teacher motivations for digital and media literacy: An examination of Turkish educators. *British Journal of Educational Technology, 48*(1), 7–22. doi:10.1111/bjet.12326

Hodgin, E., & Kahne, J. (2019). Judging credibility in un-credible times: Three educational approaches for the digital age. In W. Journell (Ed.), *Unpacking fake news: An educator's guide to navigating the media with students* (pp. 92–108). New York: Teachers College Press.

Hoeschsmann, M., & Poyntz, S. (2012). *Media literacies: A critical introduction.* Malden, MA: Wiley-Blackwell.

Holiday, R. (2012). *Trust me, I'm lying.* New York: Penguin.

Huffman, G. (2019, April 10). Twisted sources: How Confederate propaganda ended up in the South's schoolbooks. Facing South. Retrieved from https://www.facingsouth.org/2019/04/twisted-sources-how-confederate-propaganda-ended-souths-schoolbooks

Hunt, M. (2011, May 12). The bin Laden killing and American exceptionalism. UNC Press Blog. Retrieved from https://uncpressblog.com/2011/05/12/michael-h-hunt-the-bin-laden-killing-and-american-exceptionalism/

Hutzler, A. (2019, July 26). Donald Trump has appeared on Fox News eight times more than any other network. *Newsweek.* Retrieved from https://www.newsweek.com/trump-appeared-fox-news-eight-times-more-any-network-1451316

Hwang, Y., Yum, J., & Jeong, S. (2019). What components should be included in advertising literacy education? Effect of component types and the moderating role of age. *Journal of Advertising, 47*(4), 347–361. doi:10.1080/00913367.2018.1546628

Immordino-Yang, M. H., & Damasio, A. (2007). We feel, therefore we learn: The relevance of affective and social neuroscience to education. *Mind, Brain, and Education, 1*(1), 3–10.

Indiana Department of Education. (2017). Indiana state approved course titles and descriptions. Indiana Department of Education, College and Career Readiness Curriculum. Retrieved from https://www.doe.in.gov/sites/default/files/standards/17-18-ctd-all-posted.pdf

Ingraham, C. (2017, April 14). Somebody just put a price on the 2016 elections. It's a doozy. *Washington Post.* Retrieved from https://www.washingtonpost.com/news/wonk/wp/2017/04/14/somebody-just-put-a-price-tag-on-the-2016-election-its-a-doozy/?utm_term=.2e99d0f48d90

Isaac, M. (2019, November 22). Why everyone is angry with Facebook over its political ads policy. *The New York Times.* Retrieved from https://www.nytimes.com/2019/11/22/technology/campaigns-pressure-facebook-political-ads.html

Isaac, M. & Kane, C. (2020, January 9). Facebook says it won't back down from allowing lies in political ads. *The New York Times.* Retrieved from https://www.nytimes.com/2020/01/09/technology/facebook-political-ads-lies.html

Island Trees School District v. Pico, 457 U.S. 853 (1982)

Isquith, E. (2013, January 9). Hollywood's real bias is conservative (but not in the way liberals often say). *The Atlantic.* Retrieved from https://www.theatlantic.com/entertainment/archive/2013/01/hollywoods-real-bias-is-conservative-but-not-in-the-way-liberals-often-say/266960/

Iyengar, S. (2016). *Media politics: A citizen's guide* (3rd ed.). New York: Norton.

Jack, C. (2015). Fun and facts about American business: Economic education and business propaganda in an early Cold War cartoon series. *Enterprise and Society, 16*(3), 491–520.

Jack, C. (2017). *Lexicon of lies: Terms for problematic information.* New York: Data and Society.

Jackson, B., & Jamieson, K. H. (2007). *UnSpun: Finding facts in a world of disinformation.* New York: Random House.

Jarman, R., & McClune, B. (2002). A survey of the use of newspapers in science instruction by secondary teachers in Northern Ireland. *International Journal of Science Education, 24*, 997–1020. doi:10.1080/09500690210095311

Jenkins, H., Ford, S., & Green, J. (2014). *Spreadable media: Creating value and meaning in a networked culture.* New York: NYU Press.

Jenkins, H., Shresthova, S., Gamber-Thompson, L., Kligler-Vilenchik, N., & Zimmerman, A. (2016). *By any media necessary: The new youth activism.* New York: NYU Press.

Jensen, E. (2016, May 27). Did Ploughshares grant skew NPR's Iran deal coverage? National Public Radio. Retrieved from https://www.npr.org/sections/publiceditor/2016/05/27/479588582/did-ploughshares-grant-skew-nprs-iran-deal-coverage

Jewitt, C. (2008). Multimodality and literacy in school classrooms. *Review of Research in Education, 32*(1), 241–267.

Johnson, B. (2019, March 21). Deepfakes are solvable—but don't forget that "shallowfakes" are already pervasive. *MIT Technology Review.* Retrieved from https://www.technologyreview.com/s/613172/deepfakes-shallowfakes-human-rights/

Johnson, E. (2019, January 24). NYU's Jay Rosen says 2020's political journalism will be even worse than 2016's. Vox. Retrieved from https://www.vox.com/2019/1/24/18195097/jay-rosen-trump-politics-media-horse-race-recode-podcast-2020-predictions

Johnson, G. (2017, September 26). How to identify fake friend requests. YouTube. Retrieved from https://youtu.be/zDKSxb4yshs

Jolley, D., & Douglas, K. (2014). The social consequences of conspiracism: Exposure to conspiracy theories decreases intentions to engage in politics and to reduce one's carbon footprint. *British Journal of Psychology, 105,* 35–56. doi:10.1111/bjop.12018

Jowett, G., & O'Donnell, V. (2012/1986). *Propaganda and persuasion* (5th ed.). Thousand Oaks, CA: Sage.

Jubilee. (2010). Jubilee Project Spotlight: Clara Chung's Story. YouTube. Retrieved from https://youtu.be/f1stzNEVwNk

Kahne, J., & Bowyer, B. (2017). Educating for democracy in a partisan age: Confronting the challenges of motivated reasoning and misinformation. *American Educational Research Journal, 54*(1), 3–34. https://doi.org/10.3102/0002831216679817

Kahne, J., & Bowyer, B. (2019). Can media literacy education increase digital engagement in politics? *Learning, Media and Technology, 44*(2), 211–224. doi:10.1080/17439884.2019.1601108

Kahne, J., Middaugh, E., & Allen, D. (2015). Youth, new media and the rise of participatory politics. In D. Allen (Ed.), *From voice to influence: Understanding citizenship in a digital age* (pp. 35–58). Chicago: University of Chicago Press.

Kahneman, D. (2011). *Thinking, fast and slow.* New York: Macmillan.

Kaplan, T. & Almukhtar, S (2019, May 21). How Trump is outspending every 2020 Democrat on Facebook. *The New York Times.* Retrieved from https://www.nytimes.com/interactive/2019/05/21/us/politics/trump-2020-facebook-ads.html

Katz, R. (2019, January 9). A growing frontier for terrorist groups: Unsuspecting chat apps. *Wired.* Retrieved from https://www.wired.com/story/terrorist-groups-prey-on-unsuspecting-chat-apps/

Kellner, D. (1991). Film, politics, and ideology: Reflections on Hollywood film in the age of Reagan. *Velvet Light Trap, 27,* 9–24.

Kellner, D. (2003). *Media spectacle.* New York: Routledge.

Kelly, G. (2019, June 19). Lynne Dixon's misleading push poll. *Investigative Post.* Retrieved from https://www.investigativepost.org/2019/06/19/lynne-dixons-misleading-push-poll/

Kelly, T. E. (1986). Discussing controversial issues: Four perspectives on the teacher's role. *Theory and Research in Social Education, 14*(2), 113–138.

Kelly, T. M. (2013). *Teaching history in the digital age.* Ann Arbor: University of Michigan Press.

Kettmann, M. (2013, September 30). There's a hero inside of everyone, and we're not saying that to make you feel good. *Smithsonian.* Retrieved from https://www.smithsonianmag.com/innovation/theres-a-hero-inside-of-everyone-and-were-not-saying-that-to-make-you-feel-good-299563/

Klobuchar, A. (2019, July 26). Klobuchar introduces legislation to educate Americans about misinformation online, prevent the impact of foreign influence campaigns [Press release]. Retrieved from http://bit.ly/2ZlrgfJ

Kolbert, E. (2017, February 19). Why facts don't change our minds. *New Yorker.* Retrieved from https://www.newyorker.com/magazine/2017/02/27/why-facts-dont-change-our-minds

Koll, D., Schwarzmaier, M., Li, J., Li, X. Y., & Fu, X. (2017, June). Thank you for being a friend: An attacker view on online-social-network-based Sybil defenses. In *2017 IEEE 37th International Conference on Distributed Computing Systems Workshops (ICDCS)* (pp. 157–162). New York: IEEE.

Koltay, T. (2017). Data literacy for researchers and data librarians. *Journal of Librarianship and Information Science, 49*(1), 3–14.

Korbey, H. (2019, July 9). The reading wars: choice vs canon. Edutopia. Retrieved from https://www.edutopia.org/article/reading-wars-choice-vs-canon

Kovach, B., & Rosenstiel, T. (2010). *Blur: How to know what's true in the age of information overload.* New York: Bloomsbury.

Krugman, P. (2009, August 7). The town hall mob. *The New York Times.* Retrieved from https://www.nytimes.com/2009/08/07/opinion/07krugman.html

Kunzman, R. (2018). Contention and conversation in the K–12 classroom. A review essay of *Teaching controversial issues* and *The case for contention. Democracy and Education, 26*(1). Retrieved from https://democracyeducationjournal.org/home/vol26/iss1/5

Lakoff, G., & Johnson, M. (2008). *Metaphors we live by.* Chicago: University of Chicago Press.

Langer, W. (1972). *The mind of Adolf Hitler.* New York: Basic Books.

Lanier, J. (2018, April 9). Why algorithms can't save us from trolls and hate speech. Ted Ideas. https://ideas.ted.com/why-algorithms-cant-save-us-from-trolls-and-hate-speech/

Lapowski, I. (2019, May 15) Why tech didn't stop the New Zealand attack from going viral. *Wired.* Retrieved from https://www.wired.com/story/new-zealand-shooting-video-social-media/

Laskow, S. (2017, June 14). The 19th-century book of horrors that scared German kids into behaving. *Atlas Obscura.* Retrieved from https://www.atlasobscura.com/articles/original-struwwelpeter-illustrations-childrens-moral-lesson-book

Lasswell, H. D. (1938/1927). *Propaganda technique in World War I.* New York: P. Smith.

Lasswell, H. D. (1948). The structure and function of communication in society. *Communication of Ideas, 37*(1), 136–139.

Lasswell, H. D. (1995). Propaganda. In R. Jackall (Ed.), *Propaganda* (pp. 13–25). New York: NYU Press.

Latham, D., & Hollister, J. M. (2014). The games people play: Information and media literacies in *The Hunger Games* trilogy. *Children's Literature in Education, 45*(1), 33–46.

Laursen, L. (2009). Fake Facebook pages spin web of deceit. *Nature, 458*(7242), 1089.

Leary, D. (2019, May 22). Gay marriage in *Arthur* pushes the limit of social realism in children's TV. *National Review.* Retrieved from https://www.nationalreview.com/2019/05/arthur-gay-marriage-pushes-limits-social-realism-childrens-television/

Leary, M. (2018). The psychology of intellectual humility. Templeton Foundation. Retrieved from https://www.templeton.org/wp-content/uploads/2018/11/Intellectual-Humility-Leary-FullLength-Final.pdf

Lee, A., & Lee, E. (1939). *The fine art of propaganda: A study of Father Coughlin's speeches.* Institute for Propaganda Analysis. New York: Harcourt, Brace.

Lehr, D. (2014). *The birth of a nation: How a legendary filmmaker and a crusading editor reignited America's civil war.* New York: Public Affairs.

Lerner, M. (2015). Markets, movies, and media: The growing soft power threat to North Korea. *Journal of East Asian Affairs, 29*(1), 41–70.

Leung, Y. W. (2004). Nationalistic education and indoctrination. *Citizenship, Social and Economics Education, 6*(2), 116–130.

Levin, D. (2020, July 3). College revoke offers over slurs and screeds. *The New York Times,* A19.

Levine, P. (2018). Habermas with a whiff of tear gas: Nonviolent campaigns and deliberation in an era of authoritarianism. *Journal of Public Deliberation* 14(2), 4.

Lichfield, G. (2018, October 23). Facebook's ex-security boss. *MIT Technology Review.* Retrieved from https://www.technologyreview.com/s/612332/facebooks-ex-security-boss-asking-big-tech-to-police-hate-speech-is-a-dangerous-path/

Lightfoot, L. J. (2015). *Teacher perceptions on the ethics of using corporate-sponsored curriculum in the classroom* (Unpublished master's thesis). Dominican University of California.

Lippmann, W. (1997). *Public opinion.* Boston: Free Press. (Original work published 1922)

Lipton, E., Williams, B., & Confessore, N. (2014, September 6). Foreign powers buy influence at think tanks. *The New York Times.* Retrieved from https://www.nytimes.com/2014/09/07/us/politics/foreign-powers-buy-influence-at-think-tanks.html

Loewen, J. W. (2018). *Lies my teacher told me: Everything your American history textbook got wrong.* New York: New Press.

Lorentz, P. (1992). *FDR's Moviemaker: Memoirs and scripts.* Las Vegas: University of Nevada Press.

Lorenz, T. (2018, December 18). Rising Instagram stars are posting fake sponsored content. *The Atlantic.* Retrieved from https://www.theatlantic.com/technology/archive/2018/12/influencers-are-faking-brand-deals/578401/

Low-Beer, A. (2003). School history, national history and the issue of national identity. *International Journal of Historical Teaching, Learning and Research, 3*(1), 9–14.

Lowi, T., Ginsberg, B., Shepsle, K., & Ansolabehere, S. (2018). Chapter 10 outline. In *American government: Freedom and power.* New York: Norton. Retrieved from http://wwnorton.com/college/polisci/american-government12/core/ch/10/outline.aspx

Luckert, S., & Bachrach, S. (2009). *The state of deception: The power of Nazi propaganda.* New York: Norton.

Luke, A., & Freebody, P. (1997). The social practices of reading. In S. Muspratt, A. Luke, & P. Freebody (Eds.), *Constructing critical literacies* (pp. 185–226). New South Wales: Allen and Unwin.

Lukianoff, G., & Haidt, J. (2015). The coddling of the American mind. *The Atlantic.* Retrieved from https://www.theatlantic.com/magazine/archive/2015/09/the-coddling-of-the-american-mind/399356/

Lynch, M. (2005). *True to life: Why truth matters.* Cambridge, MA: MIT Press.

Lynch, P. (2009). Composition as a thermostatic activity. *College Composition and Communication, 60*(4), 728–745.

MacFarquhar, N. (2020, February 14). On the air in Kansas City: Russian propaganda. *The New York Times,* A1.

Madison, E. (2015). *Newsworthy: Cultivating critical thinkers, readers, and writers in language arts classrooms.* New York: Teachers College Press.

Maheshwari, S. (2018, November 11). Are you ready for the nanoinfluencers? *The New York Times.* Retrieved from https://www.nytimes.com/2018/11/11/business/media/nanoinfluencers-instagram-influencers.html

Malloci, M. (2018). "All art is propaganda": W.E.B. Du Bois's *The Crisis* and the construction of a black public image. *USAbroad, Journal of American History and Politics, 1,* 1. Retrieved from https://usabroad.unibo.it/article/view/7177/7504

Manjoo, F. (2017, Februrary 22). I ignored Trump news for a week: Here's what I learned. *The New York Times.* Retrieved from https://www.nytimes.com/2017/02/22/technology/trump-news-media-ignore.html

Mankoff, J. (2014). Russia's latest land grab: How Putin won Crimea and lost Ukraine. *Foreign Affairs,* 93, 60–68.

Manne, K. (2015, September 19). Why I use trigger warnings. *The New York Times,* SR5.

Marantz, A. (2019). *Antisocial: Online extremists, techno-utopians, and the hijacking of the American conversation.* New York: Viking.

Marietta, M., Barker, D. C., & Bowser, T. (2015). Fact-checking polarized politics: Does the fact-check industry provide consistent guidance on disputed realities? *The Forum, 13*(4), 577–596.

Marlin, R. (2013). Jacques Ellul's contribution to propaganda studies. In J. Auerbach & R. Castronovo (Eds.), *The Oxford handbook of propaganda studies* (pp. 348–365). New York: Oxford University Press.

Marwick, A. E., & Boyd, D. (2011). I tweet honestly, I tweet passionately: Twitter users, context collapse, and the imagined audience. *New Media and Society, 13*(1), 114–133.

Marwick, A., & Lewis, R. (2017). *Media manipulation and disinformation online.* New York: Data and Society.

Matsushima, J. (2016, December 8). Shareworthy, not sharable. *Adweek.* Retrieved from https://www.adweek.com/digital/joseph-matsushima-denizen-guest-post-shareworthy-not-shareable/

McAvoy, P. (2016). Polarized classrooms. *Teaching Tolerance*, 54. Retrieved from https://www.tolerance.org/magazine/fall-2016/polarized-classrooms

McBrayer, J. (2015, March 2). Why our children don't think there are moral facts. *The New York Times.* Opinionator. Retrieved from https://opinionator.blogs.nytimes.com/2015/03/02/why-our-children-dont-think-there-are-moral-facts/

McCall, J. (2019, June 17). Tech giants head down a 'dangerous' censorship path. The Hill. Retrieved from https://thehill.com/opinion/technology/448820-tech-giants-head-down-dangerous-censorship-path

McComiskey, B. (2017). *Post-truth rhetoric and composition.* Denver: University Press of Colorado.

McGrew, S., Breakstone, J., Ortega, T., Smith, M., & Wineburg, S. (2018). Can students evaluate online sources? Learning from assessments of civic online reasoning. *Theory and Research in Social Education*, *46*(2), 165–193.

McHangama, J. (2018, February 28). The U.N. hates hate speech more than it loves free speech. *Foreign Policy.* Retrieved from https://foreignpolicy.com/2019/02/28/the-u-n-hates-hate-speech-more-than-it-loves-free-speech/

Media Education Lab. (2018). Mind over media: Analyzing contemporary propaganda. Providence, RI. Retrieved from https://propaganda.mediaeducationlab.com

Media Smarts (ND). Facing Online Hate Tutorial. Retrieved from https://mediasmarts.ca/sites/default/files/tutorials/facing-online-hate/html5.html

Menand, L. (2018, December 3). Literary hoaxes and the ethics of authorship. *The New Yorker.* Retrieved from https://www.newyorker.com/magazine/2018/12/10/literary-hoaxes-and-the-ethics-of-authorship

Merton, R. (1995). Mass persuasion: A technical problem and a moral dilemma. In R. Jackall (Ed.), *Propaganda* (pp. 260–274). New York: NYU Press. (Original work published 1946)

Meyer, J. (2018, September 24). How Russia helped swing the election for Trump. *The New*

Yorker. Retrieved from https://www.newyorker.com/magazine/2018/10/01/how-russia-helped-to-swing-the-election-for-trump

Mihailidis, P. (2019). *Civic media literacies: Re-imagining human connection in an age of digital abundance.* New York: Routledge.

Mihailidis, P., & Gerodimos, R. (2016). Connecting pedagogies of civic media: The literacies, connected civics, and engagement in daily life. In E. Gordon & P. Mihailidis (Eds.), *Civic media: Technology, design, practice* (pp. 371–391). Cambridge, MA: MIT Press.

Mikelionis, L. (2018, July 27). Sessions says "lock her up!" chant was "perhaps" a missed opportunity to teach students about due process. *Fox News*. Retrieved from https://www.foxnews.com/politics/sessions-says-lock-her-up-chant-was-perhaps-a-missed-opportunity-to-teach-students-about-due-process

Miller, C. (2016, September 7). Who would a literary character vote for? *Teaching Tolerance.* Retrieved from https://www.tolerance.org/magazine/who-would-a-literary-character-vote-for

Miller, C. R. (1939, October). Propaganda and the European war. *Clearing House, 14*(2), 67–73.

Miller, C. R. (1941). Some comments on propaganda analysis and the science of democracy. *Public Opinion Quarterly, 5*(4), 657–655.

Miller, C. R., & Edwards, V. (1936, October). The intelligent teacher's guide through campaign propaganda. *Clearing House, 11*(2), 69–77.

Mina, A. X. (2019). *Memes to movements.* Boston: Beacon.

Moeller, F. (2015). *Forbidden films* [Motion picture]. United States: Alexander Street.

Moeller, S. (1999). *Compassion fatigue.* New York: Routledge.

Mometrix Academy. (2018, January 15). Totalitarianism vs. authoritarianism. YouTube. https://youtu.be/UAgrp4-s1r8

Moore, D. C. (2011). Asking questions first: Navigating popular culture and transgression in an inquiry-based media literacy classroom. *Action in Teacher Education, 33*(2), 219–230.

Moran, T. P. (1979). Propaganda as pseudocommunication. *Et Cetera, 2*, 181–197.

Morgan, J. (2001). The rhetoric of hate. *Teaching Tolerance,* 20. Retrieved from https://www.tolerance.org/magazine/fall-2001/the-rhetoric-of-hate

Moyers, B. (2008, February 29). Transcript. *Bill Moyers' Journal.* Retrieved from http://www.pbs.org/moyers/journal/02292008/transcript1.html

Mukherjee, A. (2011). Canons. In M. Ryan (Ed.), *The encyclopedia of literary and cultural theory.* Hoboken, NJ: Wiley.

Muñiz, J. (2019). *Culturally responsive teaching: a 50 state survey of teaching standards.* Washington, D.C.: New America Foundation.

Murrock, E., Amulya, J., Druckman, M., & Liubyva, T. (2018). Winning the war on state-sponsored propaganda: Results from an impact study of a Ukrainian news media and information literacy program. *Journal of Media Literacy Education, 10*(2), 53-85.

National Governors Association. (2010). Common core state standards. Washington, DC. retrieved from http://www.corestandards.org/

National Public Radio (2019, April 24). Fact check: Russian interference went far beyond Facebook ads. Retrieved from https://www.npr.org/2019/04/24/716374421/fact-check-russian-interference-went-far-beyond-facebook-ads-kushner-described

National Public Radio (2007, July 23). Michael Moore on Talk of the Nation. Video. Retrieved from https://youtu.be/NHCSOdkrgSw

NCTE. (2019, March 6). Resolution on English education for critical literacy in politics and media. National Council of Teachers of English. http://www2.ncte.org/statement/resolution-english-education-critical-literacy-politics-media/

Nelson, C., Dulio, D., & Medvic, S. (Eds.). (2002). *Shades of gray: Perspectives on campaign ethics.* Washington, DC: Brookings Institution.

Nelson, M.R. (2018) Research on children and advertising then and now: Challenges and opportunities for future research. *Journal of Advertising*, 47:4, 301–308.

Nelson, M. R. (2016). Developing persuasion knowledge by teaching advertising literacy in primary school. *Journal of Advertising, 45*(2), 169–182.

Nelson, M. R., Atkinson, L., Rademacher, M. A., & Ahn, R. (2017). How media and family build children's persuasion knowledge. *Journal of Current Issues and Research in Advertising, 38*(2), 165–183.

Nelson, R. A. (1995). *A chronology and glossary of propaganda in the United States.* Westport CT: Greenwood Press.

Neria, Y., DiGrande, L., & Adams, B. (2011). Posttraumatic stress disorder following the September 11 2001 terrorist attacks. *American Psychologist, 66*(6), 429–446.

New York City Mayor's Office of Media and Entertainment (2018, June 13). Press release. Commissioner Menin, Chancellor Carranza highlight Google Expeditions Pioneer Program reaching 99 NYC schools. https://www1.nyc.gov/site/mome/news/06132018-google-arvr-nyc-schools.page

News Literacy Project. (2019, January 14). Who shares "fake news"? Retrieved from https://mailchi.mp/2892e2bc585d/the-sift-ideas-and-examples-for-teaching-news-literacy-next-week-1379965?e=25372a3442

NGSS. (2013). Earth and human activity. Next Generation Science Standards. Retrieved from https://www.nextgenscience.org/dci-arrangement/ms-ess3-earth-and-human-activity

Nguyen, T. (2018, February 1). The things they made me carry: Inheriting a white curriculum. Teaching While White. Retrieved from https://teachingwhilewhite.org/blog/2018/2/1/the-things-they-made-me-carry-inheriting-a-white-curriculum

Nichols, B. (2019, March/April). What to do about documentary distortion? Toward a code of ethics. *Documentary Magazine.* https://www.documentary.org/feature/what-do-about-documentary-distortion-toward-code-ethics

Niman, M. (2019, April 4). Weaponized social media is driving the explosion of fascism. Truthout. Retrieved from https://truthout.org/articles/weaponized-social-media-is-driving-the-explosion-of-fascism/

Nix, A. (2017, April 18). Cambridge Analytica explains their microtargeting and manipulation of US voters in 2016. YouTube. https://youtu.be/HwedtPjhHeU

Nudd, T. (2016, September 12). The Ad Council and R/GA's "Love Has No Labels" wins the Emmy for best commercial. *Adweek.* Retrieved from https://www.adweek.com/brand-marketing/ad-council-and-rgas-love-has-no-labels-wins-emmy-best-commercial-173437/

Nye, J. S. (2008). Public diplomacy and soft power. *Annals of the American Academy of Political and Social Science, 616*(1), 94–109.

Nyhan, B., & Reifler, J. (2015). The effect of fact-checking on elites: A field experiment on US state legislators. *American Journal of Political Science, 59*(3), 628–640.

Oakes, G. (1995). The Cold War system of emotion management. In R. Jackall (Ed.), *Propaganda* (pp. 275–298). New York: NYU Press.

O'Brien, M. (2004). *Nazi cinema as enchantment: The politics of entertainment in the Third Reich.* Rochester, NY: Boydell and Brewer.

Odrowaz-Coates, A. (2016). Lessons on social justice: A pedagogical reflection on the educational message of The Boxtrolls. *Education as Change, 20*(2), 67–85. https://dx.doi.org/10.17159/1947-9417/2016/502

Ohlheiser, A. & Booth, W. (2015, February 3). Islamic state video claims to show burning death of Jordanian pilot. *Washington Post.* Retrieved from https://www.washingtonpost.com/news/world/wp/2015/02/03/islamic-state-video-appears-to-show-burning-death-of-jordanian-pilot/

Oliver, J. E., & Wood, T. J. (2014). Conspiracy theories and the paranoid style(s) of mass opinion. *American Journal of Political Science, 58*, 952–966. doi:10.1111/ajps.12084

Orgeron, D., Orgeron, M., & Streible, D. (Eds.). (2011). *Learning with the lights off: Educational film in the United States.* New York: Oxford University Press.

O'Sullivan, D. (2019, January). When seeing is no longer believing. CNN. Retrieved from https://www.cnn.com/interactive/2019/01/business/pentagons-race-against-deepfakes/

Ott, B. (2019, May 20). Why Trump keeps talking about a failed coup attempt. *Newsweek.* Retrieved from https://www.newsweek.com/trump-rhetoric-failed-coup-undemocratic-1430211

Papazian, E. (2013). Literacy or legibility: The trace of subjectivity in Soviet socialist realism. In J. Auerbach & R. Castronovo (Eds.), *The Oxford handbook of propaganda studies* (pp. 67–90). New York: Oxford University Press.

Pariser, E. (2011). *The filter bubble.* New York: Penguin.

Participant Media. (2018). About. Retrieved from https://participant.com/about-us

Patrick, B. (2012). *The ten commandments of propaganda.* London: Arktos.

PBS. (2018, November 8). Delete or ignore: Pretend you're a Facebook moderator. *Independent Lens.* Retrieved from http://www.pbs.org/independentlens/blog/delete-or-ignore-pretend-youre-a-facebook-content-moderator/

PBS News Hour. (2016, June 7). Understanding campaign finance law. Extra. Retrieved from https://www.pbs.org/newshour/extra/lessons-plans/understanding-campaign-finance-law/

PBS News Hour (2019, March 22). The history of Russia's 2016 election meddling in 4 minutes. Video. Retrieved from https://youtu.be/0VLQuJFMayg

Penfold-Mounce, R. (2010). *Celebrity culture and crime: The joy of transgression.* New York: Springer.

Perloff, R. (2015). A three-decade retrospective on the hostile media effect. *Mass Communication and Society, 18*(6), 701–729.

Perlroth, N. (2019, November 21). A former Fox executive divides America using Russian tactics. *The New York Times.* Retrieved from https://www.nytimes.com/2019/11/21/technology/LaCorte-edition-news.html

Pew Research Center. (2014, June 12). Political polarization in the American public. Retrieved from https://www.people-press.org/2014/06/12/political-polarization-in-the-american-public/

Pham, M. (2004). The logic of feeling. *Journal of Consumer Psychology, 14*(4), 360–369.

Phillips, W. (2018). *The oxygen of amplification.* New York: Data and Society Research Institute. Retrieved from https://datasociety.net/wp-content/uploads/2018/05/2-PART-2_Oxygen_of_Amplification_DS.pdf

Phillpott, C., & Spruce, G. (2016). *Debates in music teaching.* New York: Routledge.

Pigliucci, M. (2010). *Nonsense on stilts.* Chicago: University of Chicago Press.

Pilkington, E. (2018, January 24). How the Drudge Report ushered in the age of Trump. *The Guardian.* Retrieved from https://www.theguardian.com/us-news/2018/jan/24/how-the-drudge-report-ushered-in-the-age-of-trump

Pinkleton, B., Austin, E.W., & Fujioka, Y. (2001). The relationship of perceived beer ad and PSA quality to high school students' alcohol-related beliefs and behaviors. *Journal of Broadcasting and Electronic Media, 45*(4), 575–597.

Plutzer, E., McCaffrey, M., Hannah, A., Rosenau, J., Bereco, M., & Reid, A. (2016). Climate confusion among U.S. teachers. *Science, 12,* 664–665.

Pomerantsev, P. (2019). *This is not propaganda: Adventures in the war against reality.* New York: Public Affairs.

Popper, K. (2012). *The open society and its enemies.* New York: Routledge. (Original work published 1945)

Post, J. M., McGinnis, C., & Moody, K. (2014). The changing face of terrorism in the

21st century: The communications revolution and the virtual community of hatred. *Behavioral Sciences & the Law, 32*(3), 306–334.

Postman, N. (1979). Propaganda. *ETC: A Review of General Semantics, 36*(2), 128–133.

Postman, N. (1982). *The disappearance of childhood.* New York: Vintage.

Postman, N. (1986). *Amusing ourselves to death: Public discourse in the age of show business.* New York: Penguin.

Prince Street. (2016). These new outdoor ads in LA capture the insidious nature of domestic violence. Retrieved from https://princestreet.co/post/151751292384/these-new-outdoor-ads-in-la-capture-the

Prior, M. (2005). News vs. entertainment: How increasing media choice widens gaps in political knowledge and turnout. *American Journal of Political Science, 49*(3), 577–592.

Pullman, J. (2018, April 18). New AP U.S. history textbook implies Christians are bigots, Reagan a racist. *The Federalist.* Retrieved from https://thefederalist.com/2018/04/17/ap-u-s-history-textbook-implies-christians-bigots-reagan-racist-sexist/

Qualter, T. (1962). *Propaganda and psychological warfare.* New York: Random House.

Rapid TV News (2020, January 30). RT claims global TV news network first with over 10B YouTube views. Retrieved from https://www.rapidtvnews.com/2020013058012/rt-claims-global-tv-news-network-first-with-over-10bn-youtube-views.html#axzz6Dx9ZqOLi

Ranieri, M. (2019). Media Education for Equity and Tolerance (MEET). About. Retrieved from https://meetolerance.eu/

Rank, H. (1991). *The pitch.* Park Forest, IL: Counter-Propaganda Press.

Rank, H. (1992). Channel One/misconceptions three. *English Journal, 81*(4), 31–32.

Rapaczynski, W., Singer, D., & Singer, J. (1982). Teaching television: A curriculum for young children. *Journal of Communication, 32*(2), 46–55.

Raymond, G. (2019, February 11). Demagogues and democracy. *Blue Review.* https://theblue review.org/demagogues-and-democracy/

Reynolds, K. (2011). *Children's literature: A very short introduction.* New York: Oxford University Press.

Rich, S. (1980, April 5). Miss. must allow textbook that stresses black role. *Washington Post.* Retrieved from https://www.washingtonpost.com/archive/politics/1980/04/05/miss-must-allow-textbook-that-stresses-black-role/eee6f4b9-1b8b-4add-8aea-785a1758315a/

RobbGrieco, M. (2018). *Making media literacy in America.* Lanham, MD: Rowman and Littlefield.

Robbins, D., & Brereton, P. (2016). Claims and frames: How the news media cover climate change. *Teaching Media Quarterly, 4*(3). Retrieved from http://pubs.lib.umn.edu/tmq/vol4/iss3/5

Robinson, D., Gleddie, D., & Schaefer, L. (2016). Telling and selling: A consideration of the pedagogical work done by nationally endorsed corporate-sponsored educational resources. *Asia-Pacific Journal of Health, Sport and Physical Education, 7*(1), 37–54. doi:10.1080/18377122.2016.1145430

Robinson, P. (2015). The propaganda model: Still relevant today? In A. Edgely (Ed.), *Noam Chomsky* (pp. 77–96). London: Palgrave Macmillan.

Rock, B. (n.d.). Using movies to teach government and civics. Civic Educator. Retrieved from http://civiceducator.org/teaching-civics-ap-government-movies/

Rockefeller Foundation. (2016). Communications. Retrieved from https://rockfound.rockarch.org/communications

Rodden, J. (1991). Reputation, canon-formation, pedagogy: George Orwell in the classroom. *College English, 53*(5), 503–530. doi:10.2307/377460

Rogow, F. (2020, February 26). Personal communication. Email with the author.

Romaniuk, S., & Burgers, T. (2017, March 7). How the U.S. military is using "violent, chaotic, beautiful" video games to train soldiers. The Conversation. Retrieved from https://theconversation.com/how-the-us-military-is-using-violent-chaotic-beautiful-video-games-to-train-soldiers-73826

Ronald Reagan Presidential Foundation. (2016). The road to the White House: Election 2016. Retrieved from https://www.reaganfoundation.org/media/47306/roadtothewhitehouse6-12.pdf

Roose, K. (2019, June 8). The making of a YouTube radical. *The New York Times*. Retrieved from https://www.nytimes.com/interactive/2019/06/08/technology/youtube-radical.html

Roozenbeek, J., & van der Linden, S. (2019). Fake news game confers psychological resistance against online misinformation. *Palgrave Communications, 5*(1), 1–10.

Rose-Stockwell, T. (2017, July 15). This is how your fear and outrage are being sold for profit. Medium. Retrieved from https://medium.com/@tobiasrose/the-enemy-in-our-feeds-e86511488de

Ross, S. (2002). Understanding propaganda: The epistemic merit model and its application to art. *Journal of Aesthetic Education, 36*(1), 16–30. doi:10.2307/3333623

Rozendaal, E., Buijs, L., & van Reijmersdal, E. A. (2016). Strengthening children's advertising defenses: The effects of forewarning of commercial and manipulative intent. *Frontiers in Psychology, 7,* 1186. doi:10.3389/fpsyg.2016.01186

Rozendaal, E., Lapierre, M., van Reijmersdal, E., & Buijzen, M. (2011). Reconsidering advertising literacy as a defense against advertising effects. *Media Psychology, 14*(4), 333–354.

Rozendaal, E., Opree, S. J., & Buijzen, M. (2016). Development and validation of a survey instrument to measure children's advertising literacy. *Media Psychology, 19*(1), 72–100.

Rushkoff, D. (1994). *Media virus! Hidden agendas in popular culture.* New York: Random House.

Sanchez, T. (2016, November 11). Mountain View High history teacher on leave after comparing Trump to Hitler. *Mercury News*. Retrieved from https://www.mercurynews

.com/2016/11/11/mountain-view-high-history-teacher-on-leave-for-comparing-trump-to-hitler/

Sánchez-Arce, A. (2007). Authenticism, or the authority of authenticity. *Mosaic: A Journal for the Interdisciplinary Study of Literature, 40*(3), 139–155.

Schat, J., Bossema, F. G., Smeets, I., Burger, P., & Numans, M. E. (2018). Exaggerated health news: Association between exaggeration in university press releases and exaggeration in news media coverage. *Nederlands Tijdschrift voor Geneeskunde, 162*(1). Retrieved from https://www.ncbi.nlm.nih.gov/pubmed/30295017

Schaul, K., Uhrmacher, K. & Narayanswamy, A. (2020, February 20). Bloomberg's immense spending gets him 30,000 online ads per minute and a whole lot more. *Washington Post.* Retrieved from https://www.washingtonpost.com/graphics/2020/politics/bloomberg-ad-spending-scale/

Schiffrin, A. (2018, October 10). Fighting disinformation with media literacy—in 1939. *Columbia Journalism Review.* Retrieved from https://www.cjr.org/innovations/institute-propaganda-analysis.php

Schmidt, P. (2016, October 28). The tricky task of teaching about Trump. *Chronicle of Higher Education.* Retrieved from https://www.chronicle.com/article/The-Tricky-Task-of-Teaching/238209

Schor, J. (2004). *Born to buy: The commercialized child and the new consumer culture.* New York: Simon and Schuster.

Schudson, M. (2008). *Why democracies need an unlovable press.* London: Polity.

Schulten, K., & Gonchar, M. (2016, November 3). Election Day 2016: Teaching ideas for before and after the votes are collected. *The New York Times* Learning Network. Retrieved from https://www.nytimes.com/2016/11/03/learning/lesson-plans/election-day-2016-teaching-ideas-for-before-and-after-the-votes-are-tallied.html

Secker, T. (2017, August 7). Films are not your friends. Spy Culture. Retrieved from https://www.spyculture.com/films-not-friends-national-security-cinema-presentation-video/

Seely, M. (2019, June 10). Rising tide of students puts climate change in the classroom. *The New York Times*, A10.

Seldes, G. (1942). *The facts are . . . A guide to falsehood and propaganda in the press and radio.* New York: In Fact.

SELMA. (2019). Hacking online hate: Building an evidence base for educators. Retrieved from https://hackinghate.eu/news/hacking-online-hate-building-an-evidence-base-for-educators/

Serazio, M. (2013). *Your ad here: The cool sell of guerilla marketing.* New York: NYU Press.

Seymour, J., & Byrd, V. (1990, February 16). Has *Married . . . With Children* been muzzled? *Entertainment Weekly.* Retrieved from https://ew.com/article/1990/02/16/has-marriedwith-children-been-muzzled/

Shane, S., & Issac, M. (2017, November 3). Facebook says it's policing fake accounts. But they're still easy to spot. *The New York Times*. Retrieved from https://www.nytimes.com/2017/11/03/technology/facebook-fake-accounts.html

Shaw, T. (2002). Martyrs, miracles, and Martians: Religion and cold war cinematic propaganda in the 1950s. *Journal of Cold War Studies, 4*(2), 3–22.

Shaw, T., & Jenkins, T. (2017). From zero to hero: The CIA and Hollywood today. *Cinema Journal, 56*(2), 91–113.

Shearlaw, M. (2016, November 1). Turkish journalists face abuse and threats online as trolls step up attacks. *The Guardian*. Retrieved from https://www.theguardian.com/world/2016/nov/01/turkish-journalists-face-abuse-threats-online-trolls-attacks

Simon, S. (2017, December 16). A look at RT's "Redacted Tonight." *Weekend Edition Sunday*, National Public Radio. Retrieved from https://www.npr.org/2017/12/16/571305374/a-look-at-rts-redacted-tonight

Singer J., & Singer, D. (1980). Critical TV viewing: Helping elementary echool children learn about TV. *Journal of Communication, 30*(3), 84–93.

Singer, N. (2017, May 13). How Google took over the classroom. *The New York Times*. https://www.nytimes.com/2017/05/13/technology/google-education-chromebooks-schools.html

Slesinger, D. (1940). The film and education. *Journal of Educational Sociology, 13*(5), 263–267. doi:10.2307/2262640

Smaill, B. (2010). *The documentary: Politics, emotion, culture*. New York: Palgrave Macmillan.

Smith, J. (2011). Captivity narratives. In M. Manning & C. Wyatt (Eds.), *Encyclopedia of media and propaganda in wartime America* (Vol. 1, pp. 29–31). Santa Barbara, CA: ABC Clio.

Snow, C. E., & Uccelli, P. (2009). The challenge of academic language. In D. R. Olson & N. Torrance (Eds.), *The Cambridge handbook of literacy* (pp. 112–133). Cambridge: Cambridge University Press.

Sorkin, A. (2020, July 6). The shifting pandemic. *The New Yorker*, 15–16.

Southern Poverty Law Center. (2016). The Trump effect. *Teaching Tolerance*. Retrieved from https://www.tolerance.org/magazine/publications/after-election-day-the-trump-effect

Sproule, J. (1997). *Propaganda and democracy: The American experience of media and mass persuasion*. Cambridge: Cambridge University Press.

Sproule, J. M. (1994). *Channels of propaganda*. Bloomington, IN: ERIC Clearinghouse on Reading, English and Communication.

Stanley, J. (2015). *How propaganda works*. Princeton, NJ: Princeton University Press.

Stanley, S., Ciccone, M. & Hobbs, R. (2020). Be Internet Awesome: A Media Resource Review. Unpublished manuscript.

Starr, P. (2004). *The creation of the media: Political origins of modern communications*. New York: Basic Books.

Stelter, B. (2018, December 24). How to know if President Trump is lying. Reliable

Sources. CNN. Retrieved from https://www.cnn.com/videos/media/2018/12/24/how-to-know-if-president-trump-is-lying-rs.cnn

Sun, N. (2019, August 7). Beijing warns of dire consequences after mass Hong Kong strike. *Nikkei Asian Review.* Retrieved from https://asia.nikkei.com/Spotlight/Hong-Kong-protests/Beijing-warns-of-dire-consequences-after-massive-Hong-Kong-strike

Sunstein, C. (2016). *The ethics of influence: Government in the age of behavioral science.* Cambridge: Cambridge University Press.

Susman-Peña, T., & Vogt, K. (2017, June 12). Ukrainians' self-defense against disinformation: What we learned from Learn to Discern. IREX. Retrieved from https://www.irex.org/insight/ukrainians-self-defense-against-disinformation-what-we-learned-learn-discern

Sussman, D. (2017). From partisanship to pluralism: Teaching students how to listen to each other. *Phi Delta Kappan, 99*(4), 50–53.

Taber, N. (2018, July 5). How politics swallowed Chinese education. *Washington Examiner.* Retrieved from https://www.washingtonexaminer.com/weekly-standard/how-politics-swallowed-chinese-education

Taithe, B., & Thornton, T. (1999). Propaganda: A misnomer of rhetoric and persuasion? In B. Taithe & T. Thornton (Eds.), *Propaganda: Political rhetoric and identity 1300–2000* (pp. 1–24). Phoenix, UK: Sutton.

Talk of the Nation. (2012, June 20). "Revisionaries" tells story of Texas textbook battle. National Public Radio. Retrieved from https://www.npr.org/2012/06/20/155440679/revisionaries-tells-story-of-texas-textbook-battle

Tardaguila, C., Funke, D., & Benkelman, S. (2019, November 21). A political party has masqueraded as a fact-checker. What's next? Poynter Institute. Retrieved from https://www.poynter.org/fact-checking/2019/a-political-party-has-masqueraded-as-a-fact-checker-whats-next/

Tarr, R. (2016). Tarr's toolbox. https://www.classtools.net/blog/

Tassi, P. (2018, June 26). Study says 69% of "Fortnite" players spend money on the game. *Forbes.* Retrieved from https://www.forbes.com/sites/insertcoin/2018/06/26/study-says-69-of-fortnite-players-spend-money-on-the-game-85-spent-on-average/#138688372060

Taylor, A. (2017, June 5). American Nazis in the 1930s–the German American Bund. *The Atlantic.* Retrieved from https://www.theatlantic.com/photo/2017/06/american-nazis-in-the-1930sthe-german-american-bund/529185/

Taylor, R. (2017). Indoctrination and social context: A system-based approach to identifying the threat of indoctrination and the responsibilities of educators. *Journal of Philosophy of Education, 51*(1), 38–58.

Teaching Tolerance (2013). Toolkit for "Set in Stone." Retrieved from https://www.tolerance.org/magazine/summer-2013/toolkit-for-set-in-stone

Teach with Movies (2016). Film study worksheet for a work of historical fiction. Retrieved from http://teachwithmovies.org/film-study-worksheet-for-a-work-of-historical-fiction/

Teo, P. (2014). Making the familiar strange and the strange familiar: A project for teaching critical reading and writing. *Language and Education, 28*(6), 1–13.

Tufecki, Z. (2017). *Twitter and tear gas.* New Haven, CT: Yale University Press.

Turow, J. (2017). *The aisles have eyes: How retailers track your shopping, strip your privacy, and define your power.* New Haven, CT: Yale University Press.

UNESCO. (2018). *Journalism, "fake news" and disinformation.* UNESCO Series on Journalism Education. Paris: UNESCO. Retrieved from https://en.unesco.org/sites/default/files/journalism_fake_news_disinformation_print_friendly_0.pdf

United States Department of the Army. (1954). *Individual training: defense against enemy propaganda.* Washington, D.C.: Headquarters, Dept. of the Army.

United States Holocaust Memorial Museum (2007). Propaganda. Retrieved from https://ushmm.org/propaganda/

Uricchio, W., & Roholl, M. (2005). From New Deal propaganda to national vernacular: Pare Lorentz and the construction of an American public culture. In K. Delenay & R. Janssens (Eds.), *Over (T)here: Transatlantic essays in honor of Rob Kroes* (pp. 107–122). European Contributions to American Studies, 60. Amsterdam: VU Uitgeverij.

Uscinski, J., & Butler, R. (2013). The epistemology of fact checking. *Critical Review, 25*(2), 162–180.

Uscinski, J., & Parent, J. (2014). *American conspiracy theories.* New York: Oxford University Press.

U.S. Department of Education. (2017). Global and cultural competency. International Affairs Office. Retrieved from https://sites.ed.gov/international/global-and-cultural-competency/

U.S. Environmental Protection Agency. (2018). Greenhouse gas equivalencies calculator. https://www.epa.gov/energy/greenhouse-gas-equivalencies-calculator

U.S. Government Accountability Office. (2017, September 12). Public relations spending: Selected agencies' activities supported by contracts and public affairs staff. Retrieved from https://www.gao.gov/products/GAO-17-711

U.S. Holocaust Memorial Museum. (2007). Propaganda. Retrieved from https://www.ushmm.org/propaganda/

U.S. Institute of Education Sciences. (2018). Fast Facts: Most popular majors. National Center for Education Statistics. Retrieved from https://nces.ed.gov/fastfacts/display.asp?id=37

U.S. Senate Permanent Subcommittee on Investigations. (2019). China's impact on the U.S. education system. Washington, DC: Homeland Security and Governmental Affairs Committee.

U.S. White House (2020, July 4). Remarks by President Trump at South Dakota's Mount Rushmore Fireworks Celebration, Keystone, SD. Retrieved from https://www

.whitehouse.gov/briefings-statements/remarks-president-trump-south-dakotas-2020-mount-rushmore-fireworks-celebration-keystone-south-dakota/

Uutiset (2019, March 25). Police probe attack on foreign-background election candidate in Helsinki. Retrieved from https://yle.fi/uutiset/osasto/news/police_probe_attack_on_foreign-background_election_candidate_in_helsinki/10706355

Vara-Orta, F. (2018, August 6). Hate in schools. *Education Week.* Retrieved from https://www.edweek.org/ew/projects/hate-in-schools.html

Vilonia Schools (2017, April 13). Freshmen Academy civic students learning about propaganda. Retrieved from https://www.viloniaschools.org/blognews/2017/4/13/freshman-academy-civic-students-learning-about-propaganda

Von der Bouchard, J. (2018, Mary 21). Belgian socialist party circulates deepfake Donald Trump video. https://politico.eu/article/spa-donald-trumo-belgium-paris-climate-agreement-belgian-socialist-party-circulates-deep-fake-trump-video

Wall Street Journal (2018, January 22). Colleges in the crossfire: Moving upstream [Video]. Retrieved from https://youtu.be/cMNRt5tA1zE

Walton, D. (1997). What is propaganda, and what exactly is wrong with it. *Public Affairs Quarterly, 11*(4), 383–413.

Wardle, C. (2017, February 16). Fake news: It's complicated. First Draft. Retrieved from https://firstdraftnews.org/fake-news-complicated/

Way, T. (n.d.). Dihydrogen monoxide FAQ. United States Environmental Assessment Center. https://www.dhmo.org/facts.html

Welch, D. (2013). *Propaganda: Power and persuasion.* London: British Library.

Wertheimer, L. (2017, April 4). The alt-right curriculum. *The Atlantic.* Retrieved from https://www.theatlantic.com/education/archive/2017/04/the-alt-right-curriculum/521745/

Werz, J. (2017, July 11). Reading, writing and fracking? What the oil industry teaches Oklahoma students. *Morning Edition*, National Public Radio. Retrieved from https://www.npr.org/2017/07/11/535653913/heres-what-the-oil-industry-is-teaching-oklahomas-students

Wilkinson, M. (2013). Nudges manipulate, except when they don't. British Politics and Policy. London School of Economics and Political Science. Retrieved from https://blogs.lse.ac.uk/politicsandpolicy/nudges-manipulate-except-when-they-dont/

Wilkinson, R. (2010). Teaching dystopian literature to a consumer class. *English Journal, 99*(3), 22–26.

Williams, R. (1983). *Culture and society, 1780–1950.* New York: Columbia University Press.

Wineburg, S., & McGrew, S. (2017). Lateral reading: Reading less and learning more when evaluating digital information. Stanford History Education Group Working Paper No. 2017-A1. Retrieved from https://ssrn.com/abstract=3048994

Wolf, M., Jones, R., & Gilbert, D. (2014). Leading in and beyond the library. Alliance for

Excellent Education. Retrieved from https://all4ed.org/wp-content/uploads/2014/01/BeyondTheLibrary.pdf

Wolfe, A. (2018). *Freedom's laboratory.* Baltimore, MD: Johns Hopkins University Press.

Wolfe, D. (2008). The ecological jeremiad, the American myth, and the vivid force of color in Dr. Seuss's *The Lorax. Environmental Communication, 2*(1), 3–24. doi:10.1080/17524030801936707

Wollaeger, M. (2013). Propaganda and pleasure: From Kracauer to Joyce. In J. Auerbach & R. Castronovo (Eds.), *The Oxford handbook of propaganda studies* (pp. 278–300). New York: Oxford University Press.

Wong, C. (2019, May 22). "Arthur" creator defends gay marriage after episode following backlash. Huffington Post. Retrieved from https://www.huffpost.com/entry/arthur-creator-gay-wedding-backlash_n_5ce583a2e4b0547bd1311a34

Wonnell, C. T. (1985). Truth and the marketplace of ideas. *UC Davis Law Review, 19,* 669–728.

Wooldridge, N. (2001). Tensions and contradictions in critical literacy. In B. Comber and A. Simpson (Eds.), *Negotiating critical literacies in classrooms* (pp. 287–302). New York: Routledge.

Woodruff, J. (2016). Brief but spectacular: Fred Davis, political consultant. *PBS News Hour.* Retrieved from https://www.pbs.org/newshour/brief/158681/fred-davis

Wooley, S., & Howard, P. (2019). *Computational propaganda: Political parties, politicians and political manipulation on social media.* New York: Oxford University Press.

Worth, K. (2018, March 23). Mailings to teachers highlight a political fight over climate change in the classroom. *Frontline.* Retrieved from https://www.pbs.org/wgbh/frontline/article/mailings-to-teachers-highlight-a-political-fight-over-climate-change-in-the-classroom/

Wu, T. (2016). *The attention merchants.* New York: Vintage.

Yagoda, B. (2018, July 19). One cheer for whataboutism. *The New York Times.* Retrieved from https://www.nytimes.com/2018/07/19/opinion/one-cheer-for-whataboutism.html

Yoon, J. (2010). Media literacy education to promote cultural competence and adaptation among diverse students: A case study of North Korean refugees in South Korea. Doctoral dissertation, Temple University.

Young, A. (2014, March 3). Producing a TV series without showing a burrito, Chipotle takes a risk. *Advertising Age.* Retrieved from https://adage.com/article/digitalnext/chipotle-takes-a-risk-producing-hulu-tv-series/291914

Young, B. M. (1990). *Television advertising and children.* New York: Oxford University Press.

Zanot, E. J., Pincus, J. D., & Lamp, E. J. (1983). Public perceptions of subliminal advertising. *Journal of Advertising, 12*(1), 39–45.

Zarouali, B., Walrave, M., Poels, K., & Ponnet, K. (2019). Advertising literacy. In R. Hobbs & P. Mihailidis (Eds.), *The international encyclopedia of media literacy* (pp. 25–35). Hoboken, NJ: Wiley-Blackwell.

Zelizer, J,. & Keller, M. (2017, September 15). Is free speech really challenged on campus? *The Atlantic.* Retrieved from https://www.theatlantic.com/education/archive/2017/09/students-free-speech-campus-protest/539673/

Zeman, Z. (1995). The state and propaganda. In R. Jackall (Ed.), *Propaganda* (pp. 174–189). New York: NYU Press.

Zimdars, M. (2016, November 18). My "fake news list" went viral but made-up stories are only part of the problem. *Washington Post.* Retrieved from https://www.washingtonpost.com/posteverything/wp/2016/11/18/my-fake-news-list-went-viral-but-made-up-stories-are-only-part-of-the-problem/

Zimmerman, J., & Robertson, E. (2017). *The case for contention: Teaching controversial issues in American schools.* Chicago: University of Chicago Press.

Zuckerman, E. (2016). Effective civics. In E. Gordon & P. Mihailidis (Eds.), *Civic media: Technology, design, practice* (pp. 49–76). Cambridge, MA: MIT Press.

Zuiderveen Borgesius, F., Möller, J., Kruikemeier, S., Ó Fathaigh, R., Irion, K., Dobber, T., . . . de Vreese, C. H. (2018). Online political microtargeting: Promises and threats for democracy. *Utrecht Law Review, 14*(1), 82–96.

Index